POVERTY AND PROSPERITY IN THE USA IN THE LATE TWENTIETH CENTURY

Poverty and Prosperity in the USA in the Late Twentieth Century

Edited by

Dimitri B. Papadimitriou
Levy Institute Professor of Economics
Bard College, Annandale-on-Hudson, New York

and

Edward N. Wolff
Professor of Economics
New York University, New York

St. Martin's Press   New York

41.8

All rights reserved. For information, write:
Scholarly and Reference Division,
St. Martin's Press, Inc., 175 Fifth Avenue,
New York, N.Y. 10010

First published in the United States of America in 1993

Printed in Great Britain

ISBN 0–312–09473–6

Library of Congress Cataloging-in-Publication Data
Poverty and prosperity in the USA in the late twentieth century /
edited by Dimitri B. Papadimitriou and Edward N. Wolff.
p. cm.
Includes index.
ISBN 0–312–09473–6
1. Poor—United States.   2. Income distribution—United States.
3. United States—Economic conditions—1981–   4. Poverty—United
States.   5. United States—Economic policy—1981–
I. Papadimitriou, Dimitri B.   II. Wolff, Edward N.
HC110.P6P594   1993
330.973'092—dc20   92–39847
                                                        CIP

Contents

The Jerome Levy Economics Institute of Bard College   vii

Foreword by Dimitri B. Papadimitriou   viii

Acknowledgments   xi

Notes on the Contributors   xii

1   Introduction
    Maury Gittleman and Edward N. Wolff   1

Part I   Poverty: Trends, Composition and Sources   **19**

2   Why were Poverty Rates so High in the 1980s?
    Rebecca M. Blank   21

    Comment
    Daniel H. Weinberg   56

3   Who are the Truly Poor? Patterns of Official and Net
    Earnings Capacity Poverty, 1973–88
    Robert Haveman and Larry Buron   58

4   The Health, Earnings Capacity, and Poverty of Single-
    mother Families
    Barbara L. Wolfe and Steven Hill   89

5   Recent Trends in Economic Inequality in the United
    States: Income versus Expenditures versus Material
    Well-being
    Susan E. Mayer and Christopher Jencks   121

    Comment
    Paul Ryscavage   204

Part II   Anatomy of Income Inequality   **209**

6   Social Security Annuities and Transfers: Distributional
    and Tax Implications
    Edward N. Wolff   211

7　W(h)ither the Middle Class? A Dynamic View
　　Greg J. Duncan, Timothy M. Smeeding and
　　Willard Rodgers 240

　　Comment
　　William T. Dickens 272

8　Changes in Earnings Differentials in the 1980s:
　　Concordance, Convergence, Causes, and
　　Consequences
　　McKinley L. Blackburn, David E. Bloom and
　　Richard B. Freeman 275

　　Comments
　　Alan S. Blinder 308
　　Kevin Lang 312

9　The Changing Contributions of Men and Women to
　　the Level and Distribution of Family Income, 1968–88
　　Maria Cancian, Sheldon Danziger, and Peter
　　Gottschalk 317

　　Comment
　　Daniel H. Weinberg 354

Part III　Policy Discussion **355**

10　Policy Forum: Prospects for Future Policy
　　Robert B. Avery
　　Sheldon Danziger
　　William T. Dickens
　　Robert Haveman
　　Dimitri B. Papadimitriou (moderator)
　　Timothy M. Smeeding
　　Edward N. Wolff 357

Index 381

The Jerome Levy Economics Institute of Bard College

Founded in 1986, The Jerome Levy Economics Institute of Bard College is an autonomous, independently endowed research organization. It is nonpartisan, open to the examination of diverse points of view, and dedicated to public service.

The Institute believes in the potential for economic study to improve the human condition. Its purpose is to generate viable, effective public policy responses to important economic problems. It is concerned with issues that profoundly affect the quality of life in the United States, in other highly industrialized nations, and in countries with developing economies.

The Institute's present research agenda includes such issues as financial instability, poverty and problems associated with the distribution of income, employment and economic growth. In all its endeavors, the Institute places heavy emphasis on the values of personal freedom and justice. The opinions expressed in this volume are those of the authors and do not necessarily represent those of the Jerome Levy Economics Institute of Bard College.

Foreword

The old cliché 'the rich get richer and the poor get poorer' took particular significance during the decade of the 1980s in the United States because it was shown to be generally true. Report after report on research that focused on inequality in the 1980s provided unambiguous evidence of more gains by the richest in contrast to those of the lowest levels in the distributional ladder that experienced more declines.

This state of inequality is reminiscent of industrial America of the 1800s and early 1900s when wealth and income were concentrated at the top. Even though the Great Depression and World War II were responsible for partially reversing and equalizing these trends, the return to the growing and disturbing concentration of high income and wealth on the top 1 percent, reinforces the views of many that the US economy has undergone a structural change in the income distribution during the decade of 1980. The wealth and income research findings, including those detailed in the chapters of this volume, seem to reflect President Reagan's America which can be best described in the words of MIT economist Paul R. Krugman as 'another example of a big unprecedented jump in inequality to *Great Gatsby* levels' rather than Alexis de Toqueville's one distinguished by its egalitarian nature.

To be sure, disagreements as to the appropriateness of inequality or poverty measures abound, but all suggest that official estimates of poverty are unrealistically low and thus, they underestimate the extent of income and wealth dispersion. Nonetheless, the research findings confirm the worsening of inequality irrespective of the measure used.

It would seem, then, that the time has come for policy makers to heed the advice of economists and others who contend the United States is at serious risk if it does not address the growing inequality. The participants gathered at the Conference organized by the Jerome Levy Economics Institute of Bard College on 'Poverty and Prosperity in America at the Close of the Twentieth Century' were forceful about the need for innovative reform to train and employ the poor in order to save increasing numbers of Americans from the *underclass*. A failure to act will harm America's competitiveness by severely limiting the pool of skilled workers and further straining business and the economy. The United States simply cannot maintain its economic position unless more of its citizens become productive.

No longer are economists advocating raising welfare benefits for the able-bodied. They are focusing, instead, on areas where results are observable – namely investing in programs that encourage people to enter the labor market – such as job training and child care. While not a panacea, there is a growing consensus that full employment should be the goal. Labor market reform, targeting the working age population with low skills and aiding families with children, ought to be a national priority.

Other proposals that can accomplish this merit further discussion. For example, an employer based marginal employment subsidy like the New Jobs Tax Credit of a decade ago would target lower skilled workers for jobs; a wage rate subsidy that is highest for workers who can only be employed at minimum wage rates would also draw unskilled workers into the labor force. The subsidy would decrease as the worker's wage rose.

Relating to families, attention ought to be paid to programs that expand subsidies for child care and to make the dependent care tax credit refundable. For people who do not earn enough to pay taxes, a cash refund could be awarded. Another approach is to create a tax credit based income. For example, the range would be a non-refundable 30 percent child care tax credit for the highest income families, while the poor and near poor would receive a refundable credit up to 80 percent.

Proposals that call for a universal child support policy, and tying child care subsidies for single parents to mandatory employment or job training – not unrelated to proposals put forth by US Senator Albert Gore and Representative Thomas Downey – merit attention. Further consideration ought to be given to policies targeted to youth – such as a capital account for the young workers to improve their behavior and aspirations, as well as programs to increase opportunities for vocational training and to ease the transition from school to work.

The United States desperately needs public policy programs that must increase the employment levels of people at the bottom of the income and capability distribution scale. While not the answer to all the country's ills, programs that help overcome unemployment can improve the economic well-being of people in the lower half of the income spectrum, thereby strengthening the US.

The policy proposals derived from the research undertaken and articulated in the chapters of this book, deserve further discussion. What confronts us, is more than a divisive struggle between the haves and the havenots. When the system fails a large contingent of society, as it does currently, it creates many social problems, gives rise to inefficiency, and undermines the moral character and resolve of the nation.

DIMITRI B. PAPADIMITRIOU

Acknowledgments

We would like to thank the Board of Governors of the Jerome Levy Economics Institute of Bard College for sponsoring a year-long research project centering on the inequality in the United States at the close of the twentieth century which climaxed in a Conference on 'Poverty and Prosperity at the Close of the Twentieth Century' from which this collection of essays is drawn. We are indebted in many ways to the contributors for their cooperation and readiness in carrying out revisions. We want to thank Susan Howard and Linda Christensen of the Levy Institute and Maury Gittleman for his invaluable research assistance. Finally, sincere thanks are due to Tim Farmiloe, our publishing editor, and to Keith Povey for his editorial assistance.

DIMITRI B. PAPADIMITRIOU
EDWARD N. WOLFF

Notes on the Contributors

Robert B. Avery is Professor in the Department of Consumer Economics at Cornell University and a Research Associate at the Federal Reserve Bank of Cleveland. Prior to his arrival at Cornell, Dr Avery was Senior Economist at the Board of Governors of the Federal Reserve System (1981–8) and Assistant Professor of Economics in the Graduate School of Industrial Administration at Carnegie–Mellon University (1975–81). While at the Federal Reserve Board, he served as Project Director of the 1983, 1986 and 1989 Surveys of Consumer Finances.

McKinley L. Blackburn is Assistant Professor of Economics in the College of Business Administration at the University of South Carolina. Dr Blackburn's thesis research was devoted to analysing changes in the distribution of income among families in the US.

Rebecca Blank is Associate Professor of Economics and Education at the School of Education and Social Policy, Northwestern University. Dr Blank also taught at Princeton University, and until recently was with the Council of Economic Advisors in Washington, DC.

Alan S. Blinder is the Gordon S. Rentschler Memorial Professor of Economics, Princeton University. Dr Blinder is a regular contributor to *Business Week*, and on the editorial boards of the *Journal of Economic Literature* and the *Journal of Monetary Economics*, and is associate editor of the *Journal of Public Economics*. His publications include: *Toward an Economic Theory of Income Distribution: General Equilibrium Systems: Essays in Memory of Rafael Lusky* (ed. with P. Friedman); *Economics: Principles and Policy* (with W. J. Baumol); *Economic Policy and the Great Stagflation*, and *Hard Heads and Soft Hearts*.

David E. Bloom is Professor of Economics, Columbia University. Dr Bloom also taught at Harvard University and Carnegie–Mellon University.

Larry M. Buron is a PhD candidate in economics, University of Wisconsin at Madison.

Maria Cancian is a PhD candidate in economics, the University of Michigan.

Sheldon Danziger is Professor of Social Work and Public Policy, Faculty Associate in Population Studies, and Director of the Research and Training Program on Poverty, the Underclass and Public Policy at the University of Michigan. From 1974–88 he was at the University of Wisconsin, where he was Director of the Institute for Research on Poverty from 1983–8. He is the editor of *Fighting Poverty: What Works and What Doesn't* (Harvard University Press, 1986), and the author of numerous articles.

William T. Dickens is Associate Professor, University of California-Berkeley.

Greg J. Duncan is a Program Director in the Survey Research Center and Professor of Economics, The University of Michigan-Ann Arbor.

Richard B. Freeman is Professor of Economics at Harvard University, Research Associate at the Russell Sage Foundation and Director of Labor Studies at the NBER. He is the author of numerous books and articles.

Maury Gittleman is an economist at the Bureau of Labor Statistics.

Peter Gottschalk is Professor of Economics, Boston College. Dr Gottschalk also taught economics at Bowdoin College and was a Project Associate at the Institute for Research on Poverty at the University of Wisconsin.

Robert Haveman is the John Bascom Professor of Economics, Director, Robert M. LaFollette Institute of Public Affairs, and Fellow, Institute for Research on Poverty at the University of Wisconsin-Madison. Dr Haveman is co-editor of the *American Economic Review*. His publications include: *Earnings Capacity, Poverty and Inequality, Jobs for Disadvantaged Workers*, and *Starting Even: An Equal Opportunity Program to Combat the Nation's New Poverty*.

Steven Hill is a PhD candidate at the University of Wisconsin at Madison and a National Institute of Mental Health trainee.

Christopher Jencks is Professor of Sociology and Director of the Center for Urban Affairs and Policy Research, Northwestern University. Professor Jencks also taught at the University of California-Santa Barbara and Harvard University.

Kevin Lang is Professor of Economics, Boston University. Dr Lang is a member of the Advisory Committee, Canadian Employment Research Forum; Faculty Affiliate, Institute for Economic Development, Boston University; and was the editor of the monograph series on 'Sociology and Economics: Controversy and Integration,' Aldine de Gruyter. He is the author of many books and articles.

Susan E. Mayer is Assistant Professor, Graduate School of Public Policy Studies, University of Chicago. Dr Mayer was a Research Associate at the Center for Urban Affairs and Policy Research, Northwestern University; Equal Opportunity Specialist in the Office of Civil Rights of the U.S. Department of Health and Human Services; and taught at Indiana University.

Dimitri B. Papadimitriou is Executive Vice President and the Levy Institute Professor of Economics, Bard College; Executive Director of the Jerome Levy Economics Institute and the Bard Center. Dr Papadimitriou was a visiting scholar, Center for Economic Planning and Research (Athens, Greece); Wye Fellow, Aspen Institute. He is the general editor of the Levy Economics Institute Series, editor of *Profits, Deficits and Instability* (Macmillan Press, 1991); *Aspects of Distribution of Income and Wealth* (Macmillan Press, 1993); and, with Steven Fazzari, *Financial Conditions and Macroeconomic Performance, Essays in Honor of Hyman P. Minsky*.

Willard L. Rodgers is a Program Director in the Survey Research Center at the University of Michigan.

Paul Ryscavage is Senior Labour Economist in the Census Bureau's Housing and Household Economic Statistics Division. He serves as a staff assistant to the Assistant Division Chief of that Division and conducts research on the nation's labor force and income distribution. Mr Ryscavage has worked at the Census Bureau since 1983 and prior to that, at the US Bureau of Labor Statistics since 1962.

Timothy M. Smeeding is Professor of Economics and Public Administration, Syracuse University; Overall Project Director, Luxembourg

Income Study. Dr Smeeding also taught at Vanderbilt University, the University of Utah and Bowdoin College. He is the author of numerous books and articles, including *Poverty, Inequality and the Distribution of Income in an International Context: Initial Research from the Luxembourg Income Study (LIS) Project* (with M. O'Higgins and L. Rainwater).

Daniel H. Weinberg is Chief, Housing and Household Economic Statistics Division, US Bureau of the Census. Dr Weinberg has taught at Yale University, worked on housing research at Abt Associates, and worked for nine years at the US Department of Health and Human Services on welfare and poverty research, and policy. He is the author of numerous articles and co-author of *The Economics of Housing Vouchers*, *The Great Housing Experiment* and *Fighting Poverty*.

Barbara L. Wolfe is Professor in the Department of Economics and Preventive Medicine at the University of Wisconsin-Madison. She is also Research Associate at the National Bureau of Economic Research and Research Affiliate for the Institute for Research on Poverty at the University of Wisconsin-Madison. Professor Wolfe is a member of the Expert Group of the European Economic Community Project on the Distributive Effects of Cost Containment in Health Care. She is a Co-Editor of the *Journal of Human Resources*.

Edward N. Wolff is Professor of Economics, New York University where he has taught since 1974, and a former research associate at the National Bureau of Economic Research. He has also served as Managing Editor of the *Review of Income and Wealth* since 1987. He is the author of *Growth, Accumulation, and Unproductive Activity: An Analysis of the Post-War US Economy*, a co-author of *Productivity and American Leadership: The Long View*, and *The Information Economy: The Implications of Unbalanced Growth*.

1 Introduction

Maury Gittleman and Edward N. Wolff

1.1 BACKGROUND AND SUMMARY

The last decade witnessed an unprecedented turnaround in inequality in the United States. Inequality in the distribution of household income, which had remained virtually unchanged since the end of World War II, increased sharply during the 1980s. On the basis of U.S. Census *Current Population Reports*, it was found that the standard of living of the poorest fifth fell by 9 percent between 1979 and 1987, while that of the top fifth rose by 19 percent. The poverty rate, which had declined from 22 percent in 1960 to 11 percent by 1973, rose to 14 percent in 1990. Finally, household wealth inequality followed a similar pattern. The share of the top 1 percent fell from 32 percent in 1962 to about 18 percent in 1976 and then increased to 32 percent in 1986.

Government fiscal policy appears to have had a relatively neutral effect on this reversal. Between 1979 and 1987, government transfers (social security benefits (OASDI); Aid to Families with Dependent Children (AFDC); workers' compensation; food stamps; Supplemental Security Income (SSI); and general assistance) received by the bottom fifth fell by 9 percent, while their tax burden remained unchanged. As a result, their standard of living fell by 9 percent, slightly greater than the 8 percent decline in their private income. The government benefits received by the top fifth underwent no change, while their tax burden declined by 3 percent. The result was a 19 percent increase in their standard of living, somewhat greater than the 16 percent increase in the private income of this group. For the other income groups, government programs and tax policies had essentially no net effect on their standard of living.

The turnaround in inequality is even more puzzling in light of the much touted economic growth during the Reagan years. Normally, income inequality lessens during periods of prosperity and worsens during economic downturns. Except for the 1981–2 recession, the last decade was one of general prosperity, with stable economic growth. Moreover, the U.S. economy also experienced a reversal in

1

productivity growth over the last decade. The period from 1973–9 witnessed the slowest growth in labor productivity during the postwar period. Indeed, overall labor productivity growth fell from approximately 3 percent per annum during the 1947– 67 years to under 1 percent from 1973 to 1979. However, productivity growth has been averaging about 2 percent per year over the last decade, which is quite close to its twentieth-century average.

Another anomalous phenomenon is the pattern of real wage growth. Historically, the average real wage has moved in line with average labor productivity. Real wages have remained virtually unchanged during the 1973–87 years. This is understandable during the 1973–9 period, when productivity was almost at a standstill, but not during the ensuing years, when productivity growth picked up. Indeed, median family income (in real terms and before taxes) did not grow at all between 1979 and 1987, though disposable income per capita grew by 12 percent. (The difference is due to shrinking family size and an increasing number of adults living alone.)

The papers presented in this volume, together with a concomitant policy discussion, seek to provide a deeper understanding of these recent trends. The papers are divided into two groups, with the first focussing primarily on issues of poverty and the second on different aspects of economic inequality. While the research herein covers a broad range of topics, a number of common themes emerge in terms of key findings, methodological issues, and policy recommendations.

1.1.1 Key Findings

One finding that emerges from many of the papers is how the 1980s marked a clear break from preceding years. In particular, the economic expansion that began in 1983 did not have as equalizing an effect on the distribution of economic well-being as would have been expected on the basis of past experience. One manifestation of this development is that poverty rates remained unexpectedly high in the 1980s, as documented by Rebecca Blank. Furthermore, we see access to economic resources becoming more unequal in times of prosperity along many different dimensions of well-being. Greg Duncan, Timothy Smeeding, and Willard Rodgers document the change in earnings mobility patterns that resulted in a shrinkage of the middle class during the 1980s. Edward Wolff finds a growing intergenerational wealth gap (defined as the ratio in average wealth between elderly families and younger ones) between the early 1960s and the 1980s.

McKinley Blackburn, David Bloom and Richard Freeman find a widening of the earnings gap during the 1980s between those individuals with a college education and those with a high school degree or less, reversing previous secular trends. They also show that this change has occurred not only for white males, who have been the focus of previous research, but for females and minorities as well. Maria Cancian, Sheldon Danziger and Peter Gottschalk document an increasing dispersion of the distribution of family income during the 1980s. All told, the fact that levels of poverty and inequality remained quite high after a sustained expansion is especially worrisome, and raises concern about where these measures will stand after the current recession.

Additionally, these findings all reflect the recent widening of the earnings gap between those at the top and bottom of the male earnings distribution (see, for example, Juhn, Murphy and Pierce, 1989). Along this line, Blank argues that a key reason why poverty rates stayed high in the 1980s was that the wages of the lower portion of the income distribution did not respond to the economic growth of the 1980s as they did in the 1960s. The rising inequality in the distribution of male income also appears to be behind the shrinking of the middle class found by Duncan, Smeeding, and Rodgers, and the rising family income inequality documented by Cancian, Danziger and Gottschalk.

1.1.2 Measurement

Measurement issues also feature prominently in the papers of this volume. Given the scarcity of public resources available to aid the poverty population, one crucial concern is to be able to determine precisely who the poor are. Robert Haveman and Larry Buron find fault with the official U.S. poverty definitions, and propose, instead, one based on earnings capacity – the capability of families to generate earnings if its members fully utilized their human capital. While this approach still relies on an income-based concept, Mayer and Jencks argue that it is necessary to move beyond income to more direct measures of the living conditions of families in order to get a clearer picture of the material well-being of the low-income population. Difficulties analogous to measuring poverty impair assessment of changes in other parts of the income distribution. For example, Duncan, Smeeding, and Rodgers discuss the various definitions of the 'high income population' that have been used in past research;

Barbara Wolfe and Steven Hill discuss several problems inherent in gauging the health status of the population.

1.1.3 Policy Implications

Policy issues also provide a major focal point of the papers in this collection. One immediate concern is whether justification exists for the government to intervene or whether the market will correct itself. Notable among these papers and the Policy Forum discussion is the clear consensus that the government must intervene, for fear that the cost of doing nothing would be too high. This consensus emerges in part because, as indicated above, the economic expansion did not have its usual ameliorating effect on the problems of poverty and inequality. The one exception to the general support for intervention is from Blackburn, Bloom, and Freeman. They caution that, in the case of the widening earnings differentials between educational groups, the market is already responding, and any attempts by the government to intervene may have perverse effects in terms of economic inequality.

One area of common policy concern is the plight of children, a group that is especially vulnerable when poverty is on the rise. Haveman and Buron underscore the difficulties that low income parents face in earning enough to support their children. The need to provide adequate child care may either reduce earnings directly, by reducing the number of hours worked, or cause additional expense through the need to provide for outside child care. Wolfe and Hill show that such a problem is especially severe for single mothers who either have health problems of their own or who care for children with health problems.

Wolff documents the shift of wealth away from young families toward older ones that occurred between the 1960s and 1980s. Since children are more apt to be found in younger families, any movement in resources away from this group may have a deleterious effect on the welfare of children. Cancian, Danziger and Gottschalk emphasize the importance of women's earnings in maintaining a family's standard of living, but note that further movement by women into the labor force is hindered by the high cost of day care relative to the net wage of many mothers. The authors propose a variety of measures that would directly or indirectly aid families, especially low-income families, with children. Wolff also suggests a social security capital fund that could be used for investing in young workers. Other work discusses the need to modify child care credit allowances and to better enforce the payment of child support.

In addition to policies to aid children, proposals are also made to mitigate poverty and redistribute income. Programs to increase the human capital of labor force participants through education and training programs receive much attention, owing, in part, to the recent rise in returns to higher education. Other policy proposals focus on areas such as earning subsidies, affirmative action, and health care. Among the options mentioned to raise funds for these measures are an increase in the progressivity of the federal income tax and a new levy on household wealth. Many of the authors also urge improved data collection in order to facilitate the research that is a prerequisite of policy design.

While general support exists among the authors about the need for government intervention, there is a clear recognition of the difficulties of gaining such support. The U.S. populace as a whole seems solidly in favor of economic growth. But if economic growth is insufficient to solve the problems of poverty and inequality, a consensus must be built for other policy measures. Explicit in some papers and implicit in others is the need to develop the political will that is required to allocate resources to distributional problems. Many authors remark on the tension that exists between universal and targeted programs. Universal programs have the advantage of gaining wide political support (as evidenced by the social security system), while targeted programs are better for conserving scarce resources. Another issue is the impact of support programs on the motivation to work and other incentives. For example, Wolfe and Hill express concern about crafting a program to aid mothers with health problems without encouraging individuals to be misleading about their health status.

1.2 POVERTY: TRENDS, COMPOSITION AND SOURCES

The first part of the volume focuses on the make-up of the poverty population during the 1980s. In the first paper in this section, Rebecca Blank updates her earlier work with Alan Blinder (Blank and Blinder, 1986) on the effect of macroeconomic factors on poverty rates. The earlier paper found that changes in the poverty rate were almost completely accounted for by trends in economic growth, the unemployment rate, and transfer payments over the period from

1959 to 1983. In the new paper, Blank uses these relationships (regression coefficients) to predict poverty rates in the 1980s and finds that they lead to a considerable *underestimation* of poverty. The reason is that the correlations between poverty, on the one hand, and both unemployment and transfers, on the other, changed in unexpected ways in the 1980s. To solve this puzzle of why the poverty rate did not respond to the sustained economic growth of the 1980s, as it did during a comparable period of expansion in the 1960s, Blank first considers four possible explanations that are not related to changes in labor market behavior.

The first is whether there are serious errors in measurement stemming from the calculation of poverty levels that do not take into account in-kind income, such as Food Stamps, since most of these transfers emanate from programs that were either small or nonexistent in the 1960s. Blank eliminates this hypothesis because her various adjustments to the poverty rates for in-kind benefits produce little change in the trend of poverty for the 1983–9 period. The second is the possibility that the poor have been concentrated in central cities or regions of the country whose low rates of expansion relative to the aggregate economy limited opportunities for boosting incomes. She rejects this hypothesis because of the similarity of the geographical distribution of the poor before and after the expansion of the 1980s, but allows that other factors connected to urban location not captured by her data may have had an influence.

The third is whether changes in income transfer programs in the 1980s served to attenuate the responsiveness of the poor to economic growth. Based on simulations, she concludes that changes in Aid to Families with Dependent Children (AFDC), the primary welfare program for low-income families, did not alter trends in poverty significantly. The fourth is whether the changing demographic composition of family units – in particular, the relative increase of female-headed and elderly households, whose fortunes tend not to be influenced by the tides of economic growth – has influenced the level and trend of poverty rate. She finds that this factor does not seem to have affected the responsiveness of poverty to economic growth. Strikingly, the beneficial impact of growth on poverty rates has weakened over time for *all* family types.

Having found little support for the first four hypotheses, Blank then considers the role of labor market earnings in explaining why income has not responded to macroeconomic growth. She finds that the key factor is a lack of responsiveness of earnings among family unit heads to changing macroeconomic conditions. This, in turn, was not due to any lessening of the work effort of low-income families. In fact, the hours worked by these families responded more vigorously to the economic growth of the 1980s than of the 1960s. Rather, the primary reason is the *lack of responsiveness of wages at the lower quintiles to economic growth*. In other words, as shown by Juhn, Murphy and Pierce (1989), wages have grown more slowly for those in the lower percentiles than in the upper ones, and this has closed off avenues for escaping poverty. This result is also consistent with the findings of Blackburn, Bloom and Freeman in this volume that the earnings of high school graduates have lagged behind those of college graduates during the 1980s.

As Blank indicates, this finding points to a difficult challenge for policy makers. Economic growth has become much less effective in helping low-income families, or as Daniel Weinberg succinctly and dramatically puts it in his comments on the paper, 'trickle down is dead.' A direct implication is that it is no longer possible to rely exclusively or even primarily on economic growth to benefit the poor as well as the rich. Indeed, it no longer seems likely that the labor market by itself will serve as the prime remedy for poverty. Instead, there is a need for targeted programs that will either redistribute income in the direction of the poor or change their work behavior. But, as Blank points out, these programs are difficult to design and tend to be costly both in terms of administrative expenses and in the effort required to garner and maintain political support.

In the next chapter of this section, Robert Haveman and Larry Buron shift attention to the difficulties in identifying who the 'truly poor' are and discuss the implications that such problems pose for targeting policies. The official U.S. definition and measurement of poverty has been criticized for a wide variety of reasons (see, for example, Ruggles, 1990). Building on earlier work (Garfinkel and Haveman, 1977), Haveman and Buron introduce the concept of net earnings capacity (NEC) and use the 1973 and 1988 Current Population Surveys to estimate NEC for a sample of households. The measure NEC is designed to gauge the ability of a family to generate an income stream on the basis of the full utilization of its human and physical capital. NEC is adjusted for constraints on the use of earnings capacity – for example, due to health limitations, disabling conditions, involuntary unemployment or the like – and for the costs of acquiring acceptable child care. The authors estimate separate earnings functions for each race and gender group, which enables them to take account of race and sex discrimination. The measure overcomes some of the difficulties of the official U.S. poverty definition, as it abstracts from transitory events and from differences in tastes for leisure.

The authors find large differences in the composition of the poor as defined by NEC in comparison to that derived from the official poverty definition, based on current income. Notably, only 40 to 50 percent of the official poverty population would be considered poor according to the NEC-based definition. (Haveman and Buron choose their NEC poverty line so that the total percentage of poor families corresponds to the rate computed with the official definition.) In comparison to the NEC measure, the official poverty definition understates the incidence of poverty among blacks, Hispanics, those living in female-headed families, members of large families, and those living in families headed by a person with a low level of education. On the other hand, in comparison with the new poverty index, the official measure exaggerates the incidence of poverty among single individuals, those living in intact families, and members of families headed by a young or an old person. Likewise, changes over the 1973–88 time period in the incidence of poverty differed between the two measures. For example, minority families showed a larger reduction in their poverty rate on the basis of the NEC measure than the official definition.

This approach has a number of important policy implications. The first is the need to develop a poverty measure with fewer of the shortcomings of the official U.S. definition – that is, one that would better pinpoint those types of families that are truly in need – so that limited policy resources can be channeled to those groups most in need. The other policy measures proposed by the authors fall into two categories: (1) those designed to increase the earnings capacities of the 'truly poor', given that many of the families would remain in poverty even if they were to use their human and physical assets to full capacity; and (2) those geared to enable individuals to more fully utilize their capacities. Among the possibilities suggested by the authors are: (1) earnings subsidies for those with low earnings capacities (an expansion of the Earned Income Tax Credit, for example); (2) affirmative action programs to raise the potential earnings of women and minority groups; (3) targeted education and training programs to assist those with low levels of human capital; (4) child care subsidies to allow single parents to enter the labor force in greater numbers; and (5) improved enforcement of child support arrangements to lessen the financial burden on single parents.

In the next paper, Barbara Wolfe and Steven Hill employ the net earnings capacity concept to analyze the impact of health problems (both of the mother and her children) on single-mother families. The dramatic growth of single-mother families and the high incidence of poverty among this group are well-known phenomena. Standard explanations given for the low income of this group include the low level of schooling for many of these women, the lower earnings of women relative to men, and the constraints on labor force participation imposed by the need for child care. But, as the authors point out, another important factor is poor health, since single mothers tend to have greater health problems than other women of the same age.

The authors calculate earnings capacity corrected for the limitations imposed by health problems of single mothers and their children. They use two indices of health status in their analysis. The first is a functional one – the number of activities of daily living related to work (ADLs) an individual has difficulty performing. The second is 'poor' or 'fair' health as reported by the respondent on a five point scale. Interestingly, they find the effect of the health status of mothers on their total earnings to have its primary influence through the number of hours worked rather than through the wage rate. The authors' estimates of health-adjusted earnings capacity provide strong support for the contention that encouraging work among single mothers with health problems or children who are impaired in some way is unlikely to be a successful policy. If working at full capacity (assuming that earnings are the only source of income), one-third of the single-mother families would still be below the poverty line, with the proportion rising to 58 percent after an adjustment for child care expenses. Moreover, they find that almost all single mothers with health problems or with a disabled child would still be mired in poverty even if working at capacity. These findings are particularly relevant in light of the 1988 Family Support Act, which encourages single mothers to either work or engage in job training.

The authors suggest a number of policy options for the two key needs of these families: income to supplement the mother's earnings and adequate health insurance coverage. They argue that government programs which provide earnings subsidies are of limited use here, since constraints on time available for work is the principal reason why these families cannot earn their way out of poverty.

Instead, they propose four policy alternatives that build on existing public programs: (1) the creation of a special federal AFDC program for such families (for example, women with two or more ADLs) that would provide uniform benefits across the country as well as Medicaid coverage; (2) the modification of the existing AFDC programs to provide expanded assistance to women with significant health problems; (3) the provision of comprehensive health insurance to single parents with health problems themselves or with children who have such problems, irrespective of work status, but with benefits from this program to be adjusted based on income; and (4) the gradual expansion of the SSI program to provide increased coverage for these family types.

Susan Mayer and Christopher Jencks also analyze the well-being of the lower portion of the income distribution, but in a way quite different from the other papers in this section. Rather than focussing exclusively on income, as does most research in this area, the authors measure the standard of living through consumer expenditures and direct indicators of material well-being. The trends uncovered by this method differ markedly from those based exclusively on income, making the authors' findings quite provocative. In particular, these authors do *not* find a relative deterioration in the living conditions of the poor during the 1980s that one finds from income-based measures. One potential implication of this result is that poverty programs have had success in ensuring that basic needs are met among the low-income population.

Mayer and Jencks begin their study by noting that anti-poverty efforts in the U.S. have tended to focus not on reducing the inequality of the overall distribution of income but in ensuring that families have 'adequate' food, shelter, medical care and education. It follows that if one's goal is to measure the success of these efforts, one needs to directly measure how well these basic needs are being met. While income may provide some guidance in this regard, the research here makes it clear that the relationship between income and material well-being is incredibly complex, and that the two are far from perfectly correlated. As the authors point out, intervening between income and well-being is a long list of other factors, such as tax rates, saving and borrowing resources, non-cash benefits, physical assets, consumer efficiency, and household needs.

With these concerns in mind, the authors take a closer look at the patterns of income inequality from the 1960s to the late 1980s to see what these would imply for changes in material well-being. They find the story to be quite complicated, with trends depending on the unit of analysis, the weighting scheme, the income measure, the inequality measure, the data source and the survey used. The authors then turn to measures of consumer expenditures, using Consumer Expenditure Surveys spanning from 1960 to 1989. Mayer and Jencks find that the distribution of household expenditures is less dispersed than that of income, and that the measures of inequality derived from the two do not always move in parallel fashion. Using a variety of data sources, they examine disparities in measures of material well-being such as housing conditions, access to automobiles and telephones, health status, and access to medical and dental care. Trends in such measures do *not* tend to support the argument that the gap between the rich and poor has widened over time.

These conclusions are clearly at odds with other work (including several papers in this volume) about the well-being of the poverty population. Strikingly, Mayer and Jencks find that measures of well-being never have a correlation with reported income greater than 0.50 and in some cases this measure is less than 0.30. The implication drawn is that only a dramatic change in the income distribution would have a profound effect on measures of material well-being. The authors see the discrepancy between their conclusions and those of others as pointing to the need for additional work directly assessing living conditions of the population, starting with the collection of better data on such matters. As they note, it is ironic that while the goal of much anti-poverty legislation has been to guarantee all Americans adequate food, housing, medical care and education, few resources have been devoted to gathering consistent data on living conditions and little work has analyzed what data have been collected. In addition, future anti-poverty policies must face head on the conflict between a strategy aimed at redistributing money income and one seeking to ensure that basic needs are being met, since there is not necessarily a direct correspondence between the two.

1.3   ANATOMY OF INCOME INEQUALITY

In this section, attention shifts to aspects of the overall distribution of income and wealth. In the first chapter of this section, Edward Wolff focuses on the distribution of economic resources among the elderly as well as that between the elderly and the non-elderly. His work analyzes the effects of the social security system (in particular, the

Old Age and Survivors' Insurance or OASI program) on the in-equality of income and wealth. Using data from the 1983 Survey of Consumer Finances (SCF), Wolff divides social security benefits among retirees into two components: an *annuity* value and a *transfer* value. The annuity portion is defined by the benefit level the worker would receive on the basis of his(her) contributions into the social security system (OASI) if the system were *actuarially fair*. The cal-culation is based on the worker's earnings history and social security contributions. The transfer portion is based on the difference be-tween the actual social security benefit received and the actuarially fair annuity equivalent.

Several distributional issues arise in this context. First, in accord-ance with past analyses, he finds that the transfer portion constitutes the bulk of social security payments, 66 percent in 1983. In other words, retirees in 1983 received, on average, benefits three times the value of the contributions they made into the social security system. Second, social security payments are found to have a highly equaliz-ing effect on the distribution of income among the elderly, with most of the influence emanating from the transfer component rather than the annuity component. Third, a similar effect is evident when social security accumulations are added to the distribution of household wealth.

Wolff then considers the distributional effects of taxing the transfer portion of social security income. The justification is that, while the contributions made into the social security system were subject to income taxation, the transfer portion had not been. It is found that the new tax treatment would slightly worsen the inequality of post-tax income among the elderly.

Wolff then considers whether the additional revenues generated from such a tax could be used as a source of a 'capital fund' for young workers, in part to reduce the growing wealth gap between young households (under 45) and older ones in the U.S. (see Green-wood and Wolff, 1988). The calculations indicate that the added revenues would not be substantial relative to the wealth holdings of young families.

Even so, the paper suggests that there is still a need to tilt the age-wealth profile back in the direction of the young. Recent move-ment in the opposite direction has added to concerns about the well-being of children, who reside predominantly in households with young heads. Furthermore, investment in young workers will help improve their productivity at a time when concerns about the adequacy of the skills of the U.S. workforce are receiving increasing attention. Given the importance of these issues and the adverse implications of the new tax treatment, Wolff suggests an unbundling of the two features of the program he discusses. In other words, he recommends establishing a social security capital fund for young workers, but one that is funded by the accumulated surplus of the social security trust fund, rather than by the new tax treatment of social security income discussed above.

The paper by Greg Duncan, Timothy Smeeding, and Willard Rodgers shifts attention to a different part of the distribution of income, the middle class. While there has been a considerable amount of recent research on changes in the income distribution, almost all of it has relied upon 'snapshots' provided by cross-sectional data sources, such as the Current Population Survey. The authors, instead, utilize the Panel Study of Income Dynamics (PSID), which allows them to study *movements* into and out of the middle class over the period from 1967 to 1986. In addition, the panel allows them to use a definition of economic status that is less affected by transitory shocks, in this case an average of income over two-year periods.

The authors focus on transitions for men and women aged 25–50 over five-year intervals in an attempt to explain the recent decline of the size of the middle class. The middle class is defined (in absolute terms) as all families whose after-tax household income falls between roughly the 20th percentile and the 90th percentile of the income distribution in 1977–8. A family's 'initial' position is determined by its average income over the first two years of the span and 'final' position by the same calculation in the last two years of the period.

By construction, there are four possible transitions which govern the size of the middle class: (1) movement from the lower class into the middle class; (2) movement from the middle class into the lower class; (3) movement from the upper class into the middle class; and (4) movement from the middle class into the upper class. Interestingly, the authors find that during the 1980s all four transition probabilities changed in such a way as to reduce the size of the middle class, from 75 percent of the total population in 1979 to roughly 65 percent in 1989. In other words, over this period, families became more likely to fall from the middle to the lower class or stay in the lower class if that was their initial position, and at the same time their chances of moving from the middle into the upper class or remaining in the upper class also increased.

The authors find that differences in transition probabilities before and after 1980 could not be explained by differences in demographic characteristics, trends in macroeconomic conditions, or changes in the patterns of distance to the class boundaries. Furthermore, it was found that the likelihood of making favorable transitions declined for all groups while the probability of moving into a less favorable state increased for all groups. While women's earnings are becoming more influential over time in determining a family's income class, men's earnings continue to be the major force in spurring transitions. The implications here are that the withering of the middle class is primarily due to the worsening of earnings inequality among males. The authors also find that this widening dispersion in earnings is reinforced by changes in the wealth distribution. In other words, those experiencing the largest gains in earnings also enjoyed the biggest increases in net worth. In addition, those households with upward income class transitions achieved greater wealth gains than those who remained in the same income class or fell.

Because of the large relative gains made by the upper income class during the 1980s, the authors make several policy recommendations to aid the upward mobility of the middle and lower income classes. They favor a reversal of the decline in the progressivity of the federal income tax resulting from the tax reforms of recent years. They also recommend that some form of wealth taxation be implemented – for example, the taxation of capital gains at the time of death or transfer. They propose that the revenues generated by these changes be used to fund a child tax credit in the federal income tax (replacing the personal exemption for children) and to expand basic health and human capital programs for needy youth.

McKinley Blackburn, David Bloom and Richard Freeman focus on changes in the earnings distribution during the 1980s by education, gender and race groups. Previous work by the authors (1990), along with research by others, has documented a dramatic rise in the relative wages of the more educated among white males. To extend the analysis, the authors consider developments among female and minority workers. Their objective is to determine whether similar trends in earnings differentials occurred for other groups and whether factors accounting for the substantial earnings gains of college educated white males were the same for minorities and females.

They generally find a widening of educational earnings differences for females and minorities along with those of white males between 1979 and 1988. However, there were some important differences. While the differentials between schooling groups increased to almost the same degree for white females and white males, the return to education rose less for blacks than for whites. Indeed, for both black males and black females, earnings differences between high school graduates and those with less than a high school degree actually narrowed.

The authors achieve some success in explaining these changes in terms of measurable economic factors, such as shifts in the occupational and industrial structure of employment, changes in the industrial wage distribution, the decline in the real value of the minimum wage, falling union density, and changes in the growth rate of more-educated workers relative to their less-educated counterparts. The impact of each of these factors varied significantly by demographic group, suggesting that changes in the overall pattern of educational wage differences were the net result of movements of the various factors in sometimes opposing directions.

In addition to examining education-earnings differentials, the authors also assess the extent to which white females, black males, and black females are gaining ground on white males with the same level of schooling. In general, the earnings of white females tended to move closer to those of white males, as did earnings of black females, though to a lesser degree. For black males, the picture is mixed, as college-educated black males lost ground relative to their white counterparts, while black males with a high school degree or less gained on similarly educated white males. Again, the authors achieve mixed results in trying to account for such changes by the factors listed above.

Before examining possible policy solutions to the widening of education-earnings differentials, the authors test to see how quickly the market is responding to the changes in the wage structure. While college enrollment rates for black males and black females show too much 'noise' to draw any firm conclusions, they find that the enrollment rates of white males and white females are quite responsive to changes in the net return to education. Thus, even in the absence of government intervention, they expect the relative supply of more educated workers to grow over time, leading to a compression of earnings differences between the more and less educated.

Conceivably, the government could play a role in spurring the growth of the supply of well-educated workers by increasing the after-tax return to a college education – either through expanding tuition subsidies, adjusting marginal tax rates, or providing wage subsidies to college graduates. However, Blackburn, Bloom and

Freeman caution that it may not be appropriate for the government to intervene in such a fashion. According to conventional economic analysis, one justification for government intervention is the existence of a wedge between the social and the private return to education. The authors suggest that the social return to education may have risen in step with the private return, thus giving no cause for changes in policy (assuming that policies were at an appropriate level previously). In addition, the authors are concerned that such policies may have perverse effects on the earnings distribution, reinforcing the trend toward greater overall inequality in the distribution of income discussed in many of the papers of this volume. However, as Alan Blinder notes in his commentary, another justification for government intervention is the existence of capital market constraints, which he suggests may be more important in the 1980s, because of increased tuition bills, than previously. A program of expanded student loans may thus be warranted.

In the final paper of this section, Maria Cancian, Sheldon Danziger, and Peter Gottschalk consider the role of wives' earnings as a cause of widening inequality in the distribution of family income. Many economists have speculated that the continuing rise in the labor force participation rate of women has *reduced* the equalizing effect of the earnings of wives on the distribution of family income. The presumed reason is that the negative correlation traditionally observed between the hours worked by a wife and the earnings of her husband (that is, the wives of lower paid men work more hours) has lessened over time. This presumption is derived, at least in part, from the popular stereotype of 'yuppie' couples in which both husband and wife are professionals earning high incomes. As the authors show, such a phenomenon remains quite rare, and so has not had a major impact on the trend of family income inequality in recent years.

Rather unexpectedly, they find that wives' earnings had a *greater* equalizing effect on the distribution of income of married couples in 1988 than in 1968. This is true despite the equalization of labor force participation rates of wives across the distribution of husband's earnings. This finding is due to two factors: (1) the level of wives' earnings gained ground relative to their husbands', because of both the rising wages and participation rates of women; and (2) the distribution of earnings among wives has grown more equal, in part due to a decline in the number of non-workers in this group.

The authors also find that over the 1980s, wage and salary earnings among wives substituted for general economic growth as a major source of gain in real family income (which did increase for two-earner families), as well as preventing family income inequality from climbing to an even greater degree. But, as the authors indicate, such a trend is not sustainable in the long run for two reasons: (1) the proportion of adults living in married couple households has been falling; and (2) the labor force participation rate of women is bound to level off, given its dramatic rise in recent decades.

Cancian, Danziger, and Gottschalk make two policy recommendations to encourage more wives to enter the labor market. First, public assistance for child care expenses when both parents work can be increased, particularly for low-income families. Second, the tax code could be revised to treat home and market production more equally. In particular, they suggest a two-earner deduction for lower- and middle-income families.

References

Blackburn, McKinley L., David E. Bloom, and Richard B. Freeman (1990) 'The Declining Economic Position of Less Skilled American Men,' in Gary Burtless (ed.), *A Future of Lousy Jobs?* (Washington, D.C.: The Brookings Institution).

Blank, Rebecca M. and Alan S. Blinder (1988) 'Macroeconomics, Income Distribution and Poverty,' in S. Danziger and D. Weinberg (eds), *Fighting Poverty* (Cambridge, MA: Harvard University Press).

Garfinkel, Irwin and Robert Haveman (with the assistance of David Betson) (1977) *Earnings Capacity, Poverty and Inequality* (New York: Academic Press).

Greenwood, Daphne T. and Edward N. Wolff (1988) 'Relative Wealth Holdings of Children and the Elderly in the United States,' in John L. Palmer, Timothy Smeeding, and Barbara Boyle Torrey (eds), *The Vulnerable* (Washington, D.C.: Urban Institute Press).

Juhn, Chinhui, Kevin Murphy, and Brooks Pierce (1989) 'Wage Inequality and the Rise in Returns to Skill,' unpublished paper, University of Chicago Press.

Ruggles, Patricia (1990) *Drawing the Line* (Washington, D.C.: Urban Institute Press).

Part I

Poverty: Trends, Composition and Sources

2 Why were Poverty Rates so High in the 1980s?

Rebecca M. Blank

The longest expansion in U.S. economic history occurred during the 1960s. The economic growth of this period is typically considered one of the primary reasons for the sharp decline in the U.S. poverty rate over that decade. In fact, it was during this decade that the term 'trickling down' was first coined, to refer to the positive effect of economic growth on the well-being of the poor (Anderson, 1964). Estimates based on data from the 1960s and 1970s have consistently shown a strong negative correlation between macroeconomic expansion and the poverty rate.

Between the fourth quarter of 1982 and the fourth quarter of 1990, the U.S. experienced its second longest economic expansion. After the sharp recession of 1981–82, the poverty rate exceeded 15 percent and it would have been reasonable to expect that the strong expansion that followed would have produced a sharp decline in poverty. This did not occur. While poverty clearly declined over the entire period of the expansion, it still stood at 12.8 percent in 1989, well above its historic low of 11.1 percent in 1973, and at about the same level as in 1980. The macroeconomic expansion did not bring down poverty as quickly as historical evidence would have indicated. In 1988, for instance, when the overall economy grew by more than 4 percent, poverty fell by a statistically insignificant amount.

This paper explores the unexpectedly slow decline in poverty that occurred over the expansion of the 1980s. The next section presents evidence on the 'stickiness' in the poverty rate in the past decade, compared to earlier decades. The following section investigates several potential non-earnings-related explanations for this fact. There is little evidence that the slowdown in the response of poverty to economic growth is due to problems with the measurement of poverty, to changes in transfer policy in the early 1980s, to the regional distribution of the poor during the 1980s expansion, or to changes in family composition among the poor.

The final section of the paper investigates the decreased responsiveness of income and earnings to the macroeconomy among low-income households in the 1980s. A growing body of literature has recently begun to explore the widening in wage differentials among less-skilled and more skilled workers over the 1980s.[1] That literature indicates that substantial real wage declines occurred among low-wage workers throughout the expansion of the 1980s, while substantial real wage increases occurred among higher-wage workers. These trends are clearly correlated with the trends in poverty. Declining real wages will make it harder for low-income families to escape poverty. The point of this paper is not to describe that wage decline further, but to investigate how important this decline was relative to other factors that were operating at the bottom of the income distribution.

The lower responsiveness of poverty to economic growth is not due to changes in labor market responsiveness over the 1980s expansion. In fact, labor market involvement was more responsive during the 1980s: the unemployment rate fell more rapidly, and earners in the bottom quintile of the population increased their work effort more sharply in the 1980s than in the 1960s. The lower responsiveness of income among low-income households to the economic expansion of the 1980s is entirely due to declining real wages, which offset the increase in labor market effort, resulting in slower income growth.

The implication of these results is that the changing wage structure of the 1980s made economic growth a far less effective tool for reducing poverty than it was in the expansion of the 1960s. It is still an open question whether these trends will continue into the 1990s. If they do, economic growth cannot be expected to produce substantial declines in the poverty rate.

2.1 THE CHANGING RELATIONSHIP BETWEEN THE MACROECONOMY AND POVERTY

In 1984 Alan Blinder and I wrote a paper estimating the effect of general macroeconomic variables on the poverty rate (Blank and Blinder, 1986). Using the official data on poverty, we regressed the poverty rate against a set of control variables for the macroeconomic environment. That regression, based on data from 1959 to 1983, is presented in column 1 of Table 2.1[2] As shown at the bottom of Table 2.1, the coefficients indicate that in a steady state a 1 point increase in the male unemployment rate (a measure of core unemployment in

Table 2.1 Effect of macroeconomic variables on poverty
Dependent variable = Poverty rate
(Based on earlier work reported in Blank and Blinder, 1986)

	1959–83 (1)	*1959–89* (2)	*1959–89* (3)	
Constant	−5.532 (3.941)	−8.987 (4.740)	−5.440 (4.246)	
Male unemployment rate	0.649 (0.254)	0.078 (0.261)	0.646 (0.262)	
Inflation (CPI growth)	0.082 (0.045)	0.011 (0.050)	0.076 (0.041)	
Poverty line/ Mean income	0.386 (0.087)	0.268 (0.100)	0.386 (0.103)	
Govt transfers/ GNP	−0.295 (0.265)	0.290 (0.272)	−0.293 (0.261)	
Lag poverty rate	0.341 (0.117)	0.712 (0.082)	0.337 (0.116)	
Dummy variable (1983–9=1)			−9.112 (11.462)	
Male UR* dummy variable			−0.925 (0.320)	
Govt transfers/GNP* dummy variable			1.338 (1.105)	
Adjusted R^2	0.989	0.979	0.988	
Number of observations	24	30	30	

Steady state effect on the poverty rate of a one-point rise in:

Male UR	0.984	0.270	0.974 −0.421	(1959–82) (1983–9)
Inflation	0.124	0.038	0.115	
Transfers/GNP	−0.448	1.007	−0.442 1.576	(1959–82) (1983–9)

Standard errors in parentheses.

Figure 2.1   Predicted versus actual poverty rates

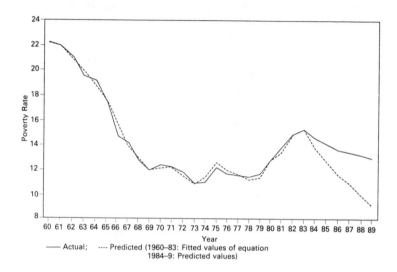

── Actual;   ---- Predicted (1960–83: Fitted values of equation
1984–9: Predicted values)

the economy) would increase the poverty rate by an almost identical
0.98 points. A 1 point rise in inflation would increase poverty by a
much smaller 0.12 points. A 1 point rise in the percent of GNP
devoted to government transfers would decrease the poverty rate by
about half a point.

This regression equation, based on the historical relationship between poverty and macroeconomic indicators, can be used to forecast
poverty for the 1980s. Multiplying the regression coefficients from
column 1 of Table 2.1 by the actual values of the macroeconomic
variables after 1983 results in a series of annual poverty rate fore-
casts. By 1989, this regression equation would have predicted a
poverty rate of 9.3 percent, largely due to a sharp decline in unemployment and inflation over these years. In reality, the poverty rate
was 12.8 percent. Figure 2.1 shows this effect, with a plot of the actual
poverty rates from 1959 to 1989, against the fitted values of the
equation in column 1 from 1959 to 1983 and the forecast values from
1984 to 1989. As Figure 2.1 indicates, the predicted values diverge
steadily from the actual poverty rate throughout the expansion of the
1980s.

Column 2 of Table 2.1 indicates the nature of this divergence. In this column, the identical regression is calculated using data from 1959 through 1989 (that is, including the 6 newly available observations). The results are astonishingly different. The coefficients change dramatically with the addition of these new observations, so that the effects of both unemployment and inflation become small and insignificant. The effect of transfers as a share of GNP changes sign.

Column 3 of Table 2.1 further investigates these differences, by adding three additional variables: a dummy variable, equal to 1 from 1983 on, which allows a shift effect in the general level of poverty over the expansion; the product of this dummy variable and the male unemployment rate, which allows the coefficient on unemployment to differ in the 1980s; and the product of this dummy variable and transfers as a percent of GNP, which allows the coefficient on this variable to differ in the 1980s. The result is a set of coefficients on the original variables similar to those found in column 1, as well as a set of additive coefficients, showing how the effects of these variables diverged during the expansion of the 1980s.

Column 3 indicates that both unemployment and transfers appear to have 'perverse' effects on poverty over the 1980s. All else held constant, for every 1 point fall in unemployment after 1982, poverty *increased* by 0.42 points. After 1982, a 1 point rise in the share of transfers in GNP is associated with a 1.58 point *rise* in poverty. This exercise indicates the difficulties of drawing causal conclusions from regression analysis. The negative correlation between unemployment and poverty in the 1980s should not be interpreted to imply that rising unemployment in the 1990s will decrease poverty. Rather, it is more likely that other (unmeasured) factors, occurring at the same time that unemployment fell, were offsetting the unemployment effects during the 1980s, resulting in a negative coefficient. The question of this paper is what those other unmeasured effects might be.

The regressions from Blank and Blinder focus particularly on the effects of unemployment and inflation on the poor. A simpler way of observing the changing relationship between economic growth and poverty is to regress the percent change in poverty against the percent change in real GNP. Using available poverty rates[3], Table 2.2 presents coefficients that estimate the percent change in poverty resulting from a 1 percent change in GNP in three different time periods. For instance, column 1 of Table 2.2 indicates that the poverty rate among all persons decreased by 2.53 percent for every 1 percent

Table 2.2   Effect of macroeconomic growth on growth in the poverty rate
of different groups among the poor

	All persons (1)	*Children (<18 yrs)* (2)	*Elderly (≥65 yrs)* (3)	*All families* (4)	*Female-headed families* (5)	*Black families* (6)
	*Dependent variable – rate of growth in poverty among*					
Constant	4.67	6.17	–1.20	5.07	1.54	2.45
	(1.04)	(1.29)	(2.15)	(1.09)	(1.44)	(1.18)
Percent change in Real GNP						
1960–69[a]	–2.53	–2.85	–1.24	–2.71	–0.92	–3.66
	(0.33)	(0.41)	(1.33)	(0.35)	(0.46)	(0.81)
1970–82	–1.58	–1.66	–0.97	–1.69	–0.69	–0.55
	(0.33)	(0.40)	(0.65)	(0.34)	(0.45)	(0.36)
1983–9	–1.69	–1.89	–0.71	–1.82	–0.76	–0.12
	(0.39)	(0.48)	(0.78)	(0.41)	(0.54)	(0.04)
Adjusted R^2	0.668	0.621	–0.019	0.681	0.058	0.488
Number of observations	30	30	23	30	30	23

Standard errors in parentheses.

[a] Data for columns 3 and 6 are available only from 1967.

Source of poverty rates: U.S. Department of Commerce, Bureau of the Census, *Money Income and Poverty Status in the U.S., 1989*, Current Population Reports, Series P–60, No. 168, September 1990.

increase in GNP over the 1960s, but decreased by only 1.69 percent for every 1 percent increase in GNP over the expansion of the 1980s.

The evidence in Table 2.2 indicates that the lower responsiveness of poverty to the expansion of the 1980s occurs among a wide range of groups in the population and is evident among both those whose incomes have historically been more responsive and those who are generally less responsive to the macroeconomy. Poverty rates calculated among families (column 4) show a pattern identical to that of poverty rates among individuals (column 1). Poverty among children (column 2) is more responsive to economic growth and poverty among the elderly (column 3) is less responsive than is the total poverty rate. For both groups, however, their responsiveness was lower in the 1980s. Female-headed families (column 5) show a markedly lower responsiveness to economic growth in both time periods.[4] Black families (column 6) escaped poverty faster than other groups when the economy grew in the 1960s, but their poverty rate has shown virtually no responsiveness to the economic growth of the 1980s.

It is worth noting that for most of these groups, poverty is also less responsive to economic growth over the 1970s and early 1980s as well. I do not focus on this fact primarily because the time period between 1970 and 1982 was a very different economic period than the 1960s and the latter part of the 1980s. The thirteen years between 1970 and 1982 contained four business cycles, with five years of negative GNP growth, and a rapid increase in both inflation and unemployment. It is perhaps not surprising that poverty is less responsive to short and sequential upturns and downturns in the economy.

In contrast, the expansion of the 1960s lasted for over nine years, and the expansion of the 1980s lasted for almost eight years. Table 2.3 indicates how similar these periods were, focussing on the seven-year periods 1963–9 and 1983–9, the two periods which we shall use extensively in the rest of this paper.[5] In both of these periods, the economy experienced sustained and continuous economic growth. As Table 2.3 indicates, in the 1960s real GNP grew by 34.7 percent over this period. In the 1980s, real GNP grew by a very similar 30.1 percent. Similarly, unemployment fell 37.0 percent over these seven years in the 1960s, while it fell by a slightly higher 45.3 percent in the 1980s. Inflation rose by 24.8 percent in the 1960s and by 26.3 percent in the 1980s. In short, these periods are quite comparable in terms of their general macroeconomic trends.[6] Since my interest is in the effect of *sustained* economic growth on the poverty rate and the

Table 2.3 Comparative macroeconomic statistics during the expansions of the 1960s and 1980s

	1963–9 (1)	1983–9 (2)
Percent change in		
Real gross national product (GNP)	+34.7%	+30.1%
Civilian unemployment rate	−37.0%	−45.3%
Inflation rate[a]	+24.8%	+26.3%

[a] GNP deflator.

income of low-income households, these two seven-year periods provide an interesting comparison.

2.2   INVESTIGATING POSSIBLE NON-EARNINGS-RELATED HYPOTHESES

The evidence in Tables 2.1 and 2.2 indicate that aggregate poverty rates appear less responsive to economic growth in recent years. This need not necessarily mean that incomes among any group are actually growing more slowly in the 1980s. A variety of possible compositional changes or measurement problems could cause the effects observed above. This section investigates four possible hypotheses. The approach of the section is to first investigate whether these issues would have affected the trend in poverty over the 1980s. If not, it is assumed that they did not affect the responsiveness of poverty to the macroeconomy. If they affect the trend in poverty, then their impact on the responsiveness of poverty is analyzed.

2.2.1   Problems in the Poverty Measurement: The Exclusion of In-kind Income

An ongoing controversy over the appropriate definition of poverty has led many analysts to question the accuracy of current poverty definitions.[7] It may be possible that the seeming differences between poverty trends in the 1980s and earlier decades are due to growing problems in the measurement of poverty, rather than any real changes in behavior among the poor. The most obvious measurement problem that might be confounding the poverty data is the exclusion of in-kind income from family resources.[8] In the 1960s, most current in-kind programs were small or nonexistent, but these programs expanded rapidly in the following decade. Official income statistics do not include the resources available to families from in-kind programs. If this income were counted, poverty rates would be lower. If these programs expanded during the macroeconomic expansion of the 1980s, family resources could be growing faster than reported income and the seeming 'unresponsiveness' of poverty to the macroeconomy could be simply a byproduct of the exclusion of in-kind income from the data.

Table 2.4 presents the changes in spending per person in the two major in-kind transfer programs, medicaid and food stamps, over the

Table 2.4   Changes in food stamp and Medicaid assistance, 1979–89

	1979 (1)	1983 (2)	1989 (3)	Percent change 1979–83 (4)	1983–9 (5)
Food Stamps					
Monthly benefits per recipient ($1989)	$46.90	$53.30	$51.90	+13.6%	−2.6%
Medicaid					
Medicaid expenditures divided by number of recipients ($1989, using the CPI for medical services)	$2236	$2407	$2547	+7.6%	+5.8%

Source: Committee on Ways and Means, U.S. House of Representatives, *1990 Green Book*, June 1990. (Appendix L, tables 9, 11, and 12.)

1980s. Monthly food stamp benefits per recipient, while expanding during the recession, contract between 1983 and 1989, indicating that poverty would not have fallen any faster over the expansion if food stamps were included in the income statistics. In contrast, medicaid expenditures per recipient continued to rise throughout the 1980s, although the rate of increase slowed after 1983.[9] There is, however, substantial debate over whether and how medical services should be counted as part of income. It seems clear that a dollar in medical services received is not equivalent to a dollar in income. Few low-income people, if given extra income, would spend it on health insurance. For these reasons, many analysts prefer not to impute the value of medicaid services into cash income.[10]

The Bureau of the Census has, for several years, provided unofficial estimates of poverty with in-kind income included in household income. A consistent series is available from 1979 through 1987.[11] Table 2.5 shows the change in poverty between 1979 to 1983 and 1983 to 1987 for the official poverty rate, the unofficial poverty rate including in-kind food and housing benefits, and the unofficial poverty rate including in-kind food, housing, and medical benefits.

The results are consistent with those in Table 2.4, indicating that no growth in food stamp and housing benefits occurred during the expansion of the 1980s. The change in poverty between 1983 and

Table 2.5   Comparative changes in official poverty and poverty including in-kind benefits

	Official poverty Rate (1)	Including in-kind income: food & housing (2)	Including in-kind income food, housing & medical (3)
1979	11.7	10.0	8.9
1983	15.2	14.1	12.8
1987	13.5	12.4	11.0
Change:			
1979–83	+3.5	+4.1	+3.9
1983–7	−1.7	−1.7	−1.8
Percent change:			
1979–83	+29.9	+41.0	+43.8
1983–7	−11.2	−12.1	−14.1

Data source: U.S. Department of Commerce, Bureau of the Census, *Estimates of Poverty Including the Value of Noncash Benefits, 1987*, Technical Paper 58, August 1988.

1989 with these two benefits included is identical to the change in the official poverty rate. The real increase in medicaid expenditures causes an additional drop of only 0.1 point in the poverty rate. Thus, the trends in poverty are virtually identical between 1983–7 in all three columns. The percentage changes in the in-kind poverty rates are slightly higher because they are calculated on a lower base. The evidence in Tables 2.3 and 2.4 provide little support for the hypothesis that poverty would have declined substantially faster during the expansion of the 1980s had a fuller measure of family income been used. Thus, the differential responsiveness of poverty to economic growth over the expansion of the 1980s is probably not due to the omission of in-kind benefits in the calculation of poverty rates.

2.2.2 The Regional Location of the Poor During the Expansion

There was an unusually high degree of regional variation in the economy during the expansion of the 1980s. For instance, in 1988, the coefficient of variation in unemployment rates across states reached a

20-year peak, indicating that there were quite large differences between unemployment levels across states.[12] While New England and the mid-Atlantic states saw enormous growth in employment and business activity, the industrial Midwest remained sluggish well into the mid-1980s.

If the poor were disproportionately located in the regions and states that experienced lower growth, their ability to expand income might have been more limited than aggregate economic growth would indicate. In other words, the seeming non-responsiveness of poverty could be due to the regional distribution of the poor and reflect dispersion in regional growth experiences rather than any aggregate decline in the overall responsiveness of poverty to economic expansion.

To investigate this question I use the March 1979 and 1989 Current Population Survey (CPS) data. This provides a random sample of the entire U.S. population. Rather than focussing on individuals, I focus on what I will call *family units*, which is essentially the combined sum of families and unrelated individuals as defined by the Census Bureau. A family unit consists of all related persons who live in the same household. Households with two unrelated single roommates consist of two family units. Households with three generations consist of one family unit. A family unit is assumed to be the appropriate economic entity for pooling income. Throughout the rest of this paper, all poverty counts and income statistics will use family units as the observational level at which the data is analyzed.[13]

Table 2.6 presents the distribution of poor and non-poor family units across the nine Census regions for 1979 and 1989. While a slightly higher percentage of the poor live in the East South Central, West South Central, and South Atlantic regions, and a slightly lower percentage live in the other regions, the distributions are quite similar in both years. As the bottom of Table 2.6 indicates, a chi-squared test of equality between the two distributions cannot reject the hypothesis that they are identical in both years. A similar test, based on the distribution of the poor and non-poor across states, also fails to reject the hypothesis that the state distributions are identical in both years.

Given the evidence in Table 2.6, it is possible to reject the theory that the regional distribution of the poor gave them less of an opportunity to experience income growth in the 1980s. Over this decade, the poor and the non-poor were distributed in essentially the same way across regions.

There is, however, a possibility that the important geographical

Table 2.6   Regional distribution of poor and non-poor family units

| | 1979 | | 1989 | |
	% poor	% Non-poor	% poor	% Non-poor
New England	4.7	5.7	3.1	5.7
Mid Atlantic	16.1	17.2	13.3	15.9
East North Central	14.9	19.5	15.5	17.7
West North Central	6.4	7.9	6.4	7.5
South Atlantic	18.7	15.2	17.5	17.0
East South Central	9.9	6.0	10.0	5.8
West South Central	13.0	9.7	15.5	10.0
Mountain	4.5	4.8	5.5	5.4
Pacific	11.7	13.9	13.1	14.9

Chi-squared test of whether 9-region distribution of poor and non-poor are identical
(10% significance level: $\chi^2 = 14.7$)

	χ^2-value
1979	6.5
1989	8.4

Chi-squared test of whether 51-state distribution of poor and non-poor are identical
(10% significance level: $\chi^2 = 63.2$)

	χ^2-value
1979	11.0
1989	12.5

Source: CPS data, March 1979 and 1989.

Region definitions:
New England: CT, MA, ME, NH, RI, VT
Mid Atlantic: NJ, NY, PA
East North Central: IL, IN, MI, OH, WI
West North Central: IA, KD, MN, MO, NE, ND, SD
South Atlantic: DE, DC, FL, GA, MS, NC, SC, VA, WV
East South Central: AL, KY, MS, TN
West South Central: AR, LA, OK, TX
Mountain: AZ, CO, ID, MT, NV, NM, UT, WY
Pacific: AK, CA, HA, OR, WA

distinction between the poor and the non-poor is not their state or regional location, but their urban location. Increasing attention in recent years has focused on the problems of low-income families and individuals living in concentrated areas of urban poverty (Wilson, 1987), often called 'underclass' areas. If increasing numbers of the

Table 2.7   Urban location of poor and non-poor family units

| | Share of the poor living in | | Share of the non-poor living in | |
	Central city	Remainder of SMSA	Central city	Remainder of SMSA
1964	32.8	17.9	35.3	35.0
1970	33.9	20.8	31.7	36.3
1980	36.9	23.0	27.7	37.4
1990	35.2	22.9	25.2	38.1

Source: CPS data. Note the data are not strictly comparable across years. Starting in 1977, a category 'not identified' is added and the population share in this category grows over time.

poor were located in urban ghettoes in the 1980s than in the 1960s, and if it is harder to find employment and escape poverty in these areas, then this could have lowered the responsiveness of poverty to economic growth.

While it is not possible to test this hypothesis thoroughly in this paper, Table 2.7 provides data on the urban location of the poor and non-poor that indicates there is little evidence of large shifts in urban location among the poor over these years. Column 1 of Table 2.7 indicates that the share of the poor living in central city locations during the expansion of the 1960s was between 33 and 34 percent. The share of the poor living in central city locations during the expansion of the 1980s was a virtually identical 35 percent. Column 2 indicates that the share of the poor living outside central cities but within major metropolitan areas increased somewhat between the 1960s and 1980s. In contrast, among the non-poor, the share in central cities (column 3) drops from 35 percent in the early 1960s to 25 percent by the end of the 1980s. Thus, a trend away from central city residence occurs among the non-poor. The non-poor also show an increased share living in metropolitan areas outside central cities (column 4).

There is little evidence in Table 2.7 that more poor were caught in central city locations in the 1980s than in the 1960s. The constant share of the poor population in urban locations over these decades suggests that changing urban location is not a primary cause of the decreased responsiveness of the poor to the macroeconomy of the 1980s. This does not, however, rule out the possibility that factors related to urban location caused the slower decline in poverty over that decade. First, it is possible that central city locations became less economically viable for residents, particularly as the non-poor population moved elsewhere. Thus, central city residents might be more disadvantaged in the 1980s than they were in the 1960s in terms of their access to jobs. Second, it is possible that 'central city location' is too aggregate a measure, and that the correct measure should be 'living in areas of concentrated urban poverty.' There is evidence that the percent of poor living in areas of high poverty increased between 1970 and 1980 (Rickets and Sawhill, 1988). Unfortunately, I lack any data on economic growth and expansion in central city versus non-central city locations, much less on such changes within particularly poor central city areas. If such effects are occurring, they will show up as part of the earnings-related effects measured in the next section of the paper.

2.2.3 Did Policy Changes in the 1980s Offset Economic Growth?

In the first two years of the Reagan Administration, there were major changes in transfer programs, particularly those aimed at the poor. Some of these changes affected the operation and administration of the programs, while others limited eligibility and benefits. It is sometimes argued that poverty stayed unduly high in the 1980s because of the policy changes in these programs in the early part of the decade.

While these program changes may have contributed to the sharp rise in poverty during the recession of the early 1980s, it is more difficult to understand why such changes would have lessened the responsiveness of the poor to economic growth over the expansion of the mid-to-late 1980s. In particular, if such cuts reduced the availability of public transfer funds, standard economic theory would predict that this should have *increased* labor supply. As employment expanded in the 1980s, one might have expected greater responsiveness to the labor market environment after the cuts (with less non-earned income to rely on) than before the cuts.

In addition, there is also evidence that many of the federal cuts in funding for state-local programs did not fully occur, because states made up the losses. A variety of federal categorical programs, many of them particularly aimed at low-income families, were abolished and their dollars diverted into newly-created block grants to the states, with less money in these block grants than had been provided earlier through the programs. Nathan and Doolittle (1987), in an extensive study of the effects of the 1981 Federal cuts on the services provided by states, found that few of the programs rolled into these block grants experienced substantial cuts, as states shifted funds from

Table 2.8   Effect on poverty rates of holding AFDC rules constant at 1979 level

| | 1978 | | 1988 | | 1988 |
	Actual *1978* (1)	*Simulated* *1978* (2)	*Actual* *1988* (3)	*Simulated* *1988* (4)	*Simulated with* *1978 Program* (5)
1. *All family units*					
Percent on AFDC[a]	5.0	3.7	3.9	3.7	3.7
Dollars of AFDC among recipients	$4173	$5732	$3245	$4523	$5307
Poverty rate	13.5	13.5	13.8	13.8	13.7
Poverty gap	$3297	$2885	$3604	$3197	$2986
2. *Female-headed families with children*					
Percent on AFDC[a]	37.6	36.7	27.2	30.0	30.4
Dollars of AFDC among recipients	$4952	$5735	$3570	$4482	$5349
Poverty rate	42.1	42.1	38.7	38.2	37.4
Poverty gap	$4620	$3451	$5302	$4246	$3545

Simulations based on CPS data, March 1979 and 1989.

[a] Actual data based on those reporting public assistance income, a somewhat more inclusive category than AFDC.

other programs, or (as the recession of the early 1980s ended) put new state revenues into these programs.

On the other hand, Nathan and Doolittle do note that the cuts in Aid to Families with Dependent Children (AFDC), the primary welfare program available to low-income families, did get passed on directly to recipients. I explore the effects of these cuts on poverty rates between 1978 and 1988 by again using the March 1979 and 1989 CPS data.[14] In Table 2.8 I tabulate the percent of the population reporting receipt of AFDC, the dollars they receive, and the poverty rate and poverty gap[15] in 1978 (column 1) and 1988 (column 3). In columns 2 and 4, I use the eligibility and benefit rules of the AFDC program for these two years in each state to simulate the percent estimated to be eligible for AFDC, the dollars they would receive, and the poverty rate and poverty gap under this simulation. In the final column, I simulate the effect on AFDC recipiency and poverty in 1988 if the 1978 programs were in effect.

Before discussing the results, let me note several caveats about the simulations performed in Table 2.8. First, the CPS data provides information on public assistance received, which is a more inclusive category than AFDC.[16] This is one reason why the simulations in row one show fewer families on AFDC than actually report receiving income from it. In the second part of Table 2.8, which calculates equivalent numbers among female-headed households, this pattern is not present, which is reassuring since the vast amount of public assistance income among these households is AFDC income.

Second, the simulation of 1978 programs on 1988 data ignores all potential labor supply changes that AFDC program changes might induce. In other words, the simulation in column 5 takes all income other than AFDC income as fixed (and by default, takes labor supply as fixed.) It is not clear whether the net effect of the program cuts was to increase or decrease labor supply. Among those whose AFDC was reduced or ended, one might expect an increase in labor supply. But the increase in tax rates on the program is generally agreed to have decreased labor supply among ongoing AFDC recipients (Moffitt, 1986). If one believes that overall labor supply increased as the availability of AFDC income fell, then the simulated effect of 1978 programs on the poverty rate in 1988 produces an underestimate; had the 1978 programs continued throughout the decade, labor supply would have been lower and poverty higher.

The simulations in columns 2 and 4 of Table 2.8 are similar to such simulation results elsewhere in the literature (for instance, see Ruggles and Michel, 1987). While the number reporting receipt of AFDC income is reasonably well estimated, the simulations allocate more AFDC dollars to these women than they report receiving.[17] The poverty rates resulting from the simulations are virtually identical to reported poverty rates, not surprising since the AFDC program in most states is too limited to move anyone out of poverty, but poverty gaps in the simulations are smaller.

The effect of changes in the AFDC program can be seen by comparing columns 4 and 5. Column 5 of Table 2.8 indicates that if the 1978 programs were available in 1988, the percent of the population on AFDC would be virtually identical to the percent who are simulated to be on AFDC (column 4) under the actual 1988 programs. The amount of money available to these recipients would be larger, however. Poverty rates would be lower by only a very small amount; poverty gaps would fall by a few hundred dollars. If the 1978 programs were in effect in 1988, the poor would surely be somewhat better off, according to these simulations, because they would have more AFDC dollars available. But the overall poverty rate would be largely unaffected by this change.

The implication of Table 2.8 is that the cuts in AFDC, the primary cash income program to experience cuts in the early 1980s, had little effect on the overall trend in poverty over the 1980s. Poverty would not have been appreciably lower in 1988 had AFDC remained unchanged. In addition, there is little theoretical reason to believe that these cuts would have decreased the responsiveness of the poor to the macroeconomy.

2.2.4 The Changing Demographic Composition of Family Units

Table 2.2 indicated that not all groups among the poor are equally responsive to economic growth. For instance, poverty among female-headed households and elderly households is less affected by the growth in overall employment opportunities. This implies that some of the shift in responsiveness during the 1980s may have been due to shifting demographic composition among the poor. Since more of the poor were in female-headed households in the 1980s than in the 1960s and 1970s, aggregate poverty could be less responsive to GNP growth, not because any group had become less responsive, but because those family types with lower responsiveness had increased their share of the poor population.

To investigate the extent to which changing demographic composition has affected poverty rates, I again turn to the March CPS data. This data is available on tape from 1964 through 1990.[18] Since data on income and poverty are based on households' experiences in the previous year, this provides me with continuous annual information from 1963 through 1989. As before, I investigate poverty and income among family units.

A sense of the importance of the demographic composition of family units to the poverty rate can be seen in Table 2.9. Column 1 of Table 2.9 reports the actual changes in poverty rates among all family units. Over the 1960s poverty falls by over 7 points, while it rises by 0.37 of a point over the 1980s.[19]

In column 2 I recalculate poverty rates, holding the demographic composition of family units constant at their 1964 levels. In particular, I hold constant the population shares of six groups: single female heads with other relatives in the family unit, single male heads with other relatives, married couples with other relatives, married couples living alone, single females living alone, and single males living alone.[20] Column 2 therefore indicates what the change in poverty rates would have been had the demographic composition of the

Table 2.9   Effect of demographic change on poverty rates, 1963–89

	Actual change in poverty rate (1)	With 1964 population weights constant (2)	Residual: change in poverty due to changing demographics (3)
1963–89	−8.42	−11.15	2.73
1963–69	−7.03	−7.91	0.88
1969–79	−1.76	−3.15	1.39
1979–89	0.37	−0.09	0.46

Data calculated from the March CPS, 1964–89. Six demographic groups are used: single females with other relatives, single males with other relatives, single females living alone, single males living alone, married couples with other relatives, and married couples living alone.

population remained constant. Column 3 reports the difference between column 2 and column 1, which is essentially the change in poverty rates that occurred solely because of the change in demographic composition.

Column 2 indicates that poverty would have fallen more rapidly (or risen more slowly) in each of the last three decades had the composition of the population remained unchanged. In particular, poverty was almost one point higher (0.88) in 1969 because of shifts toward poorer family types between 1963 and 1969. Poverty was over one point higher (1.39) by the end of the 1970s, when these demographic shifts occurred at a relatively faster rate. Over the 1980s, these shifts continued to increase poverty, but only by about one-third as much as over the 1970s.

Table 2.9 indicates that demographic shifts affected the level and trend of the poverty rate over the past three decades, but does not provide direct evidence on their effect on the responsiveness of poverty to macroeconomic growth. Table 2.10 explores this question more closely, using the same data from the CPS from 1963 through 1989. In Table 2.10 I report the results of a series of regressions of the form

$$PR_{t,i} - PR_{t-1,i} = \alpha_1 {}^* PCGNP_1 + \alpha_2 {}^* PCGNP_2 + \alpha_3 {}^* PCGNP_3, \quad (1)$$

where $PCGNP_1 =$ percent change in real GNP for years 1963–1969, 0 otherwise;

Table 2.10   Responsiveness of poverty rates among different groups to real GNP growth

	Change in share of family units below poverty line		Change in share of family units below twice poverty line	
	Coefficient on percent change in Real GNP		Coefficient on percent change in Real GNP	
	1963–9 (1)	*1983–9* (2)	*1963–9* (3)	*1983–9* (4)
All family units	–0.26	–0.09	–0.46	–0.18
	(0.05)	(0.05)	(0.10)	(0.10)
Single females	–0.30	–0.16	–0.26	–0.21
w/ other relatives	(0.12)	(0.13)	(0.16)	(0.16)
Single males	–0.13	–0.08	–0.26	–0.10
w/ other relatives	(0.17)	(0.17)	(0.29)	(0.30)
Married couples	–0.23	–0.09	–0.59	–0.25
w/ other relatives	(0.06)	(0.06)	(0.14)	(0.14)
Married couples	–0.21	–0.06	–0.39	–0.17
Living alone	(0.08)	(0.08)	(0.11)	(0.11)
Single females	–0.44	–0.19	–0.29	–0.26
Living alone	(0.12)	(0.13)	(0.10)	(0.10)
Single males	–0.38	–0.12	–0.44	–0.16
Living alone	(0.08)	(0.08)	(0.14)	(0.15)
Data with constant	–0.27	–0.10	–0.46	–0.22
population weights[a]	(0.05)	(0.06)	(0.11)	(0.11)

Standard errors in parentheses.
[a] Based on six family groups indicated above.

$PCGNP_2 =$ percent change in real GNP for years 1970–1982, 0 otherwise;

$PCGNP_3 =$ percent change in real GNP for years 1983–1989, 0 otherwise;

and $PR_{t,i}$ represents the poverty rate for time t and group i.[21] Columns 1 and 2 of Table 2.10 report the coefficients α_1 and α_3 for all family units and for the six underlying demographic groups. Each coefficient can be interpreted as the change in the level of poverty that occurs with a 1 percent increase in GNP in the indicated time period. Columns 3 and 4 use the change in the share of family units below two times the poverty line as the dependent variable, which I will refer to as the 'near-poverty rate.' The results in Table 2.10

indicate the responsiveness of the poverty rate and near-poverty rate to the economic expansion of the 1960s and the expansion of the 1980s.[22]

For all family units, a one percent increase in real GNP reduces poverty by one-fourth of a point (−0.26) between 1963 and 1969, but reduces poverty by less than one-tenth of a point (−0.09) between 1983 and 1989. The same pattern occurs for the near-poverty rate as well. The difference in responsiveness between different demographic groups can be seen in rows 2 through 7. Single males and females living alone show the biggest point changes in poverty as the economy grows in the 1960s.[23] All groups show substantially lower responsiveness to GNP growth in the 1980s.

The bottom row of Table 2.10 estimates the same regression with a new dependent variable: I create a 'constant-population-weight poverty rate' holding the demographic composition of each of these six groups constant at their starting level in the 1964 data. (This is the same variable whose poverty rate changes are reported in column 2 of Table 2.9.) The coefficients in this last row vary little from the coefficients in the first row. In both regressions, the responsiveness of poverty to GNP falls by about two-thirds between the 1960s and the 1980s. This implies that the shifting demographic composition of poverty, while it has affected the underlying poverty rate, has had little differential effect on its responsiveness to the macroeconomic expansion of the 1980s.

Table 2.11 verifies this by estimating the reduced responsiveness to GNP growth indicated by the equations in Table 2.10 among the overall poverty rate and the constant-demographics poverty rate. Row 1, column 1 indicates that the regression for all family units estimates that poverty fell 2.2 points between 1983 and 1989. If, however, poverty had been as responsive over these years as it was during a time of similar growth in the 1960s, we would have expected it to fall by 6.0 points. The difference indicates that poverty was 3.9 points higher by the end of the 1980s due to its reduced responsiveness to aggregate economic growth. Had the demographic composition of the poverty population remained unchanged, poverty would have been 3.7 points higher by the end of the 1980s (6.1 − 2.4). This indicates that 0.2 points in decreased responsiveness was due to the changing demographics of the poor population. As the bottom of Table 2.11 indicates, this is 4.4 percent of the overall decline in the reduced responsiveness of the poverty rate.

In short, the changing demographic composition among the poor

Table 2.11   Decreased responsiveness of poverty rates to GNP growth: simulated effects

	Fitted change in poverty rate 1983–9 (1)	Expected change in poverty rate if 1960s responsiveness had continued (2)
(1) All family units	−2.17	−6.05
If demographic composition had remained unchanged at 1964 weights		
(2) All family units	−2.41	−6.12
Decreased responsiveness of poverty over expansion of 1980s: (Row 1, Column 2 − Column 1)	−3.88	
Decreased responsiveness if population weights constant: (Row 2, Column 2 − Column 1)	−3.71	
Decrease in responsiveness due to changing demographics:	−0.17 (4.4%)	

has had almost no effect on the making poverty 'stickier' over the 1980s. Less than 5 percent of the reduced responsiveness of the poverty rate to real GNP growth can be explained by the changing composition of family types.

This section indicates that none of the four possible hypotheses investigated here explain the unexpectedly slow decline in poverty over the 1980s. Neither the omission of in-kind income from the poverty statistics, the change in AFDC program rules, or the distribution of the poor across regions has affected the relative trends in poverty over the 1980s. Changing demographic composition among the poor, while it has affected both the level and the trend in poverty over the past three decades, has had little effect on the responsiveness of poverty to the overall macroeconomy.

2.3   EXPLORING THE RESPONSIVENESS OF EARNINGS TO THE MACROECONOMY

The evidence above suggests that there may have been a real decrease in the responsiveness of earnings and other income components to macroeconomic growth among the poor. This section explores that possibility further.

Much of the literature on the responsiveness of the income distribution to the macroeconomy indicates that the income distribution in the United States has historically narrowed in times of economic expansion, at least in the post-World War II era. The primary reason why the poor 'catch up' in economic booms is expanded employment opportunities. The incidence of unemployment, non-employment, and part-time employment is heavily skewed toward the bottom of the income distribution; when employment grows it is the unemployed, non-employed, and part-time employed who are most able to take advantage of that growth (Blank and Blinder, or Gramlich and Laren, 1984). Persons in the upper half of the income distribution who are already working full-time have little opportunity to expand their labor market involvements in a boom (although, of course, other non-working, unemployed or part-time employed family members can always expand work hours). Thus, incomes among the poor typically grow faster in boom times because of increased labor market involvements.

Evidence on wage changes over the business cycle are more mixed. Earlier empirical evidence based on wage data from the 1940s, 1950s, and 1960s seems to indicate that wages were largely non-cyclical, but evidence from the 1970s and early 1980s indicates mild pro-cyclicality in the overall level of wages (Blank, 1990, or Keane, Moffitt and Runkle, 1988). Evidence on the relative responsiveness of wages among different groups in the income distribution is more limited. Evidence based primarily on 1970s data seems to indicate that wages changed little with the cycle for low-income groups during that time period (Blank, 1989), but one might expect that a period of sustained economic growth, particularly if it is related to underlying productivity growth, would result in real wage gains.

Note that I cannot explore the changing responsiveness of income and income components to economic growth by looking at changes among the poor and the non-poor. Because the poverty line is a fixed absolute dollar amount (it changes only with the consumer price index), the family units below the poverty line are a constantly changing group. As income expands, the poor become increasingly selected toward the least-skilled and/or least-employable. Therefore, exploring labor market involvements among the poor over the expansion will mix together the real effects of the expansion with the changing selectivity of who is poor. Therefore, in this section, rather than focussing on the poor, *per se*, I will focus on different quintiles and deciles in the income distribution. I will look particularly at the responsiveness of income and income components among the bottom two deciles (the bottom 10 percent and the 10–20 percentiles of the income distribution) to investigate the effects of macroeconomic growth on low-income households. The bottom decile is composed of 100 percent poor family units in almost all time periods, and reflects the experiences of the poorest persons in the population. The second decile is composed of between 30 to 40 percent poor family units (it varies across years) and reflects the experiences of the 'better-off' among the poor and of the near-poor. Changes among these two groups will be compared with the changes occurring in the upper four quintiles (groups between the 20–40, 40–60, 60–80 and 80–100 percentiles in the income distribution).

2.3.1 Responsiveness of Income and Income Components to Economic Growth

Table 2.12 investigates the responsiveness of different components of income to the macroeconomy among different income groups over the 1960s and the 1980s. The estimated equations in Table 2.12 are in the same format as equation (1); the dependent variable is indicated at the top of each column. Columns 1 and 2 show the level change in total income that results from a 1 percent increase in real GNP between 1963–9 and 1983–9, respectively. Among the bottom two deciles, total income rises only about one-third as fast in the 1980s in response to GNP growth as it does in the 1960s.[24] Similar patterns of somewhat slower growth in income during the 1980s are evident among the middle three quintiles as well. Income among the top quintile was far more responsive to economic growth over the 1980s.

Columns 3 and 4 look at the earnings of the head of the family unit.[25] Responsiveness of earnings is lower among all groups in the 1980s expansion. For all groups except the top quintile, it is the decreased responsiveness of earnings which is primarily responsible for the decreased responsiveness of total income to economic growth.

Columns 5 and 6 investigate the responsiveness of the earnings of spouses to economic growth. These numbers are harder to interpret, since major changes in the propensity of married women to work occur over this time period and almost surely are confounded with these coefficients on GNP growth. Among the bottom two deciles there appears to be little difference in the responsiveness of spouse's

Table 2.12 Responsiveness of income components among family units to real GNP growth

	Dependent variable							
	Total income		Head's earnings		Spouse's earnings		Other income	
	Coefficient on percent change in Real GNP		Coefficient on percent change in Real GNP		Coefficient on percent change in Real GNP		Coefficient on percent change in Real GNP	
	1963–9 (1)	1983–9 (2)	1963–9 (3)	1983–9 (4)	1963–9 (5)	1983–9 (6)	1963–9 (7)	1983–9 (8)
All family units	194 (39)	166 (40)	118 (33)	70 (34)	29 (14)	55 (14)	47 (24)	41 (24)
Bottom decile (0–10%)	48 (11)	18 (12)	30 (8)	8 (8)	5 (8)	4 (8)	13 (10)	6 (10)
Second decile (10–20%)	91 (18)	34 (18)	54 (16)	29 (16)	18 (10)	16 (10)	18 (16)	−11 (16)
Second quintile (20–40%)	138 (29)	55 (29)	91 (30)	38 (30)	14 (10)	21 (10)	34 (17)	−5 (17)
Third quintile (40–60%)	182 (40)	97 (40)	120 (43)	68 (44)	25 (12)	37 (12)	37 (20)	−8 (20)
Fourth quintile (60–80%)	235 (46)	181 (46)	144 (50)	77 (51)	58 (19)	71 (19)	33 (30)	33 (30)
Top quintile (80–100%)	348 (95)	473 (96)	196 (83)	150 (84)	49 (41)	188 (41)	102 (89)	135 (89)

Standard errors in parentheses.

earnings between the two time periods. Thus, this variable does not seem too important in explaining differences in the responsiveness of aggregate income for low-income families.

Finally, columns 7 and 8 look at the responsiveness of the residual category 'other income' to economic growth. This includes all sources of income other than primary and spouse earnings, and as a result it is a very aggregate and not very informative category.[26] For the bottom two deciles, this category is highly composed of transfer income (public and private); for top quintile groups, it contains more dividend, interest, and rental income. Only among the top quintile does this category appear to show substantial responsiveness to economic growth. Among the other groups, this category is small relative to the changes in earnings of the head.

The evidence in Table 2.12 indicates that most of the slowdown in the growth of aggregate income among poor and near-poor income groups occurs because of the slowdown in the growth of earnings among the head of family units. Thus, it is to this issue that we turn next.

2.3.2 The Responsiveness of Labor Market Involvements versus Wages

Table 2.13 looks at the relative responsiveness of four different measures of labor market involvement among family unit heads. Columns 1 and 2 indicate that the decrease in the probability of unemployment over the past year was somewhat larger during the economic growth of the 1980s than during the economic growth of the 1960s, although these numbers are small and poorly determined. Thus, unemployment appears slightly more responsive to economic growth in the 1980s than in the 1960s. This pattern occurs for all groups.

Similarly, columns 3 and 4 investigate the responsiveness of the probability that a family unit head is employed over the past year. Among the bottom two deciles, this probability is unchanged or increases slightly with GNP growth in the 1980s. For the upper four quintiles, and for the population as a whole, the probability of unemployment appears slightly less responsive to economic growth in the 1980s.

Columns 5 and 6 investigate the annual weeks of work among those who work.[27] For the top four quintiles there is little change in weeks of work over the cycle in either period. For the bottom two deciles, weeks of work grow substantially faster during the 1980s than during the 1960s expansion. Similarly, columns 7 and 8 indicate that the probability that the head is employed part-time over the year is as responsive in both expansions, except among the bottom two deciles whose part-time probabilities decline faster with the expansion of the 1980s.

In short, for the poorest 20 percent of the population, labor market involvement is generally more responsive to economic growth throughout the 1980s than it was in the 1960s: unemployment and part-time work fall more rapidly with growth in GNP, while hours of work rise more quickly. For wealthier quintiles, the difference in responsiveness between these two time periods is less striking.

There is little in Table 2.13 to indicate that poverty should be less responsive to economic growth over the 1980s than it was during the 1960s. In fact, based on these measures of labor market involvement, Table 2.13 would lead us to predict that poverty should have fallen faster in the 1980s, as the poorest groups responded more strongly to labor market opportunities.

Earned income among family unit heads is the product of weeks worked, the probability of working, and the weekly wage. If the probability of working and weeks worked expanded faster in the 1980s than in the 1960s, but earned income grew less fast, then changes in the responsiveness of weekly wages to macroeconomic growth must be responsible. Note that I have no direct information on wage rates in this data set, but I can estimate weekly wages using heads' earnings divided by the product of the probability of working times weekly hours worked.[28] But there is necessarily a lot of noise in this estimate. Therefore, I do not get very precise estimates of the effect of real GNP growth on weekly wages. There are some suggestive patterns in the data, however, although they are largely insignificant.

Table 2.14 provides estimates of the responsiveness of real weekly wages to GNP growth. During the 1960s, real wages rose with the expanding economy for all groups. For instance, the bottom decile experienced about a $2 increase in weekly wages for every 1 percent increase in GNP, while the second decile experienced a $1 increase. In the 1980s, however, the estimated coefficients indicate that real wages for these two groups actually decrease as the economy grows (although these coefficients are insignificantly different from zero). In short, there no evidence at all of any responsiveness in real wages among the bottom two deciles, and only a small effect among the

Table 2.13 Responsiveness of labor market indicators for heads of family units to real GNP growth

	Dependent variable							
	Probability of unemployment last year		Probability of employment last year		Weeks worked last year		Probability of part-time emp last yr	
	Coefficient on percent change in Real GNP		Coefficient on percent change in Real GNP		Coefficient on percent change in Real GNP		Coefficient on percent change in Real GNP	
	1963–9 (1)	1983–9 (2)	1963–9 (3)	1983–9 (4)	1963–9 (5)	1983–9 (6)	1963–9 (7)	1983–9 (8)
All family units	-0.13 (0.08)	-0.18 (0.08)	0.20 (0.08)	0.06 (0.08)	0.03 (0.02)	0.05 (0.02)	-0.02 (0.04)	-0.01 (0.04)
Bottom decile (0–10%)	-0.12 (0.11)	-0.16 (0.12)	-0.01 (0.10)	-0.01 (0.10)	-0.03 (0.19)	0.45 (0.19)	0.28 (0.18)	0.08 (0.18)
Second decile (10–20%)	-0.08 (0.10)	-0.11 (0.10)	0.20 (0.15)	0.24 (0.15)	0.09 (0.09)	0.26 (0.10)	-0.06 (0.19)	-0.19 (0.19)
Second quintile (20–40%)	-0.19 (0.12)	-0.26 (0.12)	0.31 (0.14)	0.11 (0.14)	0.06 (0.05)	0.11 (0.05)	-0.07 (0.08)	-0.07 (0.08)
Third quintile (40–60%)	-0.22 (0.11)	-0.24 (0.11)	0.21 (0.12)	0.05 (0.12)	0.05 (0.03)	0.06 (0.03)	-0.02 (0.04)	-0.02 (0.04)
Fourth quintile (60–80%)	-0.08 (0.10)	-0.20 (0.10)	0.18 (0.09)	0.03 (0.09)	0.01 (0.03)	0.02 (0.02)	-0.02 (0.05)	-0.01 (0.05)
Top quintile (80–100%)	-0.05 (0.04)	-0.08 (0.04)	0.23 (0.07)	-0.03 (0.07)	0.02 (0.01)	0.01 (0.01)	-0.01 (0.04)	0.04 (0.04)

Standard errors in parentheses.

Table 2.14   Responsiveness of weekly wages for heads of family units to real GNP growth

	Dependent variable: Weekly wages	
	Coefficient on percent change in real GNP	
	1963–9 (1)	1983–9 (2)
All family units	1.61 (0.98)	1.14 (0.99)
Bottom decile (0–10%)	2.18 (0.58)	–0.32 (0.58)
Second decile (10–20%)	1.00 (0.61)	–0.06 (0.61)
Second quintile (20–40%)	0.90 (0.48)	0.27 (0.48)
Third quintile (40–60%)	1.44 (0.76)	1.01 (0.77)
Fourth quintile (60–80%)	2.07 (0.95)	1.33 (0.96)
Top quintile (80–100%)	2.16 (1.96)	3.53 (1.98)

Standard errors in parentheses.

second quintile. In fact, real wages fall for these groups during many years in the 1980s. In contrast, among the top quintile weekly wages expand more rapidly with the economy of the 1980s than the economy of the 1960s. This dramatic difference in the responsiveness of real wages among different income quintiles over the 1980s matches the results in research cited above that reports widening real wages among different groups in the income distribution.

The story from Tables 2.12, 2.13, and 2.14 is clear: For the bottom two deciles of the income distribution, the decreased responsiveness of total income to economic growth occurred primarily because of the decreased responsiveness of head's earnings to economic growth. This in turn was due entirely to the non-responsiveness of real weekly wages to economic growth among primary earners. Indeed, labor market involvement among the bottom 20 percent expanded more rapidly in the 1980s than in the 1960s. Had wages risen with the macroeconomy as they did the 1960s, poverty would have fallen faster than in the earlier decade. Of course, had wages grown for low-income workers over the 1980s, they might not have needed to expand their labor market involvement as much as they did. In reality, however, real wages declined over the 1980s for this group, with no responsiveness to the cycle at all. This pattern occurs both among the poor and the near poor in the bottom two deciles.

Table 2.15 investigates the changes in total earnings among family unit heads in the different income categories, decomposing earnings changes into the amount due to changes in weeks of work, changes in the probability of working, and changes in the weekly wage.[29] Comparisons are made of the changes in aggregate earnings between 1963–9 and 1983–9.[30]

Patterns across the income groups are strikingly different. Among the bottom two deciles, weeks of work and the probability of working actually fell over the 1960s, so that all of the increase in earnings over this time period is due to the rise in real weekly wages for these groups. Over the 1980s, the opposite pattern is visible. Real wages fall over the 1980s in the bottom decile, while expansions in weeks of work account for much of the increase in earned income. The net result among these bottom two groups is a change in heads' total earnings that is almost identical in both periods, although arising from very different mechanisms. Among the second quintile, the comparison is not quite so striking, but the pattern is similar. Expansions in weeks of work account for far more of the earnings increase in the 1980s compared to the 1960s, and expansions in real wages account for substantially less.

Among the 3rd and 4th quintiles, there is little difference between the 1960s and the 1980s in the decomposition of earned income changes, although aggregate income changes were lower in the 1980s. There is some evidence that weeks expanded faster in the 1980s, while the probability of working expanded faster in the 1960s. Among the top quintile, increases in real wages are the dominant cause of income increases in the 1960s, but expansion in the probability of working is also important. In the 1980s, the entire rise in

Table 2.15 Decomposition of the change in earnings among family unit heads by income group

1963–9	All family units (1)	First decile (2)	Second decile (3)	Second quintile (4)	Third quintile (5)	Fourth quintile (6)	Top quintile (7)
Aggregate change in earnings of family unit head	$3228	$276	$705	$1940	$3193	$4279	$5844
Percent due to							
Change in weeks worked	4.1	–24.7	–10.3	9.0	9.7	0.8	4.0
Change in probability of employment	23.5	–35.5	12.8	30.0	23.9	25.3	33.7
Change in weekly wages	72.4	160.2	97.5	61.0	66.4	73.8	62.2
1983–9							
Aggregate change in earnings of family unit head	$1816	$235	$772	$914	$1550	$2195	$3860
Percent due to							
Change in weeks worked	21.0	124.9	60.1	46.1	29.5	14.8	–2.3
Change in probability of employment	21.4	–3.0	32.8	25.9	8.5	11.4	–3.3
Change in weekly wages	57.5	–21.9	7.1	28.0	62.0	73.8	105.6

earnings is due to expansion in weekly wages. Indeed, for the top quintile, labor market involvement decreases slightly over the 1980s.

2.4 CONCLUSION

This paper has focussed on changes in poverty rates and in income growth among low-income family units over the economic expansion of the 1980s. Poverty was surprisingly 'sticky' over this time period, declining far more slowly than previous experience would have indicated. The similarity between the sustained economic expansion of the 1960s and the sustained economic expansion of the 1980s provides an interesting comparison period to use in asking the question 'why did the expansion of the 1980s have such small affects on the poverty rate?'

My evidence shows that most of the decline in the responsiveness of poverty to macroeconomic growth was not a phenomenon of changing composition of the poor, either with regard to demographic composition or regional composition. Nor was it due to policy changes in anti-poverty programs, or to the exclusion of in-kind income in the measurement of poverty. The slower income growth among families at the bottom of the income distribution was almost entirely due to a decline in the responsiveness of earnings among family unit heads to the macroeconomy. In turn, this decline in earnings responsiveness was almost entirely due to the lack of responsiveness of real wages to the macroeconomic growth of the 1980s. It was not at all due to lower labor market involvement; in fact, labor market involvement was more responsive to the expansion of the 1980s among low-income households than it was during the 1960s.

It is not the purpose of this paper to investigate the underlying causes of the changing wage structure in the US. Other research has investigated the effects of changes in unionization, changes in technology, changes in international markets and their effects on labor demand, and changes in the relative supply of more and less-skilled workers relative to rapidly growing demand for labor market skills by employers. There is evidence that all of these issues seem to be correlated with the changing wage opportunities for low-wage workers.

The final conclusion of this paper is not a promising one for policy makers: The impact of economic growth on poverty has substantially declined in the US during the past decade. Even seven years of sustained economic expansion did little to significantly lower the poverty rate or increase incomes among low-income families. Unfortunately, other tools for reducing poverty are far less appealing: They involve focussed programs, that require large administrative organization and effort. They are also politically difficult to sustain at a high level, since upper income groups tend to experience their costs directly through increased taxes, and their benefits only very indirectly. In contrast, a reduction in poverty due to economic growth (often referred to as 'trickling down') always promised that we could have it all: We could decrease poverty at the same time that we all became richer. Unfortunately, if the changing wage patterns of the 1980s continue into the future, economic growth can no longer be relied upon as an effective weapon in future wars against poverty.

Acknowledgments

This project has been funded by the Jerome Levy Economics Institute. Support has also been provided by the Center for Urban Affairs and Policy Research, Northwestern University. Thanks are due to Sheoli Pargal for excellent research assistance and to Susan Mayer for her assistance. The comments of Christopher Jencks and of participants at the Levy Institute Conference on Inequality and the 1991 Summer Research Workshop of the Institute for Research on Poverty are gratefully acknowledged.

Notes

1. See Juhn, Murphy, and Pierce (1989), Blackburn, Bloom, and Freeman (1990), and Karoly (1990).
2. Slight differences in the results reported in Table 2.1 and in table 8.1 of Blank and Blinder are due to minor data revisions and a slightly different measure of inflation.
3. Official poverty numbers for most demographic groups are available back to 1959.
4. This is consistent with evidence in Blank (1989), based on a different data set.
5. Ideally, one would like to use the first seven years of the 1960s expansion, rather than starting in the second year, to compare to the first seven years of the 1980s expansion. Much of the empirical work of this paper, however, uses data that is not available before 1963.
6. Of course, there are real differences in the economic environment of these periods as well. The difficult economic times of the 1970s and early 1980s resulted in very different expectations and fears in 1983 than were present in 1963. In addition, the more competitive international trade environment of the 1980s affected the U.S. economy in that decade much more than did the international economy of the 1960s.
7. For the most comprehensive recent discussion of this issue, see Ruggles (1990).
8. In-kind income involves the provision of goods and services rather than cash. The largest in-kind program for low-income households is medicaid, followed by food stamps and then housing subsidies. There are also a host of relatively small in-kind programs, such as school lunch and breakfast subsidies or low-income energy assistance.
9. A wide variety of cost-control measures were implemented in the medicaid program in the early-to-mid 1980s to control medicaid budgets.
10. Imputing medical services as part of family income also has the prob-

lematic effect of making the very ill appear better off than the healthy.

11. Unfortunately, after 1987 the Bureau of the Census changed the way in which they do these estimates; the estimates currently available for 1988 and 1989 are not consistent with the earlier series. Data to calculate consistent estimates will be available from the Census at some point in the future.

12. Numbers provided by William Wascher, at the Federal Reserve Board of Governors.

13. One effect of using family units as the unit of observation is that my poverty counts do not match anything published by the Bureau of the Census. The Census reports the total number of individuals living in households whose income is below the poverty line, the total number of families (family units with at least two members) below the poverty line, and the total number of unrelated individuals below the poverty line. My poverty count is a combination of the latter two statistics. Calculating equivalent poverty definitions from my data as are reported in Census publications results in virtually identical numbers.

14. The income data from these tapes is for the preceding year.

15. The poverty gap is the average difference among all poor between family unit income and the poverty line. It shows how far below the poverty line poor families are on average.

16. For instance, it includes such items as general assistance and foster care funds.

17. This is a standard result in such simulations. There is substantial underreporting of government public assistance income among recipients.

18. For the results in the remainder of this paper, I use the Mare-Winship extracts of the March CPS for 1964 through 1988. For 1989 and 1990, I created comparable extracts from the complete CPS tapes.

19. This calculation assumes there is independence between the poverty rate of a group and its share of the population. If poverty rates change as the population share changes, due to changing selectivity into a certain family type, then the calculations in Table 2.9 are too simple.

20. In the first three groups, in most cases the 'other relatives' are children, but in some cases they are parents, siblings, grandchildren or more distant relatives. 'Living alone' means living without other relatives. These family units could be living with other unrelated family units.

21. There are no intercept terms included in equation (1). Because it is a regression of changes on changes, an intercept term for each period would measure underlying trends. But such trends may be related to the nature of economic growth over each period, and I probably want to subsume them into the coefficients on GNP change. As it turns out, in the results reported in Table 2.10 and in later tables in the paper, it makes little difference whether intercepts are included or excluded; the same conclusions will emerge. I therefore exclude intercepts from all reported results to preserve degrees of freedom.

22. All regressions in this paper rely on the percent change in real GNP as the primary independent variable. Much of this work has been duplicated using the change in unemployment rates instead. The conclusions are identical.

23. Realize that Table 2.10 uses the level change in poverty as the dependent variable. Had I instead used the percentage change – as shown in Table 2.2 – female heads would have been among the least responsive and married couples among the most responsive, because of differences in the levels of their underlying poverty rates.

24. There is not a consistent earnings series available for this entire period. The definition of earnings changes slightly between 1966 and 1967. Essentially, earnings prior to 1967 are calculated as a residual and are several thousand dollars higher than after 1967, when persons are asked their annual earnings directly. As a result, the change in earnings between these two years is omitted by including a dummy variable for this observation in all regressions for head's and spouse's earnings and for other income (which is constructed using total income minus earnings).

25. In later years, more disaggregate categories can be tabulated, but for this entire time period, it is difficult to consistently construct any additional income components.

26. The early years of CPS data do not provide information on exact weeks of work last year, but only provide a categorical variable. The midpoint of each category is used as an estimate of weeks in that category for each individual and these categories are used for all years (even those where specifics weeks are available) in order to create a consistent series. The result is to reduce variation in the microdata in this variable. Table 2.13, however, uses the means for different groups as the dependent variable and these means are probably less affected by the categorical nature of the variable.

27. I have no information on hours of work per week in the early years of the CPS (except whether the work was part-time or not.)

28. Recall that a consistent series in weeks is available only as a categorical variable.

29. The decomposition in Table 2.15 is based on the equation

$$\Delta Earnings_{t,\,t-1} = \Delta Weeks_{t,\,t-1}*ProbWk_t*Wages_t + \\ \Delta ProbWk_{t,t-1}*Weeks_{t-1}*Wages_t + \\ \Delta Wages_{t,\,t-1}*Weeks_{t-1}*ProbWk_{t-1} \quad (2)$$

Other decompositions are possible, but give similar results.

30. Because of a break in the earnings series between 1966 and 1967, earnings pre-1967 have to be adjusted. I do this by calculating an estimated 1966–7 change based on the GNP growth in that year and the coefficient on GNP growth over the 1960s expansion. I then 'backcast' from this (lower) number for 1966, using the actual reported annual percent changes in earnings between 1964, 1965, and 1966.

References

Anderson, W. H. L. (1964) 'Trickling Down: The Relationship Between Economic Growth and the Extent of Poverty Among American Families,' *Quarterly Journal of Economics*, **78**, 511–24.

Blackburn, M., D. E. Bloom, and R. B. Freeman (1990) 'The Declining Economic Position of Less Skilled American Men,' in G. Burtless (ed.), *A Future of Lousy Jobs?* (Washington, D.C.: The Brookings Institute Press).

Blank, R. M. (1989) 'Disaggregating the Effect of the Business Cycle on the Distribution of Income,' *Economica*, **56**, 141–63.

Blank, R. M. (1990) 'Why Are Wages Cyclical in the 1970s?' *Journal of Labor Economics*, **8**, 16–47.

Blank, R. M. and A. S. Blinder (1986) 'Macroeconomics, Income Distribution, and Poverty,' in S. Danziger and D. Weinberg (eds), *Fighting Poverty* (Cambridge, MA: Harvard University Press).

Gramlich, E. M. and D. S. Laren (1984) 'How Widespread are Income Losses in a Recession?' in D. L. Bawden (ed.), *The Social Contract Revisited* (Washington, D.C.: The Urban Institute Press).

Juhn, C., K. M. Murphy, and B. Pierce (1989) 'Wage Inequality and the Rise in Returns to Skill,' Paper given at the NBER Conference on Labor Markets in the 1990s, December 1989.

Karoly, L. A. (1990) 'The Trend in Inequality Among Families, Individuals, and Workers in the United States: A Twenty-Five Year Perspective,' RAND Corporation Working Paper, May 1990.

Keane, M., R. Moffitt, and D. Runkle (1988) 'Real Wages over the Business Cycle: Estimating the Impact of Heterogeneity with Micro Data,' *Journal of Political Economy*, **96**, 1232–66.

Moffitt, R. (1986) 'Work Incentives in the AFDC System: An Analysis of the 1981 Reforms,' *American Economic Review*, **76**, 219–33.

Nathan, R. P. and F. C. Doolittle (1987) *Reagan and the States* (Princeton, NJ: Princeton University Press).

Rickets, E. R. and I. V. Sawhill (1988) 'Defining and Measuring the Underclass,' *Journal of Policy Analysis and Management*, **7**, 316–25.

Ruggles, P. (1990) *Drawing the Line* (Washington, D.C.: The Urban Institute Press).

Ruggles, P. and R. C. Michel (1987) "Participation Rates in the Aid to Families with Dependent Children Program: Trends for 1967 Through 1984,' Urban Institute Working Paper, April 1987.

Wilson, W. J. (1987) *The Truly Disadvantaged* (Chicago, IL: University of Chicago Press).

Comment

Daniel H. Weinberg*

My one sentence summary of Professor Blank's paper is simple: *Trickle-down is dead*, that is, there has been a surprising decline in the responsiveness of earnings to the macroeconomy. The key question is, should we believe the message? The second question is, what should we do about it?

Blank does what so few of us do – take a critical look back at her earlier work. Her 1984 specification of the relationship between poverty and the macroeconomy did not work in the late 1980s; her paper is an attempt to ask (and answer) why? Figure 2.1 of her paper should be very sobering to social scientists, at least those doing time-series analysis of aggregates. Of course, we really should not be surprised, the world is not a simple place.

Blank turns to comparison of economic expansions to answer the key question posed above. She looks at parts of the puzzle – omission of noncash income, changes in the AFDC program, the regional distribution of the poor, demographic composition, and so forth – without finding the definitive reason(s). She has done a very clever search for (and rejection of) hypotheses. But, is that the right way to approach the question? Is it right to examine the marginals to understand the interactions? Can you examine only parts of the elephant? Probably not and I suspect that is why the paper is difficult to consider definitive.

One can discuss the margins approach piece by piece, but I will not except to say that the Census Bureau hopes to issue a consistent series on the effects of noncash benefits and taxes on income and poverty covering 1979–90 early in 1992. Rather, I ask the question: Is the comparability of the 1960s and the 1980s overdrawn in the paper? What else is different about the periods and how might those differences have affected the comparisons? For example, increased world competition, especially for products produced by low-skill workers, could have held real wages in the lower quintile down relative to

* The views expressed here do not necessarily reflect those of the Census Bureau or the Department of Commerce.

workers in other quintiles. What about the role of improved education and the continuing shift from manufacturing to services?

Doing an analysis that takes account of interactions is not easy so I appreciate Blank's efforts as a first step in that direction. But I do not think that we have the answer yet to why the economic expansion of the 1980s did not drive the poverty rate down further. Therefore, it is difficult to be definitive on the policy issue – what should we do if trickle-down is dead? If it is, should we try to resuscitate it or instead focus on different policies, such as targeted jobs programs? We need step two of this research to answer that question.

3 Who are the Truly Poor? Patterns of Official and Net Earnings Capacity Poverty, 1973–88

Robert Haveman and Larry Buron

3.1 INTRODUCTION

In this paper we study changes in the prevalence and composition of poverty in the United States over the 1973–88 period, focusing on the first and last years. Over this period, official poverty rose from 23.6 million people (11.4 percent of the population) to 31.9 million (13.1 percent), passing over a peak in the recession of 1981–83 of over 15 percent of the population.[1]

The official definition of poverty in the United States compares the total income of families to an officially designated 'poverty line' that varies with the size and composition of the family. If the income of a family falls below its poverty line, it is said to be poor. Total poverty in the nation is the sum of the individuals living in families whose income falls below their poverty line.

For a large number of reasons, the official U.S. definition and measurement of poverty have been widely criticized. Based on current cash income, the measure fails to reflect the recipient value of either in-kind transfers (e.g., food stamps and Medicaid) or taxes paid. Similarly, the official poverty measure inadequately reflects assets held by individuals and the value of leisure time. Furthermore, the designation of the particular dollar line taken to reflect 'poverty' has been criticized as lacking a sound conceptual basis, and hence as being arbitrary. Adjustments in the poverty line to account for different family sizes and structures have also been criticized on similar grounds. Finally, the data base on which the official poverty measure rests has been faulted for failing to accurately capture true cash income (especially those components deriving from public transfers, income from assets, and illegal activities; see Rector *et al.*, 1990; Ruggles, 1990).

One of the most persistent and fundamental criticisms of the official definition is its reliance on a single year of cash income of a family. For many families, annual income is a fluctuating figure. Unemployment, layoffs, income flows from self-employment, the decision to undertake mid-career training or to change jobs, or health considerations may all cause the money income of a household to change substantially from one year to the next. A second fundamental problem with the official definition is its heavy dependence on tastes – in particular, the tastes of the members of the household unit for income versus leisure. Holding all other considerations constant, a household with strong preferences for leisure (relative to income) is more likely to be counted as officially poor than is a family with less strong tastes for leisure. For example, a two-parent family choosing to keep a parent at home will have a higher chance of being counted as poor than a similar family in which both husband and wife choose to work.

Both theoretical and empirical work in economics have recognized these limitations of money income as a measure of economic well-being. Many studies have relied on the average of a number of years of a household's income in order to gain a better estimate of 'normal' income – income purged of its transitory elements. Others have taken observed, annual consumption to be a better estimate of real economic well-being than annual income (e.g. Mayer and Jencks, 1991). Consistent with the multiyear perspective, early work by Ando and Modigliani (1963) emphasized a life-cycle perspective. They argued for a measure based on a household's optimal level of real consumption in a period, given the presence of the unit's total resources over its remaining lifetime. Becker's (1965) concept of 'full income' extends this concept still further, and includes the time available to the household to be allocated either work or leisure. A further refinement of this full income measure would adjust for differences in the size and composition of the consumption unit, arriving at a concept of *potential real consumption per equivalent consumer unit*. Such a concept forms a definition of economic welfare or economic position which rests on economic theory and which reflects a more comprehensive set of considerations than one year of cash income (Moon and Smolensky, 1977).

Here we set forth an empirically tractable measure of economic

position – *Net Earnings Capacity* – which seeks to reflect such potential real consumption. This measure abstracts from transitory events
and phenomena, unlike current cash income. It also abstracts from
individual tastes for income relative to leisure, again differing from
the current income measure. And, it reflects the potential of the
consumer unit to generate real consumption. Finally, it adjusts for
the size and composition of the family unit. Net Earnings Capacity is
designed to measure the potential of a family to generate an income
stream (which can then be used to support its members) were it to use
its human and physical capital to capacity. Individuals living in those
households with the lowest levels of Net Earnings Capacity relative to
their needs are considered to be the nation's 'truly poor' (Garfinkel
and Haveman, 1977).

In the next section of the paper, we define the concept of Net
Earnings Capacity more rigorously, and discuss the empirical techniques that we use in measuring it. Section 3.3 presents our empirical
estimates of the prevalence and composition of Net Earnings
Capacity poverty over the 1973–88 period. We contrast the nation's
'truly poor' families with those families designated as the nation's
'official poor.' In Section 3.4, we estimate the probability that a
variety of prototypical families – families with particular constella-
tions of characteristics – will be either officially poor or Net Earnings
Capacity poor. Changes in these probabilities over time will indicate
both changes in the underlying character of true poverty in the
United States and the extent to which the standard poverty measure
conveys an inaccurate picture of the true patterns of low economic
position. In the final section, we summarize our findings and indicate
some of their policy implications.

3.2 EARNINGS CAPACITY POVERTY: CONCEPT AND MEASUREMENT

In estimating Net Earnings Capacity for individual families, we rely
on the microdata from the public use files of the March Current
Population Survey (CPS) of the U.S. Bureau of the Census. This
annual survey, which covers some 55 000 households each year in a
rotating panel, serves as the basis for the official U.S. measure of
poverty and for the annual statistics on income distribution, earnings,
income, and labor force patterns. When appropriately weighted, the
CPS yields a reliable picture of the demographic and economic struc-

ture of the U.S. population in each year. We employ the CPS surveys from March 1974 (for income year 1973) and from March 1989 (for income year 1988).

Our estimates of the Net Earnings Capacity of families in the CPS are constructed from estimates of the earnings capacities of the head and (if present) the spouse of the family. In particular, we define family Gross Earnings Capacity (GEC_F) as the earnings capacity of the head (EC_H) plus the earnings capacity of the spouse (EC_S) plus property income (μ). That is:

$$GEC_F = EC_H + EC_S + \mu$$

To estimate the earnings capacities of the head and spouse, we fit an identical two-equation model for four race-gender categories in both 1973 and 1988.[2] The use of separate race-gender groups presumes that the structure of the labor markets in which these race-gender groups sell labor services differs across the groups. Discrimination against racial minorities and women is one factor that justifies the presumption of such differences in structure.

In the first equation, the correlates of the labor force participation of adults of each race-gender category are estimated for 1973 and 1988 using a reduced form Probit specification. Individuals are assigned a value of 1 if they have positive log earnings in the year; 0 otherwise. The independent variables include variables that affect the expected market wage (e.g., education and age), the incentive to work (e.g., nonlabor income and AFDC benefits), and labor market conditions (e.g., unemployment rate). Estimates from the first-stage probit equations are used to construct the Heckman selectivity correction term (λ) for each individual. λ is used in a second-stage earnings equation to correct for the bias in estimating an earnings equation using data only on individuals who have selected into the work force.

The second-stage earnings equation is fit over those individuals with positive earnings, and the dependent variable is defined as the logarithm of observed earnings (LOGEARN). Choice of the independent variables in this equation is guided by the human capital model, and include education, age, region of the country, rural–suburban–urban location, marital status, number of children and their ages, hours worked in the year, health status indicators, and the estimated λ term.

The coefficient estimates from the eight race-gender equations for each year are shown in Appendix A; a description of the variables used in these estimates is presented in Appendix B. The estimated results conform to the expectations of the human capital model. Changes in the estimated coefficients over the years reflect changes in labor supply, labor demand, and the structure of the labor market over time.

To obtain the estimated earnings capacity for a person (EC), we employ coefficients from the appropriate LOGEARN equation and the person's family and individual characteristics. Because we define individual earnings capacity to be the earnings that the person would be expected to receive if he/she worked full-time, full-year, the hours worked variable is set at 2000 hours (50 weeks × 40 hours). By adopting this procedure, each individual with the same set of characteristics is assigned the same value of EC.[3]

The concept of earnings capacity presumes that individuals are fully utilizing their ability to earn income at capacity, i.e., that they work full-time, full-year. However, individuals are constrained from utilizing their EC at capacity for several reasons. For example, health limitations, disabling conditions or involuntary unemployment due to insufficient aggregate demand restrict the total number of hours that an individual is able to work. To take account of such exogenous limitations on the use of earnings capacity, we adjust the estimated EC values by a factor which reflects the time that each individual loses in a year because of health limitations, disabling conditions, or involuntary unemployment. This factor is defined as:

$$\Gamma = (50 - WC)/50$$

where WC is reported weeks constrained from working because of sickness, disability, or unemployment.[4] In summary:

$$\hat{EC} = \exp(\text{pred. LOGEARN at 2000 hours}) \times \Gamma$$

To obtain the gross earnings capacity of a family, GEC, we sum the $\hat{EC}$ of the head and the spouse (if present), and add the value of observed property income (that is, interest, dividends, rents, alimony, and miscellaneous other property-related income sources).[5] Note that the value of public transfer payments are excluded from GEC, whereas they are included in the current income figure on which the official poverty definition is based.

Our GEC estimate neglects the costs which must be borne by a family to attain the full use of earnings capacity. Some of these costs may be specific to particular jobs, and therefore reflected in the market wage rate. Others, however, result from the obstacles to full-time, full-year work for both the head and spouse which are inherent in the structure or location of families, in combination with socially established standards for overcoming these obstacles. The most prominent of these obstacles is the presence of young children, for whom care requirements may impede the ability of single parents or spouses to work at capacity. Families can overcome this obstacle by arranging – and paying – for socially acceptable child care for young children.

To reflect the costs of overcoming this child-related obstacle to the full use of earnings capacity, we subtract from each family GEC estimate the amount required to purchase acceptable child care.[6] We assume the cost of child care to be $1.50 per hour in 1988, and that each child less than 6 years of age requires 2000 hours of child care per year.[7] Hence,

$$NEC = GEC - (\$3000 \times \text{number of children less than } 6)$$

In the analyses of earnings capacity poverty that follow, the estimate of family NEC is divided by the poverty line for the family, and families are then ranked from highest to lowest by the resulting 'Net Earnings Capacity welfare ratio'. Families at the bottom of the 'NEC welfare ratio' distribution are the earnings capacity poor – those families least capable of earning sufficient income to lift the family above the poverty line. We take these families to be the nation's truly poor.

3.3 POVERTY COMPOSITION AND PREVALENCE, 1973–88

The official poverty rate, indicating the prevalence of income poverty in the United States, has fluctuated over the 1973–88 period from about 11 to 15 percent for the entire population. In the population with family heads under age 65 – which we use for our analyses – current income poverty has fluctuated a little more widely, from about 10.5 to 15.5 percent of the population. The official current-income-based poverty rates for individuals in families with nonaged heads in the first, last and a middle year of our study are: 1973, 10.5 percent; 1980, 12.8 percent; 1988, 13.3 percent.

In this section, we compare the composition and prevalence of poverty in the United States (and the changes in composition and prevalence) using two definitions of economic well-being – current money income (the basis of the official definition of poverty) and Net Earnings Capacity (as defined in Section 3.2). For both the beginning and ending years of the 1973 and 1988 period – and for both indicators of economic position – we identify the 13.3 percent of individuals in families with the lowest ratio of current money income (Net Earnings Capacity) to the poverty line.[8] We then compare the composition and prevalence rates of the alternative poverty populations.

Appendix C presents the full set of tables describing the composition and incidence of poverty by the two poverty definitions for 1973 and 1988. Table 3.1 extracts basic information on poverty composition from these tables. Table 3.2 presents information on poverty incidence for 1973 and 1988.

3.3.1 Poverty Composition and Poverty Incidence – CY versus NEC

Perusal of Tables 3.1 and 3.2 reveals substantial differences in the extent to which individuals with various selected characteristics are concentrated in the two poverty populations – CY and NEC – and in the incidence of CY and NEC poverty among these groups. Taking the NEC measure to be the superior indicator of true poverty status, the official poverty measure is seen to *understate* the incidence of (and the concentration within) poverty of *blacks, Hispanics, those living in very large families, those in families headed by a person with a very low level of schooling*, and *those living in families headed by a female*.

Conversely, official statistics *overstate* the incidence of (and concentration within) poverty of *those living in families headed by a young or old person, single individuals, and those living in intact (husband/wife) families*.

Hence, relying on the official definition of poverty creates the impression that those groups commonly viewed as the nation's most vulnerable populations – racial minorities, female heads, and the unschooled – are *less* concentrated in the poverty population (and have a *lower* incidence of poverty) than is in fact the case. Stated alternatively, the poverty problem for these vulnerable groups is substantially more serious than is indicated in the official statistics.

A few examples taken from Table 3.2 make this conclusion clear. For the most recent year, 1988, the official statistics indicate that about 32 percent of blacks are in poverty; however, nearly 37 percent

Table 3.1 Composition of individuals in current income (CY) and net earnings capacity (NEC) poverty by selected characteristics of the family head, 1973–88 (Head aged less than 65 years)

Characteristic	Percentage of poverty population with indicated characteristic				Percentage of national population with indicated characteristic	
	1973		1988		1973	1988
	CY	NEC	CY	NEC	% Pop.	% Pop.
Black	32.4	39.9	29.8	34.4	11.4	12.4
Hispanic	12.5	14.7	17.9	19.3	5.5	8.9
Head aged 16–21	6.8	3.8	6.8	5.1	2.6	2.0
Head aged 61–64	5.8	4.5	4.7	5.5	5.0	5.3
Educ. < 9 years	35.7	40.0	21.5	24.1	16.8	8.1
One-person unit	11.6	3.1	16.8	8.3	6.3	11.8
Family size > 8	9.0	13.8	2.9	5.2	2.8	1.0
White female head with children < 18	12.8	24.4	13.9	19.5	4.2	4.9
Non-white female head with children < 18	20.5	26.4	24.6	29.9	3.8	5.2
Female head without children < 18	10.7	11.3	13.9	14.3	5.4	9.0
Male head without children < 18	5.5	2.2	9.4	6.7	4.2	8.2
Husband-wife families	49.8	34.0	36.0	26.2	81.7	71.1

Table 3.2 Incidence of current income (CY) and net earnings capacity (NEC) poverty by selected characteristics of the family head, 1973–88 (head aged less than 65 years)

Characteristic	1973		1988	
	CY	NEC	CY	NEC
Black	37.8	46.4	31.9	36.5
Hispanic	30.1	35.1	26.8	28.7
Head aged 16–21	35.3	19.8	44.6	33.0
Head aged 61–64	15.6	12.1	11.9	13.7
Educ. < 9 years	28.3	31.3	35.3	39.3
One-person unit	24.7	6.6	18.9	9.3
Family size > 8	42.4	64.3	39.6	70.1
White female head with children < 18	39.8	67.5	37.7	52.4
Non-white female head with children < 18	72.6	88.6	63.1	76.0
Female head without children < 18	26.5	27.8	20.4	18.9
Male head without children < 18	17.3	6.9	15.2	10.7
Husband-wife families	8.1	5.5	6.7	4.9

of blacks are in NEC poverty. For those living in non-white female-headed families with children under 18 in 1988, the comparable incidence rates are 63 percent (official) and 76 percent (NEC). While official statistics indicate a poverty rate of 35 percent for those living in families headed by a person with less than 9 years of schooling, the NEC rate is 39 percent. The incidence gap between the two poverty measures is the most stark in the case of those living in very large families – official statistics record a poverty rate for this group of 40 percent; the NEC poverty incidence rate is over 70 percent.

3.3.2 Changes in Poverty Incidence, 1973–88 – CY versus NEC

The two poverty definitions also convey quite different pictures of changes over time in the extent to which various population groups have *escaped* (or *fallen into*) poverty over the past two decades. As Table 3.2 indicates, official statistics indicate that racial minorities have experienced 11 to 16 percent decreases in their poverty rate; in fact, NEC poverty rates have fallen by a more substantial 18 to 22 percent for blacks and Hispanics. For families headed by a person age 61 to 64 and one-person families, the two measures of economic well-being have gone in different directions. While the CY poverty rate has fallen over time for these groups, the NEC poverty rate has actually increased. White and non-white single mother families have seen their CY and NEC poverty rates decline from 1973 to 1988; however the patterns for each of these families were different. Among non-white single mother families, CY and NEC poverty incidence dropped by the same proportion; while for individuals in white single mother families, the CY rate dropped slightly while the NEC rate dropped by 22 percent.

3.4 OFFICIAL AND NEC POVERTY PROBABILITIES FOR PROTOTYPICAL FAMILIES

While Tables 3.1 and 3.2 present an overview of *poverty rates and composition* among various demographic and economic groups under the two definitions, it is difficult to discern from that data which family characteristics are the most important determinants of poverty status in each case. In this section, we identify 10 family types – ranging from large intact families to single individuals – and calculate poverty rates for each of them using both the current income and the

Table 3.3   Probability that various family types are net earnings capacity and current income poor, 1973 and 1988

Characteristic	1973 CY	1973 NEC	1988 CY	1988 NEC
Intact rural families				
Midwestern farm family	0.28	0.05	0.36	0.12
Rural black family	0.90	0.96	0.91	0.86
Non-rural intact families				
Blue-collar family	0.01	0.00	0.05	0.01
Suburban black family	0.05	0.01	0.05	0.01
White low-education family	0.29	0.06	0.39	0.12
Black low-education family	0.52	0.40	0.52	0.27
Single mothers				
AFDC stereotype	0.93	0.99	0.97	0.98
Suburban, single mother	0.08	0.82	0.17	0.68
Single males				
Ghetto youth	0.88	0.65	0.85	0.60
Independent student	0.70	0.01	0.57	0.04

Net Earnings Capacity definitions of economic position. We do this for both 1973 and 1988. The poverty rate calculations are predictions from empirically fitted functions which measure the independent contribution of a wide variety of characteristics to poverty status. These probit equations are presented in Appendix D.[9]

Table 3.3 presents the predicted probability that each of the 10 prototypical families will be poor by the CY and the NEC indicators of economic position. The prototypical families chosen include those non-aged family types which figure most prominently in discussions of poverty and poverty policy. The constellation of characteristics defining each of these families is described in Appendix E. The predicted probabilities are estimated by simulations in which the specified values of the various sets of characteristics are introduced into the estimated probit equations.

Irrespective of the year (1973, 1988) or the measure of economic status (CY, NEC), four of the prototypical families have a very high probability of being poor – the black AFDC stereotype, the large black rural family, the black low-education family, and the ghetto youth. For these family types, there is no predicted poverty rate that falls below 27 percent.

The families with the lowest probability of being poor are the blue-collar family and the suburban black family. Probabilities recorded for these families do not exceed 5 percent.

For four of the prototypical households, substantial differences are recorded in the probability of being counted as poor by the two measures. For the midwestern farm family, the white low-education family, and the independent student, the NEC poverty rate is below the national average, while the CY poverty rate is substantially above the average. The CY poverty rate is at least three times that of the NEC measure for all of these groups. Indeed, the average NEC poverty rate for these family types (averaged over types and years) is 6.5 percent; the average CY rate is 43 percent. For each of these family types, the high levels of CY poverty appears to be more a matter of 'choice' than of 'circumstance' or 'capabilities.'[10]

In only one case – that of the suburban single mother – is this pattern reversed. Using the official poverty definition, a relatively low poverty rate is estimated – an average of 12.5 percent. However, the average NEC poverty rate is 75 percent. In this case, the official, CY-based poverty measure implies a far less serious problem of low economic position than does the NEC measure.

3.4.1 Changes in CY Poverty Rates – 1973–88

Table 3.4 summarizes the patterns of change from 1973 to 1988 in predicted CY and NEC poverty rates for those prototypical family types for which NEC poverty is judged to be a serious problem.[11] The

Table 3.4 Percentage-point changes in the probability of being poor, CY and NEC measures of economic status, from 1973 to 1988

Characteristic	Current income 1973–88	Net earnings capacity 1973–88
Midwestern farm family	+8	+7
Rural black family	+1	−10
White low-education family	+10	+6
Black low-education family	0	−13
AFDC stereotype	+4	−1
Suburban single mother	+9	−14
Ghetto youth	−3	−5

percentage-point changes summarized in the table are calculated from Table 3.3.

The patterns of change observed in Table 3.4 vary substantially over the prototypical household types. A few deserve to be noted:

- For *all* the families with children (the first six types), the official CY poverty rate either increased over the period or remained constant. Both of the mother-only family types increased their CY poverty rates over the period by at least five percentage points from an already high base. Conversely, the CY poverty rates for the ghetto youth decreased over the period.
- A quite different pattern of changed poverty incidence is shown using the NEC measure. All of the categories except the two intact white families (the Midwestern farm and low-education families) showed decreases in the NEC poverty rate. The largest reductions are for the two black intact families and the suburban single-mother family, where poverty rate decreases of at least 10 percentage points are recorded.

3.5 SUMMARY AND POLICY IMPLICATIONS

The estimates presented above have important implications for both the measurement of poverty and for public policies toward the poor. Table 3.5 summarizes some of the important patterns revealed in our estimates, and sketches out a few of their implications.

Official U.S. poverty statistics, released annually by the Census Bureau, are the nation's official antipoverty report card, indicating the success made in combating poverty. The results of this report card carry substantial weight. Political leaders rely on it for evidence of the success or failure of the policies that have been put in place and of the need for additional resources or altered strategies.

An important implication of our research is that the official measure is a weak reed on which to rest assessments of the nation's progress against poverty, resting as it does on recorded cash income. A superior measure of poverty status, we argue, would rest on an assessment of the capabilities of individuals and families, rather than on their observed outcomes. Our Net Earnings Capacity measure is such an indicator.

Overall, we find that only about 40 to 50 percent of the CY poor are indeed poor in terms of their ability to be independent and

Table 3.5 Summary of poverty patterns and changes in poverty incidence, 1973–88, and their policy implications

Family	Accuracy of official poverty measure	Poverty status	Change in poverty status	Policy implications
Midwestern farm family	Seriously over-states poverty	CY – high NEC – low	CY – increased poverty NEC – increased poverty	Little NEC poverty problem
Rural black family	Relatively accurate	CY and NEC poverty very high	CY–increased poverty NEC–decreased poverty	Very low income and earnings capacity; target for policy action
Blue-collar family	Substantially overstates poverty	CY and NEC poverty very low	CY – small increase NEC – small increase	Little poverty policy concern
Suburban black family	Substantially overstates poverty	CY and NEC poverty very low	CY – no change NEC – no change	Little poverty policy concern
White, low-education family	Seriously over-states poverty	CY – high NEC – below average	CY – sizable increase NEC – sizable increase	Increase in CY and NEC poverty troublesome
Black, low-education family	Substantially overstates poverty	CY and NEC poverty very high	CY – no change NEC – substantial decrease	High NEC poverty, but decrease is encouraging
AFDC stereotype	Slightly under states poverty	CY and NEC poverty extremely high	CY – some increase NEC – small decrease	NEC poverty very severe, and stable
Suburban single mother	Dramatically understates poverty	CY – about average NEC – very high	CY – substantial increase NEC – substantial decrease	NEC and CY poverty very high, but decrease in NEC rate encouraging
Ghetto youth	Substantially overstates poverty	CY and NEC poverty very high	CY and NEC small decrease	Serious CY and NEC poverty problem
Independent student	Dramatically overstates poverty	CY – very high NEC – very low	CY – substantial decrease NEC – very small	No poverty problem, in spite of high CY rate

self-sustaining. Hence, for some of our 10 prototypical groups, we find that the official measure seriously overstates the incidence of poverty (e.g., the independent student and intact white families). For others, the incidence of true poverty is severely understated by the official measure (e.g., the suburban single mother). For these groups, already perceived to be among the nation's most vulnerable, their economic plight is even more severe than is conveyed by the official poverty statistics.

For example, consider family types for which the poverty rate averages 30 percent or more over the two years. The NEC and CY measures agree that four of the family types are in this high poverty category – the rural black family, the black low-education family, the AFDC stereotype, and ghetto youth. However, the official measure would also include three other family types in this seriously vulnerable category – the Midwestern farm family, the independent student, and the low- education white family. It would fail to include the suburban single mother family, which records one of the highest NEC poverty rates.

Similarly, for some groups (e.g., the black low-education family, the blue-collar family, and the suburban single mother) the time trend in official poverty is quite different from the trend in the NEC measure.

These comparisons suggest that a new definition of national poverty is in order, one which would attend to the longer-term capabilities of individuals and families, rather than to their current cash income. Perhaps a National Commission composed of poverty researchers, statisticians, and policy makers should be organized for the purpose of devising a poverty measure that can reliably identify those among us who are truly at the bottom of the distribution of economic capabilities.

On the basis of the NEC estimates, a number of family types are seen to have shockingly high poverty and vulnerability problems. They, together with their average NEC poverty rates, are as follows:

- the rural black family (91 percent)
- the black low-education family (34 percent)
- the AFDC stereotype (99 percent)
- the suburban single mother (75 percent)
- the ghetto youth (63 percent)

These family types would seem to be prime candidates for focused social policy efforts. Note that four of the five groups are black and three of the five are headed by a black male. Two of the five are single parents. All of these groups have shown some progress in reducing the incidence of NEC poverty over the past two decades.

Are there any policy directions that would seem to follow from this evidence regarding who are in fact the truly poor? Because these truly poor families are of working age, two sorts of policy measures would seem to be in order: (1) Policies designed to increase the earnings capacities of these groups, and (2) policies designed to enable them to more fully utilize the capacities that they do possess. The goal would be to move these truly poor and vulnerable families toward economic independence through the exercise of their own earnings abilities.

Some of the following strategies would seem to be particularly interesting measures for experimentation and testing:[12]

- Earnings (or wage rate) subsidies for those with low earnings capacities (that is, low wage rates) could be targeted on both the supply and demand side of the labor market, generating increased work effort and take-home pay for those with the least skills and capacities.
- Effectively implemented affirmative action programs could reduce the effect of labor market (or wage rate) discrimination among racial and gender minorities.
- Education-training efforts targeted on those with few skills or little education could effectively benefit those at the very bottom of the distribution of earnings capacities.
- Child care subsidies could enable additional adults in large families or additional single mothers to enter the work force and increase the utilization of their earnings capacities.
- Child support enforcement – or the adoption of a new child support system (involving the mandatory withholding of child support payments from absent fathers together with an assured benefit arrangement) – would offset to some extent the low earnings capacities of mother-only families, and would enable single mothers to increase the utilization of their earnings capacities.

Appendix A

Probit Estimates of Determinants of Labor Force Participation in 1973

Variable	White males n = 30 407 Coefficient	T-ratio	Non-white males n = 4538 Coefficient	T-ratio	White females n = 35 025 Coefficient	T-ratio	Non-white females n = 6098 Coefficient	T-ratio
ED	-0.026	-1.17	-0.020	-0.44	0.101	5.09	0.068	2.29
EDSQ	0.001	0.17	-0.001	-0.54	0.001	1.04	0.003	2.87
AGE	0.060	10.55	0.109	6.34	0.031	6.39	0.074	6.66
AGESQ	0.009	-19.06	-0.001	-8.97	-0.001	-13.36	-0.001	-7.91
AGESCH	0.00	5.03	0.001	1.33	-0.001	-3.82	-0.001	-3.17
NORTHEAST	-0.108	-2.92	0.053	0.48	-0.037	-1.45	-0.221	-3.20
SOUTH	-0.211	-6.10	-0.068	-0.81	-0.040	-1.64	0.151	2.76
WEST	-0.270	-5.53	-0.246	-1.90	-0.013	-0.38	-0.114	-1.35
SUB	-0.023	-0.90	-0.012	-0.18	-0.045	-2.52	-0.127	-2.27
CITY	-0.057	-2.04	-0.020	-0.27	-0.028	-1.41	-0.180	-3.71
MARRIED	0.101	3.18	0.158	2.26	—	—	—	—
SNC	—	—	—	—	0.694	18.53	0.400	5.05
SWC	—	—	—	—	0.334	9.01	0.066	1.17
MNC	—	—	—	—	0.132	4.74	-0.085	-1.33
TOT	—	—	—	—	-0.682	-27.73	-0.376	-7.20
NUMKID	0.005	0.53	0.011	0.53	-0.100	-10.95	-0.086	-5.85
NONLAB	0.006	-3.12	0.008	1.17	-0.022	-21.633	-0.027	-4.73
SCHOOLLW	-0.580	-6.57	-1.198	-7.56	-0.584	-6.714	-0.589	-3.52
OLD	-0.840	-18.74	-0.341	-2.60	-0.615	-14.30	-0.416	-3.60
HEALTHPG	-0.802	-25.934	-1.179	-16.49	-0.544	-13.24	-0.914	-14.09
WELFGEN	0.001	3.02	-0.001	-1.76	0.001	0.26	-0.001	-0.17
UE	-0.037	-2.12	0.043	0.87	-0.019	-1.52	0.001	0.04
ONE	0.810	3.35	-0.088	-0.16	-0.271	-1.40	-1.078	-3.09

Probit Estimates of Determinants of Labor Force Participation in 1988

Variable	White males n = 34 527		Non-white males n = 7869		White females n = 39 616		Non-white females n = 10 189	
	Coefficient	T-ratio	Coefficient	T-ratio	Coefficient	T-ratio	Coefficient	T-ratio
ED	0.038	1.74	-0.064	-2.41	0.206	9.78	0.636	2.86
EDSQ	0.001	1.15	0.002	2.24	-0.001	-1.34	0.004	5.52
AGE	0.071	12.68	0.068	6.39	0.077	16.16	0.106	12.15
AGESQ	-0.001	-21.47	-0.001	-10.56	-0.001	-22.72	-0.001	-13.59
AGESCH	0.00	-0.31	0.001	2.67	-0.002	-7.56	-0.001	-4.78
NORTHEAST	0.034	1.07	0.155	2.03	-0.139	-5.72	-0.150	-2.70
SOUTH	-0.166	-5.57	0.022	0.34	-0.116	-4.95	0.072	1.51
WEST	-0.186	-6.24	0.226	3.46	-0.034	-1.44	0.181	3.56
SUB	0.025	1.11	0.147	2.74	0.005	0.28	-0.047	-1.18
CITY	-0.063	-2.26	0.086	1.84	-0.011	-0.47	-0.059	-1.68
MARRIED	-0.009	-0.34	0.061	1.26	—		—	
SNC	—		—		0.267	7.11	0.040	0.65
SWC	—		—		0.129	3.75	-0.129	-3.01
MNC	—		—		-0.783	-2.42	-0.200	-3.57
TOT	—		—		-0.516	-19.66	-0.292	-6.89
NUMKID	0.003	-0.23	-0.040	-2.16	-0.167	-13.23	-0.142	-8.23
NONLAB	0.003	4.25	0.005	2.89	-0.006	-15.84	0.003	-3.64
SCHOOLLW	-0.937	-13.31	-1.217	-11.37	-0.822	-14.58	-0.683	-8.37
OLD	-0.536	-12.91	-0.397	-3.95	-0.422	-10.60	-0.246	-2.70
HEALTHPG	-0.997	-30.98	-1.313	-21.19	-0.818	-21.15	-0.852	-13.99
WELFGEN	-0.001	-2.91	-0.001	-4.99	-0.001	-1.35	-0.004	-3.33
UE	-0.016	-2.38	-0.041	-3.14	-0.050	-9.70	-0.072	-7.30
ONE	0.329	1.41	1.051	3.16	-1.335	-6.60	-1.251	-4.58

Least Squares Estimates of Semilogarithmic Yearly Earnings Equations for 1973

Variable	White males n = 25 255		Non-white males n = 3759		White females n = 17 138		Non-white females n = 3347	
	Coefficient	T-ratio	Coefficient	T-ratio	Coefficient	T-ratio	Coefficient	T-ratio
ED	0.006	0.72	0.016	1.03	-0.033	-1.92	-0.065	-3.05
EDSQ	0.001	3.49	0.002	4.27	0.004	6.89	0.006	8.22
AGE	0.050	18.84	0.057	8.07	0.040	10.25	0.040	4.45
AGESQ	-0.001	-18.86	-0.001	-7.90	-0.001	-11.71	-0.001	-5.87
AGESCH	0.001	6.02	0.00	-0.99	0.00	1.30	0.00	1.12
NORTHEAST	0.017	1.70	0.005	0.17	0.060	3.90	0.115	3.08
SOUTH	-0.023	-2.28	-0.075	-2.94	0.012	0.77	-0.191	-6.35
WEST	0.034	3.01	0.109	3.89	0.00	-0.01	0.001	0.02
SUB	0.219	24.96	0.310	10.52	0.186	13.03	0.242	6.65
CITY	0.160	15.83	0.290	11.05	0.192	12.63	0.243	7.70
MARRIED	0.171	13.66	0.120	4.38	—		—	
SNC	—		—		0.093	3.12	-0.074	-1.53
SWC	—		—		0.035	1.35	-0.072	-2.23
MNC	—		—		0.035	1.63	-0.044	-1.09
NUMKID	0.025	7.91	0.010	1.56	-0.040	-4.56	-0.018	-1.52
LOG HOURS	0.974	108.41	0.947	46.06	1.156	157.10	1.103	73.08
HEALTHPT	-0.193	-2.38	-0.416	-2.74	-0.085	-0.68	-0.102	-0.72
HEALTHPY	-0.010	-0.51	-0.030	-0.70	0.083	2.84	-0.027	-0.60
ONE	0.100	0.90	-0.101	-0.42	-1.313	-7.66	-0.756	-2.60
LAMBDA	-0.392	-11.90	-0.408	-6.33	-0.007	-0.21	-0.077	-1.03
R^2	0.532		0.584		0.651		0.713	

Least Squares Estimates of Semilogorithmic Yearly Earnings Equations for 1988

Variable	White males n = 27 086 Coefficient	T-ratio	Non-white males n = 6181 Coefficient	T-ratio	White females n = 24 092 Coefficient	T-ratio	Non-white females n = 6112 Coefficient	T-ratio
ED	0.050	4.38	0.006	0.50	0.093	6.47	-0.061	-4.13
EDSQ	0.001	2.22	0.003	6.36	0.001	2.09	0.005	11.31
AGE	0.055	18.53	0.055	10.15	0.064	18.82	0.039	6.10
AGESQ	-0.001	-13.44	-0.001	-8.58	-0.001	-17.50	-0.001	-6.90
AGESCH	0.00	-0.82	0.00	0.69	-0.001	-3.03	0.001	3.10
NORTHEAST	0.126	11.29	0.015	0.52	0.171	14.40	0.155	5.48
SOUTH	0.014	1.34	-0.167	-6.58	0.055	4.90	-0.038	-1.54
WEST	0.034	2.80	-0.037	-1.39	0.046	3.67	0.042	1.59
SUB	0.208	23.32	0.137	6.42	0.206	21.80	0.151	7.36
CITY	0.138	12.01	0.047	2.46	0.173	14.40	0.140	7.42
MARRIED	0.143	13.21	0.100	4.90	—	—	—	—
SNC	—	—	—	—	0.016	0.84	-0.014	-0.39
SWC	—	—	—	—	-0.019	-1.14	-0.070	-3.30
MNC	—	—	—	—	-0.049	-2.89	-0.065	-2.20
NUMKID	0.020	4.68	0.003	0.36	-0.078	-9.61	-0.031	-2.66
LOG HOURS	0.918	131.06	1.049	75.71	1.040	210.49	1.070	112.62
HEALTHPT	-0.186	-1.48	-0.395	-2.09	-0.111	-1.23	0.071	0.41
HEALTHPY	-0.001	-0.04	0.011	0.24	-0.040	-1.51	0.033	0.75
ONE	0.670	5.53	0.003	-0.02	-1.023	-6.99	0.205	0.98
LAMBDA	-0.367	-10.95	-0.037	-0.66	0.167	5.15	0.060	1.02
R^2	0.555		0.617		0.716		0.751	

Appendix B Alphabetical Listing of Variable Definitions

AGE — Age in single years.

AGESCH — Age times number of years of schooling completed.

AGESQ — Age squared.

CITY — D.V.[a] equal to 1 if from central city.

ED — Number of years of schooling beyond kindergarten completed.

HEALTHPG — D.V. equal to 1 if person participates in disability program.
Program participation:
1. Receives social security or railroad retirement benefits and
    a. is not in school, is age 19–22, and is not widowed, divorced or separated with dependent children.
    b. is age 23–59, and is not widowed divorced or separated with dependent children.
2. For 1988, receives SSI.
For 1973, receives welfare/public assistance and is not unemployed and not separated, divorced or widowed with dependent children.
3. Receives Workers' Compensation.
3. Receives veteran disability benefits, is a veteran, and is not in school.

HEALTHPT — D.V. equal to 1 if person limited to part time work for health reasons.

HEALTHPY — D.V. equal to 1 if person limited to part year work for health reasons.

LAMBDA — Selectivity correction variable.

LOG HOURS — Natural log of total hours worked in the year.
Total hours equals (No. of weeks worked in year) × (No. of hours usually worked per week).
For 1973, we only have information on individual's part-time/full-time status and weeks worked category (e.g. 1–13 weeks). The mean of the person's weeks worked category is multiplied by 20 if he/she was a part-time worker and 40 if a full time worker to get to total hours worked in 1973.

MARRIED — D.V. equal to 1 if person married, spouse present.

MIDWEST — D.V. equal to 1 if from midwest region of country.

MNC — D.V. equal to 1 if married, no children < age 18.

MWC — D.V. equal to 1 if married, with children < age 18.

NONLAB — Non-labor income equals family income minus individual's earnings minus family income dependent on individual's labor supply decision (in thousands of dollars).

[a] D.V. = dummy variable.

NORTHEAST   – D.V. equal to 1 if individual from northeast region of the country.

NOTID   – D.V. equal to 1 if survey does not identify whether individual is from city, suburb or rural area.

NUMKID   – The number of own, never married children less than 18.

OLD   – D.V. equal to 1 if person age 65 or older.

ONE   – Constant, equal to 1 for everyone.

SCHOOLLW   – D.V. equal to 1 if school major activity last week.

SNC   – D.V. equal to 1 if single, no children < age 18.

SOUTH   – D.V. equal to 1 if from Southern region of country.

SUB   – D.V. equal to 1 if from metropolitan area, but not central city.

SWC   – D.V. equal to 1 if single with children < age 18.

TOT   – D.V. equal to 1 if have a child < age 6.

UE   – State unemployment rate. For 1973, individuals are only identified as being from one of 23 groups of states. The ue rate reported for them is a weighted average (by population) of the group's ue rates.

WELFGEN   – Maximum state AFDC payment for a family of four. For 1973, individuals are only identified as being from one of 23 groups of states. The AFDC benefits reported for them is a weighted average (by population) of the group's AFDC benefits.

Appendix C
Composition and Incidence of Current Income (CY) and Net Earnings Capacity (NEC) Poverty

Characteristic	Percentage of poverty population with indicated characteristic 1973 CY	NEC	1988 CY	NEC	Percentage of national population with indicated characteristics 1973	1988	Incidence of poverty in selected groups from the national population 1973 CY	NEC	1988 CY	NEC
Race of head										
White	53.4	43.8	47.1	42.2	81.8	75.3	8.7	7.1	8.3	7.4
Black	32.4	39.9	29.8	34.4	11.4	12.4	37.8	46.4	31.9	36.5
Hispanic	12.5	14.7	17.9	19.3	5.5	8.9	30.1	35.1	26.8	28.7
Other	1.7	1.6	5.2	4.1	1.3	3.4	17.6	16.1	20.2	15.8
Sex of head										
Male	56.0	38.0	47.6	36.3	86.6	80.9	8.6	5.8	7.8	5.9
Female	44.0	62.1	52.4	63.7	13.4	19.2	43.8	61.8	36.4	43.9
Family structure										
Husband-wife	49.8	34.0	36.0	26.2	81.7	71.1	8.1	5.5	6.7	4.9
Single non-white mom[a]	20.5	26.4	24.6	29.9	3.8	5.2	72.6	88.6	63.1	76.0
Single white mom	12.8	24.4	13.9	19.5	4.2	4.9	40.4	67.5	37.7	52.4
Single dad	0.7	1.7	2.1	3.4	0.7	1.5	12.5	32.8	19.0	29.7
Single male headed[b]	5.5	2.2	9.4	6.7	4.2	8.2	17.3	6.9	15.2	10.7
Single female headed[b]	10.7	11.3	13.9	14.3	5.4	9.0	26.5	27.8	20.4	20.9
Age of head										
16-21	6.8	3.8	6.8	5.1	2.6	2.0	35.3	19.8	44.6	33.0
22-30	22.7	21.0	30.2	29.0	20.2	19.6	14.9	13.7	20.5	19.5
31-40	28.4	31.4	31.8	30.7	27.3	33.4	13.8	15.2	12.7	12.1
41-50	21.4	24.9	15.2	17.2	26.6	24.8	10.7	12.4	8.2	9.2
51-60	15.0	14.3	11.3	12.6	18.4	15.0	10.8	10.3	10.1	11.1
61-64	5.8	4.5	4.7	5.5	5.0	5.3	15.6	12.1	11.9	13.7

continued on page 80

Appendix C (*continued*)

	Percentage of poverty population with indicated characteristic				Percentage of national population with indicated characteristics		Incidence of poverty in selected groups from the national population			
Education of head										
0–8	35.7	40.0	21.5	24.1	16.8	8.1	28.3	31.3	35.3	39.3
9–12	52.2	54.6	62.3	65.5	53.1	49.1	13.1	13.6	16.9	17.6
13–16	10.8	5.6	14.5	10.1	22.6	32.0	6.3	3.2	6.0	4.2
17+	1.4	0.2	1.7	0.3	7.6	10.8	2.4	0.4	2.1	0.4
Family size										
1	11.6	3.1	16.8	8.3	6.3	11.8	24.7	6.6	18.9	9.3
2	11.3	8.2	14.3	12.5	15.6	18.3	9.6	6.9	10.4	9.0
3 to 4	26.7	30.4	36.7	41.2	40.5	46.9	8.8	9.9	10.4	11.6
5 to 6	27.4	26.8	23.1	25.4	26.8	19.4	13.6	13.2	15.8	17.3
7 to 8	14.0	17.7	6.3	7.4	8.0	2.6	23.4	29.3	31.5	37.0
9 +	9.0	13.8	2.9	5.2	2.8	1.0	42.4	64.3	39.6	70.1

[a] The non-white category includes Hispanics.

[b] Single male headed family structure includes male individuals plus families headed by an unmarried male without children < age 18. Single female headed family structure is similarly defined.

Appendix D
Probit Estimates of Correlates of Current Income Poverty

Variable	1973 N = 30 369[a] Coefficient	T-Ratio	1988 N = 31 000[a] Coefficient	T-Ratio
RACE OF HEAD				
White	—	—	—	—
Black	0.588	15.25	0.352	8.42
Hispanic	0.316	6.55	0.260	5.74
Other	0.139	1.31	0.222	2.96
AGE OF HEAD				
16–21	0.695	9.41	0.422	5.23
22–30	0.213	5.27	0.180	4.39
31–40	—	—	—	—
41–50	–0.089	–2.31	–0.034	–0.76
51–60	0.033	0.62	0.039	0.62
61–64	–0.066	–0.90	–0.452	–5.52
ED OF HEAD				
0–8	0.317	5.98	0.205	3.02
9–11	0.264	7.22	0.268	6.65
12	—	—	—	—
13–15	–0.009	–0.20	–0.136	–3.23
16	–0.083	–1.23	–0.156	–2.43
17+	–0.147	–1.72	–0.213	–2.45
AGE*EDUCATION OF HEAD	–0.001	–4.03	–0.001	–6.11
FAMILY STRUCTURE				
Husband-Wife	—	—	—	—
Non-white single mom	0.510	8.27	0.373	6.40
White single mom	0.487	9.23	0.416	7.55
Single dad	–0.363	–2.49	–0.138	–1.53
Other male headed	0.331	5.75	0.205	3.89
Other female headed	0.586	11.09	0.400	8.02
NUMBER OF OWN CHILDREN < 18	0.216	26.94	0.289	23.96
OCCUPATION OF HEAD				
Professional	—	—	—	—
Manager	–0.162	–2.40	0.179	2.38
Sales	0.045	0.59	0.411	5.87
Clerical	–0.184	–2.72	0.066	.88
Craftsman	–0.133	–2.41	0.293	4.40
Operator	–0.136	–2.32	0.235	3.22
Transportation	–0.024	–0.36	0.107	1.29
Laborer	0.220	3.35	0.432	5.09
Private HH	0.699	5.35	0.559	3.99

continued on page 82

Appendix D (*continued*)

Variable	1973 N = 30 369[a] Coefficient	T-Ratio	1988 N = 31 000[a] Coefficient	T-Ratio
Service	0.190	3.13	0.537	8.61
Farmer	0.909	13.73	0.898	11.25
Military	−0.190	−1.67	0.219	1.61
Unemployed/NILF	−0.318	−4.41	0.127	1.75
REGION				
Northeast	0.043	1.17	−0.147	−3.45
South	0.203	5.92	0.107	3.01
West	0.239	6.65	0.047	1.15
Midwest	—	—	—	—
LOCATION				
Suburban	—	—	—	—
City	0.075	2.29	0.125	3.49
Nonurban	0.303	9.84	0.329	8.88
Not ID	X	X	0.113	2.71
WEEKS WORKED				
Full-time (head)	−0.037	−36.74	−0.041	−43.90
Part-time (head)	−0.022	−14.66	−0.024	−18.53
Full-time (spouse)	−0.015	−16.96	−0.024	−25.16
Part-time (spouse)	−0.005	−4.46	−0.013	−10.0
STUDENT STATUS				
Student (head)	0.126	1.34	0.013	0.16
Student (spouse)	0.186	1.12	−0.033	−0.22
HEALTH STATUS[b]				
Disabled (head)	−0.023	−0.65	−0.261	−6.26
Disabled (spouse)	−0.035	−0.64	−0.216	−3.30
GHETTO[c]	−0.125	−0.61	−0.074	−0.39
CONSTANT	−0.387	−3.54	−0.016	−0.14

Probit Estimates of Correlates of Net Earnings Capacity Poverty

Variable	1973 N = 30 369[a] Coefficient	T-Ratio	1988 N = 31 000[a] Coefficient	T-Ratio
RACE OF HEAD				
White	—	—	—	—
Black	1.355	27.84	0.566	12.01
Hispanic	1.180	19.47	0.576	11.10
Other	1.005	7.08	0.372	4.42
AGE OF HEAD				
16–21	0.429	4.03	0.562	6.23
22–30	0.508	8.91	0.433	9.03
31–40	—	—	—	—
41–50	0.127	2.44	0.210	4.19
51–60	0.553	8.24	0.413	5.87
61–64	0.725	7.55	0.405	4.37
ED OF HEAD				
0–8	0.693	9.96	0.567	7.46
9–11	0.435	8.75	0.322	7.18
12	—	—	—	—
13–15	−0.500	−6.79	−0.428	−8.62
16	−0.874	−6.88	−1.001	−9.86
17+	−1.321	−6.17	−0.990	−6.79
AGE*EDUCATION OF HEAD	−0.001	−6.12	−0.001	−5.44
FAMILY STRUCTURE				
Husband–Wife	—	—	—	—
Non-white single mom	2.930	30.20	2.029	29.50
White single mom	3.816	49.02	2.231	35.78
Single dad	1.454	11.96	1.400	15.94
Other male headed	1.200	13.77	1.157	17.48
Other female headed	2.607	34.86	1.657	26.47
NUMBER OF OWN CHILDREN < 18	0.517	41.16	0.493	33.53
OCCUPATION OF HEAD				
Professional	—	—	—	—
Manager	0.323	2.72	0.008	0.09
Sales	0.353	2.71	0.010	0.12
Clerical	0.154	1.48	0.133	1.65
Craftsman	0.189	1.96	−0.008	−0.10
Operator	0.296	3.06	0.195	2.39
Transportation	0.395	3.70	0.096	1.02
Laborer	0.530	5.09	0.110	1.14
Private HH	0.512	2.85	0.257	1.56
Service	0.335	3.32	0.152	2.05

continued on page 84

Appendix D (*continued*)

Variable	1973 N = 30 369[a] Coefficient	T-Ratio	1988 N = 31 000[a] Coefficient	T-Ratio
Farmer	0.336	2.89	0.242	2.43
Military	−0.323	−1.15	0.348	2.15
Unemployed/NILF	−0.975	−8.23	−0.240	−2.80
REGION				
Northeast	−0.161	−3.09	−0.504	−10.35
South	0.211	4.58	0.039	0.95
West	−0.090	−1.76	−0.038	−0.81
Midwest	—	—	—	—
LOCATION				
Suburban	—	—	—	—
City	0.004	0.09	0.009	0.20
Nonurban	0.924	19.97	0.438	10.08
Not ID	X	X	0.478	10.10
WEEKS WORKED				
Full-time (head)	−0.031	−21.92	−0.030	−29.61
Part-time (head)	−0.021	−9.88	−0.024	−15.70
Full-time (spouse)	−0.006	−4.95	−0.014	−11.94
Part-time (spouse)	−0.003	−1.56	−0.009	−5.01
STUDENT STATUS				
Student (head)	−0.525	−3.27	−0.363	−4.06
Student (spouse)	0.221	0.61	0.225	1.20
HEALTH STATUS[b]				
Disabled (head)	−0.075	−1.23	0.969	22.20
Disabled (spouse)	−0.094	−0.73	0.783	12.11
GHETTO[c]	0.156	0.21	0.249	1.37
CONSTANT	−2.798	−17.17	−1.730	−11.92

[a] Due to computational limitations, a random 80 percent sample from 1973 and a random 70 percent sample from 1988 were used for these calculations.
[b] A person is labelled disabled if they received transfer payments from a disability program or listed health reasons/disability as the reason they didn't work or only worked part-time or part-year in the previous year.
[c] GHETTO is a dummy variable equal to 1 if the head of the family is a non-white male, less than age 25, has less than 12 years of education and lives in a central city.

Appendix E   Descriptions of Prototypical Families

Midwestern farm family
    White, age 41 to 50, education = 9 to 11, intact, 3 children, farmer, midwest, rural, head worked 52 weeks full-time, spouse nonworker.
Rural black family
    Black, age 31 to 40, education = 0 to 8, intact, 5 children, farmer, south, rural, head worked 44 weeks full-time, spouse nonworker.
Blue-collar family
    White, age 41 to 50, education = 12, intact, 2 children, craftsman, midwest, suburban, head worked 45 weeks full-time, spouse nonworker.
Suburban black family
    Black, age 31 to 40, education = 12, intact, 2 children, machine operator, northeast, suburban, head worked 52 weeks full-time, spouse nonworker.
White, low education family
    White, age 31 to 40, education = 9 to 11, intact, 4 children, laborer, west, city, head worked 40 weeks full-time, spouse worked 20 weeks part-time.
Black, low education family
    Black, age 31 to 40, education = 9 to 11, intact, 4 children, laborer, west, city, head worked 40 weeks full-time, spouse worked 20 weeks part-time.
AFDC stereotype family
    Black, age 22 to 30, education = 9 to 11, single mom, 3 children, nonworker, northeast, central city.
Suburban single mother family
    White, age 41 to 50, education = 12, single mom, 3 children, clerical, midwest, suburban, 40 weeks full-time.
Ghetto youth
    Black, age 16 to 21, education = 9 to 11, single male, service worker, not in school, northeast, city, worked 10 weeks full-time, inner-city interaction term.
Independent student
    White, age 16 to 21, education = 13 to 15, single male, laborer, northeast, city, head worked 12 weeks full-time, student.

Notes

1. The 1973 poverty thresholds used for calcuations reported in this paper were constructed by using a deflated (CPI-U) version of the current poverty thresholds. The new poverty thresholds have been used by the Census Bureau since 1981 and differ from the old thresholds in three ways: (1) There are no longer separate thresholds for male- and female-headed families; (2) farm and nonfarm residences have the same poverty cutoffs; and (3) the poverty matrix has been extended to families of 9 or more persons from the previous cutoff of 7 or more persons. Use of the revised poverty thresholds raises the poverty count from 11.1 to 11.4 percent of the population in 1973.
2. Race is categorized as either white or non-white. Non-white is composed

of those individuals reporting their race as black or non-black *and* non-white, plus those who reported their ethnic origin as Hispanic.

3. By assigning the same expected earnings capacity to each individual with the same set of independent variables, we are neglecting the role of unobserved human capital characteristics, unmeasured labor demand circumstances, and 'luck' in the earnings determination process. As a result, the distribution of predicted EC for each race/gender group is artificially compressed, as is the EC distribution of the entire population. We also estimate an EC value for each individual which accounts for earnings variation within each race/gender category by distributing individual observations within a cell randomly about the cell mean. The random number generator technique employed assumes that the distribution of observations within cells is normal, with a standard deviation equal to the standard error of a separately estimated race/gender earnings equation fit over only *full-time, full-year workers* (including an appropriately estimated variable). The estimates of the composition and incidence of earnings capacity poverty resulting from this randomization adjustment generally dampen the differences between current income (official) poverty and the EC estimates without the variance adjustment reported. However, the overall patterns are little changed.

4. In addition, if a person reported they worked part time because of a health limitation, a disabling condition, or the inability to find full time employment, their EC was multiplied by 0.5, implying that these exogenous factors constrain capacity work to 20 hours per week. These adjustments, it should be noted, implicitly assume that the observed illness, disability, or unemployment circumstance is a 'permanent' characteristic of the individual, consistent with the concept and definition of earnings capacity. To the extent that the circumstance is transitory, our procedure may bias the EC estimate for any particular individual. However, if the incidence of illness, disability or unemployment among the population is roughly constant over time within broad population groups, the effects of these constraints on our group estimates of earnings capacity are appropriately reflected by this adjustment.

5. This implicitly assumes that the observed value of these flows is an accurate measure of the family's ability to generate income from its assets. To the extent that these flows are underreported in the data, our estimates of GEC will be biased downward.

6. The contribution of children to family economic status (real consumption) is a controversial issue. If the presence of a child conveys utility to the other members of the family unit, this contribution to well-being should be reflected in an ideal indicator of family economic position. Although our GEC measure does not include this child-based source of well-being, we nevertheless subtract the cost of child care necessary to enable the full use of family GEC. We justify the implicit neglect of children's contribution to family well-being on grounds that: (1) not all children are 'desired' (especially at the low end of the earnings capacity distribution); (2) if children's well-being is included in the family utility function, the simulated returns from parental use of earnings capacity entails a loss of parental care time which is not accounted for; and (3)

reliable estimates of a money measure of the family utility gain from children are non-existent.

7. Data on the costs of 'acceptable' child care are from Sandra Hofferth's 1987 Congressional testimony as reported in the Institute for American Values' policy brief in March 1989, titled 'How the Child Care Market Works: An Economic Analysis.' Communication with experts on the child care market suggest that the variation in hourly child care costs across regions is negligible, and that the real cost of child care has been virtually constant through the 1970s and 1980s.

8. The 13.3 percent figure was chosen because that is the size of the nonaged current income poverty population in 1988 and is a rough approximation of the poverty population over the time of our study. Our objective of comparing the composition and prevalence of poverty using the two definitions of well-being is facilitated by holding constant the percentage of individuals in the bottom tail of the two distributions.

9. Appendix D presents four probit regressions, two each for 1973 and 1988. In each equation, the dependent variable takes on the value of 1 for a family which is in poverty (either current income or net earnings capacity poverty, depending on the regression), and 0 if not in poverty. The independent variables in each regression are the same, and include many of the family characteristics employed in Appendix C to describe the composition of poverty – race, education, age, occupation, gender, family size, region, urbanicity, and weeks and hours worked of the family head and the spouse. In addition, student and health status are included as independent variables. While the signs and magnitudes of the coefficients, and their t-statistics, convey some information regarding the independent contribution of each variable to the probability of a family being in poverty, the non-linear specification of probit equations renders direct comparison of the coefficients from different years impossible.

10. Two considerations could modify this conclusion. First, these family types may possess characteristics not recorded in our data that could reduce their 'true' earnings capacity below that which we estimate for them. Illiteracy (in spite of years of schooling) or non-standard language usage are examples that come to mind. If measures of these characteristics could be incorporated into our estimates, the NEC poverty rate would be greater than that indicated in the table. Second, the presence of unreported (or 'underground') income may vary over the groups. To the extent that such income is substantial, the measured CY poverty rate would overstate the 'true' CY poverty rate.

11. All of the family types included in Table 3.4 had predicted NEC poverty rates of at least 12 percent in 1988.

12. These suggestions parallel those discussed in Ellwood (1988) and Haveman (1989).

References

Ando, Albert and Franco Modigliani (1963) 'The "Life Cycle" Hypothesis of Saving: Aggregate Implications and Tests,' *American Economic Review*, **53**, 55–84.

Becker, Gary S. (1965) 'A Theory of the Allocation of Time,' *The Economic Journal*, **75**, 493–517.

Ellwood, David T. (1988) *Poor Support: Poverty in the American Family* (New York: Basic Books).

Garfinkel, Irwin and Robert Havemam (with the assistance of David Betson) (1977) *Earnings Capacity, Poverty and Inequality* (New York: Academic Press).

Haveman, Robert (1989) *Starting Even: An Equal Opportunity Program to Combat the Nation's New Poverty* (New York: Simon and Schuster).

Mayer, Susan E. and Christopher Jencks (1991) 'Recent Trends in Economic Inequality in the United States: Income vs. Material Well-Being.' Paper presented at Levy Conference on Inequality at the Close of the Twentieth Century.

Moon, Marilyn L. and Eugene Smolensky (eds) (1977) *Improving Measures of Economic Well-Being* (New York: Academic Press).

Rector, Robert, Kate Walsh, O'Beirne, and Michael McLaughlin (1990) *How "Poor" are America's Poor? (Washington, D.C.: The Heritage Foundation)*.

Ruggles, Patricia (1990) *Drawing the Line: Alternative Poverty Measures and Their Implications for Public Policy* (Washington, D.C.: Urban Institute Press).

Schwartz, Saul (1986) 'Earnings Capacity and the Trend in Inequality among Black Men,' *Journal of Human Resources*, **21** (1), 44–63.

4 The Health, Earnings Capacity, and Poverty of Single-mother Families

Barbara L. Wolfe and Steven Hill

Approximately 1.4 million single mothers have substantial health problems. Even if they were to work full time, they would be unlikely to earn enough to adequately provide for themselves and their children. Many of these women are not likely to find employment that offers health insurance coverage for themselves or their children. Employment is thus not an option that would provide sufficient resources – in terms of income or insurance – for them to live at or above the poverty line. Those single mothers who have a disabled child are at additional disadvantage. These children may require increased time from an adult and are likely to have considerable medical care needs and expenditures. For these families, employment of the mother may not provide adequate resources in terms of either time available to meet the disabled child's special needs, income, or adequate health insurance.

We explore these issues, first examining the health status of single mothers compared to other women. We next estimate their earnings capacity – the amount they would earn were they to join the work force on a full-time basis, taking into account their health status and that of their children. We then investigate the percentage of single mothers and their children who would be poor if they had to rely on the earnings capacity of the women (working 40 hours per week, adjusting for health). Finally, we explore the policy implications of our findings, which seem particularly timely in the face of the new work requirements of the 1988 Family Support Act. The Act requires most single mothers currently receiving or applying for Aid to Families with Dependent Children (AFDC) to enroll in training or register to work.

4.1 INTRODUCTION

More than 12 percent of GNP is now spent on health. The health services component of welfare benefits, Medicaid, has grown rapidly over the last two and a half decades, yet there has been little study of the link between health and labor force participation, earnings capacity, and poverty among single mothers.[1] This is surprising given (1) the important role of health (disability) in explaining the early retirement decisions of men and male labor supply decisions in general, and (2) basic statistics, discussed below, that suggest a generally low level of health among women and children in low-income families.

Health appears to play a role in poverty. If we look at the health profile of the U.S. population (as reported in National Center for Health Statistics, 1990), limitation of activity and self-reports of poor and fair health are higher among the low-income population than middle- and higher-income persons: as of 1989, 23.2 percent of those with family incomes under $14 000 reported some limitation of activity, while 14.8 and 8.4 percent of those in families with incomes between $14 000 and $25 000 and above $50 000, respectively, reported such limitations. Similarly, nearly 20 percent of the lowest income group reported fair or poor health compared to 10, and less than 4, percent of those in these middle- and higher-income groups.[2] Table 4.1 illustrates another link between health and income. In it, the adult population of this country is divided into income deciles using equivalent income, and data from the 1980 National Medical Care Utilization and Expenditure Survey are used to calculate the distributions of two measures of poor health: that associated with one or more limitations on physical activity; and self-reports of poor health. Both measures indicate that poor health is concentrated among those with low incomes. These raw data point to a correlation of health and income.

Health status, labor force status, and employment status are all quite clearly related. As of the mid-1980s, the percentage of currently employed persons who reported fair or poor health was relatively low (3.8 percent among those aged 18–44), whereas the percentage among those not in the labor force was much higher (12.6 percent).[3] And a number of studies have demonstrated a link between health and labor force participation and earnings, particularly among men.[4]

The growth of single-mother families and the fact of their low family incomes are well known. There are now some 6.7 million families without fathers in the U.S. About 50 percent of the children

Table 4.1 Distribution of poor health among U.S. adults, by income level, 1980–81

Income decile	% with limitation	% in poor health
Lowest	21.44	30.69
2	16.2	19.02
3	12.45	11.93
4	10.33	10.4
5	8.63	9.29
6	6.85	4.9
7	6.44	4.38
8	5.32	2.25
9	5.73	4.3
10	6.60	2.85
Gini coefficient	–0.244	–0.411

Source: Calculations using National Medical Care Utilization and Expenditure Survey data as reported in Peter Gottschalk and Barbara Wolfe, 'How Equal Is the Utilization of Medical Care in the United State?' 1991, mimeo. Institute for Research on Poverty, University of Wisconsin-Madison.

living in these families are below the poverty line. Among black children in such families, nearly three-quarters live in families with incomes below the poverty line.

As of 1987, slightly more than 50 percent of all single mothers with children under 18 worked; among them, nearly three-quarters worked full time. Six percent of single mothers receiving welfare (AFDC) worked, and of these about one third worked full time. Only about 40 percent of single mothers earn enough to raise their families out of poverty. This economic condition has been explained by the relatively low level of education of many of these women, the lower earnings of women compared to men, and the need of single parents to arrange for child care. Another factor, however, may be poor health.

The evidence on single mothers from the Survey of Income and Program Participation (SIPP) is that approximately one quarter report that they are in poor or fair health, and 2 percent of them need help doing housework.[5] More of those in families with incomes below the poverty line (nearly 60 percent of these women) report poor or fair health than do those in families one to two times the poverty line, and the incidence is even less among those in higher-income families. Approximately 10 percent of the children of the single mothers in

SIPP have some form of disability. The disability of a child is likely to influence the hours worked and hence the earnings capacity of a single parent.

4.2   HEALTH STATUS

Are single mothers at risk particularly of health problems? They face the stress of raising a child or children alone; they live on the earnings of one person combined with any transfers for which they are eligible; many have relatively low levels of education compared to the general population (adjusting for age). All of these factors indicate that they are likely to have a greater probability of experiencing health problems than other persons of similar age.

Although health can be measured a number of ways, all of the available measures have limitations. The most commonly used means are self-reports of health on a four- or five-dimension scale ranking it poor through excellent. This has the disadvantage of being self-reported and hence depends in part on individuals' expectations of their health; e.g., a blind person may feel better than anticipated and reply excellent, while an able-bodied person with sight may feel somewhat depressed for a short period and respond fair or good. Studies comparing this measure to others find it is a good predictor of future health (see for example Maddox and Douglass, 1973). Other measures are self-reported disability or the presence of a health problem that prevents or limits the amount of work that a person can do. This is a commonly used measure in the disability area. Another measure that is sometimes used is the presence of specific health conditions. Unfortunately, small sample sizes limit the usefulness of such conditions. This is the case with the data set (SIPP) used in this analysis. Researchers now are turning to measures of functional ability – and using scales such as Activities of Daily Living (ADLs) and Instrumental Activities of Daily Living (IADLs) as better, more continuous measures of disability – and the need for additional services. We use self-reported disability or the presence of a health problem that prevents or limits work as the basis of our comparison of single mothers and other women. We also use self-reported poor or fair health and a variation of ADLs in our analysis that uses SIPP. These are more detailed and hence are likely to be better, more continuous measures of health status. They include difficulty in (1) lifting ten pounds, (2) seeing with the aid of corrective lenses, (3)

Table 4.2   Disability among women, by marital, family, work, and welfare status

Status	Self-reported disability or health problem limits work	Disability indicator: work or program participation
Single	8%	11%
Married	4	6
Not working	12	14
Working	2	4
Mothers	4	7
Not mothers	7	9
Mothers		
Single	7	13
Married	3	5
Not working	7	10
Working	2	5
Single mothers		
Not working	12	18
Working	2	9
AFDC recipient	11	10
Not AFDC recipient	5	14

Source: Calculations by the authors with data from the Current Population Survey, March 1989.

hearing normal conversation, and (4) walking a quarter of a mile. They are not available on the more recent data set, the Current Population Survey (CPS) that we use for our broader comparisons.

We begin our analysis by using information on women aged 18–60 from the March 1989 CPS. Most of the subsequent analysis is conducted with a different sample, single mothers from the SIPP for 1984, which has much more extensive data on the health status of adults, and also contains information on the work effort of these women, their education, hours worked, and work experience. The CPS is used as a point of comparison because it is more recent.

Table 4.2 shows the simple average of those in poor health by our preferred CPS measure, self-reported disability or presence of a health problem that prevents or limits work, and a second gauge, the 'Haveman–Wolfe' measure,[6] which uses information on work limitation as well as participation in a disability-related transfer program.[7] The extent of poor health as measured by both of these indicators provides evidence that single women have poorer health than married women, that nonworking women have poorer health than working women, and that mothers have better health than women who are not mothers. The highest rate of reported poor health is among single mothers who are not working. AFDC recipients are less healthy than other women according to these measures. The evidence cited here is generally consistent with our expectations regarding the greater extent of health problems among single mothers than among most other women of similar age.

Next we examine the extent of disability among women who work and do not work, among women who are mothers and those who are not, among single versus married mothers, and among single mothers who receive or do not receive AFDC benefits, controlling for age and race by dividing the sample into four age groups (18–24, 25–34, 35–44, and 45–60) and two racial groups (white and nonwhite) (see Table 4.3). We also performed these calculations for education groups, but the results are not reported here. For these comparisons, only the preferred measure of disability (as used in column 1 of Table 4.2) is presented. The proportions of women with disabilities are calculated using the population weights assigned by the U.S. Bureau of the Census to each woman. A test for whether the proportions are statistically different across each (subgroup) was conducted using a one-tailed t-test of the difference between the weighted proportions within each subgroup defined in terms of age, education, or race by the work, maternal, marital, or AFDC recipiency status, adjusted for the number of tests run using the Bonferroni technique.[8] We find that about 80 percent of the t-tests conducted and reported in Table 4.3 are statistically significant at the 5 percent level; the Bonferroni inequality implies that the simultaneous results of all the tests of differences are significant at the 5 percent level. Another statistical test is conducted to test whether the incidence of disability is the same across these women defined in terms of marital status and maternal status. For this a nonparametric test – the Friedman F_r test – is used.[9]

The results suggest:

- Older (aged 45–60) single mothers receiving AFDC are the most likely women among those aged 18–60 to report poor health. Forty-one percent of these women report health problems.
- Among single mothers with more than a high school education (not shown on table), a significantly higher percentage of AFDC recipients report poor health than do those who are not AFDC recipients.

Table 4.3 Comparative health of women by marital, maternal, and work status and by race. (Sample size in parentheses)

	Self-reported disability or health problem that limits work			
	Ages 18–24 (7 356)	Ages 25–34 (12 718)	Ages 35–44 (10 968)	Ages 45–60 (11 420)
Work status				
Not working	4%*	6%*	14%*	22%*
White	4*	7*	12*	20*
Nonwhite	3	6*	18*	27*
Working	1*	2*	2*	4*
White	1*	2*	3*	3*
Nonwhite	1	1*	2*	6*
Maternal status				
Mothers	3	3*	4*	7*
White	2	3	4*	6*
Nonwhite	3	2	6*	10*
Non Mothers	2	4*	9*	12*
White	2	4	9*	11*
Nonwhite	1	4	11*	17*
Marital status for mothers				
Single mothers	4	5*	8*	15*
White	4	6*	7*	14*
Nonwhite	4	4*	10*	16*
Married mothers	2	2*	3*	6*
White	2	3*	3*	5*
Nonwhite	2	1*	4*	7*
AFDC status for single mothers				
AFDC recipient	4	8*	20*	41*
Not AFDC recipient	4	3*	5*	9*

* Significantly different at 5 percent level, compared to matched age and race subgroup in same panel (for example, not working 25–34 white women compared to working 25–34 white women).

Source: Calculations by the authors with data from the Current Population Survey, March, 1989.

• Across racial groups, single mothers report more health limitations than do married mothers.
• A lower level of reported health limitations prevails among working women than among nonworking women, across race, education (not shown in the table), and age groups.

- Somewhat surprisingly, reported health among mothers is better on average than among women who are not mothers.

The nonparametric results provide evidence that

- The distribution of health problems differs significantly among the four marital-maternal groups using all of the 43 age groups as blocks (F_r = 66.8, significant at the 1 percent level).
- The distribution of health problems also differs among the four maternal-marital status groups using the age and education groups (F_r = 11.1, significant at the 5 percent level).

In general, the results are consistent with our expectations regarding the greater incidence of health problems among certain subgroups of women. These include a statistically significant greater incidence of limitations among single mothers compared to other mothers, non-working women relative to working women, and recipients of transfers oriented to single mothers versus single mothers who do not receive such aid. These patterns generally hold across the age, education, and race subgroups. The only unexpected results are poorer health of women who are not mothers than that of mothers, among those aged 35–60, but this may be consistent with fecundity problems of some of the women who are not mothers. Nevertheless, these cross-tabulations do not simultaneously control for a number of characteristics of these women at the same time. For this, we turn to a probit estimate on the determinants of self-reporting of disability or health problems that limit work.

Table 4.4 provides the estimates from three probit equations on the probability of health problems among women aged 18–60. The results suggest that older women, women with less schooling, single mothers, other unmarried women, and women in lower-income households are all more likely to report greater health problems. Women with more children aged 6–18 tend to be healthier than those with fewer children in this age bracket, and there is also some (surprising) evidence that women with more children under 6 report fewer health problems. These results are generally consistent with the analysis above. All of this evidence supports the view that single mothers relative to married mothers are more likely to have health problems. The evidence also supports the view that working women tend to have better health than women who do not work. Finally, the evidence is consistent with the view that low income and poor health are related.

Table 4.4 Probit models of disability (dependent variable: self-reported disability or health problem limits work)

Variable	Coefficient (stnd error)	Coefficient (stnd error)	Coefficient (stnd error)
Intercept	-1.63** (0.072)	-1.59** (0.073)	-1.43** (0.075)
Age	0.026** (0.00096)	0.025** (0.0099)	0.026** (0.0010)
Race (non-white)	-0.14** (0.026)	-0.13** (0.026)	0.19** (0.027)
Education	-0.093** (0.0037)	-0.094** (0.0037)	-0.068** (0.0040)
South	0.068** (0.022)	0.059** (0.022)	0.031 (0.023)
Single mother	0.35** (0.039)	0.43** (0.049)	0.19** (0.050)
Married mother	-0.042 (0.031)	0.049 (0.045)	-0.0027 (0.046)
Single, not mother	0.46** (0.029)	0.46** (0.029)	0.30** (0.030)
Number of unmarried children under 18		-0.044* (0.019)	-0.079 ** (0.020)
Number of children under 6		-0.035 (0.025)	-0.062* (0.025)
Income/poverty line			-0.11** (0.0058)
Log likelihood	-8310.6	-8305.3	-8084.8

* Significant at 5 percent level.
** Significant at 1 percent level.

Source: Calculations by the authors with data from the Current Population Survey, March, 1989; 42,462 observations.

We turn our attention now to the group of primary interest, single mothers, drawing on SIPP data and its greater detail on health. We note first that in the SIPP data set, using the same definition of poor health as used in CPS, older women are more likely to self-report disability or health problems that limit work, and that there is more reported poor health among recipients of AFDC than among non-recipients. These differences, as well as whether or not there are statistically different levels of disability in the SIPP sample of single women, are reported in Table 4.5. The same tests of statistical

Table 4.5   Comparative health of single mothers receiving AFDC and
other single mothers, by age, education, and race
(Numbers of observations in parentheses)

| | Self-reported disability or health problem limits work | | | | |
| | AFDC recipient | | Not AFDC recipient | | Difference |
	Frequency	Proportion	Frequency	Proportion	of proportion t-statistic
Age					
18–24 (340)	7	0.05	2	0.01	2.013
25–34 (684)	20	0.10	18	0.04	* 2.923
35–44 (487)	24	0.25	25	0.06	** 5.594
45–60 (191)	16	0.50	29	0.19	** 3.812
Education					
Did not complete high school (496)	32	0.14	33	0.13	0.392
Completed high school (727)	27	0.13	25	0.05	** 3.946
More than high school (479)	8	0.11	16	0.04	2.396
Race					
White (1094)	33	0.12	54	0.07	* 2.753
Nonwhite (608)	34	0.14	20	0.06	** 3.771
Region					
Midwest (440)	10	0.06	4	0.01	2.492
Northeast (334)	12	0.15	25	0.09	1.350
South (613)	24	0.16	34	0.07	** 3.191
West (315)	21	0.19	11	0.06	** 3.779
All single mothers (1702)	67	0.13	74	0.06	** 4.715

Note: Positive t-statistics indicate poorer health among AFDC recipients.
* Significant at 5 percent level.
** Significant at 1 percent level.

Source: Calculated by the authors with data from the Survey of Income and Program
Participation, 1984 panel.

significance were run. Overall, and in the majority of age and race
categories, there is a statistically significant difference between the
higher reported rates of disability among AFDC recipients than
among non-recipients. These patterns are similar to those found
using the 1989 CPS and the percentage reporting a disability or
limitation is nearly identical in both samples (8 and 7 percent).[10]

4.3 EARNINGS CAPACITY

Persons with health problems are likely to have reduced earnings capacity relative to their able-bodied peers.[11] This may occur because of decreased productivity due to lower energy levels, the inability to perform certain tasks and hence reduced labor market options, fewer hours available to work owing to time needed for health-related activities, greater time requirements to perform everyday tasks, etc. Parents with a disabled child are also likely to face increased time demands and have fewer hours available to participate in the paid work force. We explore these issues for single mothers.

We estimate a tobit two-stage model of hours worked and wages.[12] The model is similar to a three-stage model in which the first equation concerns whether the woman works at all, and the second equation estimates hours of work and another wages. Like the three-stage model, the two-stage model takes into account the fact that a number of these single mothers do not participate in the paid labor force. These women have both zero hours of work and zero wages. The final equation in both models is identical – an equation of wages among only those single mothers in the paid labor force. We estimate both versions but prefer the tobit two-stage model, which allows for a clearer direct representation of the influence of health on hours worked.

The first stage is an equation which has as its dependent variable log of hours worked. It is estimated as a maximum likelihood tobit equation in order to take into account the truncation at zero hours.

The tobit hours equation estimated is

$$HRS = \mathbf{X_1}' \, \beta_1 + \mathbf{Y_1}' \, \alpha_1 + \mathbf{H_1}' \, \gamma_1 + \epsilon_1$$

The equation is also the selection criterion for the second stage, which is estimated only over those for whom $HRS > 0$. The wage equation is specified as a log wage equation, and the two-stage model includes a selection control for the decision to work positive hours, that is, to enter the paid labor force. The selection correction is identical to the more commonly used one based on a probit equation of labor force participation, except that the tobit parameter estimates are used in the normal distribution and density (see Maddala, 1983, p. 240).

The wage equation estimated is

$$WAGE = \mathbf{X_2}' \, \beta_2 + \mathbf{Y_2}' \, \alpha_2 + \mathbf{H_2} \, \gamma_2 + \lambda \, \xi + \epsilon_2$$

where the X vector contains personal characteristics of the woman, the Y vector contains family characteristics of the woman's family, and the H vector contains health information on the woman and her children. The α, β, and γ vectors and ξ are parameters to be estimated. The subscripts are used to indicate that the vectors need not be identical in the two equations.

The variables included in the hours equation are those designed to measure alternative demands on a mother's time (number of children under age 6 and aged 6–18; the presence of a disabled child), labor market opportunities (unemployment rate), human capital (education and education squared, experience prior to this time period and its squared term), other personal characteristics (race measured as two variables, Hispanic and black; and non-public transfer, non-earnings of the mother which provide additional income and hence may increase an income effect), another potential source of income to also capture a potential income effect (maximum state AFDC benefits), attitudes toward work (captured by income of other family members), and own health (self-reported fair or poor health and a modified version of the Activities of Daily Living scale which measure functional status – the modification highlights the work-related nature of some ADLs). (Appendix B contains more exact variable definitions.) The variables measuring alternative demands on the mother's time, except for presence of a disabled child, are only included in the hours equation, as are measures of other income and maximum AFDC benefits. Once their influence is captured in the hours equation, there is little reason to believe that these factors should influence the wage rate. Otherwise the included variables are the same (with, of course, the exception of the selection term in the wage equation).

The results of this model are reported in Table 4.6. The first column of results reports the log hours tobit estimates; the second column reports the log wage results. The means and standard deviations of the independent variables are in columns three and four. The model is estimated only over the 1605 single mothers in the sample who report 60 or fewer hours per week as their regular hours worked and over those with consistent responses on earnings and hours worked (both positive or both zero).

The mother's own health clearly plays a large and significant role in influencing hours worked. The coefficient on poor-fair health is -0.9 in the log hours specification, while the coefficient on work ADLs is -0.67. Both are significant at the 1 percent level.

Table 4.6   Estimated model of earnings capacity of single mothers: two-stage tobit estimates ($N = 1605$)

	Ln hours	Ln wage	Mean	Standard deviation
		Those with HRS > 0		
Constant	0.20(0.68)	1.54(0.33)**		
Health				
Poor-Fair	−0.90(0.20)**	−0.15(0.10)	0.18	0.38
Work ADLs	−0.67(0.09)**	−0.06(0.06)	0.36	0.91
Time demands				
Children under 6	−0.64(0.12)**		0.58	0.73
Children 6–18	−0.13(0.08)		1.19	1.10
Disabled child	−0.43(0.24)*	0.09(0.11)	0.09	0.29
Personal characteristics				
Hispanic	−0.29(0.24)	−0.01(0.11)	0.09	0.29
Black	−0.47(0.14)**	0.04(0.06)	0.34	0.48
Mother's other income (000's)	−0.74(0.18)**		0.18	0.39
Human capital				
Education	0.11(0.10)	−0.13(0.05)**	11.8	2.58
Education^2	0.003(0.004)	0.01(0.002)**	146.9	56.9
Prior Exp.	0.36(0.02)**	0.05(0.02)**	8.86	7.93
Prior Exp.^{2}	−0.01(0.001)**	−0.001(0.56^{-4})**	141.3	220.9
Unempl. rate	−0.08(0.03)**	0.01(0.01)	7.79	2.26
Other sources of income				
Other family income (000's)	0.12(0.06)*			
Max AFDC benefits (000's)	−1.93(0.47)**			
Sigma	2.25(0.06)			
λ		0.16(0.14)		
Covariance	0.29			
Log likelihood	−5060			

** Significant at 5 percent level; * significant at 10 percent level.

Note: Standard errors in parentheses.

The presence of a disabled child also is associated with fewer hours worked. In this case the coefficient is −0.43 and is significant at the 10 percent level. Other factors that measure time demands – the number of children by two age groups – are also negative, as expected. The coefficient on number of children under 6 is −0.64 and is significant at the 1 percent level. The coefficient on number of children aged 6–18 is −0.13 but is not quite significant. The smaller coefficient on older children is consistent with greater time demands of pre-school-age children. If a disabled child is present, he or she is included in the number of children in his or her age bracket – hence the impact of disability is over and above the presence of a child.

Among personal characteristics, being black and having an amount of other own income are statistically significant. Other potential sources of income (maximum AFDC benefits) are negative and statistically significant at the 1 percent level. Income of other family members is positive, perhaps suggesting unobserved attitudes rather than an income effect. Among human capital variables, education is not significant but increases in both the linear and quadratic terms. Prior work experience (measured up to the period of the factors under analysis) is positively associated with hours worked, but decreasingly so. Finally, the unemployment rate in the community, which measures employment opportunities facing the woman, has the expected negative sign and is statistically significant at the 1 percent level. (The sigma reported is the standard deviation of the residual error term.)

The log wage equation is only estimated over those with positive hours in the labor force. Note, however, that the selection correction factor, although not statistically significant, has a large effect on wage rates. Thus, the single mothers who command the highest wage rates are already in the labor force.

For wages, own health is not significant. This suggests that the big impact of health among single mothers lies in reducing the potential to work and the hours that can be worked. Time demands other than the presence of a disabled child are not included in the model, since a priori they should not play a role. The presence of a disabled child does not significantly influence wages, and its sign is positive. The two personal characteristics, both of which measure race, are also not statistically significant. Human capital values – education and experience – are significant in explaining wages, as expected. Education again shows a nonlinear relationship, and the positive effect dominates beginning at 8.7 years of education. For prior work experience the positive effect dominates until 21.3 years of experience – or throughout the relevant range for most of these women. Employment opportunities as captured by the unemployment rate are not significant, although they have the expected negative sign.

These log equations do not directly convey the impact of the right-hand-side variables on earnings capacity. Thus, we now use these equations to calculate the earnings capacity of single mothers. We use 40 hours per week as the basis of our calculation of how much these women could earn were they to work full time.[13] For women with poor health or one or more ADLs, we reduce their potential hours of work by using the coefficients on the relevant health variables from our hours equation. We do the same thing for the presence of a disabled child. The third row of Table 4.7 provides the weekly capacity hours worked for each of these categories of women. The highest reported number is 37.9 for those with no ADLs; the lowest is 4.49 for those with three ADLs. The average for all mothers is 32.3 hours per week. In the calculation of earnings capacity, because nonlinear transformations are not mean preserving, we correct our exponentiated log earnings capacity by a multiplicative factor, 1.3866. This factor is the ratio of the mean of the distribution of actual wages among workers divided by the mean of the distribution of wages of workers predicted by the two stage model. The earnings capacities thus calculated are reported in the first row of Table 4.7.

Over all of these women, the mean of annual earnings capacity in 1984 dollars is $9117. For women who report fair or poor health, the mean earnings capacity is $2440 per year, while for women with good or better health it is $10 724 per year. Thus, women with poor or fair health have an earnings capacity less than one quarter that of healthier women.

Women who report no ADLs (functional limitations) have an average earnings capacity of $10 714 per year. Those with ADLs have significantly lower average annual earnings capacity – $4466 for those with one ADL, $1919 for those with two, and only $973 for those with three ADLs.[14] The effect of having a disabled child on the earnings capacity of the single mothers with one or more disabled children is to reduce it to $8135 per year, on average.

None of the estimates just discussed take into account the cost of child care. We do this in the next row of Table 4.7. We link a child care payment to the hours the single mother would work at capacity (40 hours, adjusting for health). The dollar value of our calculation is based on a per hour, per child payment of $1.25 for child care.[15] When we adjust for needed child care – needed during the hours these women are to work, exclusive of the time the children are in school, adjusting for school vacation and exclusive of care for children in school or in families with children over age 14 – we reduce earnings capacity on average to $7092 per year. Women who report fair or poor health have an average earnings capacity of $1859 per year, while those with three ADLs have an earnings capacity of $855 per year, on average. (Clearly, the differences between the

Table 4.7 Earnings capacity of single mothers: mean (and standard deviation) of annual earnings and weekly hours (N = 1702, 1984 data and dollars)

Weighted	All	Women with poor/fair health	Women with good health	Those with disabled child	Disabled child and adj. for own health	Those with no ADLs	Those with 1 ADL	Those with 2 ADLs	Those with 3 ADLs	Current workers
Earnings capacity	$9 117(4521)	2 440(1523)	10 724(3502)	8 135(1844)	6 634(2622)	10 714(3514)	4 466(2075)	1 919(1092)	973(460)	10 713(4126)
Earnings capacity corrected for child care	7 092(4365)	1 859(1367)	8 299(3974)	5 023(3522)	4 054(3341)	8 262(4041)	3 445(2108)	1 569(1082)	855(486)	8 886(4054)
Weekly hours worked at capacity (adjusted for health)	32.33(12.5)	11.1(6.0)	37.75(7.1)	26.7(0)	17.0(9.9)	37.9(6.5)	16.8(5.7)	8.26(3.0)	4.49(1.4)	35.06(10.0)
N	1 702	294	1 408	160	160	1 398	142	82	43	967

unadjusted earnings capacity and the child-care-adjusted ones are greater for healthier women who work more hours. Note as well that no adjustment is made for the potentially greater hourly cost of care for disabled children.)

4.4 EARNINGS CAPACITY AND POVERTY

Another way to interpret these earnings capacity measures is to ask what proportion of these single mothers and their children would have family incomes below the poverty line if the mothers were to work at their earnings capacity. This assumes that the only source of income for the woman and her children is her earnings.

The results are reported in Table 4.8. There are four sets of reported proportions of single-mother families below the poverty line: the first is estimated from earnings capacity unadjusted for child care expenses, the second adjusts that set for child care expenses, the third reports actual percentages below the poverty line, and the fourth reports actual earnings, relative to the poverty line. The reported results are weighted; they differ little from the unweighted proportions.

If all of these women were to work at their earnings capacity – 40 hours per week adjusted only for health – more than a third of their families would still be below the poverty line. Once we adjust for child care expenses, the proportion increases to 58 percent. Clearly, then, labor force participation will not provide sufficient income for most of these single-mother families. If we turn our attention to women with health problems, we see that a substantial share will live in poverty even if they work at their capacity: among women who report poor or fair health, all would reside in poverty under these circumstances; among women with one ADL about 94 percent (or about 96 percent adjusted for child care) would find themselves and their children living in poverty under these circumstances; among women with two or more ADLs, all would live in poverty. For single mothers with health problems, relying on their earnings capacity would mean that nearly all of them and their children would live in poverty. Finally, we present our predictions of the effect on family poverty status that a disabled child has through the earnings capacity of the mother. If we adjust hours that could be worked solely to account for the presence of a disabled child, we find that about 60 percent (72 percent adjusting for ordinary child care expenses) of

Table 4.8   Prediction of poverty among single mothers as based on earnings capacity and family size (N = 1702; weighted proportions[a])

	Percentage poor, based on earnings capacity	Percentage poor, based on earnings capacity and child care costs	Actual percentage poor, based on all family income	Actual percentage poor, based on earnings alone
All	37.0%	58.4%	52.5%	87.7%
If *only* child disabled	60.5	72.2	—	—
Child disabled actual mom health	77.7	84.6	55.3	92.1
Women in poor or fair health	100	100	73.1	97.3
Women in good health	22.3	48.5	48.1	85.6
Women with 0 ADLs	22.5	48.6	49.6	85.8
Women with 1 ADL	94.3	95.6	57.5	94.0
Women with 2 ADLs	100	100	73.7	97.5
Women with 3 ADLs	100	100	67.2	97.4
Women with 4 ADLs	100	100	88.5	100
Current workers	21.8	40.2	25.4	78.2

[a] The proportion below the official poverty line if the family received the maximum AFDC benefit for their family in their state is 100 percent for all categories of single mothers.

these families are predicted to live in poverty. If we also take the mother's own health into account in our hours calculation, we instead predict that nearly 78 percent (about 85 percent when we adjust for child care) of families with a disabled child would be living in poverty. Clearly then, encouraging work among single mothers with health problems or with a disabled child is not an approach that will provide adequate income to the majority of these single-parent families.

The third column shows the percentage of single-mother families with actual incomes below the poverty line. It provides an interesting comparison: a somewhat lower percentage of these families live in poverty now (that is, 1984) than if the mothers worked at their earnings capacity, taking child care into account. However, this average masks a pattern. Women with health problems would be worse off, in terms of income, if they were required to work at their earnings capacity and did not receive supplementary funds. Alternatively, 'healthy' single-parent families would have about the same rate of poverty that they actually experience if the mother worked at her earnings capacity. The final column shows the percentage of these families who would live in poverty if their only income were the mother's actual earnings. In every case, except for women with one to three ADLs, this is greater than actual poverty levels and levels that depend on earnings capacity. Finally, we calculated (not shown on table) the proportion of women in each of these categories who currently receive AFDC. Thirty-one percent receive AFDC; of them, about 4 percent also receive SSI benefits.

4.5 POLICY IMPLICATIONS

If single mothers with substantial health problems – some 1.4 million families – are to avoid facing a situation of very low incomes for themselves and their children, there may be a need for a transfer program designed specifically for them. This is particularly the case if the public sector continues to pursue and even intensifies the move toward encouraging single mothers to work, exemplified in the work and training requirements of the 1988 Family Support Act.[16]

Similarly, if single mothers with disabled children are to secure a reasonable income for themselves and their children, a specific policy may be required for them. Having a disabled child puts increased demands on these single mothers – in terms of spending time with the disabled child and the need for generous health insurance coverage for the care required by the child.

Our study of the earnings potential of single mothers with health problems and of single mothers who have a disabled child estimates that the earnings capacity of a single mother in poor or fair health is about $2200 per year in 1990 dollars, after adjusting for child care needs. Based on these projections, all of these women and their children could expect to live in poverty if they worked at their capacity and received no transfers. (This projection does not take into account needed expenditures for medical care for the uninsured, out-of-pocket expenses for the insured, additional costs of child care to cover travel time, and the higher cost of care for disabled children.)

Using a functional index of health, we find that all of the women with two or more ADLs would live below the poverty line, even if they worked at their capacity. We estimate that a woman with two ADLs would have an earnings capacity of about $2300 annually, and a woman with three ADLs would on average have an earnings capacity of about $1200 annually.

A single mother with a disabled child also has limited earnings capacity. We estimate that the mean earnings capacity of such mothers is about $8000 per year. This estimate does not take into account any special surcharges for child care for a disabled child. Our estimates suggest that her average hours worked at capacity would be 17 per week (starting at a base of 40 hours per week and adjusting for the effects of child's health and her own health). We expect that about four out of five of these families would live below the poverty line if forced to rely on the mother's earnings as their only source of income.

Under the more generous provision of private health insurance benefits existing in 1984, only 39 percent of single mothers with poor or fair health would expect to be offered health insurance at their place of employment if they were to work. Thirty-two percent are expected to be offered family coverage while 7 percent are expected to be offered individual coverage only. More than 60 percent would not be offered coverage of either kind (see Moffitt and Wolfe, 1990, Table 14.)

There are two central problems for single-parent families in which the mother has significant health problems and/or there is a disabled child: the need for an adequate income independent of the parent's earnings, and for generous and comprehensive financing of medical care, including coverage for chronic conditions. The solution cannot take the form of a wage subsidy, since the earnings limitation facing these families is primarily one of limited time available to work. Hence there is need for provision of adequate income through a transfer program as well as a generous insurance package containing the benefits generally covered by Medicaid. As of 1984, the maximum AFDC benefit for women with poor or fair health was $331 per month, slightly less than $4000 per year. Because these benefits differ owing to geographic location and family size rather than health, they would not lift these families out of poverty.

What are the options to increase the family income of these families and to provide health insurance coverage as well? Several policy alternatives could be based on modification of existing public programs: (1) creating a special federal AFDC program for these women and their families that would provide uniform benefits across the country and to provide Medicaid coverage as well; (2) modifying the current state-based AFDC programs to provide extra payments to such families; (3) providing comprehensive health insurance to these persons regardless of their work status, a coverage that would continue if their income were to increase substantially but would require income-conditioned premiums and copayments at the time of utilization; and (4) providing coverage to many of these persons under the existing SSI program along with AFDC participation for other family members. Each option is discussed in more detail below.

Increasing the generosity of AFDC for these families would best be achieved in the form of a federal program with uniform payments across states. The program would be directed at a limited group – women with significant health problems, such as those with two or more ADLs. The payment schedule would depend on family size and would include coverage under Medicaid. The women would not be expected to enroll in a training program or to register for work. The payment schedule would be sufficient to enable them to live reasonably comfortably, certainly out of poverty. They might be encouraged to work part time to augment their income up to some specified limit. After a certain dollar disregard, any additional earnings could be taxed at a 33 to 50 percent rate.

The second option is to modify the current AFDC program to include a special benefit for women with significant health problems. AFDC could have a multiplicative adjustment factor which increased the payments to families if the single parent met a specific health criterion or if she qualified for benefits owing to the health condition of a dependent child. This would be a simple adjustment formula that could easily be established to take into account the extra needs of these families. These women would be exempted from the work-training requirements of AFDC.

The difficulty with such a program is that it might create an incentive for other persons on AFDC to attempt to qualify. Some health conditions are rather difficult to establish. Avoiding giving extra payments to those who should not receive them could require substantial resources for determination of who is (or ought to be) eligible to receive the additional benefits. If the benefits are tied specifically to each health problem, the administrative chore becomes even greater. It would be clearly desirable to limit the options for adjustment. These might depend only on whether the mother has a health condition or the number of ADLs she has, with a separate consideration of the presence of a disabled child, perhaps differentiating the payment by the child's age.

A third (or perhaps complementary) policy would be to provide extensive health insurance benefits in order to relieve financial uncertainly and increase willingness to join the work force.[17] These insurance benefits should be modeled on the Medicaid benefits that provide coverage for chronic conditions. The families would be permanently covered by this insurance although, as their income increased, coverage would continue but income-conditioned premiums and copayments at the time of utilization would be required. The only condition for maintaining the insurance would be the continuation of the mother's (or the child's) significant health condition(s).

Yet another alternative would be to modify the Supplemental Security Income (SSI) program to cover such families. SSI is a program which had expenditures of $13.7 billion in 1988, or 4.1 percent of public income-maintenance program expenditures. It is a somewhat smaller program than AFDC, which had expenditures of $18.4 billion. Measured by number of recipients, AFDC is far larger, with 10.9 million recipients (3.75 million families and 7.3 million children) in 1987 compared to 4.5 million for SSI, including 2.9 million disabled. SSI eligibility is based on low income plus disability, blindness, or elderly status. Disability requires that a person not be able to engage in a 'substantial gainful activity,' defined as earnings of more than $500 per month over an extended period of time. (Many of the single mothers in our sample with health problems would qualify for benefits under this criterion – including about 90 percent of women with poor or fair health, 60 percent of women with one ADL,

97 percent of women with two ADLs, and all women with three or more ADLs. However, very few women in the sample actually receive SSI.[18]) The average monthly payment to individuals under SSI is greater than that under AFDC on average, but is well below the payment to AFDC families. As of 1988, average monthly payments were $379 for AFDC families, and $294 for SSI disabled persons – 29 percent less than under AFDC (*Statistical Abstract of the United States 1990*, Table 607, p. 367). The primary reason for this difference is that SSI does not provide benefits for dependents. A single-parent family with a severely disabled person can receive benefits under both programs – the severely disabled person under SSI, the others under AFDC. Yet only a small proportion (less than 5 percent) of single-parent families receiving AFDC also have a person receiving SSI.

There are several other differences in the two programs. SSI is primarily a federal program providing nationally uniform benefits. (There are also state-based programs covering additional persons and providing small additional benefits, but these differences are not considered here.) SSI coverage is targeted on those with very low earnings capacity owing to disability; it is not conditioned on family structure. Eligibility for SSI confers Medicaid coverage, as does AFDC.[19]

The fourth policy option is to encourage women having a significant disability or a child with a significant disability to apply for SSI. As part of this special program, dependents' benefits might be added. Modifying the payment schedule for SSI to provide additional funds for the dependents of disabled persons – or the families of disabled children – would put these families under a uniform national standard and would separate them from state-based AFDC programs. Since eligibility for SSI requires establishment of a significant level of disability, and since SSI is an entirely separate program from AFDC, this option may have limited effects on women who do not have a significant long-term health problem.

In sum, if single mothers having significant disabilities (or children with significant disabilities) were to fall under a program designed for them – a special category of SSI, or a national AFDC program – they might obtain financial security with minimal incentives for others to join or even apply for the program. It may also be possible to use the existing administrative structure of SSI disability determination to facilitate this process. The 1986 amendments under section 1619 permit a number of deductions from earnings in determining continued eligibility for SSI. These include 'impairment-related work expenses, work expenses of the blind, the cost of a plan to achieve self support and publicly funded attendant care services' (*1990 Green Book*, pp. 738–9). Using these deductions in initial eligibility determinations for single parents, making the standard more lenient for single parents and adding a dependents' allowance might permit these women to work and attain a decent living standard.

Under current law, severely disabled children in families receiving AFDC can receive SSI. The child found eligible receives a minimum payment of $30 per month. Above this amount, payments are determined by family income. There is a disregard of the first $2000 of a single parent's income in calculating eligibility and the payment level. If a single parent's income is more than $12 500, the child is not eligible to receive other payments from SSI. The child covered by SSI is not regarded as a member of the family when AFDC benefits are calculated. In states with low AFDC payments, SSI can make a sizable contribution to the family income of single parents with a disabled child, even though benefits under both programs are generally reduced because of the receipt of benefits from the other program.[20] In our sample, only 2 percent of families received SSI, and among them 72 percent also received AFDC. Of families with a disabled child, 7 percent received SSI, compared to only 1.6 percent of single-parent families without a disabled child.

Could these programs be combined (or could there be joint eligibility) for single mothers with substantial health problems? As stated above, SSI provides payment only for a disabled person, not for his or her dependents. AFDC laws do not consider SSI payments in determining eligibility or payments – nor is the SSI recipient considered in calculating the AFDC benefit amount or eligibility. Thus, AFDC laws need not be modified to facilitate joint SSI and AFDC eligibility. However, substantial effort would be required to *inform* these single parents as well as AFDC administrators of the possibility of joint eligibility. By using SSI eligibility, no new administrative structure would be required for AFDC. Using SSI modified disability standards should minimize the extra AFDC payments that may be required under joint eligibility. If the standards were too strict, however, the problem of providing adequate income to these single parents and their children would remain. Combining AFDC with SSI removes the need to add dependents' benefits to SSI.[21] However, to provide an adequate income, in most states the combined benefits would have to be raised to the poverty line.

4.6 CONCLUSIONS

We have documented the lower health status, on average, of single mothers as compared to married mothers and of nonworkers as compared to workers. Health status influences the earnings capacity of single mothers: poor health substantially reduces potential earnings. We have estimated that the earnings capacity of a single mother in poor or fair health is about $2900 per year. Based on these projections, all of these women and their children could expect to live in poverty if they worked at their capacity and received no transfers. (This projection does not take into account needed expenditures for medical care for the uninsured and out-of-pocket expenses for the insured.)

We also used a functional type index of health in our study. It adds the number of activities of daily living (ADLs) that a person experiences difficulty in performing. The ADLs include seeing with the aid of corrective lenses, hearing normal conversation, lifting ten pounds, walking a quarter of a mile, and climbing stairs. Using this alternative measure of health, we find that all of the women with two or more ADLs would live below the poverty line even if they worked at their capacity. We estimate that a woman with two ADLs would have an earnings capacity of about $2300 per year, and a woman with three ADLs would on average have an earnings capacity of about $1200 per year.

A single mother with a disabled child also has limited earnings capacity. We estimate that the mean earnings capacity of such mothers is about $8000 per year. This estimate does not take into account any special surcharges for child care of her disabled child. Our estimates suggest that her average expected hours worked would be 17 per week, adjusting 40 hours per week only for the role of child's health and her own health. For these families, we expect that more than half would live below the poverty line if forced to rely on the mother's earnings as the only source of income.

This evidence suggests that labor force participation by itself may not raise a single-mother-headed family above the poverty line. The central problem is not so much low earnings – which would suggest the possibility of designing a special earnings supplement for single mothers with health limitations – as it is a limitation on hours available to work. Hence, policy should concentrate on designing a welfare program that provides more generous benefits to single mothers with health limitations than to single mothers in good health.

Appendix A   Disability among Women, Mothers, and Single Mothers by Five Definitions

		Women	Mothers	Single mothers
Self-reported disability or health problem which prevents working or which limits the kind or amount of work performable	Frequency Proportion	2448 0.06	755 0.04	299 0.07
Self-reported 'ever retired or left a job for health reasons'	Frequency Proportion	1115 0.03	340 0.02	131 0.03
Indicator by program participation	Frequency Proportion	2009 0.05	839 0.04	407 0.09
Indicator by work limitation	Frequency Proportion	2084 0.05	682 0.03	253 0.06
Indicator by work limitation or program participation	Frequency Proportion	3373 0.08	1371 0.07	589 0.13
Total observations		42 462	19 867	3576

Data source: Current Population Survey, March, 1989.

Program participation:

1. Receives social security or railrod retirement benefits and
   a. is not in school, is age 19 to 59, and is not widowed, divorced, or separated with dependent children,
   b. is in school and is age 23 to 59, or
   c. is age 19 to 59, and is widowed, divorced, or separated with dependent children.
2. Receives SSI.
3. Receives workers compensation.
4. Receives veterans disability benefits, is a veteran, and is not in school.

Work limitation:

1. Major activity last week is 'unable to work.'
2. Works fewer than 35 hours, and the reason for part-time work is 'own illness' or the reason for working part year is 'own illness.'
3. Works fewer than 35 hours and was absent from work last week, and the reason for absence is 'own illness.'

Correlation coefficient between 'Self-reported disability or health problem limits work' and 'disability indicator: work or program participation' = 0.453.

Appendix B   Definitions of Selected Variables

Our ADL measure was constructed from the Activities of Daily Living questions most clearly related to ability to work. Dummy variables for difficulty performing the following activities were summed: reading with glasses or contact lenses, hearing normal conversation, having one's speech understood, walking a quarter mile, lifting ten pounds, climbing a flight of stairs, moving without a walking aid, and getting around outside one's home. Thus the measure ranges from 0 to 8. In this sample about 9 percent report difficulty lifting ten pounds or walking a quarter mile; about 8 percent have difficulty climbing stairs and 5 percent seeing with corrective lenses. About 1 percent report each of the other ADLs.

Experience was derived from the work history section of topical module on Wave 3 of SIPP. It is the minimum of age-education-5 and the maximum of the number of years the woman worked six months or more, the sum of the complement periods to spells without employment and time at current and last employer, and length of time holding this type of job. The experience gained during the 5 months of Wave 3 used in this study was eliminated from all relevant variables in this calculation.

Hours is the usual number of hours worked each week.

Maximum AFDC benefits are maximum monthly benefits available to the mother in 1984 based on the number of her children and her state of residence.

Mother's other income is the four month average of the difference between total personal income and earned income, less public transfers. Negative incomes were not included in the average.

Other family income is the four month average of the difference between total family income and total mother's income. Negative incomes were not included in the average.

Unemployment rate is the average unemployment rate over the four months surveyed in Wave 3 for the woman. SMA rates were used for SMA residents, otherwise state rates were used.

Wage is the average of monthly earnings over months with positive earnings in the past four months, divided by the usual number of hours the woman worked each week. Geographic variations were removed by dividing by the ratio of average weekly earnings of workers in each state's unemployment compensation system and the national average of workers in the unemployment compensation system. Reported earnings capacities by health status and poverty rates, are also normalized. The coefficients of the wage and hours equations are similar to those using non-normalized wages and geographic dummy variables.

Appendix C   Joint Eligibility for SSI and AFDC

A person who is unable to do any kind of work for which he or she is suited owing to a medically determined physical or mental impairment,[22] who has been out of work for six months or more, and whose disability is expected to last for at least a year or result in death is eligible for SSI. This includes children who have an impairment comparable to that of adults. In the case of children, the work component is changed to the inability to attend school.

A single-parent family which meets the income and assets tests is generally eligible for AFDC in the state in which it resides.

If a woman is sufficiently disabled to receive SSI, her child(ren) can receive AFDC under the stipulation that they are a deprived child – deprived of the care of one parent. (They might also receive AFDC in a two-parent household if one parent is sufficiently disabled to be on SSI. However, in the latter case, the family will be subject to the income and assets tests.) In the case of a single mother, the woman faces an income test of $407 per month (1991) and an assets test of $2000 in determining her SSI benefits.[23] The maximum she can receive in most states is a total monthly income of $407, or $4884 per year. Her child can receive AFDC benefits. These benefits are determined as though the mother were not part of the household – so that a single child would receive the single or first-person payment. In the United States as a whole in 1991, on average, this would be $133 (*1990 Green Book* projection, p. 576); in Wisconsin this would be $248 per month for one child. The total for this mother and child would then be $655, or $7860 per year in Wisconsin including both SSI and AFDC benefits.

If a child is so severely disabled as to be eligible for SSI, his or her payments would depend on the income of the parents. The child would be eligible to receive payments if a single parent's income were less than $1454 per month (1991). The maximum payment for a person on SSI would again apply – $407. The actual amount would depend on the source of the mother's income (earned income is treated more generously than unearned income), as well as her total income. The single mother would be potentially eligible for AFDC as the caretaker of a deprived child. Her actual AFDC payment would depend on her other income, not the SSI payment to her child.

As of 1988, only 1.9 percent of AFDC families also received federal SSI (*1990 Green Book*, p. 582).

Notes

1. The exceptions to this are the few studies that analyze the role of Medicaid in influencing welfare participation. See for example Blank (1989), Winkler (1991), and Moffitt and Wolfe (1990).
2. Rates of poor or fair health are also greater among blacks than whites – 15.9 compared to 8.2 percent. This holds after controlling for broad income categories: the percentages for 1985–7 are 18 versus 11.1 percent among blacks and whites with family incomes less than $10 000 (National Center for Health Statistics, 1990).
3. See Ries (1990).
4. See for example Luft (1975), Lee (1982), and Haveman, Stone, and Wolfe (1989).
5. See Table 4 in Moffitt and Wolfe (1990).
6. This measure has been used in a number of studies conducted by Haveman and Wolfe (e.g., 1990a, 1990b).

7. These measures are compared with several others in Appendix A.
8. The standard error for each test is the square root of the product of the proportion of disabled women among the entire subgroup (e.g., ages 18–24), the proportion nondisabled and the sum of the reciprocals of the numbers of observations by either the work–nonwork classification, maternal or marital status, or recipiency status. Take as an example women 18–24 who work or do not work; for this test, the appropriate calculation is the square root of the product of the proportion disabled among all women 18–24, the proportion nondisabled among all women 18–24, and the sum of the reciprocals of the numbers of observations in the work and nonwork subgroups among women 18–24. Since there is a high probability of type-I errors when a large number of t-tests are conducted, the Bonferroni technique is applied to reduce the possibility of spurious claims of significance. This simple correction requires dividing the desired significance level by the number of t-tests to be performed in order to derive a new critical level to determine statistical significance for the t-tests.
9. The population of women is divided into four mutually exclusive categories (called treatments): married mothers, married women without children, single childless women and single mothers. Blocks such as age serve as the basis of the test calculation. Employing a block for each age, 18–60 (or the four age and three education groups: 0–11, 12, and more than 12 years), the proportion disabled in each block is calculated (4 * 43), and these proportions of disabled are then ranked for each block (each age) across the four maternal, marital groupings. Within each marital, maternal category, the rankings are then summed across the age blocks; these values are squared and summed and the resulting value is multiplied by a constant (12), divided by the number of blocks multiplied by the number of treatments (4) times the number of treatments plus one (5). Next, we subtract a constant (3) times the number of blocks times the number of treatments plus one. The resulting value is then compared to the critical value in a chi-square table using the degrees of freedom equal to the number of treatments (4) minus 1 in this case.
10. Using a chi-squared test, we tested the hypothesis that the distribution of our preferred health measure among single mothers is the same in CPS and SIPP samples. We stratified both samples into twelve groups by our four age groups and three education groups. For each of the twelve groups, we calculated the weighted proportion with a work limitation in the pooled CPS and SIPP sample. The difference between the CPS and pooled proportion was squared, multiplied by the CPS group sample size, and divided by the product of the pooled proportion and its complement. The same calculation was performed for the SIPP proportion, and then the CPS and SIPP numbers were added and summed across the twelve groups. Our test statistic is 20.77, and thus we reject the hypothesis at the 5 percent significance level. However, the overall difference in disability is small: 8 percent in SIPP versus 7 percent in CPS. There may be several reasons why SIPP has a slightly larger number of single mothers with disabilities. First, the question in SIPP is worded differently – it specifically mentions mental and physical disabilities, and so it may

prompt greater responses. Second, SIPP asked the question initially and then verified the status at the beginning of the health section of the topical module, and this pattern of questions would encourage positive responses. Finally, varying attrition rates between the nondisabled and disabled may not be accounted for in the Census Bureau's weighting scheme. The 1 percent difference between CPS and SIPP is not large, and, both show the same pattern of disability – rising with age and decreasing with education.

11. See the Haveman and Buron paper in this volume for a fuller discussion of the concept of earnings capacity.

12. We also estimated a maximum likelihood simulations system with the same specification. Results are nearly identical to the tobit two-stage model reported in the paper.

13. Among our sample of healthy single mothers who work, the median number of actual hours worked is 40. The hours available to work at capacity are derived in the following way. First, we calculated the value of the latent log hours (the right-hand-side of the hours equation) that would yield a mean of the log of 40 hours – used as our standard base in calculating earnings capacity. From this value we subtract the product of the variables for a woman's own health and that of her children and their respective coefficients. From this, we have an estimate of mean log hours which is used to calculate health-adjusted earnings capacity hours.

14. We also calculate these values for women with four, five or six ADLs. They are not reported, owing to their small sample size.

15. This figure is from data on the costs of 'acceptable" child care reported in the Institute for American Values (1989). A similar figure can be derived from tables published by the U.S. Bureau of the Census (1987).

16. Under current law, all able-bodied women with children aged 6 or older must be registered for work or for job training. Furthermore, according to the Family Support Act, a state at its discretion can lower this requirement to cover women with children over one year of age. No special provision is included for mothers with a disabled child. Women with substantial health problems are clearly not 'able-bodied,' but it may be difficult for them to establish that fact. It is not at all clear whether the majority of women who report themselves in poor or fair health would be considered able-bodied, nor is it clear how many ADLs a woman would be required to have in order to be classified as 'not able-bodied'.

17. Moffitt and Wolfe (1990, Table 12) estimate that the value of health insurance to a single mother with fair or poor health is three or four times the value to a single mother with very good or excellent health, i.e., about $4000 in 1984 dollars.

18. In our sample (using weights), only among women with six ADLs do all (100 percent) receive SSI. Among women with five ADLs, 38 percent are on SSI, while for women with fewer ADLs, less than 10 percent in any category receive SSI.

19. In 13 states, there are further restrictions on Medicaid coverage under 209B provisions. In these states, those covered under SSI must be covered by a medical 'spend-down' option.

20. For AFDC calculations, the SSI benefits of a child are ignored. A study

done in 1979 suggested that, of those children covered under SSI by their own disability and not living in a foster home, 42 percent lived in families receiving AFDC or local general assistance (*1990 Green Book*, p. 732).

21. Increasing SSI eligibility for single mothers with substantial health problems will reduce AFDC payments somewhat, decreasing the AFDC expenditures of both states and the federal government. This would be offset by increased federal expenditures on SSI – and state expenditures to the extent that they provide SSI supplements. The alternative of adding dependents' benefits to SSI along with modified leniency standards for single parents would decrease AFDC – hence state payments – to a greater extent while increasing federal payments to a greater extent.

22. Over half of those receiving SSI on the basis of disability are eligible on the basis of a mental disability. Among children this is largely mental retardation. More than one-fifth of those eligible via disability are over age 65.

23. A number of states provide a state supplement. In these cases, the income test is also increased and is usually equal to the higher benefit level. Less than 10 percent of beneficiaries qualify because of state supplementation.

References

Blank, R. (1989) 'The Effect of Medical Need and Medicaid on AFDC Participation,' *Journal of Human Resources*, 24 (Winter), 54–87.

1990 Green Book, Committee on Ways and Means, U.S. House of Representatives (Washington, D.C.: U.S. Government Printing Office).

Haveman, R., and B. Wolfe (1990a) 'The Economic Well–Being of the Disabled, 1962–1984,' *Journal of Human Resources*, 25(1), 32–54.

Haveman, R., and B. Wolfe (1990b) 'Trends in the Prevalence of Disability, 1962–1984,' *The Milbank Quarterly*, 68(1), 53–80.

Haveman, R., M. Stone, and B. Wolfe. (1989) 'Market Work, Wages and Men's Health.' Working Paper No. 3020, National Bureau of Economic Research, Cambridge, Mass.

Institute for American Values (1989) 'How the Child Care Market Works: An Economic Analysis.' Family Policy Brief, New York.

Lee, L. F. (1982) 'Health and Wage: A Simultaneous Equation Model with Multiple Discrete Indicators,' *International Economic Review*, 23, 199–221.

Luft, H. (1975) 'The Impact of Poor Health on Earnings,' *Review of Economics and Statistics*, 57, 43–57.

Maddala, G. S. (1983) *Limited Dependent and Qualitative Variables in Econometrics* (Cambridge: Cambridge University Press).

Maddox, G. L., and E. B. Douglass (1973) 'Self-Assessment of Health: A Longitudinal Study of Elderly Subjects,' *Journal of Health and Social Behavior*, 14 (March), 87–93.

Moffitt, R. (1987) 'Work and the U.S. Welfare System: A Critical Review.' Final Report to the Department of Health and Human Services.

Moffitt, R., and B. Wolfe (1990) 'The Effects of Medicaid on Welfare Dependency and Work.' Special Report no. 49, Institute for Research on Poverty, University of Wisconsin-Madison.

National Center for Health Statistics (1990) *Health of Black and White Americans, 1985–87* (Hyattsville, Maryland: Public Health Service) Series 10, no. 171.

National Center for Health Statistics (1991) *Health, United States, 1990* (Hyattsville, Maryland: Public Health Service).

Ries, P. (1990) *Americans Assess Their Health: United States 1987* (National Center for Health Statistics, Hyattsville, Maryland).

Winkler, A. (1991) 'The Incentive Effects of Medicaid on Women's Labor Supply,' *Journal of Human Resources*, **26**(2), 308–37.

U.S. Bureau of the Census (1987) *Who's Minding the Kids? Child Care Arrangements: Winter 1984–85*. Current Population Reports, Series P-70, No. 9 (Washington, D.C., U.S. Government Printing Office).

5 Recent Trends in Economic Inequality in the United States: Income versus Expenditures versus Material Well-being[1]

Susan E. Mayer and Christopher Jencks

Official income statistics suggest that the United States did not protect the economic interests of its poorest citizens very effectively during the 1970s and 1980s. According to the Census Bureau's best published estimates, the average American family's real annual pretax money income rose 12 percent during the 1970s and 11 percent during the 1980s. Among the poorest fifth of all families, in contrast, real income rose 6 percent during the 1970s and fell 4 percent during the 1980s.[2] By 1989 the distribution of family income was more unequal than at any time since the Census Bureau began collecting such data in 1947.[3]

Most commentators assume that because income inequality has increased, disparities in families' expenditures, consumption, and material well-being have also increased. This may be true, but it is not self-evident. As Figure 5.1 indicates, the links between income, expenditure, consumption, and material well-being are extremely complex. If all else remains equal, changes in the distribution of reported income will obviously lead to parallel changes in the distribution of expenditures, consumption, and material well-being. But all else may not remain equal. The distributions of reporting errors, taxes, saving and borrowing, noncash benefits, physical and financial assets, consumer efficiency, household size, age, physical and mental health, and work-related expenses have all changed over the past generation. As a result, changes in the distribution of income need not imply parallel changes in the distribution of material well-being.

121

Figure 5.1 Determinants of material well-being

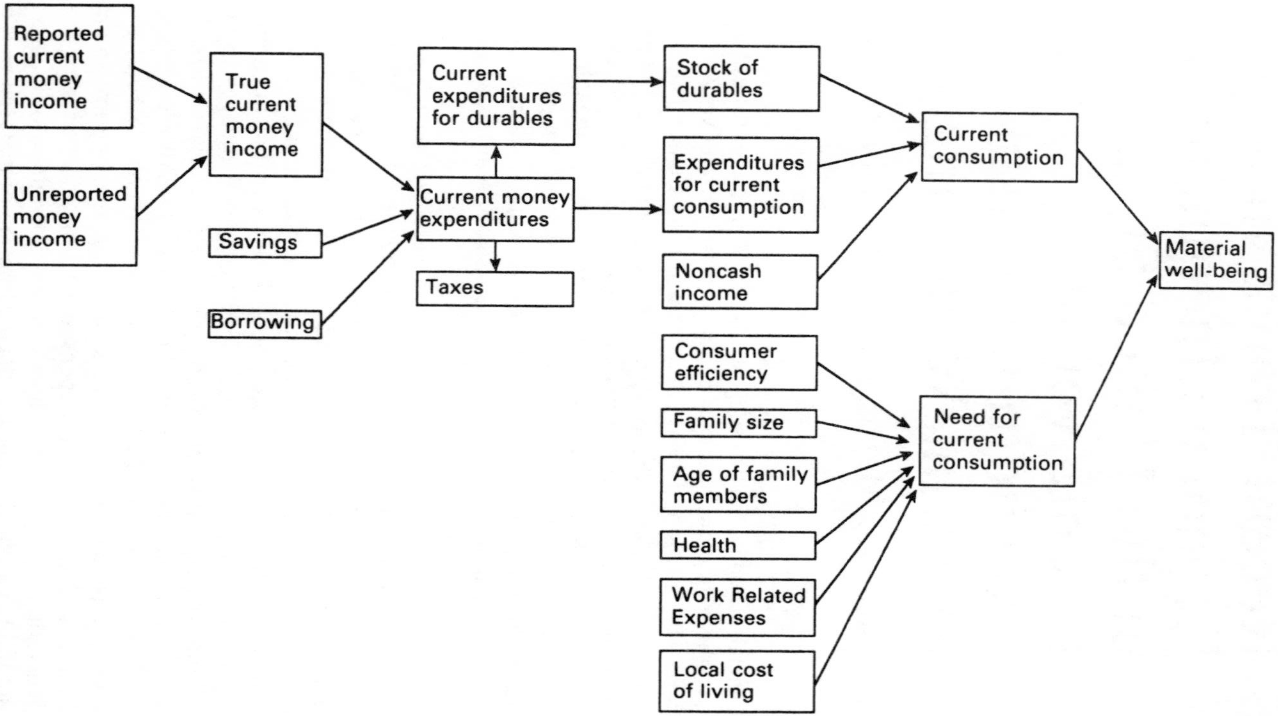

Our discussion has three parts. We begin by examining changes in the distribution of income since the early 1960s, showing that trends in inequality differ for families and households, that trends for households differ when we weight all persons equally instead of weighting all households equally, that trends for total household income differ from trends for per capita household income, that trends in the top half of the distribution do not always mirror trends in the bottom half of the distribution, and that the decennial Census tells a somewhat different story from the Current Population Survey (CPS) about the 1960s and 1970s. Nonetheless, all measures derived from the CPS indicate that income inequality grew in the early 1980s and remained unusually high in the late 1980s. (The 1990 Census was not available when we wrote this chapter, so we could not use it to check conclusions about the 1980s based on the CPS.)

We next examine changes in the distribution of expenditures and consumption. Like others before us, we find that both expenditures and consumption are more equally distributed than income. We also find that while income inequality has grown quite a lot since the early 1970s, consumption inequality has changed far less.

Finally, we describe changes in the distribution of material well-being, using data on housing conditions, automobile ownership, telephone service, doctor and dentist visits, bed days, and restricted activity days. We find that income is only moderately correlated with these material advantages. Furthermore, changes in the distribution of income have almost no effect on the distribution of these advantages.

5.1 CHANGES IN THE DISTRIBUTION OF INCOME

Most discussions of change in the distribution of income rely on data collected by the Census Bureau's Current Population Survey (CPS). The CPS currently surveys about 60 000 households a month and succeeds in interviewing someone in 96 percent of them. Every March the CPS asks detailed questions about household members' income from earnings, assets, and transfer payments during the previous calendar year. (The CPS did not begin to collect data on noncash income until 1979, and these data are still very limited.)

The Census Bureau reports income distributions for three groups: households, families, and unrelated individuals. Household income is the total money income of everyone living in a house or apartment, regardless of their economic or familial relationship to one another.

Family income is the total income of any group of two or more household members who are related by blood, marriage, or adoption. The Bureau does not treat individuals who live alone or with nonrelatives as members of families. Instead, it calls them 'unrelated individuals' and reports their incomes separately.

When the Census Bureau describes trends in inequality, it presents two kinds of statistics: the Gini coefficient and the share of all income received by the poorest fifth, the next poorest fifth, and so on.[4] The Gini coefficient is popular among economists because it summarizes the level of inequality in a single number, but unlike quintile shares its meaning is not easy to explain to nonspecialists. From our perspective, moreover, the fact that the Gini coefficient summarizes the degree of inequality in a single number is a disadvantage rather than an advantage.

Both the likely causes and the likely consequences of a change in the distribution of income depend on whether the change occurs in the top or bottom half of the distribution. If recent increases in income inequality derived mainly from a widening gap between the poor and everyone else, for example, it might make sense to think about the growth of an underclass as a possible cause of the change and perhaps also as a likely consequence of such a change. It would also make sense to think about changes in low-wage labor markets as a possible cause, and to think about transfer payments, minimum wages, and job training as possible remedies.

If recent increases in the overall level of income inequality were mainly attributable to growing inequality between the rich and everyone else, in contrast, the growth of an urban underclass could hardly be the explanation. Instead, we might want to ask why America's professional and managerial elite had been more successful than other groups at insulating itself from the ravages of economic instability and international competition, why blue-collar labor unions were so much less successful in pursuing this goal, why the social norms that had limited inequality within organizations during the 1950s and 1960s eroded during the late 1970s and 1980s, and why legislators made no effort to offset the consequences of these changes by making taxes more progressive.

We therefore look at the top and bottom halves of the income distribution separately. To measure inequality in the top half of the distribution we compare the mean income of those in the top quintile to the mean income of those in the middle quintile. To measure inequality in the bottom half of the distribution we compare the mean income for the bottom quintile to the mean for the middle quintile.[5] This is almost the same as comparing the means for the top and bottom quintiles to the median.

Readers who prefer a single measure of overall inequality can divide the ratio of the top to the middle by the ratio of the bottom to the middle. This calculation will allow them to compare the mean income of the top quintile to the mean for the bottom quintile. Readers should also bear in mind that when inequality increases in the top and bottom halves of the distribution simultaneously, inequality between the top and the bottom increases multiplicatively. Suppose, for example, that the bottom quintile's income drops from 30 to 27 percent of the middle quintile's income (a drop of a tenth) and that the top quintile's income rises from 200 to 220 percent of the middle quintile's income (an increase of a tenth). The top quintile's income will then rise from $200/30 = 6.67$ times the bottom quintile's income to $220/27 = 8.15$ times the bottom quintile's income (an increase of 22 percent).

Family income. Because Census Bureau publications have traditionally emphasized trends in family income, most popular discussions of income inequality do the same thing. Figures 5.2a and 5.2b compare the mean income of the top and bottom quintiles to the mean of the middle quintile for the entire post-war period (1947–89). Contrary to popular belief, the percentage difference between the bottom and the middle quintiles is consistently greater than that between the top and the middle quintiles. This becomes obvious if one takes the reciprocals of the ratios shown on the right side of Figure 5.2b and calculates the ratio of the middle quintile's income to the bottom quintile's income.[6] For the post-war period as a whole, the income of the middle quintile ranges from 3.2 to 3.8 times that of the bottom quintile, while the income of the top quintile ranges from 2.3 to 2.7 times that of the middle quintile.[7] This difference may help explain why most middle-income Americans feel they have more in common with families near the top of the distribution than with families near the bottom.[8]

Our main concern here, however, is not the shape of the distribution but how it has changed over time. From 1947 to 1979, the top and bottom halves of the family income distribution seemed to respond to different influences. Inequality between the top and the middle declined somewhat between 1947 and 1957, while inequality between the bottom and the middle fluctuated with the business cycle, exhibiting no clear secular trend.[9] From 1957 to 1968 inequality

Figure 5.2a   Income of highest quintile as a proportion of middle quintile

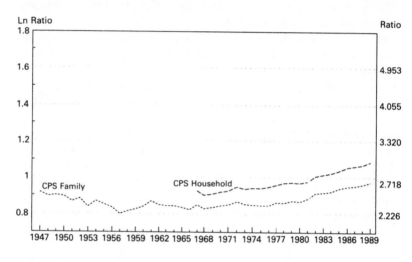

Figure 5.2b   Income of lowest quintile as a proportion of middle quintile

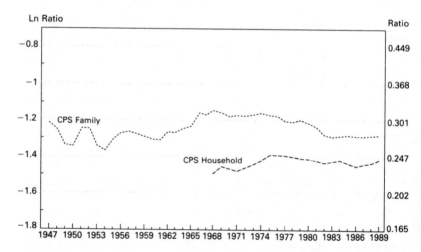

Sources: U.S. Bureau of Census, *Current Population Survey*, Series P-60, no. 168, table 6. Bureau of Labor Statistics *Consumer Expenditure Survey*: Bulletin 2225, (80–81); *Integrated Survey Data*, (84–89) and subsequent press releases.

between the bottom and the middle narrowed as the labor market tightened, but inequality between the top and the middle showed no clear trend. From 1968 to 1974 there was little change of any sort. From 1974 to 1980, inequality grew in the bottom half of the distribution but not in the top half. It was only during the early 1980s that family income inequality grew in both the top and bottom halves of the distribution.

Household income. Although the Census Bureau has traditionally emphasized trends in family income, trends among families are not a reliable guide to trends in the population as a whole, because a rising fraction of the population consists of unrelated individuals, and trends among unrelated individuals have not paralleled those among families. One can deal with this problem in two ways. If one thinks that kinship is crucial and physical proximity secondary, one can define unrelated individuals as families of one and combine them with families of two or more. If one thinks physical proximity is crucial and kinship secondary, one can make households the basic unit of analysis, ignoring their composition. The first approach treats two unrelated individuals in the same household as if they lived in separate households. The second approach treats them like a married couple or adult siblings.

In 1940, when the Census Bureau's conventions for dealing with income were established, lodgers and live-in domestic servants were still common, so it seemed sensible to treat nonrelatives differently from relatives in the same household. But both lodgers and live-in domestic servants have almost disappeared, largely because Americans have come to dislike the formal codes of behavior that make it possible for unequals to share living space. Most Americans are now reluctant to share their living space with people they cannot treat like family members. This still leaves room for a wide range of economic relationships. But when nonrelatives who share living quarters have a sexual relationship, they usually seem to make short-term economic arrangements that fall within the same spectrum as the arrangements of married couples. And when nonrelatives have no sexual ties, their economic arrangements appear to be much like those of extended families.

If this argument is correct, contemporary studies of income inequality that rely on CPS data should probably ignore kinship and treat households as their basic unit of analysis.[10] This conclusion does not mean we think income inequality within households is unimportant. But we do not believe that the CPS is a useful tool for analyzing the distribution of economic resources within households.[11]

Figures 5.2a and 5.2b compare trends in family and household income inequality.[12] Because the household distribution includes a lot of one-person households with very low incomes, the measured level of inequality among households is even higher than among families. Nonetheless, the trend in the top half of the distribution is almost identical for households and families (see Figure 5.2a). It is only in the bottom half of the distribution that trends for families and households differ (see Figure 5.2b). Whereas inequality between the bottom and middle quintiles widened between 1967 and 1989 for families, it narrowed slightly for households, largely because unrelated individuals' incomes rose faster than family incomes.

Persons versus households. When the Census Bureau estimates the distribution of income for households or families, it weights each household or family equally, regardless of its size. But most Americans care about the welfare of individuals. If two people who maintain separate households decide to marry, for example, we do not want them to have less weight in our economic statistics. We just want to measure their level of well-being differently, taking account of the fact that living together reduces some of their expenses.

If we want to weight all individuals equally, regardless of their living arrangements, we must weight households unequally, giving them weights proportional to their size. Figures 5.3a and 5.3b show how such reweighting alters the distribution of household income. The estimates designated TOT–HHWT are taken from the published data in Figures 5.2a and 5.2b and weight all households equally. The estimates designated TOT–PWT come from CPS data tapes and weight households by size.[13] Contrasting the two series leads us to three conclusions:

- Weighting all persons equally makes the overall distribution of household income look somewhat more equal. (The TOT–PWT line is below the TOT–HHWT in Figure 5.3a and above it in Figure 5.3b.)
- Weighting all persons equally makes the gap between the top and the middle almost constant from 1963 through 1980 and accentuates the increase in inequality during the early 1980s (see Figure 5.3a).[14]
- Weighting all persons equally also changes the trend in the bottom half of the distribution (see Figure 5.3b). Whereas inequality between the bottom and the middle appears to diminish from 1967 to

Figure 5.3a   Household income of highest quintile as a proportion of middle quintile, using alternative measures from CPS data

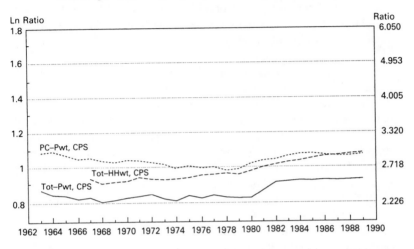

Figure 5.3b   Household income of lowest quintile as a proportion of middle quintile, using alternative measures from CPS data

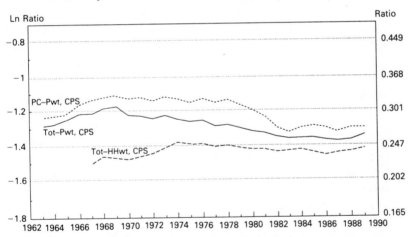

Notes: Tot–Pwt = Total household income with each person weighted equally.

Tot–HHwt = Total household income with each household weighted equally.

PC–Pwt = Per Capita household income with each person weighted equally.

Source: Tabulations by David Rhodes from *Current Population Survey*. Data tapes provided by Robert Mare and Christopher Winship.

1974 when we weight all households equally, it widens slightly when we weight all persons equally. And whereas inequality between the bottom and the middle appears roughly constant from 1974 to 1989 when we weight all households equally, it widens when we weight all persons equally.

Even when we weight individuals equally, therefore, the CPS tells quite different stories about trends in the top and bottom halves of the distribution. The relative position of the bottom quintile began to deteriorate around 1970 and continued to deteriorate at a fairly steady rate until 1987 – a trend that is broadly consistent with claims that America has been creating a new 'underclass' whose situation differs dramatically from that of 'mainstream' Americans. In the top half of the distribution, in contrast, there is no clear trend from 1963 to 1980. Instead, there is a sudden increase in inequality in 1981 and 1982, which persists for the rest of the decade. While this change was presumably linked to the Volcker recession, it is not obvious why this particular recession affected the top half of the distribution when earlier recessions had not. Nor is it obvious why the effects of the recession persisted during the subsequent recovery. Shortages of highly educated labor may have been a factor, but we suspect that the changes in political and social attitudes associated with Ronald Reagan's arrival in Washington played a larger role. We doubt, for example, that the extraordinary increases in top executives' compensation during the 1980s derived either from a sudden increase in demand for skilled CEO's or a sudden decline in the supply of such individuals.

Adjusting income for need. Up to this point we have ignored the fact that different households need different amounts of money in order to live equally well. As Figure 5.1 indicates, a household's need for money depends on a multitude of factors, many of which are not measured in the CPS. The CPS does, however, measure the most important determinant of a household's monetary needs, namely its size.[15]

In order to adjust for differences in household size, we need an equivalence scale that tells us how much money households of different sizes need in order to be equally well off. Unfortunately for social science, no scale can make households of different sizes equally well off in all respects. Scales that try to equalize the distribution of material hardship require very large adjustments for household size.[16] Scales that try to equalize the extent to which households consume 'luxuries' rather than 'necessities' require somewhat smaller adjustments (Lazear and Michel, 1980; Van der Gaag and Smolensky, 1981). Scales that try to equalize adults' subjective satisfaction with their material standard of living require still smaller adjustments (Rainwater, 1974; Vaughan, 1984).[17] We do not know what sort of adjustment would be needed to equalize children's material well-being, children's subjective satisfaction with their standard of living, or children's life chances.[18]

Nonetheless, everyone agrees that a household of two needs more money than a household of one. Everyone also agrees that a household of two needs less than twice as much money as a household of one. It follows that any plausible adjustment for household size will yield results somewhere between those for total household income and those for per capita household income. If the trend lines for these two measures are parallel, we can have considerable confidence that we would see the same trend for any measure of inequality based on households' size and income. If the trend lines for total and per capita income are not parallel, the 'true' trend depends on our choice of equivalence scales, which in turn depends on what we want to equalize.

Figures 5.3a and 5.3b allow us to compare trends in total and per capita household income (which we denote as TOT–PWT and PC–PWT). Both these measures weight households by size. Comparing the two trend lines leads us to five conclusions:

- Substituting per capita income for total income makes inequality between the bottom and the middle look smaller while making inequality between the top and the middle look larger.
- Substituting per capita income for total income has little effect on our story about trends during the 1960s. So long as we weight all persons equally, inequality shrank from 1963 to 1969 in both the top and bottom halves of the distribution.
- Substituting per capita income for total income does not greatly alter our picture of what happened to the bottom half of the distribution during the 1970s, but it does alter our picture of what happened to the top half. Inequality between the top and the middle hardly changed from 1970 to 1980 using total income; it narrowed slightly using per capita income. Thus we cannot say what 'really' happened to inequality in the top half of the distribution during the 1970s unless we define what we mean by equality among households of different sizes.

- Substituting per capita income for total income does not alter our picture of the early 1980s. Inequality increased rapidly from 1980 to 1984 using either measure, although the increase at the bottom was greater using per capita income.
- Substituting per capita income for total income does not change our conclusions about the late 1980s. No matter what equivalence scale we use, inequality was about the same in 1989 as in 1984.

Changes in the quality of income data. CPS respondents have become increasingly reluctant to answer questions about their income. In 1948 the CPS got complete income data on 95 percent of the adults in its target population. By 1968 the figure had fallen to 89 percent and by 1982 it was down to 73 percent (Lillard, Smith, and Welch, 1986). Fortunately, there was no further change between 1982 and 1988 (Karoly, 1990). But because many families include more than one individual with income, roughly a third of all families now fail to report some component of at least one family member's income. Missing data have become more common partly because the CPS now asks more detailed questions about income than it asked a generation ago. But respondents are also less likely to answer those questions that the CPS has always asked.

When a CPS respondent cannot or will not answer a question, the Census Bureau estimates the missing value by setting it equal to the value reported by the last previous respondent with similar demographic and economic characteristics.[19] This imputation procedure is known as the 'hot deck.' It will yield unbiased estimates of income inequality so long as income *per se* does not affect response rates. But if, as seems likely, income does affect response rates independent of the characteristics that the Census Bureau uses to impute missing values, imputations may well bias both the estimated mean and the estimated dispersion.[20] If that happens, growing reliance on imputed data could also lead to biased estimates of the trend in inequality, although we doubt that the bias would be large.[21]

The CPS versus the Census The decennial Census differs from the CPS in several potentially important respects. Starting in 1970 the Census began to rely largely on mailback questionnaires, whereas the CPS relies on a mix of face-to-face and telephone interviews.[22] Face-to-face and telephone interviewing have the advantage that interviewers can clarify ambiguous questions. Mailback questionnaires have the advantage that a conscientious respondent who does not know another household member's income from a particular source has time to inquire. It is not intuitively obvious which approach should yield the best overall results. The Census also asks somewhat less detailed income questions than the CPS, although experience with earlier versions of the CPS suggests that this should not greatly affect the estimated level of inequality.[23]

The median Census household reported almost exactly the same income as the median CPS household in both 1970 and 1980. The amounts reported by households at the 20th and 80th percentiles were also very close. Indeed, even the 10th and 90th percentiles were fairly close. But households below the 10th percentile of the Census distribution reported considerably less income than those at the same point in the CPS distribution. Conversely, households above the 90th percentile of the Census distribution reported considerably more income than their counterparts in the CPS.[24] The distribution of per capita household income was also more unequal in the Census than in the CPS (see Figures 5.4a and 5.4b).

The fact that households in the top decile report more income to the Census than to the CPS makes it hard to argue that the CPS gets consistently better income data than the Census. We strongly suspect that the CPS does a better job with households in the bottom tail of the distribution, while the Census does a better job with those in the top tail.[25]

Our primary concern, however, is whether the Census and CPS tell the same story about trends over time. If the introduction of mailback questionnaires accounted for the higher level of inequality in the Census, we would expect the level of inequality to increase more during the 1960s in the Census than in the CPS. Exact comparisons are impossible because CPS data on household income in 1959 have not survived, but the CPS data on families in Figure 5.2 suggest that the trend in inequality from 1959 to 1963 was very similar to that from 1963 to 1969. It therefore seems reasonable to estimate inequality in CPS household income for 1959 by projecting trend lines for 1963–9 backwards to 1959. When we do this we find that the 1959 CPS results are almost identical to the 1959 Census results (see Figures 5.4a and 5.4b). This finding supports our conjecture that the introduction of mailback questionnaires explains why more households report very high and very low incomes to the Census than to the CPS.

If the introduction of mailback questionnaires were the sole explanation for differences between the Census and the CPS, the two surveys should tell almost identical stories about trends during the 1970s. This is in fact the case for the top half of the distribution (see

Figure 5.4a   Household income of highest quintile as a proportion of middle quintile, using alternative surveys

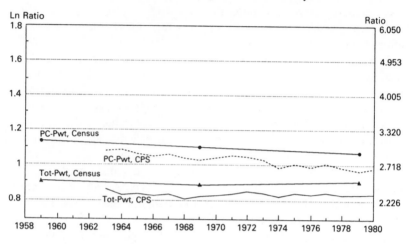

Figure 5.4b   Household income of lowest quintile as a proportion of middle quintile, using alternative surveys

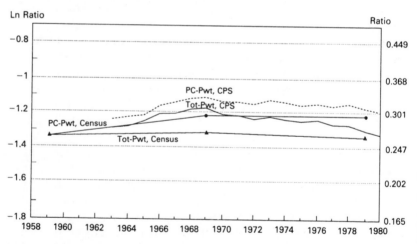

Notes: Tot–Pwt = Total household income with each person weighted equally.

PC–Pwt = Per Capita household income with each person weighted equally.

Source: Tabulations by David Rhodes from *Current Population Survey*. Data tapes provided by Robert Mare and Christopher Winship. Also, 1/1,000 Public Use Census Samples.

Figure 5.4a). Unfortunately, it is not the case for the bottom half of the distribution. In the CPS, inequality between the bottom and the middle quintile declines by 0.029 for total income and 0.021 for per capita income during the 1970s. In the Census, the declines are only 0.010 and 0.003 (see Appendix B, Table B.1).

The reader who is now totally confused should be. Figures 5.2 to 5.4 show that conclusions about trends in inequality are quite sensitive to whether we focus on families or households, whether we weight households by size, whether we measure income adequacy using total income or per capita income, whether we look at the Census or the CPS, and which years we choose to start and end our time series. Nonetheless, so long as we weight all persons equally, four broad conclusions seem justified:

- During the 1960s inequality declined slightly in both the top and bottom half of the distribution, regardless of how we adjust for changes in household size.
- During the early 1980s inequality increased in both the top and bottom half of the distribution, regardless of how we adjust for size.
- During the late 1980s inequality hardly changed in either half of the distribution, regardless of how we adjust for size.
- During the 1970s the trend in inequality depends on how we adjust for changes in household size and which half of the distribution we look at.

The first three conclusions are familiar to anyone who has examined the voluminous literature on income inequality. The sensitivity of conclusions about the 1970s to whether one looks at the top or bottom of the distribution and how one adjusts for changes in household size has been less widely noted, and it helps explain why economic analysts have often reached different conclusions about trends in inequality.

If one looks at total household income, for example, one finds that inequality in the bottom half of the distribution began to increase in the early 1970s, when America's dominance of the world economy began eroding and stagflation began. This does not necessarily mean that foreign competition or economic uncertainty *caused* the change, but it certainly suggests that possibility. The gap between the top and middle quintiles follows a different trajectory, increasing sharply in the early 1980s. This change coincides with changes in the cultural and political climate that made organizations more willing to boost managers' pay while constraining almost everyone else's pay. If one conflates changes in the top and bottom halves of the distribution, sorting out these distinct trends becomes more difficult.

Distinguishing between inequality in total and per capita household income also draws attention to the complex effects of demographic change on economic inequality. A full analysis of these influences would have to distinguish the effects of changes in adult living arrangements from the effects of changes in fertility. The spread of one-adult households almost inevitably increases inequality, both because women have less income than men and because any arrangement in which two or more earners pool their income is likely to produce a more equal distribution than an arrangement in which no pooling occurs. Declining fertility has more ambiguous effects. On the one hand, it makes households' economic needs more uniform, which is likely to reduce measured inequality. On the other hand, declining fertility is associated with increased labor force participation among wives, which can either increase or decrease measured inequality in household income depending on which wives already work and which wives enter the labor force when there are fewer children at home.

Disentangling the effects of demographic change on economic inequality is beyond the scope of this chapter. Nonetheless, it is important to recognize that demographic changes had an important impact on measured inequality during the 1970s, making trends in inequality highly sensitive to judgments about how much money households of different sizes need to be equally well off. This does not appear to be as true during the 1960s or 1980s, when inequality in total and per capita income moved in tandem (at least in the CPS).

5.2 CHANGES IN THE DISTRIBUTION OF EXPENDITURES

We now turn to the question of whether trends in the distribution of household income have led to parallel changes in the distribution of household expenditures and consumption. As Figure 5.1 indicated, reported expenditures can differ from reported income for two reasons. First, households can save or borrow. Second, those who report, record, or impute income and expenditures can make mistakes. We have no a priori reason to believe that the distribution of saving and borrowing by income level has changed appreciably over the past generation.[26] We do, however, have reason to suspect that errors in income measurement have increased. We also know that many households report extraordinarily low annual incomes, and that far fewer households report very low expenditures. While many economists assume that this difference reflects widespread borrowing by low-income households, we believe it also reflects widespread underreporting by poor households (Edin, 1992; Edin and Jencks, 1992). If this belief is correct, trends in expenditure inequality could provide a more accurate measure of the true trend in income inequality than trends in reported income do.

As Figure 5.1 indicates, a household's current consumption can also differ from its current expenditures. This occurs for at least four reasons. First, expenditures include outlays for taxes, retirement plans, insurance, and gifts that have little or no influence on current consumption. Second, the current cost of home ownership can be substantially higher or lower than a home's rental value, especially for elderly homeowners who have paid off their mortgages. Third, current outlays for consumer durables (especially motor vehicles) are often a poor proxy for the value of the 'service flows' that a household derives from its stock of such durables. Fourth, many households get significant amounts of noncash income from the government (Medicaid and Food Stamps, for example), from employers (health insurance and business lunches, for example), and from relatives in other households (free childcare, for example).

Trend data are not available on most of the factors that make consumption differ from expenditure. We do know, however, that the distributions of taxes and home ownership have changed over the past generation, that the relationship between homeowners' current outlays and the rental value of their homes has changed, and that noncash government benefits for the poor have grown dramatically. Inequality in current consumption could therefore have changed in somewhat different ways from inequality in current expenditures.

In order to track these changes we rely on the Consumer Expenditure Survey (CEX), conducted by the Bureau of Labor Statistics (BLS) in 1960–1, 1972–3, and continuously since 1980. Unfortunately, we did not have access to the CEX data for 1980–81 when we were writing this chapter, and the 1982–3 CEX was restricted to urban households. Our discussion therefore focuses on changes over three intervals: 1960–61 to 1972–3, 1972–3 to 1984–5, and 1984–5 to 1988–9.[27]

Our expenditure measure includes all out-of-pocket expenditures except for investments. We include personal taxes. We exclude money spent for stocks, bonds, and real estate, including the portion of a homeowner's mortgage payment that reduces the principal.[28]

Our estimate of current consumption differs from expenditures in three ways:

(1) It excludes income taxes, social security taxes, pension contributions, and gifts.[29]

(2) It replaces the current cost of home ownership (property taxes, mortgage interest, and home maintenance) with an estimate of each home's rental value.[30]

(3) It excludes the purchase price of motor vehicles. In principle, it should include an estimate of vehicle depreciation, but because of data limitations this was impossible. We doubt that this affects our results appreciably.[31]

In principle, our consumption measure should also exclude expenditures on other durables, such as furniture, refrigerators, and stereo equipment. Instead, we should include the estimated value of the 'service flows' from each household's stock of such durables. But we do not have inventories of durables for most years, so we used current expenditures on durables as a proxy for the value of the missing service flows. This estimate will be accurate if households smooth expenditures on durables over time (by buying a new sofa one year, a new washing machine the next year, and so on). If expenditures on durables vary from year to year, as they surely do, our estimate exaggerates consumption inequality. Fortunately, the bias is unlikely to change much over time.[32]

Our consumption measure includes food outlays covered by Food Stamps. It does not include the value of other noncash benefits, such as federal housing subsidies, employer-financed health insurance, Medicare and Medicaid, or childcare provided by relatives living elsewhere.

Comparing the CEX and CPS. Comparing trends in expenditure and consumption inequality to trends in income inequality is complicated by four considerations: the fact that the CEX and CPS use different units of observation, the low quality of the CEX income data, changes in the way the CEX defines expenditures, and changes in the design of the CEX.

Whereas the CPS aggregates individuals into families and households, the CEX aggregates them into what it calls 'consumer units' (CUs). The CEX always treats a household head's spouse and unmarried children as part of the head's CU. It assigns other household members to separate CUs if the head says that they pay their bills with 'their own money.' Because individuals who live with their extended family or nonrelatives tend to be poor, assigning them to a separate CU is likely to increase measured inequality in total resources, though it is not likely to have much effect on inequality in per capita resources. Fortunately, BLS splits only 3 percent of all households into multiple consumer units, and this figure appears to have been fairly stable over time.[33] In the absence of other differences, therefore, we would expect the CEX and CPS to yield very similar trends in economic inequality.

Nonetheless, neither the level of income inequality nor the trend over time is the same in the CEX as in the CPS. We suspect that the two income series diverge mainly because they treat missing income data differently.[34] Since the CPS treatment of missing data is superior to the CEX treatment, trend estimates based on the CPS should be somewhat more accurate than those based on the CEX. We therefore treat the CPS income data as our benchmark and ask whether changes in the CPS income distribution lead to parallel changes in the CEX distributions of expenditures and consumption.

But because BLS has changed the way it treats certain transactions, our expenditure estimates for the 1960s cannot be made precisely comparable to those for the 1980s. Fortunately, we can make the 1972–3 data almost comparable both to that gathered in 1960–61 and to that gathered in the 1980s. Our 1972–3A samples try to replicate 1960–61 definitions and coverage. Our 1972B and 1973B samples try to replicate the definitions and coverage used in the 1980s.

Nonetheless, our estimates of expenditure and consumption inequality in 1960–61, 1972–3, and 1984–9 are not perfectly comparable, because of other changes in the design of the CEX. Four changes were especially important.

- In 1972 BLS stopped trying to reconcile a CU's reported income with its reported expenditures.
- Whereas the 1960–61 survey covered the previous twelve months, subsequent surveys conducted four quarterly interviews, each of which asked about expenditures over the previous three months.
- Whereas the 1960–61 survey substituted a CU at another address

when the first CU on its list was difficult to reach or uncooperative, subsequent surveys made more effort to get data from the original sample. This raised the participation rate.

- In 1972–3 the target population consisted of CUs living at a sample address in the last quarter of the survey. When a CU had moved to a sample address during the survey year or missed an interview for some other reason, the CEX asked the CU to estimate its expenditures during the missing quarters. After 1980 the target population changed every quarter and consisted of CUs living at a sample address during that quarter. Because the CEX did not try to reconstruct data for missing quarters, roughly a quarter of the weighted sample has less than four quarters of expenditure data in 1984–9.

The cumulative effect of these design changes is uncertain, but if the real world had not changed we would make four predictions:

(1) Higher participation rates and the elimination of account balancing should increase the measured level of inequality between 1961 and 1972.

(2) Including CUs with less than four quarters of expenditure data and estimating their annual expenditures by multiplication should increase the measured level of inequality between 1973 and 1984.

(3) Eliminating CUs with less than four quarters of data and reweighting the sample should reduce the measured level of inequality between 1973 and 1984.

(4) In the 1980s, the downward bias introduced by eliminating CUs with less than four quarters of data and reweighting should be smaller than the upward bias introduced by including such CUs and estimating their annual expenditures by multiplication. We therefore emphasize results for CUs with four quarters of data.

Appendix A discusses these and other changes in the CEX, as well as their potential effects on inequality, in more detail.

Findings. Table 5.1 compares the expenditures and consumption of CUs in the bottom, middle, and top quintiles during 1960–61, 1972–3, and 1984–9. Like earlier investigators (e.g. Friedman, 1957; Garner, 1989), we find that annual expenditures are more equally distributed than annual income. The difference is especially marked in the bottom half of the distribution. When we rank CPS households by income, the poorest fifth report incomes between 25 and 30 percent those of the middle fifth. When we rank CUs by total expenditures, the poorest fifth report spending 34 to 39 percent of what the middle fifth spends (see Figures 5.5 and 5.6). Consumption is even more equal than expenditures, with the poorest fifth consuming 38 to 45 percent of what the middle fifth consumes.

Our concern here, however, is whether the distribution of expenditures has changed over time in the same way as the distribution of income. Table 5.2 shows how different quintiles' relative income, expenditures, and consumption changed during three intervals: 1960–61 to 1972–3, 1972–3 to 1984–5, and 1984–5 to 1988–9. Negative changes indicate growing inequality, while positive changes indicate shrinking inequality.

1960–61 to 1972–3. Both the Census and the CPS suggest that income inequality declined from 1960 to 1973 (see rows 1 and 2 of Table 5.2). The CEX, in contrast, shows that expenditure inequality increased during this period on three of our four measures, and even on the fourth measure expenditure inequality decreases less than income inequality (see row 3). The discrepancy between trends for income and expenditure could mean that patterns of saving and borrowing changed. We suspect, however, that what changed was the pattern of reporting errors. Account balancing eliminated many random errors in both the income and expenditure estimates in 1960–61. Once BLS dropped account balancing, such errors increased the apparent level of inequality.[35]

1972–3 to 1984–5. When we compare the total resources of the bottom and middle quintiles, making no adjustment for size, income inequality increased significantly from 1972–3 to 1984–5, expenditure inequality increased far less, and consumption inequality actually declined. When we look at per capita resources rather than total resources, all three outcomes show increases in the gap between the bottom and middle quintiles, but the increase is still largest for income, slightly smaller for expenditures, and still smaller for consumption. The difference between CPS income trends and CEX expenditure trends (shown in line 8 of Table 5.2) could be due to methodological changes in the CEX.[36] The difference between CEX expenditure and consumption trends (shown in line 10) cannot be so easily dismissed as a methodological artifact. It strongly suggests that consumption inequality really did rise less than income or expenditure inequality during this period.

Turning to the top half of the distribution and looking first at total resources, we see a significant increase in income inequality, an even

Table 5.1 Relative expenditure and consumption of consumer units in the bottom, middle, and top quintiles of each distribution: consumer expenditure surveys for 1960–61, 1972–3, and 1984–9

	1960–1	1972–3A	1972B	1973B	1984	1985	1986	1987	1988	1989
Total CU expenditures										
Low/Middle Quintile										
All CUs			0.356	0.365	0.307				0.307	
CUs with full data	0.389	0.375				0.345	0.335	0.342		0.362
Middle/High										
All CUs			0.459	0.462	0.381				0.383	
CUs with full data	0.491	0.467	0.465	0.464	0.405	0.411	0.406	0.408	0.415	0.398
High/Middle										
All CUs			2.179	2.165	2.625				2.611	
CUs with full data	2.038	2.141	2.153	2.154	2.471	2.435	2.463	2.450	2.411	2.510
CU expenditures per person										
Low/Middle										
All CUs			0.390	0.398	0.326				0.305	
CUs with full data	0.385	0.405				0.342	0.335	0.339		0.348
Middle/High										
All CUs			0.377	0.384	0.333				0.328	
CUs with full data	0.392	0.386	0.378	0.384	0.347	0.348	0.351	0.347	0.345	0.347

High/Middle	2.553	2.590						
All CUs	2.604	2.653		3.003			3.003	3.049
CUs with full data	2.644	2.606	2.878	2.877	2.847	2.884	2.896	2.885
Total CU consumption								
Low/Middle	0.417	0.431	0.445	0.436	0.436	0.439	0.444	0.458
Middle/High	0.496	0.489	0.471	0.480	0.472	0.476	0.477	0.444
High/Middle	2.015	2.043	2.123	2.085	2.117	2.102	2.095	2.255
CU consumption per person								
Low/Middle	0.426	0.431	0.410	0.397	0.391	0.395	0.378	0.388
Middle/High	0.425	0.427	0.421	0.421	0.422	0.418	0.410	0.401
High/Middle	2.354	2.343	2.375	2.375	2.368	2.394	2.441	2.493

Sources: Karen Rolf did the tabulations for 1960–61 and 1972–3A using data tapes assembled by Larry Radbill. Tony Maier did the tabulations for 1972–3B and 1980s using data tapes assembled by John Sabelhaus. The decile means for the 'full data' samples appear in Appendix B, Table B.2. All estimates weight CUs by their size.

Samples: The samples labelled 'all CUs' exclude CUs with zero or negative expenditures. When CUs in this sample had less than four quarters of expenditure data, as they often did in 1984–9, we estimated their annual expenditures by multiplication. The samples labelled 'CUs with full data' exclude CUs with zero or negative expenditures, CUs with less than four quarters of expenditure data, and CUs with what BLS calls incomplete income data. Because of changes in survey design, these restrictions mean that CUs which moved during the survey year or missed an interview for other reasons were excluded in 1984–9 but not in 1972–3B. CUs formed after the start of the survey period were excluded from all 'full data' samples except 1972–3A (see Appendix B).

Figure 5.5a   Ratio of high to middle quintile for income, expenditures, consumption

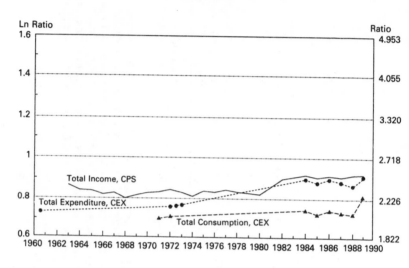

Figure 5.5b   Ratio of low to middle quintile for total income, expenditures, and consumption

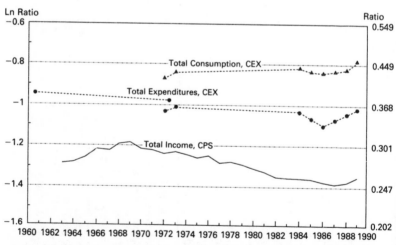

Sources: *Current Population Survey* data tapes provided by Robert Mare and Christopher Winship. Tabulations by David Rhodes. *Consumer Expenditure Survey* data tapes constructed by John Sabelhaus. Tabulations by Tony Maier.

Figure 5.6a   Ratio of high to middle quintile for per capita income, expenditures, and consumption

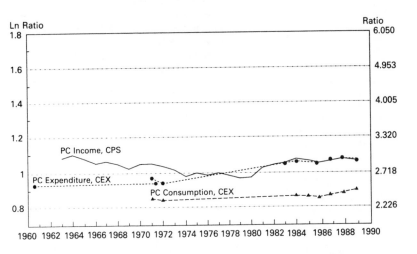

Figure 5.6b   Ratio of low to middle quintile for per capita income, expenditures, and consumption

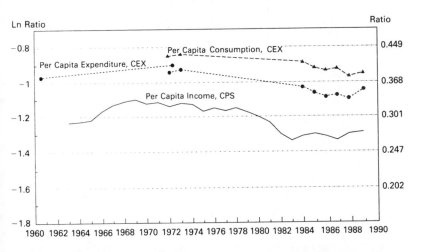

Sources: *Current Population Survey* data tapes provided by Robert Mare and Christopher Winship. Tabulations by David Rhodes. *Consumer Expenditure Survey* data tapes constructed by John Sabelhaus. Tabulations by Tony Maier.

Table 5.2   Percentage increase or decrease in relative income, expenditures and consumption of bottom, middle, and top quintiles: CEX CUs with full data versus CPS and census

Period, survey, and resource measure	Change in ratio of bottom to middle quintile		Change in ratio of middle to top quintile	
	Total resources	Per capita resources	Total resources	Per capita resources
1960–61 to 1972–3				
CPS household income				
(1963 to 1973)	0.015	0.034	0.011	0.023
Census household income				
(1959 to 1969)	0.005	0.027	0.034	0.024
CEX expenditures				
CUs with full data	−0.014	0.020	−0.024	−0.006
CEX expenditures minus				
CPS income	−0.029	−0.014	−0.035	−0.029
1972–3 to 1984–5				
CPS household income	−0.033	−0.048	−0.032	−0.014
CEX expenditures	−0.011	−0.043	−0.057	−0.033
CEX consumption	0.017	−0.025	−0.017	−0.005
CEX expenditures minus				
CPS income	0.022	0.005	−0.025	−0.019
CEX consumption minus				
CPS income	0.050	0.023	0.015	0.009
CEX consumption minus				
CEX expenditures	0.028	0.018	0.040	0.028
1984–5 to 1988–9				
CPS household income	0.000	0.000	−0.004	0.000
CEX expenditures	0.005	−0.012	−0.001	−0.002
CEX consumption	0.010	−0.021	−0.015	−0.015
CEX expenditures minus				
CPS income	0.005	−0.012	0.001	−0.002
CEX consumption minus				
CPS income	0.010	−0.021	−0.003	−0.015
CEX consumption minus				
CEX expenditures	0.005	−0.009	−0.004	−0.013
1972–3 to 1988–9				
CPS household income	−0.033	−0.048	−0.036	−0.014
CEX expenditures	−0.006	−0.055	−0.058	−0.035
CEX consumption	0.027	−0.046	−0.032	−0.020

Source: Percentage changes are calculated from ratios shown in Table 5.1 and in Appendix B, Table B.1.

larger increase in expenditure inequality, and a smaller increase in consumption inequality. All the changes over time are smaller when we look at per capita resources, but the pattern of differences between income, expenditures, and consumption is the same as for total resources. The fact that expenditure inequality grew more than income inequality could mean that savings fell more in the top quintile than in the middle quintile. But a change of that kind should also have made consumption inequality grow more than income inequality. The fact that consumption inequality grew less than expenditure inequality cannot be easily blamed on design changes in the CEX.

Taken as a whole, the CEX data leave little doubt that consumption inequality increased less than expenditure inequality between 1972–3 and 1984–5. This difference probably reflects changes in the distribution of taxation and home ownership, although other factors could also have played some role.

1984–5 to 1988–9. Income inequality in the CPS hardly changes between 1984–5 and 1988–9. The CEX suggests a small increase in inequality between the top and middle quintiles as the economy expanded during the late 1980s. The apparent trend in inequality between the bottom and middle quintiles depends on one's choice among the many possible equivalence scales.

Overall, the degree of consistency between the CPS and the CEX is not impressive. Some of the inconsistencies are probably due to methodological changes in the CEX, but some resist such explanations. In particular, the differences between expenditures and consumption in the CEX strongly suggest that income data exaggerate the increase in consumption inequality during the late 1970s and early 1980s. If we had data on the value of housing subsidies and Medicare, the discrepancy between trends in income and consumption during this period would presumably be even greater.

Cutler and Katz (1991) and Slesnick (1991) have also compared changes in CPS income inequality to changes in CEX consumption inequality. Cutler and Katz conclude that the trends are similar. Slesnick concludes that they are different. We find this disagreement reassuring, since it confirms our belief that the raw data tell a very mixed story. Table 5.3 compares their numerical findings for the period 1972–3 to 1988–9 with our own. For the top half of the distribution, all three studies tell essentially identical stories: inequality between the top and the middle increased between 1972 and 1989, it increased more for total resources than for per capita resources, and the increase for consumption is roughly comparable to

Table 5.3   Change in income and consumption inequality from 1972–3 to
1988–9 in Cutler–Katz, Slesnick, and Mayer–Jencks

	Ratio of bottom to middle fifth			Ratio of middle to top fifth			Ratio of top to bottom fifth		
	1972–3	*1988–9*	*Dif.*	*1972–3*	*1988–9*	*Dif.*	*1972–3*	*1988–9*	*Dif.*
Total resources									
CEX consumption									
Slesnick	0.400	0.408	0.008	0.477	0.427	–0.050	5.24	5.74	0.50
Mayer–Jencks	0.424	0.451	0.027	0.493	0.461	–0.032	4.78	4.81	0.03
CPS income									
Mayer–Jencks	0.291	0.258	–0.033	0.432	0.396	–0.036	7.95	9.79	1.84
Per capita resources									
CEX consumption									
Cutler–Katz	0.468	0.384	–0.084	0.434	0.423	–0.011	4.92	6.16	1.24
Mayer–Jencks	0.429	0.383	–0.046	0.426	0.406	–0.020	5.47	6.43	0.96
CPS income									
Mayer–Jencks	0.321	0.273	–0.048	0.359	0.345	–0.014	8.68	10.62	1.94

Sources: Cutler and Katz (1991, July version); Slesnick (1991); and Table 5.2 and
Appendix B, Table B.1 of this paper. Mayer–Jencks estimates are means of 1972B and
1973B and 1988–9. Because CU's enter the sample continuously after 1980, the twelve
months of expenditure data collected from any given CU seldom cover a calendar year.
As a result, the 1988 and 1989 samples are not precisely the same in different papers.
The Cutler–Katz estimates are for what they call 1988.

that for income. When we turn to the bottom half of the distribution,
however, consensus vanishes. Cutler and Katz find a dramatic
increase in consumption inequality between the bottom and the
middle, so they conclude that the CEX tells the same story as the
CPS. Slesnick finds a very small decline, so he concludes that the
CEX tells a very different story from the CPS.

The big difference between Cutler–Katz and Slesnick is the way
they adjust for differences in household size. Cutler and Katz make
strong adjustments for size.[37] As the reader can see by examining our
results, a large adjustment for size makes consumption inequality
appear to increase and makes trends in the CPS and CEX consistent.
The Slesnick estimates shown here make no adjustment for size.[38]
Again, the reader can see that this makes consumption inequality in
the bottom half of the distribution diminish rather than increase and
makes the CEX look very different from the CPS.

Our overall conclusion is that one can find whatever one wants in
these data, depending on where you look. In an effort to underline
this point, the last three columns of Table 5.3 rearrange the data in

the first six columns so that they compare the resources of the top quintile to those of the bottom quintile. This comparison makes changes over time look much larger. It also dramatizes the difference between our results for income and consumption, as well as the difference between Slesnick and ourselves – a difference that looked far smaller in columns 3 and 6.

5.3   DISPARITIES IN MATERIAL WELL-BEING

One can think of material well-being in two quite distinct ways, which we will call 'individualistic' and 'social.' The individualistic approach, familiar to all economists, assumes that each person is the best judge of what will maximize his or her well-being. Individuals may need to make different claims on society's collective resources because of differences in their health status, employment status, or the efficiency with which they use these resources, but when two individuals have the same objective needs and the same level of current consumption they are *by definition* equally well off. The same logic applies to households. From this perspective, therefore, all we need to convert data on household consumption into estimates of material well-being is some kind of equivalence scale that adjusts for differences in household needs.

The 'social' approach to material well-being, which we adopt here, differs from the individualistic approach in its willingness to assert that some forms of consumption are more important than others. Public discussions of material well-being tend to emphasize consumers' long-term interests at the expense of their short-term interests. Almost all public discussions assume, for example, that the distribution of fruit and vegetables is more important than the distribution of beer or pretzels. The social approach to material well-being also tends to emphasize 'necessities' (which in practice are usually things almost everyone has) while deemphasizing 'luxuries' (things a lot of people seem willing to do without).

Society can assign a good or service special importance for many different reasons. Some goods get a lot of attention because they consume a large fraction of household income and virtually everyone wants them. Homes and automobiles are obvious examples. Some goods are symbolically important because they relate to bodily functions (kitchens and bathrooms, for example). Some goods and services have become important because professional experts say they are important (the idea that everyone should see a doctor at least once a year, for example). Some standards have become important largely because the Census Bureau has used them for a long time (the idea that housing is crowded if there is more than one person per room, for example).

The correlation between income and material well-being obviously depends on how we define material well-being. If we allow individuals to define well-being for themselves, it depends entirely on the relationship of current consumption to need (see Figure 5.1). If we use socially defined benchmarks to judge material well-being, the correlation between income and well-being will also depend on the extent to which our benchmarks reflect individuals' subjective preferences or tastes. If everyone agreed that going hungry at the end of the month was by far the worst thing that could happen to them, for example, no one with enough money to buy food would ever go hungry, and the correlation between income and hunger would be very high. If significant numbers of people go hungry because they are saving money for a stereo or have spent their money on drugs, the correlation between income and hunger will be lower.

In 1983 and 1985 we conducted two surveys that tried to measure the extent of material hardship in Chicago. We asked respondents whether there had been a time in the past year when they could not afford to buy food, pay the rent, pay their utility bills, or see a doctor or dentist they needed to see. We also asked whether the respondent's home had physical problems such as a leaky roof or plumbing that did not work. Finally, we asked how much money a household spent on food each week and coded households as experiencing a hardship if they spent less than the federal Food Stamp budget for a family of that size. Using this 'social' approach to measuring well-being, our index of material hardship correlated only -0.372 with the logarithm of household income (Mayer and Jencks, 1989).[39]

There are no national data on most of the matters about which we asked in Chicago, but the decennial Census and the Annual Housing Survey (AHS) have collected data on housing conditions, access to automobiles, and access to telephones, and the Health Interview Survey (HIS) has collected data on people's health status and the frequency with which they see doctors and dentists. Unfortunately, these surveys tell us more about trends during the 1960s and 1970s than about trends during the 1980s. The 1990 Census was not available when we wrote this chapter, so we could not use it to assess trends during the 1980s. The Department of Housing and Urban

Development discontinued the Annual Housing Survey after 1983, and the new American Housing Survey covered a somewhat different sample and asked somewhat different questions, so our analysis of housing conditions ends in 1983. Finally, the National Center for Health Statistics changed the HIS questionnaire in 1982, so we cannot construct a uniform time series on health status, doctor visits, or dental visits covering the 1960s, 1970s, and 1980s. Our analyses of the 1980s are further limited by the fact that we have not yet been able to examine individual-level data from the AHS or the post-1980 HIS, and published results from these surveys are quite limited.

Ideally, we would like to construct a measure of material well-being comparable to our measures of income, expenditures, and consumption. We would like to be able to say, in other words, that Household A's consumption meets its needs twice as well as Household B's consumption does. In order to do this, however, we would have to be able to measure all the factors that make some households need to spend more for consumer goods and services than other households do. These factors include not only household size but the age and health of household members, the household's work-related expenses, the local cost of living, and the efficiency with which the household uses its money. We would also have to devise a convincing procedure for deciding when households with different needs were equally well off. We have not attempted that task here. Instead, we have adopted the 'social' approach to measuring material well-being. In practice, this means we examine a set of measures that public officials have judged sufficiently important to include year after year on the Census, the AHS, or the HIS. We then ask whether changes in the distribution of income have led to parallel changes in inequality between rich and poor on these measures.

Measuring material inequality between the rich and poor raises potentially controversial statistical issues. When the outcome that concerns us is continuous (the number of bathrooms in a housing unit, for example), we can divide the mean for the rich by the mean for the poor, just as we do for income. But when the outcome that concerns us is dichotomous (whether a housing unit has a complete kitchen, for example), division can lead to confusion.

Suppose, to take a hypothetical example, that the percentage of households reporting complete kitchens rises from 67 to 80 percent in the bottom income decile ('the poor') and from 98 to 99 percent in the top income decile ('the rich'). The most common way of deciding whether inequality has risen or fallen is to compare the percentage increase in the fraction of each group that has a complete kitchen. This calculation shows an increase of $(80 - 67)/67 = 19$ percent among the poor, compared to only $(99 - 98)/98 = 1$ percent among the rich. In this case, such a comparison implies that inequality between the rich and poor declined.

Calculating percentage changes in percentages turns out to be a mistake, however. The difficulty is that we could equally well calculate the percentage change in the fraction of each group *without* kitchens. Had we done this we would have concluded that the percentage without kitchens fell by $(2 - 1)/2 = 50$ percent in the top decile compared to only $(33 - 20)/33 = 39$ percent in the bottom decile, and hence that inequality increased. Since there is no obvious way of deciding whether to focus on the proportion of people with or without kitchens, this general approach soon leads to total confusion.

In an effort to avoid arbitrary decisions of this kind, many social scientists now look at changes in the logged odds that rich and poor households have complete kitchens. In the example just given, the odds that a poor household has a complete kitchen roughly double (from $67/33 = 2/1$ to $80/20 = 4/1$). The odds that a rich household has a complete kitchen also roughly double (from $49/1$ to $99/1$). The logged odds therefore increase by about the same amount for both the rich and the poor. It does not follow, however, that the rich and the poor really gained the same amount or that inequality really remained constant. No one would claim that raising the overall proportion of families with complete kitchens from 98 to 99 percent represented as much progress as raising the overall proportion from 67 to 80 percent. If that is true for society as a whole, it is equally true for subgroups within society.

If we want to measure inequality between the rich and poor using a dichotomous outcome, our best measure is the arithmetic difference between the proportions of rich and poor with each advantage that interests us. In our kitchen example, this difference is $98 - 67 = 31$ points at Time 1 and $99 - 80 = 19$ points at Time 2. Like logged odds, this measure of inequality yields the same answer regardless of whether we measure the presence or absence of kitchens. Unlike logged odds, however, this measure also yields answers consistent with everyday understandings of inequality. It tells us that when the poor acquire a lot of kitchens and the rich acquire only a few, inequality between the rich and poor has declined. When the rich acquire a lot of kitchens and the poor acquire only a few, inequality has increased. If we want to measure the *reduction* in inequality using this measure, we can subtract inequality at Time 2 (19 percentage points) from inequality at Time 1 (31 percentage points). If we want to measure the percentage change in inequality, we can divide inequality at Time 2 by inequality at Time 1.

This method makes trends in inequality depend partly on the initial distribution. If the rich all have complete kitchens at Time 1, any increase in the overall proportion of households with kitchens is bound to reduce the gap between rich and poor. Sensitivity to the initial distribution is not an argument against the method, however. The world in which inequality is debated is also sensitive to initial distributions. A measure of change in a dichotomous outcome that is insensitive to the initial distribution is therefore a poor measure.

Because societies seldom define an item as a 'necessity' until most middle-income households have it, necessities tend to become more equally distributed when real incomes rise, even if the distribution of income remains constant. But when incomes rise societies also tend to expand the list of things they regard as necessities. In equilibrium, this process can mean that every specific necessity becomes more equally distributed over time but that the overall distribution of necessities shows no tendency to become more unequal. Readers should beware of this potential bias in our data.

Housing conditions, automobiles, and telephones. The 1960, 1970, and 1980 Censuses asked household heads whether they owned the building in which they lived, how old it was, and whether it had central heat. They also asked how many complete bathrooms the respondent's unit had, how many other rooms it had, whether it had an air conditioner or a telephone, and how many automobiles the household had available for its use. The Annual Housing Survey also asked about most of these matters from 1973 to 1983.[40] Extending our inquiry through 1983 is important because the distribution of income took a marked turn for the worse in the early 1980s, and we want to know whether that change had a detectable effect on housing conditions.

Table 5.4 shows how household size and income affect a household's probability of having the amenities that the Census measures.[41] At any given income level, increases in household size are associated with living in a newer building, owning the residence in which you live, having more rooms, having more automobiles, and (in 1980) having more bathrooms. Large households pay for these amenities partly by saving less and partly by making sacrifices in other domains. Table 5.4 shows, for example, that once income is held constant large

Table 5.4   Regressions of housing conditions, automobiles, and telephones on ln Income and ln Size: 1960, 1970, and 1980 censuses

| Dependent | Regression coefficients and standard errors | | | | | |
| | Ln Income | | | Ln Size | | |
	1960	1970	1980	1960	1970	1980
Number of autos						
B	0.320	0.412	0.422	0.120	0.184	0.272
(SE)	(0.004)	(0.002)	(0.002)	(0.006)	(0.003)	(0.003)
Number of rooms						
B	0.521	0.538	0.665	0.711	0.878	0.884
(SE)	(0.004)	(0.004)	(0.004)	(0.007)	(0.006)	(0.006)
Owner-occupied residence						
B	0.127	0.137	0.166	0.005	0.040	0.054
(SE)	(0.002)	(0.001)	(0.001)	(0.002)	(0.002)	(0.002)
Age of building (in years)						
B	−2.165	−2.187	−1.410	−0.719	−0.116	−0.213
(SE)	(0.036)	(0.029)	(0.027)	(0.057)	(0.045)	(0.043)
Number of bathrooms						
B	0.215	0.145	0.110	−0.104	−0.032	−0.014
(SE)	(0.001)	(0.001)	(0.001)	(0.002)	(0.001)	(0.001)
Access to a telephone						
B	0.195	0.119	0.078	−0.110	−0.060	−0.038
(SE)	(0.001)	(0.001)	(0.001)	(0.002)	(0.001)	(0.001)
Air conditioner						
B	0.074	0.140	0.120	−0.037	−0.118	−0.104
(SE)	(0.002)	(0.001)	(0.001)	(0.003)	(0.002)	(0.002)
Central heat						
B	0.216	0.156	0.103	−0.132	−0.086	−0.076
(SE)	(0.001)	(0.001)	(0.001)	(0.002)	(0.002)	(0.002)

Source: Tabulations by David Rhodes from 1/1000 public use Census samples of households, weighted by size. Except for owner occupancy, the data cover only persons living in households. The number of persons is usually 175 125 in 1960, 197 466 in 1970, and 220 918 in 1980, but in 1960 the estimates for air conditioners are based on a 20 percent subsample, the estimates for bathrooms, type of dwelling, and central heating are based on an 80 percent subsample, and the estimates for automobiles are based on a 20 percent subsample of urban households and an 80 percent subsample of rural households (reweighted to be representative of the entire country).

households are less likely than small households to have central heating, air conditioning, and telephone service. Nonetheless, per capita income seldom predicts these measures of material well-being as accurately as total household income does. We therefore expect the distribution of these amenities to change more when the distribution of total household income changes than when the distribution of per capita income changes.

Space. Tables 5.5 and 5.6 show that the number of rooms in housing units changed very slowly from 1960 to 1980 and that increases in household income had very modest effects on the number of rooms a household rented or owned. In 1980, for example, middle-income households had only 24 percent more rooms than poor households, even though they had six or seven times more income. Likewise, rich households had only 25 percent more rooms than middle-income households, even though they had three times as much income. Since the CEX shows that the fraction of income spent on housing does not vary much by income level, the low income elasticity of room consumption implies that people who spend a lot for housing are mostly buying bigger and better maintained rooms in nicer locations.

The number of rooms available to poor households grew slightly less rapidly than the number of rooms available to middle-income households from 1960 to 1980. If we want to measure material inequality, however, we also need to take account of changes in household size. Unfortunately, we do not know how many rooms a large household needs to feel as well housed as a small household, so we cannot say what distribution of rooms would represent complete equality. But we can ask whether the effects of income changed with size held constant. Table 5.4 shows that any given percentage increase in household income had more effect on number of rooms in 1970 than in 1960, even with household size controlled. The increased effect of any given income change more than offset the effect of declining income inequality, so the 'room gap' between rich and poor households widened. During the 1970s, in contrast, neither the coefficient of income nor income inequality changed much, so inequality in number of rooms between the top and bottom deciles did not change much.[42]

An alternative way of looking at space is to concentrate on the minority of households that appear to suffer from severe crowding. The Census Bureau defines housing as crowded when a unit has more than one person per room. Using this standard 22 percent of the

156

Table 5.5 Housing conditions, access to automobiles, and access to telephones, by household income decile: 1960, 1970, and 1980 censuses

	1	2	3	4	5	6	7	8	9	10	Mean of middle decile
Household's income in previous year as a proportion of the median[a]											
Census											
1960	0.137	0.394	0.602	0.778	0.924	1.08	1.24	1.45	1.79	3.16[b]	$19 521[a]
1970	0.144	0.398	0.600	0.775	0.925	1.08	1.24	1.46	1.78	3.07[b]	26 846
1980	0.147	0.375	0.558	0.738	0.914	1.09	1.27	1.51	1.85	3.09[b]	30 273
CPS											
1964	0.153	0.402	0.600	0.777	0.924	1.08	1.24	1.46	1.77	2.95	20 654
1970	0.182	0.426	0.616	0.780	0.926	1.07	1.24	1.45	1.75	2.76	26 886
1980	0.167	0.382	0.563	0.737	0.915	1.09	1.28	1.50	1.85	2.74	30 062
											Grand mean
Mean number of rooms											
1960	4.48	4.69	4.84	4.99	5.20	5.28	5.43	5.60	5.75	6.41	5.27
1970	4.57	4.77	5.00	5.20	5.35	5.57	5.73	5.87	6.15	6.75	5.50
1980	4.61	4.85	5.08	5.29	5.59	5.81	6.03	6.28	6.58	7.13	5.72
Mean rooms per person											
1960	1.84	1.57	1.44	1.42	1.39	1.39	1.40	1.47	1.52	1.61	1.51
1970	2.20	1.76	1.61	1.53	1.50	1.51	1.50	1.52	1.57	1.71	1.64
1980	2.32	2.08	1.98	1.89	1.83	1.82	1.82	1.83	1.87	1.98	1.94
Proportion with more than one room per person											
1960	0.732	0.707	0.706	0.748	0.764	0.786	0.807	0.851	0.865	0.875	0.784
1970	0.839	0.781	0.788	0.793	0.812	0.841	0.847	0.857	0.879	0.905	0.834
1980	0.880	0.872	0.883	0.895	0.913	0.921	0.921	0.933	0.940	0.946	0.911

Mean number of complete baths

1960	0.552	0.672	0.792	0.864	0.939	0.966	0.994	1.019	1.052	1.159	0.900
1970	0.838	0.883	0.942	0.997	1.020	1.059	1.079	1.115	1.168	1.259	1.036
1980	0.967	1.009	1.043	1.069	1.098	1.128	1.153	1.198	1.238	1.322	1.122

Proportion with at least one complete bathroom

1960	0.536	0.657	0.774	0.845	0.912	0.933	0.941	0.962	0.970	0.983	0.851
1970	0.804	0.853	0.902	0.944	0.959	0.972	0.976	0.984	0.989	0.990	0.937
1980	0.919	0.953	0.966	0.976	0.981	0.986	0.985	0.992	0.995	0.995	0.975

Mean age of building (in years)

1960	24.1	23.4	22.3	21.2	20.5	19.2	18.6	18.3	18.2	18.3	20.4
1970	23.5	22.9	21.8	20.8	20.1	19.3	18.6	18.1	17.8	17.4	20.0
1980	22.3	21.8	21.0	20.8	19.9	19.6	19.2	18.7	18.6	18.3	20.0

Proportion in buildings less than 10 years old

1960	0.160	0.183	0.213	0.268	0.291	0.344	0.367	0.379	0.385	0.386	0.297
1970	0.164	0.174	0.207	0.231	0.268	0.279	0.301	0.321	0.323	0.339	0.261
1980	0.205	0.221	0.243	0.250	0.278	0.284	0.290	0.301	0.297	0.290	0.266

Proportion with central heat

1960	0.359	0.407	0.507	0.601	0.700	0.758	0.787	0.836	0.859	0.907	0.672
1970	0.561	0.600	0.666	0.751	0.788	0.844	0.872	0.889	0.914	0.941	0.783
1980	0.689	0.724	0.771	0.806	0.822	0.858	0.873	0.902	0.923	0.943	0.831

Proportion with air conditioner

1960	0.054	0.067	0.077	0.099	0.115	0.122	0.122	0.160	0.167	0.277	0.126
1970	0.188	0.231	0.272	0.320	0.338	0.387	0.401	0.419	0.475	0.553	0.359
1980	0.381	0.440	0.496	0.525	0.560	0.579	0.597	0.621	0.653	0.680	0.553

continued on page 158

Table 5.5 (continued)

	1	2	3	4	5	6	7	8	9	10	Grand mean
Proportion in owner-occupied unit											
1960	0.483	0.494	0.512	0.561	0.624	0.679	0.721	0.744	0.779	0.830	0.643
1970	0.479	0.490	0.521	0.598	0.657	0.716	0.759	0.789	0.825	0.863	0.670
1980	0.427	0.500	0.551	0.614	0.702	0.766	0.800	0.845	0.881	0.911	0.700
Mean number of automobiles											
1960	0.615	0.795	0.946	1.033	1.079	1.168	1.239	1.282	1.430	1.659	1.126
1970	0.659	0.911	1.096	1.264	1.360	1.457	1.547	1.671	1.819	1.989	1.378
1980	0.733	0.988	1.178	1.325	1.457	1.571	1.696	1.834	1.980	2.157	1.492
Proportion with access to an automobile											
1960	0.535	0.670	0.783	0.843	0.881	0.920	0.918	0.926	0.937	0.952	0.837
1970	0.544	0.728	0.837	0.905	0.931	0.949	0.964	0.971	0.975	0.979	0.878
1980	0.583	0.773	0.866	0.907	0.938	0.956	0.968	0.979	0.983	0.980	0.893
Proportion with access to a truck or automobile											
1980	0.606	0.794	0.891	0.932	0.961	0.973	0.980	0.989	0.991	0.987	0.910
Proportion with access to a telephone											
1960	0.478	0.543	0.647	0.737	0.811	0.869	0.889	0.926	0.942	0.960	0.780
1970	0.700	0.727	0.789	0.865	0.899	0.929	0.938	0.964	0.977	0.983	0.877
1980	0.795	0.853	0.891	0.924	0.948	0.972	0.980	0.985	0.989	0.991	0.933

[a] Incomes were converted to 1987 dollars using the fixed-weight price index for Personal Consumption Expenditures from the National Income Accounts.

[b] Estimates for different years are not precisely comparable because of top coding. For detailed breakdowns see footnote 24.

Source: See Table 5.4.

Table 5.6 Changes in housing conditions, access to automobiles, and access to telephones for the low, middle, and high income deciles: 1960s and 1970s

	Lowest decile as a percent of middle quintile			Highest decile as a percent of middle quintile			Correlation with log of income		
	1960	1970	1980	1960	1970	1980	1960	1970	1980
Household income[a]									
CPS	15.3[b]	18.2	16.7	294.6[b]	276.1	273.8			
Census	13.7	14.4	14.7	316.4[c]	307.1[c]	308.5[c]			
Number of rooms	83.1	80.5	76.3	122.4	123.8	125.0	0.282	0.378	0.363
Rooms per person	132.4	146.2	127.1	115.7	113.9	108.2	-0.066	-0.149	-0.090
Number of baths	58.0	80.6	86.9	121.7	121.2	118.8	0.422	0.349	0.332
Age of building	121.4	119.3	112.9	92.2	88.0	92.7	-0.170	-0.175	-0.118
Number of autos	54.7	46.8	48.4	147.7	141.2	142.5	0.391	0.470	0.475

	Middle quintile mean minus lowest decile's mean			Highest decile mean minus middle quintile's mean			Correlation with log of income		
	1960	1970	1980	1960	1970	1980	1960	1970	1980
At least one room per person	0.043	-0.013	0.037	0.100	0.078	0.029	0.121	0.059	0.082
Complete bath	0.386	0.161	0.064	0.061	0.025	0.011	0.377	0.235	0.139
Building less than ten years old	0.157	0.110	0.076	0.069	0.066	0.009	0.162	0.124	0.065
Central heat	0.370	0.255	0.151	0.179	0.125	0.103	0.363	0.284	0.206
Air conditioner	0.064	0.175	0.188	0.158	0.190	0.111	0.172	0.207	0.174
Owner-occupied	0.168	0.207	0.307	0.179	0.176	0.177	0.258	0.304	0.368
Access to an auto	0.365	0.396	0.365	0.052	0.039	0.033	0.327	0.384	0.355
Access to a phone	0.362	0.214	0.165	0.120	0.070	0.031	0.369	0.276	0.242

[a] All incomes are for previous year.
[b] 1960 data not available. Estimate is for 1964.
[c] Estimates are not fully comparable over time because of top coding. For detailed breakdowns see footnote 24.

Source: Table 5.5.

population was crowded in 1960, 17 percent in 1970, and 9 percent in 1980. It is not clear that the victims of crowding regard it as a serious problem, however. If everyone hated crowding, we would expect the problem to be concentrated in the bottom income decile. Yet by 1980 the proportion of households with more than one person per room was as high in the second and third income deciles as in the bottom decile (see Table 5.5). Indeed, there was a significant amount of crowding even in the top decile (5 percent in the top decile compared to 12 percent in the bottom decile). These figures suggest that many crowded households at all income levels were relatively indifferent to the fact that they had more members than rooms. Otherwise, affluent households would have used their money to acquire more rooms.

Nonetheless, crowding still looms large in many public discussions of housing conditions, so we cannot afford to ignore it entirely. Table 5.5 shows that during the 1960s crowding declined faster in the bottom income decile than in any other. This change was largely traceable to the fact that low-income households grew smaller, not to the fact that they moved to larger quarters. During the 1970s, crowding declined fastest among middle-income households, but this change was also driven largely by declines in household size, not by increases in the number of rooms that middle-income households rented or owned. Thus while changes in crowding follow the same pattern as changes in the distribution of household income from 1960 to 1980, the connection does not seem to be causal.

Figure 5.7 uses the AHS to extend our analysis of crowding through 1983.[43] According to the AHS, crowding declined between 1979 and 1983 in the top two-thirds of the income distribution but increased in the bottom third.[44] This is consistent with the hypothesis that fewer poor families and unrelated individuals could afford their own living quarters and that more of them had to double up.[45]

Bathrooms. The Census Bureau defines a bathroom as complete if it has hot and cold running water, a sink, a flush toilet, and a shower or bathtub. Table 5.5 shows that the number of bathrooms increased for all income deciles both during the 1960s and during the 1970s, despite the fact that households had fewer members. Table 5.5 also shows steady increases in the proportion of households with at least one complete bathroom. Table 5.6 shows that the 'bathroom gap' between the bottom and the middle income deciles fell dramatically during the 1960s, when income inequality was declining. It continued to fall during the 1970s, when income inequality hardly changed, perhaps partly because more low-income families were getting rent

Figure 5.7   Percentage of households with one or more rooms per person by income percentile

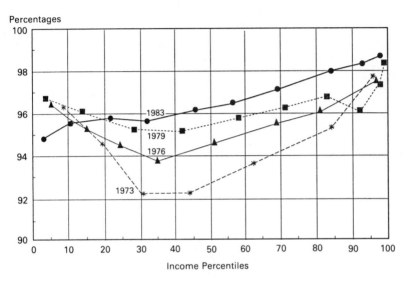

Percentages

Source: *Annual Housing Survey, Parts B, C and F. Indicators of Housing and Neighborhood Quality by Financial Characteristics*, 1973–1983.

subsidies. The bathroom gap between the top and the middle does not change much in either decade. Figure 5.8 extends the story to 1983. Despite the severe recession of the early 1980s and the apparent increase in crowding among low-income households between 1979 and 1983, the percentage of poor households living in units that lacked a complete bathroom continued to decline.

These changes were driven partly by the spread of housing codes that made it harder to rent units without complete bathrooms and partly by turnover in the housing stock. It is cheaper to install complete plumbing at the time a housing unit is built than later, and once they are installed, bathrooms last a long time. (Landlords may not repair broken plumbing promptly, but they seldom disconnect a toilet, shower, or hot water heater altogether.) Almost all housing units built since World War II have complete bathrooms. Thus as the fraction of the housing stock built since World War II increases, the relative cost of a 'used' bathroom tends to fall.

Temperature control. Central heating was moderately related to income in 1960 ($r = 0.363$), but over the next two decades central

Figure 5.8   Percentage of households with complete bathroom by income decile

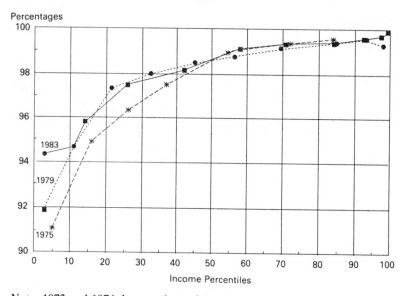

Note: 1973 and 1974 data are inconsistent, hence the use of 1975 data.

Source: *Annual Housing Survey, Parts B, C and F. Indicators of Housing and Neighborhood Quality by Financial Characteristics*, 1973–1983.

heating spread fastest among the poor. As a result, the 'heating gap' between the bottom and the middle income deciles narrowed both during the 1960s and during the 1970s. This change was presumably related to the fact that the poor were moving from rural single-family residences that had few modern amenities to urban tenements that usually had electricity, modern plumbing, and central heat.

Unlike all the other household amenities on which we have data, air conditioners were relatively rare in 1960: only 13 percent of the population had access to one. Since air conditioners were also relatively expensive, we would expect them to have spread fastest among the rich, slower among middle-income households, and still slower among the poor during the 1960s. That is indeed what happened. By 1970 more than half the nation's rich households had air conditioners. The surprise is that during the 1970s air conditioning spread almost as fast among the poor as among those in the middle of the income distribution, despite the fact that many middle-income households still lacked it in 1970. Furthermore, despite growing

Figure 5.9   Percentage of households with air conditioning (central air or units) by income percentile

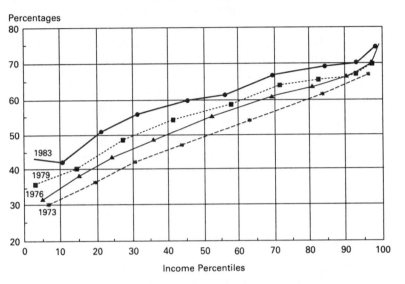

Percentages

Source: *Annual Housing Survey, Parts B, C and F. Indicators of Housing and Neighborhood Quality by Financial Characteristics*, 1973–1983.

income inequality in the early 1980s the AHS shows no change in the 'cooling gap' between those at the bottom and those in the middle from 1979 to 1983 (see Figure 5.9).

Age of building. Although living in a new building offers few advantages over living in a well maintained older building, older buildings are not always well maintained. As a result, a building's age is to some extent a proxy for its general condition. Nonetheless, the correlation between age of building and household income was only −0.170 in 1960 and −0.175 in 1970 (see Table 5.6). By 1980 the correlation had fallen to −0.118, apparently because federal subsidies allowed more low-income families to move into new housing units.[46]

Home ownership. Home ownership has long been a symbol of middle-class status in America. This symbolism has several sources. To begin with, home mortgages require payments of principal as well as interest. As a result, homeowners tend to save more than tenants and enjoy greater financial security once their mortgage is paid off. The financial consequences of ownership have, however, changed over time. Ownership was not an especially lucrative way of saving during the 1950s or 1960s, so many affluent families chose to rent and invested their savings in other ways. During the 1970s, in contrast, real estate was by far the best available hedge against inflation, so even households that lived in multi-family dwellings began to buy their apartments rather than renting. This change led to some redistribution of home ownership. But if home ownership was redistributed solely because real estate became a better investment, this fact would not necessarily imply any change in the distribution of material well-being, at least in the short term.

A second reason why ownership has become a symbol of middle-class status is that owner-occupied housing usually has more amenities than rental housing in the same geographic area. Here again, however, the significance of ownership has changed over time. In 1960, when the rural poor often owned their own homes and the urban middle class often rented, the correlation between ownership and amenities at the national level was quite low. As the rural poor became urban apartment dwellers and the urban middle class became suburban home owners, the correlation between ownership and amenities rose. This means we cannot use changes in the distribution of ownership as a proxy for changes in the distribution of housing conditions.

A third reason why home ownership has come to symbolize membership in the middle class is that ownership allows a household to customize its residence to fit its distinctive tastes and needs. Making one's home into a physical expression of one's self has always been important to Americans, and this benefit of ownership appears to have been relatively constant over time. This argument suggests that changes in the distribution of home ownership may, in fact, tell us something about changes in well-being.

Home ownership was only moderately correlated with income in 1960 ($r = 0.26$). Despite declines in income inequality, the correlation between income and home ownership rose during the 1960s, because the rural poor were selling their homes and moving to cities and middle-income apartment dwellers were buying suburban homes. The distribution of income did not change much during the 1970s, but the correlation between income and home ownership continued to rise, partly housing became a good investment and partly because the incomes of the elderly (most of whom owned their homes) were rising faster than the incomes of the young (many of whom were tenants). Figure 5.10 also shows that home ownership

Figure 5.10   Percentage of home owners by income percentile

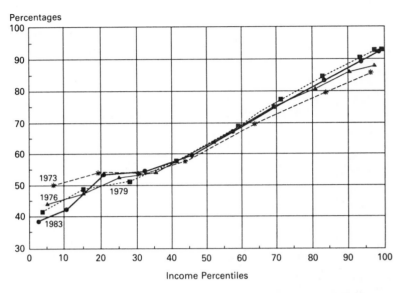

Source: *Annual Housing Survey, Parts B, C and F. Indicators of Housing and Neighborhood Quality by Financial Characteristics*, 1973–1983.

was redistributed from the poor to the rich between 1973 and 1983. But this change occurs mainly between 1973 and 1976, when the income distribution was fairly stable, not between 1979 and 1983, when income inequality was increasing.

Complete kitchens. Although the decennial Census collects data on whether households have complete kitchens, the definition of a complete kitchen was not the same in 1960 as in later years. We therefore focus on data collected by the AHS from 1973 to 1983. Figure 5.11 shows a gradual decline in the fraction of housing units without a complete kitchen. This decline is especially marked for those near the bottom of the income distribution. Census data on kitchens (not shown) tell the same story for the 1970s.

Automobiles. In 1960 and 1970 the Census asked how many automobiles household members 'owned or regularly used'. In 1980 it asked a slightly more restrictive question about how many automobiles were 'kept at home' for use by household members, but we doubt that this change in wording had much effect. The Census did not ask about trucks in 1960 or 1970, so it underestimates access to

Figure 5.11   Percentage of households with complete kitchen by income percentile

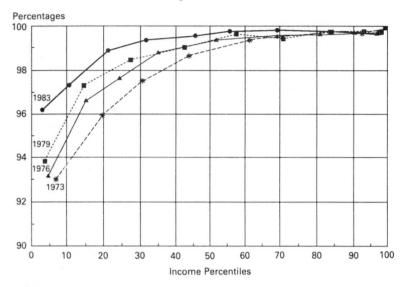

Source: *Annual Housing Survey, Parts B, C and F. Indicators of Housing and Neighborhood Quality by Financial Characteristics*, 1973–1983.

motor vehicles in these years, but it did ask about trucks in 1980. Including trucks reduces the proportion of households without a vehicle from 10.7 to 9.0 percent. Including trucks would have had a somewhat smaller effect in 1970 and 1960.[47] Fortunately, including trucks does not appreciably alter the association between income and access to vehicles.

Income is more strongly correlated with access to motor vehicles than with any of the housing conditions we measured (see Table 5.6). We would therefore expect changes in the distribution of income to have more effect on the distribution of vehicles than on housing conditions. In reality, however, the correlation between income and vehicle ownership rose during the 1960s, even though poor people's ability to buy cars was rising at an unprecedented rate. This development presumably reflected the fact that the poor were moving to big cities, where they needed cars less than they had in rural areas. The correlation between income and vehicle ownership hardly changed during the 1970s, which is what we would expect given stability in the distribution of income.

Notice, however, that while the disparity between rich and poor in total vehicles hardly changed during the 1970s, the disparity in their chances of having at least one vehicle fell slightly. Another way to characterize this result is to say that the distribution of first cars became slightly more equal while the distribution of second cars became slightly less equal.

Telephones. In 1960, having a telephone was about as highly correlated with income as having an automobile, a complete bathroom, or a lot of rooms. The correlation between income and having telephone service declined steadily between 1960 and 1980. This trend shows no obvious relationship to trends in the distribution of income. It may, however, be related to the fact that many states forced local telephone companies to keep the price of residential telephone service low, while raising charges to business customers and long-distance users. After deregulation, this pattern of cross-subsidies ended, and the price of residential service rose. The correlation between income and having a telephone may therefore have risen since 1980.

Taking the data on housing conditions, automobiles, and telephones as a whole, we see little evidence that changes in the distribution of income had any consistent effect on material inequality between the rich and the poor. Instead, we see three other patterns:

- When an amenity is already commonplace among the affluent and incomes are rising, the amenity tends to become more equally distributed as everyone acquires it. Telephones, bathrooms, kitchens, and central heating all illustrate this pattern.
- When a relatively expensive new amenity is introduced, it initially tends to spread fastest among the rich, exacerbating inequality. Air conditioning follows this pattern in the 1960s.
- When an amenity is not spreading rapidly, its correlation with income can either rise, fall, or remain constant. Motor vehicles and new buildings illustrate this pattern.

Our findings suggest that technical innovations had more impact than changes in the distribution of income on the distribution of housing conditions, automobiles, and telephones. Technical innovations led millions of Americans to move from rural areas to central cities, and they allowed millions of others to move from central cities to suburbs. These two migrations have led to much larger changes in patterns of consumption than anything that happened to the distribution of money income over the past generation. Technical innovation also led to big changes in many products' relative prices, which also altered patterns of consumption. In addition, government spending almost certainly improved poor people's housing conditions during the 1970s, and regulatory policy may have helped the poor acquire telephones during the 1960s and 1970s.

We are not suggesting, of course, that the distribution of income has no effect whatever on material well-being. But because a household's income is only moderately correlated with its consumption of the goods and services on which the Census collects data, the distribution of income must change a lot before we can expect to see a significant change in the distribution of any specific good or service. When the effects of changes in income inequality are small and the effects of other influences are large, it is difficult to trace any particular change in material inequality to a change in income inequality.

Health status. No one imagines that income has as much effect on people's health status as on their chances of owning a Rolls-Royce. Nonetheless, people in rich countries live longer than people in poor countries, and within any given country rich people live longer than poor people. If the bottom decile of the income distribution stops gaining ground economically, many people expect this to have some impact on the distribution of illness.

Starting in the late 1950s the Health Interview Survey (HIS) has asked a representative sample of individuals (or their parents, when the individual was a child) about their health. We look at two measures of health: how many days the individual had to restrict his or her usual activities because of illness during the past two weeks ('restricted activity days') and how many days the individual spent in bed because of the illness ('bed days'). We investigate the effects of income and family size on both outcomes using the 1962–3, 1970, and 1980 HIS data tapes and tables compiled by the National Center for Health Statistics for 1982 through 1989.[48] We present separate estimates for individuals of different ages, partly because the direction of the causal linkage between household income and individual health is clearer for children than for adults and partly because restricting one's usual activities has a different meaning for individuals of different ages.

The average American reported 10.9 restricted activity days in 1962–3, 9.4 in 1970, and 11.6 in 1980. The mean for each of these years is roughly comparable to that for the immediately preceding and following years, so both the implied decline in illness during the 1960s and the implied increase during the 1970s are probably genuine. Bed days follow the same trajectory, falling from 4.6 in 1962–3 to 4.4 in 1970 and then rising to 5.2 in 1980. The HIS changed its measure of bed days after 1981, but the number of bed days continued to increase from 1982 to 1989 using the new measure. No one has proposed an entirely convincing explanation for these trends.

Table 5.7 shows the effects of income and household size on the number of days an individual restricted his or her 'usual' activities because of illness. The last column of Table 5.7 uses the regression coefficient of income to estimate the percentage increase in restricted activity days associated with having an income half the national average rather than at the national average, assuming one lives in a household of average size. For respondents between the ages of 25 and 44 in 1980, for example, cutting household income from the mean to half the mean is associated with a 27.6 percent increase in restricted activity days. Table 5.8 presents analogous results for bed days.

If we set aside the elderly, the association between income and restricted activity days increased steadily from 1962–3 to 1980. The absolute number of restricted activity days also increased among low income respondents. These changes occurred both during the 1960s, when incomes were becoming more equal, and during the 1970s, when income inequality changed relatively little. The trend for bed days was less consistent, but income had more effect in 1980 than in 1963 at all ages.

Table 5.9 extends this analysis from 1982 to 1989 using published data on a broader set of health measures. These data do not allow us to make comparisons between 1980 and 1982, but they are still of interest because many public health experts believe that an increase in income inequality should have a cumulative effect on poor people's health. Income-related disparities in bed days were larger at the end of the 1980s than earlier in the decade, but the percentage of low-income respondents in 'fair' or 'poor' health showed the opposite trend. The percentage of poor people with some chronic limitation on their activity rose slightly during the 1980s, but the distribution of acute conditions shows no clear relationship to income.

The fact that different health measures exhibit different trends during the 1980s raises serious questions about whether we can use data on bed days or restricted activity days to draw general conclusions about

Table 5.7 Effect of income and family size on restricted activity days in past two weeks: 1963, 1970, and 1980 Health Interview Surveys

| Age | Regression coefficients and standard errors | | | | | | R^2 | Mean | SD | Percent increase if income falls 50%[a] |
| | Ln Income | | Ln Size | | Constant | | | | | |
	B	(SE)	B	(SE)	B	(SE)				
Under 7										
1963	0.036	(0.016)	-0.128	(0.032)	0.346	(0.159)	0.001	0.447	1.651	-5.6
1970	-0.042	(0.019)	-0.177	(0.036)	1.106	(0.196)	0.002	0.424	1.572	6.8
1980	-0.056	(0.021)	-0.169	(0.055)	1.267	(0.204)	0.002	0.492	1.696	7.9
7 to 17										
1963	0.008	(0.012)	-0.127	(0.025)	0.532	(0.116)	0.000	0.319	1.609	-1.7
1970	-0.012	(0.012)	-0.063	(0.021)	0.556	(0.125)	0.003	0.330	1.381	2.5
1980	-0.075	(0.016)	-0.027	(0.037)	1.193	(0.153)	0.001	0.417	1.639	12.4
18 to 24										
1963	-0.011	(0.019)	0.003	(0.031)	0.500	(0.166)	0.000	0.412	1.766	1.8
1970	-0.071	(0.020)	-0.003	(0.029)	1.061	(0.178)	0.001	0.376	1.684	13.0
1980	-0.095	(0.021)	-0.008	(0.034)	1.411	(0.183)	0.002	0.512	1.993	12.8
25 to 44										
1963	-0.144	(0.017)	0.028	(0.024)	1.746	(0.163)	0.002	0.539	2.137	18.4
1970	-0.265	(0.021)	0.123	(0.027)	2.968	(0.209)	0.006	0.507	2.090	36.1
1980	-0.256	(0.020)	0.047	(0.028)	3.128	(0.191)	0.007	0.639	2.338	27.6
45 to 64										
1963	-0.376	(0.021)	0.139	(0.036)	3.933	(0.174)	0.012	0.855	2.875	30.3
1970	-0.387	(0.024)	0.003	(0.037)	4.552	(0.228)	0.012	0.767	2.767	34.8
1980	-0.661	(0.030)	-0.102	(0.048)	7.500	(0.280)	0.028	1.006	3.174	45.3
65 and over										
1963	-0.526	(0.043)	0.519	(0.081)	5.247	(0.321)	0.012	1.444	3.886	25.1
1970	-0.385	(0.046)	0.433	(0.085)	4.381	(0.389)	0.007	1.180	3.543	58.4
1980	-0.639	(0.058)	0.426	(0.105)	7.110	(0.503)	0.010	1.529	4.002	28.8

[a] Estimated as (Column 1) (ln.5)/(Column 8). These estimates should be approximately correct when initial income is at the mean.

Source: Tabulations by Tony Maier, Karen Rolf, and Tim Veenstra from Health Interview Survey public use samples. Income is total

Table 5.8 Effect of income and family size on bed days in past two weeks: 1963, 1970, and 1980 Health Interview Surveys

| Age | Regression coefficients and standard errors | | | | | | | R^2 | Mean | SD | Percent increase if income falls 50%[a] |
| | Ln Income | | Ln Size | | Constant | | | | | | |
	B	(SE)	B	(SE)	B	(SE)					
Under 7											
1963	-0.012	(0.009)	-0.039	(0.019)	0.361	(0.087)	0.000	0.197	0.987	4.2
1970	-0.055	(0.013)	-0.057	(0.024)	0.812	(0.128)	0.002	0.192	1.026	19.8
1980	-0.047	(0.013)	-0.040	(0.035)	0.736	(0.129)	0.001	0.231	1.080	14.0
7 to 17											
1963	-0.015	(0.007)	-0.051	(0.015)	0.390	(0.073)	0.005	0.179	0.924	5.8
1970	-0.012	(0.007)	-0.005	(0.014)	0.265	(0.735)	0.000	0.156	0.811	5.3
1980	-0.038	(0.008)	-0.011	(0.020)	0.567	(0.082)	0.001	0.182	0.877	14.4
18 to 24											
1963	-0.020	(0.011)	0.017	(0.018)	0.332	(0.084)	0.000	0.185	1.001	7.5
1970	-0.018	(0.011)	-0.004	(0.016)	0.346	(0.102)	0.000	0.165	0.963	7.5
1980	-0.055	(0.010)	-0.024	(0.016)	0.685	(0.089)	0.002	0.188	0.975	20.2
25 to 44											
1963	-0.064	(0.009)	0.009	(0.013)	0.509	(0.089)	0.001	0.212	1.179	20.8
1970	-0.101	(0.011)	0.026	(0.014)	1.156	(0.113)	0.003	0.194	1.127	35.9
1980	-0.114	(0.010)	0.006	(0.015)	1.357	(0.101)	0.005	0.237	1.237	33.2
45 to 64											
1963	-0.122	(0.011)	0.056	(0.010)	1.293	(0.104)	0.004	0.307	1.572	27.4
1970	-0.162	(0.014)	-0.003	(0.021)	1.874	(0.129)	0.007	0.287	1.563	38.9
1980	-0.231	(0.015)	0.035	(0.025)	2.557	(0.145)	0.012	0.320	1.637	49.8
65 and over											
1963	-0.272	(0.028)	0.396	(0.053)	2.497	(0.211)	0.008	0.615	2.544	30.5
1970	-0.213	(0.031)	0.378	(0.057)	2.220	(0.264)	0.006	0.537	2.405	27.4
1980	-0.225	(0.034)	0.267	(0.061)	2.410	(0.292)	0.003	0.514	2.316	30.2

[a] Estimated as (Column 1) (ln.5)/(Column 8). These estimates should be approximately correct when initial income is at the mean.

Source: See Table 5.7.

Table 5.9   Measures of health status by income, 1982–9[a]

Health measure and income level	1982	1983	1984	1985	1986	1987	1988	1989
Bed days								
Under $10 000	11.2	12.2	11.6	11.2	11.2	11.4	12.2	12.2
$10 000–19 999	6.3	6.7	6.7	7.0	7.7	7.5	7.9	8.2
$20 000–34 999	4.4	4.6	4.7	4.6	5.2	4.9	4.9	5.2
$35 000 or more	3.9	4.1	4.4	3.9	4.3	3.9	3.8	4.0
Difference (top minus bottom)	7.3	8.1	7.2	7.3	7.2	7.5	8.4	8.2
Percent reporting 'fair' or 'poor' health								
Under $10 000	23.8	22.6	21.8	21.8	21.6	21.9	22.1	22.6
$10 000–19 999	12.6	12.6	13.1	12.9	13.7	13.7	14.3	14.3
$20 000–34 999	6.4	6.1	6.9	6.9	6.6	6.7	7.4	7.3
$35 000 or more	3.8	3.9	4.0	3.9	3.6	4.0	4.0	3.8
Difference (top minus bottom)	20.0	18.7	17.8	17.9	18.0	17.9	18.1	18.8
Percent with chronic limitation[b]								
Under $10 000	na	24.9	24.0	25.7	25.3	25.3	26.0	26.8
$10 000–19 999	na	16.1	15.3	16.3	17.3	17.0	18.1	19.4
$20 000–34 999	na	9.8	10.3	10.8	10.4	10.7	11.5	11.9
$35 000 or more	na	8.5	8.0	8.1	8.6	7.8	7.9	8.2
Difference (top minus bottom)		16.4	16.0	17.6	16.7	17.5	18.1	18.6
Number of acute conditions per 100 respondents[c]								
Under $10 000	na	194.8	187.6	176.0	200.2	198.2	199.2	208.1
$10 000–19 999	na	168.6	181.0	186.6	174.5	171.3	166.4	166.3
$20 000–34 999	na	187.0	179.8	178.4	207.7	177.6	174.5	197.0
$35 000 or more	na	168.9	189.0	175.2	195.7	173.9	184.7	183.9
Difference (top minus bottom)		25.9	–1.4	0.8	4.5	24.3	14.5	14.2

[a] Measured in current dollars.
[b] Definition varies by age and involves limitations in play for children under 6, schooling for children ages 6 to 17, work for adults ages 18 to 69, and independent living for those over 69.
[c] Acute conditions must have been first noticed within three months of the interview, must not be the type of conditions classified as chronic and must be sufficiently severe to result in either a doctor visit or a restricted activity day.

Source: National Center for Health Statistics: 'Current Estimates from the National Health Interview Survey, United States,' *Vital and Health Statistics*. Series 10 (Washington, Government Printing Office, various years).

the distribution of health during the 1960s and 1970s. But if one accepts bed days and restricted activity days as valid indicators, the data suggest that changes in income inequality did not have much effect on the distribution of illness. The correlation between income and the number of days people spent in bed appears to have risen fairly consistently from 1963 to 1989, regardless of what happened to the distribution of income.

Use of doctors and dentists. Most Americans believe that everyone should be able to see a doctor when they need to. Starting in 1965 the federal government initiated a series of programs to improve medical care for the poor. The government sought to increase the number of physicians, especially in areas that had traditionally been under-served. It also assumed primary responsibility for paying people's medical bills if they were elderly or receiving public assistance.

The HIS asks how many doctor visits each household member made during the last year and when they last saw a doctor. Published HIS data show no consistent trend in the mean number of doctor visits from 1963–4 to 1981 or (using the revised measures) from 1982 through 1989.[49] Published data also suggest that the disparity in total number of physician visits between the rich and the poor narrowed during the 1960s and had disappeared by 1970 (National Center for Health Statistics, various years).

Published data do not allow us to adjust income for changes in family size, and we cannot do this with our 1962–3 HIS data tape either, because it does not contain information on doctor visits. We can, however, use the 1970 and 1980 tapes to look at the effects of income controlling family size.[50] Table 5.10 shows the coefficients of income and family size when we predict two different outcomes: whether individuals had seen a doctor in the past year and how often they had seen a doctor in the past year.[51] The contrast between having seen a doctor at all and how many times one had seen a doctor is important because the determinants of a first visit may be different from the determinants of follow-up visits. If the poor wait longer to see a doctor, for example, they may have more years without a visit but more visits per year.

Two striking facts emerge from Table 5.10:

- Income does not have much effect on doctor visits for any age group in either 1970 or 1980.
- The advantages enjoyed by the affluent declined between 1970 and 1980 for all age groups.

Table 5.10 Effect of income and family size on doctor visits in past year: 1970 and 1980 Health Interview Surveys

Age and year	Ln Income B	(SE)	Ln Size B	(SE)	Constant B	(SE)	R^2	Mean	SD	N
Visited doctor at least once										
Under 7										
1970	0.089	(0.005)	−0.234	(0.009)	0.387	(0.043)	0.071	0.820	0.384	14 062
1980	0.029	(0.004)	−0.157	(0.011)	0.828	(0.040)	0.025	0.877	0.329	9 601
7 to 17										
1970	0.095	(0.004)	−0.217	(0.008)	0.123	(0.039)	0.044	0.630	0.483	24 414
1980	0.044	(0.005)	−0.182	(0.010)	0.538	(0.044)	0.020	0.693	0.461	17 079
18 to 24										
1970	0.020	(0.005)	−0.118	(0.007)	0.722	(0.040)	0.024	0.770	0.421	12 182
1980	−0.001	(0.005)	−0.091	(0.007)	0.846	(0.041)	0.017	0.742	0.437	12 234
25 to 44										
1970	0.038	(0.004)	−0.001	(0.006)	0.384	(0.039)	0.003	0.731	0.444	25 793
1980	0.020	(0.004)	−0.022	(0.005)	0.563	(0.037)	0.001	0.732	0.443	26 582
45 to 64										
1970	0.037	(0.004)	−0.028	(0.006)	0.393	(0.035)	0.004	0.696	0.460	22 035
1980	0.022	(0.004)	−0.053	(0.007)	0.570	(0.042)	0.003	0.738	0.440	18 382
65 or over										
1970	0.033	(0.006)	−0.018	(0.011)	0.456	(0.044)	0.004	0.721	0.449	10 060
1980	0.020	(0.006)	−0.024	(0.011)	0.621	(0.052)	0.001	0.792	0.406	9 828

Number of
doctor visits

Under 6										
1970	0.620	(0.148)	-2.578	(0.281)	2.413	(1.394)	0.007	3.956	12.059	14 062
1980	0.329	(0.091)	-2.038	(0.236)	3.850	(0.893)	0.008	4.076	7.222	9 601
7 to 17										
1970	0.348	(0.049)	-1.307	(0.095)	1.151	(0.459)	0.009	2.160	5.521	24 414
1980	0.154	(0.051)	-1.224	(0.116)	2.633	(0.496)	0.007	2.294	5.125	17 079
18 to 24										
1970	0.231	(0.087)	-0.788	(0.127)	2.620	(0.717)	0.003	3.802	7.427	12 182
1980	-0.382	(0.076)	-0.092	(0.120)	7.022	(0.670)	0.003	3.317	7.063	12 234
25 to 44										
1970	0.374	(0.072)	0.234	(0.093)	6.765	(0.661)	0.001	3.646	7.449	25 793
1980	-0.646	(0.074)	0.203	(0.100)	9.586	(0.715)	0.003	3.488	8.497	26 582
45 to 64										
1970	-0.486	(0.075)	-0.429	(0.118)	8.865	(0.655)	0.004	4.062	8.558	22 035
1980	-1.145	(0.091)	-0.294	(0.140)	15.390	(0.852)	0.011	3.941	8.924	18 382
65 or over										
1970	-0.072	(0.140)	0.173	(0.262)	5.755	(1.094)	0.000	5.264	11.029	10 060
1980	-0.718	(0.140)	0.391	(0.245)	11.223	(1.211)	0.003	4.909	9.385	9 828

Source: See Table 5.7.

Cutting household income from the national average to half the average lowered the probability that children under seven had seen the doctor within the past year by only two points in 1980 (86 versus 88 percent), compared to six points in 1970 (76 versus 82 percent). Among adults aged 45 to 64, the effect of cutting household income from the national average to half the average on the chances of having visited the doctor within the past year fell from three points in 1970 (67 versus 70 percent) to two points in 1980 (72 versus 74 percent).

When we look at total doctor visits over the previous twelve months, the story for children is much the same as when we look at whether they visited the doctor at all. Among adults, however, we find that the poor make *more* total visits than the rich, presumably because the poor are more likely to have serious medical problems that require many visits. The fact that income has a negative effect on the chances of making one doctor visit but a positive effect on the total number of visits supports our hypothesis that income has more effect on routine checkups and first visits for any given illness than on return visits.

Nonetheless, the medical cost of being poor seems to have fallen during the 1970s, even when we look at total doctor visits. The average 45 to 64 year old made 4.1 doctor visits in 1970 and 3.9 in 1980. If he or she lived in a household of the same size but with an income half the national average, the mean number of doctor visits rose from 4.4 in 1970 to 4.7 in 1980.

Why doctor visits rose among the poor while falling among the more affluent is far from clear. The spread of Medicaid coverage during the 1970s was probably a factor, but the effect of insurance coverage on doctor visits was quite small even in 1980. The increase in poor people's restricted activity days may also have been a factor, but restricted activity days also have a quite modest effect on doctor visits in 1980.[52]

One way to put the effect of income in perspective is to compare it with the effect of household size. Table 5.10 shows that doubling household size reduces children's doctor visits far more than doubling household income increases them. We suspect that this is because parents with a lot of children use medical advice more efficiently than parents with only one or two children. When your first child gets chickenpox, you take the child to the doctor. When your third child gets chickenpox, no professional advice seems necessary. The same is true for many other ailments.

Table 5.11   Number of doctor visits in the last year by income, 1982–9

	Year							
Income[a]	1982	1983	1984	1985	1986	1987	1988	1989
Under $10 000	6.2	6.1	6.1	6.2	6.8	7.1	6.6	6.8
$10 000–19 999	4.9	4.9	5.0	5.3	5.5	5.6	5.6	5.8
$20 000–34 999	5.0	4.8	4.9	5.2	5.2	5.1	5.2	5.3
$35 000 or more	5.0	5.1	5.0	5.2	5.1	5.1	5.3	5.2
All	5.2	5.1	5.1	5.3	5.4	5.4	5.4	5.4

[a] Measured in current dollars.

Source: National Center for Health Statistics (various years). Estimates are not age standardized. Age standardized estimates are almost identical.

Table 5.11 extends our story about doctors from 1982 through 1989. Despite cutbacks in programs that provided medical care for the poor, doctor visits among individuals from poor households continued to increase during the 1980s. The increase is clearly larger among the poor than among the more affluent. Once again we cannot say to what extent this change reflects a growing correlation between income and health status and to what extent it reflects differential improvements in access to doctors.

Table 5.12 uses HIS data to examine the effect of income on whether individuals had seen a dentist within the past year. Income had far more effect on people's chances of seeing a dentist than on their chances of seeing a doctor in both 1970 and 1980 (compare Tables 5.12 and 5.10). But the effect of income on people's chances of seeing a dentist decreased during the 1970s, just as it did for doctors. This is significant because relatively few people had dental insurance even in 1980, and public policy made far less effort to ensure that poor people got dental care than to ensure that they got doctor care. The declining effect of income on dental visits may be a byproduct of improvements in dental technology that made dental visits less painful and hence a better 'buy' for the poor. Whatever the explanation, the change was not caused by reductions in income inequality.

5.4   SUMMARY AND POLICY IMPLICATIONS

We began by asking how income inequality had changed over the past generation. Answering that question required a series of

Table 5.12 Effect of income and family size on visiting a dentist within past year: 1970 and 1980 Health Interview Surveys

Age and year	Ln Income B	(SE)	Ln Size B	(SE)	Constant B	(SE)	R^2	Mean	SD	N
Under 7										
1970	0.121	(0.005)	0.043	(0.010)	-0.881	(0.051)	0.036	0.274	0.446	14 062
1980	0.066	(0.006)	0.031	(0.015)	-0.368	(0.057)	0.015	0.312	0.463	9 601
7 to 17										
1970	0.165	(0.004)	-0.188	(0.007)	-0.435	(0.034)	0.094	0.751	0.433	24 414
1980	0.110	(0.004)	-0.169	(0.009)	-0.016	(0.038)	0.056	0.799	0.401	17 079
18 to 24										
1970	0.078	(0.005)	-0.148	(0.008)	0.191	(0.043)	0.034	0.719	0.450	12 182
1980	0.060	(0.005)	-0.114	(0.007)	0.281	(0.042)	0.021	0.730	0.444	12 234
25 to 44										
1970	0.151	(0.004)	-0.082	(0.006)	-0.603	(0.041)	0.047	0.674	0.469	25 793
1980	0.117	(0.004)	-0.090	(0.005)	-0.331	(0.037)	0.038	0.715	0.451	26 582
45 to 64										
1970	0.179	(0.004)	-0.065	(0.007)	-1.000	(0.037)	0.077	0.554	0.497	22 035
1980	0.175	(0.005)	-0.092	(0.006)	-1.001	(0.045)	0.069	0.626	0.484	18 382
65 or over										
1970	0.154	(0.006)	-0.187	(0.011)	-0.838	(0.045)	0.069	0.322	0.467	10 060
1980	0.215	(0.007)	-0.231	(0.012)	-1.417	(0.061)	0.089	0.411	0.492	9 828

Source: See Table 5.7.

methodological judgments. We argued that the right unit of analysis was the household rather than the family, that households should be weighted by size, and that there was no one 'best' way to adjust income for differences in household size. We therefore concluded that the best way to measure trends in inequality was to compare trends for total and per capita household income. If the two trend lines are parallel, the 'true' trend is clear. If the two trend lines are not parallel, no unequivocal conclusions are possible. Finally, we argued that changes in inequality between the bottom and the middle are likely to have different causes and different cures from changes in inequality between the top and the middle.

Because income data have inherent limitations and the CPS only gathers complete data from about two-thirds of its target population, we also argued that policy analysts should check conclusions based on the CPS against data from other sources. To illustrate this approach we compared CPS measures of income inequality to Census measures of income inequality, CEX measures of expenditure and consumption inequality, and measures of material inequality derived from the Census, the AHS, and the HIS.

The best way to summarize our findings is to look at trends for four separate periods: the 1960s, the 1970s, the early 1980s, and the late 1980s.

The 1960s. The CPS suggests that the distribution of household income grew more equal from 1963 to 1969, regardless of whether we look at the top or bottom half of the distribution and regardless of whether we look at total or per capita income. CPS data on families show the same trend from 1959 to 1963. The Census, in contrast, shows a much smaller decline in income inequality. The CEX expenditure data suggest a small increase in inequality during the 1960s, but this is probably because of methodological changes in the CEX.

Our measures of material well-being show growing inequality between the rich and the poor during the 1960s for number of rooms, number of automobiles, air conditioning, home ownership, and restricted activity days. But inequality declined for bathrooms, crowding, age of building, central heating, telephone service, and doctor visits.

The 1970s. The CPS tells an ambiguous story about trends in income inequality during the 1970s. The trend depends on whether one looks at the top or bottom half of the distribution and whether one looks at total or per capita income. The Census is equally ambiguous. We do not have data on changes in the distribution of expenditures or consumption between 1970 and 1980, but we do have data on changes in material well-being. Income-related inequality rose during the 1970s for home ownership and restricted activity days. It fell when we look at people's chances of living in a new building, seeing the doctor, seeing the dentist, or having a complete bathroom, central heat, an automobile, or a telephone. The trend is either flat or ambiguous for number of rooms, crowding, total number of automobiles, total number of bathrooms, and air conditioning.

The early 1980s. CPS data show an unambiguous increase in income inequality between 1979 and 1984, regardless of whether we look at the top or bottom half of the distribution and regardless of whether we focus on total or per capita income. Our consumption data, which cover 1972–84, tell the same story as the CPS about the top half of the distribution but show no clear trend in the bottom half. The AHS shows that crowding grew at the low end of the income distribution and fell at the high end between 1979 and 1983, which is what we would expect based on changes in the distribution of income. The AHS also shows that home ownership declined more in the bottom of the income distribution than in the middle or the top during these years. But the bottom deciles gained more than the middle or the top in terms of complete bathrooms, complete kitchens, and air conditioners.

The late 1980s. From 1984 to 1989 we see almost no change on any CPS measure of income inequality. Inequality in expenditures and consumption shows no consistent trend either. We do not have measures of housing conditions or access to automobiles and telephones for these years. Income-related inequality in health status shows no clear trend, while doctor visits increased faster among the poor than among the affluent.

These findings lead us to three general conclusions:

- The CPS, the Census, and the CEX tell somewhat different stories about trends in income and consumption inequality.
- Trends in material inequality, at least as the government currently measures it, are very weakly related to trends in income inequality.
- Different kinds of material inequality respond to very different technical, economic, political, and social forces. Trends in one domain are therefore weak predictors of trends in other domains.

Over the past generation anti-poverty programs for the nonelderly have placed more and more emphasis on noncash programs like

Medicaid, compensatory education, Food Stamps, and Section 8 rent subsidies. (Recent increases in the Earned Income Tax Credit are a notable exception to this pattern.) Legislators have supported noncash programs because they are more interested in guaranteeing everyone adequate food, housing, medical care, and education than in guaranteeing everyone enough income to ensure that they buy these things in the open market. Yet despite the dramatic growth of noncash programs aimed at the poor, federal statistical agencies have made relatively little effort to track changes in the quality of poor people's food intake, housing conditions, medical care, education, or health. Official surveys ask only a handful of questions about these matters and largely ignore those problems that dominate public debate (the incidence of hunger and the number of people deterred by cost from seeing a doctor when they are sick, for example).

Nonetheless, the surveys we have examined do tell us some important things. By almost every yardstick except home ownership, poor people's housing conditions improved during the 1970s, when federal housing programs were growing. After 1980, when growth in federal housing programs slowed, the evidence is more fragmentary. Some indicators show progress between 1979 and 1983 while others show retrogression. We will not have reliable data for the rest of the decade until the 1990 Census is released. And even the Census will not tell us anything about the poorest of the poor, because it does not cover the homeless, who became considerably more numerous during the 1980s.[53]

Our data also show that poor people's access to medical care improved during the 1970s. This may have been partly because the number of physicians was growing and partly because Medicaid was paying more poor people's bills, but it is hard to be sure. Poor households' use of doctors also appears to have risen in the late 1980s, despite cutbacks in Medicaid and related programs.

Such findings do not imply that Americans should ignore the distribution of money income or abandon efforts to make incomes more equal. But economic inequality has many dimensions, of which income is only one. Legislators have always known this and have developed a wide range of policies that seek to reduce material inequality among people whose incomes are very unequal. Scholars and policy analysts who want to assess trends in economic inequality need to become at least as eclectic as the legislators whose behavior they seek to influence.

Appendix A   Design Changes in the Consumer Expenditure Survey

The Bureau of Labor Statistics (BLS) redesigned the Consumer Expenditure Survey (CEX) in 1972 and again in 1980. This appendix summarizes the changes that seem most likely to have had an influence on the measured distribution of income and expenditures.

Definition of the Consumer Unit. According to the BLS (1989, p. 142), a consumer unit (CU) is composed of either (a) all relatives who live in the same household, or (b) an individual who lives alone or with nonrelatives but is financially independent, or (c) two or more unrelated individuals who live in the same household and pool their income to make joint expenditure decisions. This description is misleading in two respects. First, while BLS publications indicate that the income pooling test is applied only to nonrelatives, BLS officials told us that it was actually applied to all household members except married couples and their unmarried children. Second, BLS does not ask whether household members pool their income or make joint expenditure decisions. Instead, it asks whether they pay their bills with 'their own money' – a quite different question.

In 1960–61 the CEX asked the respondent (who was initially the household head or his wife), 'In financial matters, did you consider _____ part of your family or a separate family in (1960/1961).' If the answer was yes, the CEX also asked the individual in question, 'Were you financially independent last year – that is did you pay for food, rent, and clothing with your own money?' It is not clear what happened if the individual was neither 'part of the family' nor 'financially independent.'

In 1972–3 the interviewer was told to define the CU as including the 'head of household, wife, never married children, and any other person [living in the household] who is considered part of that family.' If an individual was neither the head, the head's wife, nor the head's unmarried child, the interviewer was supposed to ask, 'Is _____ financially independent, that is, does _____ pay for food, shelter, and clothing with his own money?'

In the 1980s BLS asked three questions: (1) 'Does _____ pay for all his/her housing expenses with his/her own money?' (2) 'Does _____ pay for all his/her food expenses with his/her own money?' (3) 'Does _____ pay for all his/her other living expenses such as clothing, transportation, etc. with his/her own money?' If the answer to at least two of these questions was yes, and if the individual in question was neither the spouse nor the unmarried child of the household head, BLS treated the individual as a separate CU.

In 1984–5, 3.0 percent of all households contained two or more CUs, and 6.5 percent of all CUs lived in households that contained two or more CUs. Comparing the Census Bureau count of households to the BLS count of CUs suggests that these percentages were slightly lower in 1972–3, but the counts in question may not cover precisely the same population or the same month, so we cannot be sure of this.

Although a CU is normally limited to individuals who live in the same household, BLS treated most students living away from home as part of their parents' CU in 1960–61 and 1972–3. In 1960–61, all young adults living away from home were included in their parents' consumer unit if their parents provided most of their support. In 1972–3 students were classified as part of their parents' household if they lived in a dormitory or gave their parents' address as their usual address. Starting in 1980, students living away from home were treated as separate CUs. Treating students as separate CUs presumably makes the distributions of income and expenditures slightly more unequal, so we eliminated students from our tabulations for 1984–9. This sample restriction had almost no impact on our results.

Missing income data. The CEX income questions are not quite as detailed as those currently used in the CPS, but the amount of missing data is roughly comparable. Unlike the CPS, however, the CEX has never used a 'hot deck' to impute missing income data. Instead, missing data have always been recoded as zeros. In an effort to minimize errors arising from this practice, BLS designates CUs with especially severe missing data problems as having 'incomplete' income data. In 1960–61 BLS excluded such CUs both from its publications and from its public use data tape. Starting in 1972–3 BLS presented separate results for CUs designated as having incomplete income data and flagged them on its public use data tapes. Starting in 1980 the public use data tapes also flag each imputed income value, so users can define 'incomplete' reporters differently from BLS if they wish. One cannot do this in earlier years, however, so most analysts use the BLS definition in all years. Unfortunately, this practice is not sufficient to ensure that samples are subject to comparable selection bias in different years.

We have not been able to determine how BLS defined complete income reporters in 1960–61, how many CUs were excluded because their income data were incomplete, or how many of those defined as having complete data answered all the income questions. Given what we know about the CPS, missing data were probably quite rare.

In 1972–3 BLS designated CUs as having incomplete income data if the respondent reported that a member of the CU worked but failed to report the individual's earnings, or if the respondent reported that the CU received income from Social Security but failed to report the amount (Bureau of Labor Statistics, 1978, p. 126). If the respondent reported that someone worked but had no earnings, BLS accepted this as a legitimate response. Likewise, if the respondent reported earnings or Social Security income but failed to answer other income questions, BLS treated the CU as having complete income data. Using these criteria, 5 percent of the weighted sample had incomplete income data. Judging by CPS experience, 10 to 15 percent of all persons and 15 to 20 percent of all CUs probably had some missing income data in 1972–3. If these estimates are correct, 10 to 15 percent of all CUs with nominally complete data must have failed to answer at least one of the income questions and must have been assigned values of zero. We cannot identify these CUs on the public use data tape.

In the 1980s BLS defined CUs as having incomplete data only if the CU reported *no* major source of income. Using this criterion, 10 to 15 percent of all CUs had incomplete income data, with the exact value fluctuating unpredictably from year to year. Since 32 percent of all CUs failed to answer at least one of the income questions, something like 22 percent of all CUs with nominally complete income data had some missing values that had been set to zero. (We are indebted to Thesia Garner of the Bureau of Labor Statistics for these estimates.)

In an effort to minimize the effect of changes in the definition of a complete income reporter between 1972–3 and 1984–9, we treated CUs with no reported income as incomplete income reporters in all years.

Missing expenditure data. BLS currently imputes missing expenditure data using a 'hot deck' routine. We have been told that this was done in 1972–3 as well. We do not know what was done in 1960–61. BLS officials have told us that they currently impute about 5 percent of total expenditures. We do not know how this figure has changed over time or how the imputation procedures have changed.

Account balancing. The 1960–61 CEX asked CUs whose reported income and expenditures differed by more than 10 percent to explain the difference. This request led to changes in both estimated income and estimated expenditures. CUs that had initially reported very low incomes or expenditures tended to revise their estimates upward, while CUs that had initially reported high incomes or expenditures tended to revise their estimates downward (Ray Geisman, Bureau of Labor Statistics, personal communication). As a result, the distributions of income and expenditures that interviewers eventually recorded were almost certainly more equal than those that respondents initially reported. The CEX did not engage in this kind of account balancing after 1961. Thus if nothing else had changed we would expect to see an increase in both income and expenditure inequality between 1961 and 1972.

Recall period. The 1960-61 CEX asked about expenditures over the previous twelve months. Because of high refusal rates and doubts about the accuracy of consumers' recollections over such a long period, BLS introduced quarterly interviews in 1972. The shorter recall period presumably reduced random reporting errors, which should reduce estimated expenditure inequality. But the shorter recall period may also affect rich and poor consumers differently. We know, for example, that the correlation between income and reported food expenditures is higher in surveys that ask respondents to record their food expenditures for a week than in surveys that ask for an estimate of average food expenditure during the previous three months.[54] If shortening the recall period from twelve to three months had a similar effect, the estimated level of expenditure inequality could rise.

Movers. Although several interviews were usually necessary to collect the 1960–61 data, these interviews were all conducted in a fairly short period, so movers posed a negligible problem. When BLS introduced quarterly interviews in 1972, movers became a major problem. For budgetary reasons, BLS has never followed CUs that moved to a new address. In 1972–3 BLS defined its target population as those who lived at a sample address during the final quarter of the survey. If the CU had not lived at the sample address throughout the survey period, BLS asked it to reconstruct its expenditures for earlier quarters so as to get a full year of expenditure data. In the 1980s, in contrast, BLS treated the CEX as a series of independent quarterly surveys. Expenditure data were still collected at each sample address for four consecutive quarters, but individuals who moved in were no longer asked about their expenditures in earlier quarters.[55] As a result, the CEX no longer provided a full year of expenditure data for CUs that moved during the survey year.[56]

One way to deal with movers is to calculate their mean expenditures over as many quarters as one has available and estimate their annual expenditures by multiplication. Unfortunately, this approach exaggerates inequality in movers' annual expenditures. The reason is that quarterly expenditures are more unequally distributed than annual expenditures. To see why this is so one need only recognize that a CU's expenditures in any one quarter are not perfectly correlated with its expenditures in earlier or later quarters. Thus while summing expenditures over four randomly selected quarters will raise mean expenditures by a factor of four, it will raise the standard deviation by a factor of less than four. This means that the coefficient of variation falls, and the same is almost invariably true for all other standard measures of inequality.

An alternative approach would be to assume that the covariance between quarterly and annual expenditures was the same for CUs with less than four quarters of data as for those with all four quarters of data. If this assumption were correct, we could use a regression equation plus a random error term to estimate movers' annual expenditures. Unfortunately, moving is usually associated with significant changes in expenditures, so we doubt that this approach would yield unbiased results.

Fluctuating response rates. BLS describes the response rate in 1960–61 as 80.8 percent (Bureau of Labor Statistics, 1971, p. 25), but this statistic is misleading. When BLS constructed its 1960–61 sample, it drew up two matched lists of addresses. If the interviewer could not find anyone at the first address after two visits, or if the CU at the first address refused to participate, BLS sought an interview at the second address. According to BLS, 23.1 percent of its final urban sample was drawn from the second list. Of this group, 23 percent replaced vacant addresses, 38 percent replaced CUs that were never at home, and 39 percent replaced CUs that refused (*op. cit.* p. 25). Replacing vacant addresses should pose no problem for the representativeness of the final sample, but CUs that are not at home or refuse can never be fully replaced. Since the latter two groups constitute 17.8 percent of the final sample, only about $(100 - 17.8)(80.8) = 66$ percent of the CUs on the initial list actually participated.

In 1972–3 the participation rate was 88.6 percent (Bureau of Labor Statistics, 1978, p. 4).

In the 1980s the quarterly participation rate among eligible CUs averaged about 85 percent (Bureau of Labor Statistics, 1989b, p. 150). In a weighted sample of respondents with at least one quarter of data who entered the CEX in 1984 or early 1985, 74 percent had four quarters of data. This implies that about 63 percent of the target population provided four quarters of data.

BLS weights its final sample to make it resemble the CPS with respect to race, sex, age, and home ownership, but BLS does not try to correct for underrepresentation of high or low income CUs within these strata. Since participation rates are usually lower among the rich and the poor even with race, sex, age, and home ownership held constant, nonparticipation is likely to bias the distributions of both income and expenditures towards equality. This bias, while small, is likely to be larger in 1960–61 than in 1972–3, and when we focus on CUs with four quarters of data it is also likely to be larger in 1984–9 than in 1972–3.

Newly formed consumer units. About 3 percent of all CUs interviewed in the CEX during 1960–61 and 1972–3 had come into existence during the previous calendar year, so they could not provide a full year of expenditure data. BLS did not include these part-year CUs in its 1960–61 tabulations, and it does not appear to have included them on its 1960–61 data tape. BLS did include part-year CUs on the 1972–3 data tape, but it only included their income and expenditures for the portion of the year during which the CU existed. We should therefore have excluded part-year CUs from our 1972–73A sample. Due to an error that we discovered too late to correct, we failed to do so. Part-year CUs are, however, excluded from our 1972–73B 'full data' sample. Since the 1972B and 1973B 'full data' samples yield results very similar to those for our 1972–73A sample, this error appears to be inconsequential.

Appendix B Supplementary Income and Expenditure Tables

Table B.1 Mean household income in 1987 dollars for bottom, middle, and top quintiles, weighted by household size in the Census and CPS

Year	Total household income					Per capita household income				
	Quintile means			Ratios		Quintile means			Ratios	
	1st	3rd	5th	1/3	3/5	1st	3rd	5th	1/3	3/5
CPS										
1963	5727	20 652	48 804	0.277	0.423	1464	5029	14 865	0.291	0.338
1964	5950	21 318	49 196	0.279	0.433	1511	5165	15 370	0.292	0.336
1965	6363	22 256	51 291	0.286	0.434	1610	5452	15 828	0.295	0.344
1966	7088	23 756	53 931	0.298	0.440	1802	5754	16 365	0.313	0.352
1967	7272	24 412	55 611	0.298	0.439	1937	6013	17 227	0.322	0.349
1968	7801	25 723	57 677	0.303	0.446	2105	6432	18 107	0.327	0.355
1969	8175	26 862	60 640	0.304	0.443	2233	6781	18 935	0.329	0.358
1970	7944	26 981	61 593	0.294	0.438	2206	6844	19 380	0.322	0.353
1971	7906	26 891	61 735	0.294	0.436	2246	6954	19 723	0.323	0.353
1972	8107	27 988	65 028	0.290	0.430	2359	7440	20 881	0.317	0.356
1973	8425	28 808	66 325	0.292	0.434	2530	7787	21 574	0.325	0.361
1974	8042	28 004	63 534	0.287	0.441	2472	7672	20 670	0.322	0.371
1975	7899	27 729	63 977	0.285	0.433	2420	7716	21 133	0.314	0.365
1976	8149	28 507	65 465	0.286	0.435	2554	8013	21 673	0.319	0.370
1977	7995	28 789	66 629	0.278	0.432	2584	8262	22 410	0.313	0.369
1978	8247	29 652	68 092	0.278	0.435	2721	8612	23 190	0.316	0.371
1979	8265	30 066	68 971	0.275	0.436	2735	8875	23 564	0.308	0.377
1980	7889	29 112	66 818	0.271	0.436	2609	8699	23 257	0.300	0.374

continued on page 188

Table B.1 (continued)

Year	Total household income					Per capita household income				
	Quintile means			Ratios		Quintile means			Ratios	
	1st	3rd	5th	1/3	3/5	1st	3rd	5th	1/3	3/5
1981	7650	28 648	68 252	0.267	0.420	2506	8626	24 132	0.290	0.357
1982	7317	28 202	69 478	0.259	0.406	2347	8593	24 457	0.273	0.351
1983	7229	28 103	69 812	0.257	0.403	2316	8724	24 876	0.265	0.351
1984	7519	29 119	72 998	0.258	0.399	2465	9061	26 242	0.272	0.345
1985	7644	29 630	74 117	0.258	0.400	2530	9230	26 811	0.274	0.344
1986	7751	30 449	76 395	0.255	0.399	2577	9503	27 388	0.271	0.347
1987	7661	30 522	76 457	0.251	0.399	2570	9590	27 416	0.268	0.350
1988	7786	30 602	77 195	0.254	0.396	2656	9775	28 232	0.272	0.346
1989	8082	30 980	78 435	0.261	0.395	2704	9875	28 716	0.274	0.344
Mean	7625	27 547	65 128	0.278	0.425	2325	7795	21 942	0.300	0.355
S.D.	662	2 775	8 239	0.016	0.017	359	1430	4018	0.022	0.011
C.V.	0.087	0.101	0.127	0.059	0.040	0.155	0.183	0.183	0.072	0.031
CENSUS										
1959	5184	19 521	50 083	0.266	0.390	1282	4809	15 363	0.267	0.313
1969	7277	26 846	63 285	0.271	0.424	2004	6808	20 209	0.294	0.337
1979	7899	30 273	72 255	0.261	0.419	2578	8846	25 106	0.291	0.352

Source: Tabulations by David Rhodes from CPS data tapes for 1964–88 assembled by Robert Mare and Christopher Winship, 1989 and 1990 CPS public use tapes, and 1960–80 Census public use tapes. All calculations exclude individuals in group quarters and correct for top coding using procedures described in the text. All estimates are converted to 1987 dollars using the fixed-weight price index for Personal Consumption Expenditures from the National Income Accounts.

Table B.2 Mean income, expenditures, and consumption in 1987 dollars for the bottom, middle, and top quintiles: CEX consumer units with complete income and four quarters of expenditure data in 1960–61, 1972–3, and 1984–9

	1960–1	1972–3A	1972B	1973B	1984	1985	1986	1987	1988	1989
Income by decile										
1st	4 900	5 543	5 619	5 375	3 097	3 663	2 962	4 129	4 451	4 832
2nd	9 608	12 202	11 606	12 356	9 074	8 695	9 130	9 326	9 441	10 205
5th	19 115	27 335	26 753	27 892	24 114	23 251	24 392	24 126	24 382	25 052
6th	21 831	31 901	31 059	32 733	29 316	28 958	30 290	29 563	29 776	30 251
9th	34 811	51 400	50 517	53 139	53 659	54 471	55 365	53 339	53 735	55 968
10th	56 614	84 891	80 961	88 054	85 335	83 327	82 917	84 192	82 257	85 408
All	23 023	26 931	32 399	34 225	31 508	31 238	31 789	31 651	31 624	32 714
Per capita income by decile										
1st	1 257	1 929	1 798	1 574	996	1 217	959	1 322	1 420	1 540
2nd	2 445	3 593	3 414	3 583	2 988	2 957	3 034	3 269	3 191	3 388
5th	4 753	7 250	7 012	7 432	7 738	7 614	8 046	7 935	7 799	8 222
6th	5 605	8 591	8 329	8 805	9 422	9 317	9 870	9 621	9 603	9 897
9th	10 452	15 967	15 578	16 308	18 750	19 162	19 474	19 143	19 353	19 746
10th	18 710	29 404	28 429	29 471	33 741	34 121	34 143	34 594	34 414	35 051
All	5 983	8 071	9 716	10 142	11 016	11 113	11 349	11 341	11 297	11 653

continued on page 190

Table B.2 (continued)

	1960–1	1972–3A	1972B	1973B	1984	1985	1986	1987	1988	1989
Expenditures by decile										
1st	5 374	6 509	6 614	6 993	7 002	6 814	6 823	6 601	6 922	7 182
2nd	9 678	11 657	12 013	12 672	12 096	11 544	11 503	11 255	11 358	11 837
5th	18 062	22 432	23 963	24 889	24 362	24 169	24 986	23 863	23 930	23 918
6th	20 650	26 041	27 794	28 857	28 807	29 033	29 703	28 406	28 112	28 678
9th	31 995	41 105	43 567	46 041	50 797	51 247	52 743	49 965	49 181	50 770
10th	46 888	62 687	67 851	69 712	80 569	78 293	81 940	78 082	76 316	81 229
All	21 360	26 931	28 697	29 870	31 406	31 211	32 123	30 674	30 388	31 540
Per capita expenditures by decile										
1st	1 387	2 010	2 033	2 123	2 245	2 110	2 237	2 151	2 024	2 157
2nd	2 427	3 355	3 394	3 669	3 867	3 780	3 759	3 723	3 625	3 947
5th	4 578	6 134	6 424	6 744	7 746	7 759	8 097	7 915	7 856	8 038
6th	5 332	7 099	7 517	7 812	9 299	9 471	9 820	9 404	9 289	9 502
9th	9 442	12 646	13 546	13 968	18 064	18 321	18 764	18 210	18 088	18 543
10th	15 854	21 628	23 314	23 963	30 993	31 257	32 251	31 743	31 560	32 066
All	5 983	8 071	8 556	8 895	10 882	11 011	11 350	10 967	10 885	11 204
Consumption by decile										
1st			6 241	6 625	7 057	6 818	6 846	6 641	6 928	7 048
2nd			10 469	11 170	11 081	10 614	10 626	10 441	10 489	10 750
5th			18 633	19 262	19 067	18 619	18 664	18 117	18 242	18 076

6th	21 408	22 025	21 723	21 329	21 424	20 832	20 985	20 774
9th	32 698	34 265	35 043	34 138	34 340	33 135	33 227	34 316
10th	47 972	50 103	51 538	49 140	50 517	48 755	48 967	53 282
All	21 905	22 829	22 874	22 294	22 496	21 846	22 005	22 582
Per capita consumption by decile								
1st	1 805	1 890	2 068	1 945	2 021	2 002	1 919	1 958
2nd	2 919	3 106	3 426	3 378	3 352	3 286	3 152	3 287
5th	5 150	5 387	6 189	6 190	6 346	6 206	6 184	6 231
6th	5 932	6 193	7 213	7 229	7 379	7 165	7 218	7 282
9th	9 992	10 367	12 444	12 538	12 536	12 355	12 558	12 755
10th	16 094	16 760	19 386	19 336	19 968	19 660	20 156	20 931
All	6 493	6 778	7 897	7 869	7 986	7 818	7 892	8 065

Source: Tabulations for 1972–3B and 1980s by Tony Maier from Consumer Expenditure Survey data tapes constructed by John Sabelhaus. Tabulations for 1960–61 and 1972–3A by Karen Rolf using data tapes constructed by Larry Radbill. Current dollars are converted to 1987 dollars using the fixed-weight price index for Personal Consumption Expenditures from the National Income Accounts (see *Economic Report of the President*, 1991).

Sample coverage. Estimates are for respondents with positive expenditures and complete income data. CUs with no reported income are defined as having incomplete income data in all years. CUs that did not exist at the beginning of the year are excluded in all years except 1972–3A. Excluding respondents with less than four quarters of data eliminates CUs that moved to a sample address after the first quarter or missed an interview for other reasons in 1984–9 but not in 1972–3. Estimates for earlier years treat students living away from home. Estimates for 1984–9 exclude students not living at home but dependent on their parents as members of their parents' CU.

Notes

1. We are grateful to the Jerome Levy Economics Institute, the Russell Sage Foundation, the Ford Foundation, the Sloan Foundation, and the Center for Urban Affairs and Policy Research at Northwestern University for financial support, to Robert Mare and Christopher Winship for making available their extracts from the 1963-86 Current Population Survey, to Larry Radbill and John Sabelhaus for creating extracts from the Consumer Expenditure Survey, and to Gary McClelland for creating extracts from the decennial Census. Tony Maier, Karen Rolf, and David Rhodes provided invaluable programming assistance. Tim Veenstra provided research assistance and made the graphs. Rebecca Blank, Thesia Garner, Robert Haveman, Lawrence Katz, and Paul Ryscavage made unusually careful and helpful comments on earlier drafts.

2. The estimates come from US Bureau of the Census (1990a), Table E-4. They are adjusted for inflation using the CPI-U-X1 rather than the CPI-U. If one uses the more widely cited but less accurate CPI-U, the average family gained 16 percent between 1969 and 1989 while the poorest fifth lost 5 percent (*ibid*, Table 6). Allowing for means-tested noncash benefits would reduce and perhaps eliminate the apparent trend towards inequality during the 1970s but would not appreciably alter the picture during the 1980s (see Rebecca Blank's chapter in this volume). Here and throughout we use the difference between the last year of a decade and the last year of the previous decade (e.g. 1989 and 1979) to estimate change during that decade.

3. From 1947 to 1979 the Gini coefficient for family income fluctuated between a high of 0.378 (1949) and a low of 0.348 (1967 and 1968). After 1979 the Gini coefficient began to rise steadily, moving from 0.365 in 1979 to 0.401 in 1989 (US Bureau of the Census, 1989, Table 12, and 1990, Table 6.)

4. Like almost all other measures of inequality (e.g. the ratio of the standard deviation to the mean or the standard deviation of the logarithm) these measures assume that when everyone's income rises by the same percentage, inequality remains unchanged. From a social or psychological viewpoint, this assumption is quite problematic. Empirical research suggests that at any given time socioeconomic distance is probably a function of *both* the percentage difference *and* the absolute difference between two individuals' or families' incomes. Rainwater (1974) and Coleman, Rainwater, and McClelland (1978) present evidence suggesting, for example, that the perceived socioeconomic distance between families is a linear transformation of $(Income)^{1/3}$. But while cross-sectional evidence suggests that socioeconomic distance depends on absolute as well as proportional income differences, we have been unable to find any evidence that this rule holds when we compare incomes over time. In the absence of such evidence, we have deferred to the long-standing economic presumption that doubling everyone's real income leaves inequality unchanged. For a fuller discussion of these issues see Atkinson (1970).

5. We divide by the mean for the middle quintile rather than the grand

mean because we want our measures of inequality in the top and bottom halves of the distribution to be independent of one another.

6. In order to keep the vertical axes in Figures 5.2a through 5.6b comparable, we have made their endpoints reciprocals of one another and converted them to logarithmic scales.

7. The claim that there is more inequality in the bottom half of the distribution than in the top half also holds if we compare the richest and poorest 5 percent of all families to those in the middle. In 1989 the top 5 percent of all families reported incomes averaging $148 438, while the middle quintile reported incomes averaging $34 206 (US Bureau of the Census, 1990a, Table E-4). The Census Bureau does not report the mean income of the bottom 5 percent, but it publishes enough information for us to estimate such a mean fairly accurately. In 1989, 3.6 percent of all families had incomes below $5000 and 6.3 percent had incomes between $5000 and $9999. The distribution of income among those with incomes between $5000 and $9999 was almost rectangular, so the cutoff point for the poorest 5 percent was about $6100, and the mean for those with incomes between $5000 and $6100 was about $5550. The mean for those with incomes below $5000 was $2575 in 1987 (US Bureau of the Census, 1989, Table 13), and it seems likely that the 1989 mean was similar. The 1989 mean for the bottom 5 percent must therefore have been about $3410. These estimates imply that the bottom 5 percent reported incomes averaging 10 percent of the mean for the middle quintile, while the middle quintile reported incomes averaging 23 percent of the mean for the top 5 percent. One cannot make analogous calculations for the top and bottom 1 percent, because published tables do not provide enough detail on these groups and public use data tapes are top coded. Furthermore, it is not clear how one would apply this method to households that report incomes of zero or incomes that are negative because of business losses.

8. The apparent asymmetry of the logged distribution could be caused partly by measurement error. Census Bureau data indicate that households report about as much income from wages and salaries as employers claim to have paid out. The same is true for Social Security. Income from self-employment, dividends, interest, public assistance, and unemployment compensation is much less fully reported. This situation implies that CPS data underestimate the incomes of the top and bottom quintiles relative to the middle three quintiles. If so, the true distribution of family income is more nearly log-normal than conventional calculations indicate. Consumption data also come much closer to being log-normal (see below).

9. The apparent decline in inequality between the top and the middle from 1947 to 1957 could be a byproduct of the way the Census Bureau estimated the incomes of the rich during this period. The estimates for 1947–57 were not derived from respondents' original reports (which have been destroyed) but from published data on the percentage of families with incomes of $25 000 or more and the percentage with incomes between $15 000 and $24 999. The Bureau estimated the mean income of families in each group by assuming that income follows a Pareto distribution (US Bureau of the Census, 1989, p. 177). This assumption is seldom

exactly true, so the pre-1957 estimates must be treated quite cautiously.

10. An ideal income series would probably treat lodgers and live-in domestic workers as separate economic units, while pooling the incomes of all other household members, but this was not possible using our extracts from the CPS. Because lodgers and live-in domestic workers were relatively rare even in 1960, we doubt that distinguishing them from other household members would appreciably alter any of the findings reported in this chapter.

11. While we prefer data on households to data on families plus unrelated individuals, trends in inequality are quite similar using either approach. Karoly (1990) provides an excellent analysis of trends in inequality among families plus unrelated individuals. She finds essentially the same trends in the bottom half of the distribution for families and unrelated individuals that we find for households. She finds less increase in inequality in the top half of the distribution for families and unrelated individuals than we find for households, but that is probably because her analysis does not take account of trends among those above the 90th percentile.

12. Published data on the distribution of household income are not available prior to 1967.

13. The CPS does not cover inmates of institutions or members of the armed forces living on bases. It does cover individuals living in group quarters (most of whom live in residential hotels and lodging houses), but pre-1976 data tapes do not include such individuals' income. Our tabulations are therefore restricted to household members in all years. When we tried adding individuals in group quarters and treating them as households of one, our post-1976 results were almost unchanged.

14. Estimating inequality between the top and the middle from public-use data tapes is complicated by the fact that the Census Bureau imposes an arbitrary upper limit on the amount of income it will record on public use data tapes. CPS income questions were supposedly top-coded at $99 999 from 1963 to 1966, but we found no internal evidence of this. Starting in 1967, CPS income questions were top-coded at $50 000. From 1967 through 1974 total household income was also top-coded at $50 000. After 1974 the top code was applied only to the components of income, not the total. The proportion of individuals living in households affected by top-coding rose steadily from 1967 to 1974, reaching 1.2 percent of the population in 1974. Since 1974 the figure has been much smaller.

To keep the distributional effects of top-coding uniform over time, one must impose uniform top-coding rules in all years. The cutoff point for top coding was 3.447 times the mean in 1974, so we top-coded households with incomes more than 3.447 times the mean in all years. Since our newly top-coded households had actually had incomes 4.223 times the mean in 1975, we assigned all top-coded households a value 4.223 times the mean in the relevant year. This procedure has two drawbacks. First, if the distribution of income among households with incomes more than 3.445 times the mean has changed over time, our procedure will miss these changes. Second, since some households in the top 1 percent of the distribution were top-coded even in 1975, the value we assign top-coded households is too low in all years.

15. The CPS also measures age, location, and whether respondents have disabilities, all of which should in principle be incorporated in a need measure. But there is no general agreement about how much these characteristics affect a household's need for money, and neither is there an easy way to set upper and lower bounds on their likely effect, so we ignore them here.

16. When Mayer and Jencks (1989) regressed an index of material hardship (H) derived from a survey of Chicago households on the natural logarithm of household income (Y), the natural logarithm of household size (S), and a dummy variable for having a head over the age of sixty-five (A), they obtained:

$$H = -0.876Y + 0.799S -0.901A$$

This result implies that when family size doubles family income must rise by $0.799/0.876 = 91$ percent to keep the level of hardship constant.

17. Adults presumably try to have the number of children they think will maximize their subjective well-being, given their expected income. If households achieve this goal, or if the costs of positive and negative errors are approximately equal, adults with the same income and different numbers of children should all have the same mean level of subjective well-being. If that were in fact the case, equivalence scales for adults could ignore the number of children in a household, on the grounds that spending money on children is no different from spending money on fancy restaurants, a nicer house, or a more enjoyable vacation.

18. Adjustments aimed at equalizing material well-being might well be similar for children and adults. Adjustments aimed at equalizing subjective well-being are less likely to be similar for children and adults, because children have little influence on the size of their household and there is little evidence that they prefer having more siblings to seeing more movies, living in a better neighborhood, or taking more vacations. Although we know no work that tries to compare the elasticities of children's adult life chances with respect to family income and family size, many investigators have shown that extra siblings (except perhaps for the first) have substantial adverse effects on children's cognitive development, educational attainment, and economic success in adulthood with income controlled (see e.g. Sewell and Hauser, 1975; Jencks *et al.*, 1979).

19. If a wife does not report her husband's earnings, for example, the Bureau sets his earnings equal to the earnings of the last previous husband of the same age and race who had the same amount of education, the same occupation, the same number of weeks worked, and so on. If no good match can be found, the process is repeated using less strenuous matching requirements. This approach to missing data is equivalent for our purposes to doubling the weight assigned the person from whom income data have been 'borrowed.'

20. A woman who does not answer a question about dividends, for example, is more likely to have some dividend income than a randomly selected woman with similar demographic characteristics. The same principle applies when respondents fail to answer questions about income from public assistance, interest, self-employment, and so on. Lillard, Smith, and Welch (1986) and Coder (1991) also provide data suggesting that response rates for questions about earnings depend partly on the amount earned.

21. Even when CPS respondents answer the interviewer's questions, the answers may not be accurate. The CPS relies on a single informant to report all household members' incomes. This informant may not know how much income other household members get from various sources. Indeed, many informants have only the vaguest notion of how much income they themselves received from various sources during the previous calendar year. Errors also creep in because people have memory lapses, make errors when adding or multiplying, use the wrong accounting period, deliberately conceal or understate certain kinds of income, or exaggerate their income in order to put themselves in a more favorable light.

    Unlike nonreporting, underreporting does not appear to have increased over time. The Census Bureau periodically compares CPS estimates of total money income to estimates from the National Income and Product Accounts (NIPA), which are derived from independent sources like payroll records, corporate reports of interest and dividends paid to individuals, and governmental reports of transfer payments to individuals. The most recent comparison suggests that CPS respondents reported about 71 percent of their income in 1987. After adding the income imputed to households with missing data, the CPS estimate of total household income was 89 percent of the NIPA estimate (US Bureau of the Census, 1991, p. 389). This ratio has been quite stable for many years.

22. The 1980 Census relied almost exclusively on mailback questionnaires. The 1970 Census relied mainly on a mailback questionnaire but used some face-to-face interviews. The 1960 Census relied entirely on face-to-face interviews.

23. Although both the Census and the CPS use a 'hot deck' to impute missing data, the details of their imputation routines differ somewhat. The sampling frames also differ to some extent. The CPS relies largely on the last previous Census for its sampling frame. Census population counts by age, race, and sex are then adjusted upwards each year on the basis of data derived from birth and death certificates and immigration estimates, and the CPS sample is reweighted so that it reproduces these estimates. If this procedure works well, CPS population estimates by race, sex, and age will predict the counts in the next Census quite accurately, but that does not always happen. In theory, reweighting the CPS after a new Census could alter the estimated level of income inequality, but the change has never been large.

24. If we weight all households by size and express their total income as a percentage of the median, the relative income of households at different points in the distribution is as follows:

					Percentile						
	1	*2*	*5*	*10*	*20*	*50*	*80*	*90*	*95*	*98*	*99*	*Median*
Census												
1960	0	4	15	27	50	100	161	205	266	380	NA	$5 650
1970	0	6	15	28	51	100	159	202	256	350	462	9 600
1980	0.5	7	16	27	47	100	163	210	262	358	NA	19 835
CPS												
1970	7	11	20	32	52	100	157	198	244	316	401	9 548
1980	5	11	19	29	48	100	164	211	258	NA	NA	19 600

The zeros shown for the first percentile of the Census distribution in 1960 and 1970 are not a product of rounding; they are literally correct. An 'NA' in the 98th or 99th percentile of a distribution indicates that we cannot estimate the income of such households because of top-coding. (In the Census, responses to any given income question were top-coded if they exceeded $25 000 in 1960, $50 000 in 1970, and $75 000 in 1980. In the CPS, responses were top-coded if they exceeded $50 000 in either 1970 or 1980.)

25. One way to check the accuracy of income reports by households in the bottom half of the distribution is to compare their reported income to their reported rent. The Census asks tenants how much they pay per month for rent and utilities and calls the sum of these two amounts 'gross rent.' Multiplying this figure by twelve gives us an estimate of each household's gross annual rent. In 1960, 35.8 percent of tenants in the lowest income decile reported gross annual rents that exceeded their reported income for 1959. In 1970 the figure was 39.0 percent, and in 1980 it was 43.8 percent. Some of these households were presumably paying part of their rent from savings or borrowing. Some presumably relied on friends or relatives to pay their rent. Some had presumably experienced large recent increases in income that had allowed them to move to a more expensive residence. Nonetheless, these data strongly suggest that many poor households underreport their income in the Census. Unfortunately, we do not have comparable figures from the CPS.

26. Low-income households' expenditures could have risen faster than their incomes if they had easier access to credit or if they had more savings than in the past. Changes of this kind would be quite likely if year-to-year fluctuations in income were growing, lowering the correlation between annual and permanent income. Data from the Panel Study of Income Dynamics provide little evidence of such a trend, however.

27. We work exclusively with what BLS calls the 'interview' survey, which does not ask about expenditures for household supplies, personal care, or prescription drugs. In the 1980s these items accounted for about 4 percent of total expenditure (5 percent in the two lowest income quintiles, 4 percent in the next two income quintiles, and 3 percent in the top income quintile).

28. Our estimate of federal income tax liabilities differs from that on the

public use data tapes in the 1980s. According to John Sabelhaus, who computed the values we used, the public use data tapes systematically understate federal income tax liabilities in the 1980s. Sabelhaus recomputed tax liabilities using the CEX income data. Our expenditure measure also includes the entire purchase price of consumer durables, even when the purchase is partially financed by borrowing.

29. Because BLS includes sales taxes in the purchase price of specific items and does not record the state in which a CU lived on public use data tapes, we were unable to exclude sales taxes. We would also have preferred to exclude the cost of insurance coverage, but Sabelhaus's 1972–89 data tape does not allow us to do this.

30. Our estimate of a home's rental value is taken from Sabelhaus's 1972–89 data tape. This estimate is based on owners' estimates of their home's market value multiplied by the ratio of aggregate rental value to aggregate market value for owner-occupied housing in the relevant year. The numerator of this ratio comes from the National Income Accounts, while the denominator comes from the Flow of Funds accounts.

31. Cutler and Katz (1991) report that the treatment of vehicle depreciation has little effect on trends in consumption inequality. This is not surprising, since the distribution of vehicle ownership by expenditure level did not change much from 1960 to 1989.

32. If expenditures on durables fluctuate more than most other expenditures over the course of a business cycle, the bias introduced by substituting current expenditures for service flows might be greater near the peak of a business cycle than near the trough.

33. For details see Appendix A.

34. Appendix A describes these differences in detail.

35. This hypothesis is supported by the fact that the CEX income data, which are subject to similar methodological biases, also show growing inequality at a time when the CPS and Census suggest that inequality was declining.

36. If Sabelhaus's weights do not fully compensate for the exclusion of CUs with less than four quarters of data from our 1984–9 CEX samples, our trend estimates for 1972–3 to 1988–9 are likely to underestimate the true increase in inequality. But we can see no obvious reason why this bias should be larger for total than per capita resources, and neither can we see any reason why it should affect consumption more than expenditures.

37. In the published version of their paper Cutler and Katz present results for consumption divided by the federal poverty threshold rather than for consumption divided by household size. The two sets of results are quite similar, because the federal poverty threshold makes a large adjustment for family size. We present their per capita estimates here in order to maintain comparability with the estimates elsewhere in this paper.

38. Slesnick also presents results adjusted for household size, but his adjustment also takes account of changes in race, age, location, and sex of the head. Slesnick's adjustments for these latter characteristics are very large and often counterintuitive. As a result, his adjusted measures show little change in consumption inequality.

39. For analogous data from Great Britain, see Townsend (1979) and Mack and Lansley (1985).

40. The AHS actually asks about a wider range of housing conditions than the Census, but the additional questions proved to be of limited value for our purposes. The AHS asked, for example, about exposed wiring, water leakage, cracks and holes in interior walls and floors, mice and rats, and whether various neighborhood conditions were 'bothersome.' But all these measures show large, statistically significant year-to-year fluctuations that do not parallel fluctuations in either macroeconomic conditions or public policy. Some of these fluctuations appear to be traceable to methodological changes. The reported incidence of exposed wiring and cracks and holes in walls and floors declined from 1973 to 1977, rose sharply in 1978 because of a change in the way questions were grouped, and then began to decline again. But water leakage declined from 1973 to 1976, was stable from 1976 through 1978, jumped in 1979, fell from 1979 to 1981, and jumped in 1983, for reasons we cannot explain. And reports of mice and rats fluctuated unpredictably, perhaps because of variations in weather conditions but perhaps for other reasons. Respondents' reports of neighborhood conditions that are 'bothersome' appear to be distorted by class-related differences in what people find 'bothersome.' High-income respondents are as likely as low-income respondents to report bothersome levels of crime, for example, even though the National Crime Survey always finds that high-income respondents are less likely to be victimized.

41. Although some of the dependent variables in Table 5.4 are dichotomous, we present OLS rather than logistic regressions because the OLS coefficients are easier to interpret and the standard errors are of no importance. Just as in previous sections, our analyses weight all individuals equally. Because the Census does not ask individuals living in institutions or in group quarters about their housing conditions, our analyses of housing conditions are also restricted to household members. Adding individuals in group quarters to our Census samples increased the number of individuals in the bottom income decile by about a fifth in all three Census years but had almost no effect on the number of individuals in any other decile. It follows that unless conditions in group quarters changed dramatically between 1960 and 1980 excluding individuals in group quarters should not bias trend estimates for the bottom decile. We do not know what would happen if we were to include inmates of institutions and the homeless.

42. This conclusion appears to be at odds with the results for rooms per person in Table 5.6, which show a marked decline in inequality between the bottom and the middle during the 1970s. Note, however, that the poor have substantially *more* rooms per person than middle-income households in both 1970 and 1980. This surprising situation reflects the fact that elderly homeowners often continue to live in relatively large houses even if their incomes are very low.

43. When we analyzed the Census, we worked with public use samples. Since we assumed that all household members derived some benefit from the

amenities we measured, we weighted all persons equally. Unfortunately, our AHS data come from published tables that weight all households equally. Because the AHS weights large and small households equally, crowding appears to be less common in Figure 5.7 than in Table 5.5.

44. Figures 5.7 through 5.11 are based on published tables that divide households into about a dozen income categories. We assigned all households in a given income category to the percentile of the income distribution occupied by the median household in that income category. These midpoints are indicated by dots, squares, and triangles in Figures 5.7 through 5.12.

45. Using CPS data on the eight largest metropolitan areas in the United States, Blank and Rosen (1989) found strong evidence that doubling up increased between 1977 and 1987, especially among the poor. They had no measure of crowding, however, and they found only a small and statistically unreliable increase in the mean size of poor households. Their results therefore provide only equivocal support for the conclusion that doubling up led to more crowding in the early 1980s. Their findings could differ from ours because they use different dependent variables, because they focus exclusively on large cities, because they measure the mean annual change from 1977 to 1987 rather than the from 1979 to 1983, or because of random sampling error.

46. The Census does not ask households whether they got a federal housing subsidy, but it does show a sharp increase between 1970 and 1980 in the proportion of low-income households living in units that were less than ten years old. The AHS, in turn, shows a parallel increase in the proportion of low-income households receiving federal housing subsidies.

47. Trucks accounted for 22.0 percent of total registrations in 1980, 17.7 percent in 1970, and 16.5 percent in 1960 (US Bureau of the Census, 1990b, Table 1029). The 1980 Census data also indicate that 22 percent of vehicles kept at home were trucks, so we assume that the figure was about 18 percent in 1970 and 17 percent in 1960. If these estimates are correct, the bias introduced by ignoring trucks is likely to have increased from 1960 to 1980, but not enough to be of much practical importance.

48. There is no public use version of the 1962–3 HIS, but the National Center for Health Statistics (NCHS) provided us with an extract from the 1962–3 data. We are grateful for NCHS's considerable investment of time and effort in creating this extract.

49. Freeman *et al.* (1987) report that the number of people who visited a physician in the previous year decreased between 1982 and 1986. They also report that the decrease was greatest among the poor. Their results come from two telephone surveys. The first was done by Louis Harris and Associates and included information on 6700 adults and children. The second consisted of 10 130 respondents. These surveys differed in several important ways from the HIS survey. They also differ in important respects from one another, so we do not have much confidence in trend estimates derived from them.

50. Public use data on doctor visits are not available from the HIS until 1969.

51. Once again we present results from OLS rather than logistic regressions because the OLS coefficients are easier to interpret and the standard

errors are of little interest. The HIS income data are categorical. We estimated the mean for the top interval from Census data. We coded all other intervals at the midpoint of the interval. We then took the logarithms of these values.

52. For a more detailed analysis of doctor visits in 1980 that controls self-reported health status, the presence of acute and chronic conditions, and bed days in the past year, see Mayer (1991).

53. The 1990 Census did make some effort to count the homeless, but based on observers' accounts we have no confidence in the results. For data on the rise of homelessness during the 1980s see Burt (1992).

54. Since 1972 the CEX has conducted both a quarterly 'interview' survey and a 'diary' survey covering a single week. In the 1984 interview survey, the top income quintile spent 2.5 times more than the bottom quintile on food (Bureau of Labor Statistics, 1989a, Tables 5 to 8). In the 1984 diary survey, the top quintile spent 3.1 times more than the bottom quintile on food (Bureau of Labor Statistics, 1989b, Table 21). The bottom quintile reported mean annual food expenditures of $2065 in the interview survey compared to only $1886 in the diary survey, suggesting that poor respondents may not keep very complete diaries. The top quintile, in contrast, reported mean food expenditures of $5852 in the diary survey compared to $5190 in the interview survey, suggesting that the top quintile tended to forget a lot of small expenditures on food, perhaps especially when it was consumed away from home.

55. Sample addresses are actually visited five times, but the first visit is used only to collect demographic and 'bounding' data. Four quarters of detailed expenditure data are collected at any given address.

56. The CPS finds that about 19 percent of all household heads have moved to their present address within the past twelve months (US Bureau of the Census, 1990b, Table 1275). Most of these movers are filling a vacancy created when another household moved out, but some are moving into newly constructed units or units that have been vacant for a long time. When turnover occurred at a sample address during the 1980s, BLS retained both the old and the new CU in its quarterly samples. When we combine quarterly samples to get an annual sample we must retain both CUs (as separate units of observation) and make their weights proportional to the number of quarters they spent at the sample address. This means that while the unweighted percentage of CUs with less than four quarters of data is quite high (43.4 percent in 1984–5), the weighted percentage is considerably lower (25.5 percent in 1984–5). Even the weighted percentage with less than four quarters of data exceeds the percentage of movers, however, because some CUs miss an interview for reasons unrelated to moving.

References

Atkinson, Anthony B. (1970) 'On the Measurement of Inequality,' *Journal of Economic Theory*, **II**, 244–63.

Blank, Rebecca, and Harvey Rosen (1989) 'Recent Trends in Housing Conditions among the Urban Poor.' Cambridge: National Bureau of Economic Research, Working Paper No. 2886.

Bosworth, Barry, Gary Burtless, and John Sabelhaus (1991) 'The Decline in Savings: Evidence from Household Surveys,' *Brookings Papers on Economic Activity*, No. 1, pp. 183–255.

Bureau of Labor Statistics (1971) *Consumer Expenditures and Income* (Bulletin 1684) (Washington: US Government Printing Office).

Bureau of Labor Statistics (1978) *Consumer Expenditure Survey: Integrated Diary and Interview Survey Data, (1972–73* (Bulletin 1992) (Washington: US Government Printing Office).

Bureau of Labor Statistics (1989a) *Consumer Expenditure Interview Survey: Quarterly Data, 1984–87* (Bulletin 2332) (Washington: US Government Printing Office).

Bureau of Labor Statistics (1989b) *Consumer Expenditure Survey: Integrated Survey Data, 1984–86* (Bulletin 2333) (Washington: US Government Printing Office).

Burt, Martha (1992) *Over the Edge: The Growth of Homelessness in the 1980s* (New York: Russell Sage Foundation).

Coder, John (1991) 'Exploring Nonsampling Errors in the Wage and Salary Income Data from the March Current Population Survey.' Washington: Housing and Household Economic Statistics Division, US Bureau of the Census.

Coleman, Richard, Lee Rainwater, and Kent McClelland (1978) *Social Standing in America* (New York: Basic Books).

Council of Economic Advisors (1991) *Economic Report of the President* (Washington: US Government Printing Office).

Cutler, David and Lawrence Katz (1991) 'Macroeconomic Performance and the Disadvantaged.' Cambridge: National Bureau of Economic Research (forthcoming in *Brookings Papers on Economic Activity*, 1992).

Edin, Kathryn (1992) 'Surviving the Welfare System: How Welfare Recipients in Chicago Make Ends Meet,' *Social Problems*, **38**, 462–74.

Edin, Kathryn and Christopher Jencks (1992) 'Reforming Welfare,' in Christopher Jencks, *Rethinking Social Policy* (Cambridge: Harvard University Press) pp. 204–35.

Freeman, H. E. and R. J. Blendon, L. H. Aiken, S. Sudman, C. F. Mullinix and C. R. Corey (1987) 'Americans Report on Their Access to Health Care,' *Health Affairs* (Spring).

Friedman, Milton (1957) *A Theory of the Consumption Function* (Princeton: Princeton University Press).

Garner, Thesia (1989) 'Consumer Expenditures and Inequality: An Analysis Using the Gini Coefficient.' Washington: U.S. Department of Labor, Bureau of Labor Statistics, Working Paper 197.

Jacobs, Eva, and Stephanie Shipp (1990) 'A History of the US Consumer Expenditure Survey.' Washington: US Department of Labor, Bureau of Labor Statistics.

Jencks, Christopher, Susan Bartlett, Mary Corcoran, James Crouse, David Eaglesfield, Gregory Jackson, Kent McClelland, Peter Mueser, Michael

Olnecks, Joseph Schwartz, Sherry Ward, and Jill Williams (1979) *Who Gets Ahead?* (New York: Basic Books).

Karoly, Lynn (1990) 'The Trend in Inequality among Families, Individuals, and Workers in the United States: A Twenty-five Year Perspective' (Santa Monica: The Rand Corporation).

Lazear, Edward and Robert Michel (1980) 'Family Size and the Distribution of Real Per Capita Income.' *American Economic Review*, **70**, 91–107.

Lillard, Lee, James P. Smith, and Finis Welch (1986) 'What Do We Really Know about Wages? The Importance of Nonreporting and Census Imputation,' *Journal of Political Economy*, **94**, 489–506.

Mack, Joanna and Stewart Lansley (1985) *Poor Britain* (London: George Allen and Unwin).

Mayer, Susan E. and Christopher Jencks (1989) 'Poverty and The Distribution of Material Hardship,' *Journal of Human Resources*, **24**, 88–114.

Mayer, Susan E. (1991) 'Are There Economic Barriers to Seeing a Doctor?' University of Chicago, Harris School of Public Policy Studies, Working Paper, 92–6.

National Center for Health Statistics (1964–1991) 'Current Estimates from the National Health Interview Survey, United States,' issued annually. *Vital and Health Statistics*, Series 10 (Washington: US Government Printing Office).

Rainwater, Lee (1974) *What Money Buys* (New York: Basic Books).

Sewell, William and Robert Hauser (1975) *Education, Occupation, and Earnings* (New York: Academic Press).

Slesnick, Daniel (1991) 'Consumption, Needs, and Inequality' (Austin: Department of Economics, University of Texas).

Townsend, Peter (1979) *Poverty in the United Kingdom: A Survey of Household Resources and Standards of Living* (Los Angeles: University of California Press).

US Bureau of the Census (1989) 'Money Income of Households, Families, and Persons in the United States: 1987,' *Current Population Reports*, Series P-60, No. 162 (Washington: US Government Printing Office).

US Bureau of the Census (1990a) 'Money Income and Poverty Status in the United States: 1989,' *Current Population Reports*, Series P-60, No. 168 (Washington: US Government Printing Office).

US Bureau of the Census (1990b) *Statistical Abstract of the United States, 1990* (Washington: Government Printing Office).

US Bureau of the Census (1991) 'Money Income of Households, Families, and Persons in the United States: 1988 and 1989,' *Current Population Reports*, Series P-60, No. 172 (Washington: US Government Printing Office).

Van der Gaag, Jacques and Eugene Smolensky (1981) 'True Household Equivalence Scales and Characteristics of the Poor in the United States,' *Review of Income and Wealth*, **28**(1), 17–28.

Vaughan, Denton (1984) *Using Subjective Assessments of Income to Estimate Family Equivalence Scales: A Report of Work in Progress* (Washington: Social Security Administration).

Comment

Paul Ryscavage

The paper by Mayer and Jenks is a continuation of their work in the area of material well-being. It is set in the context of the recent concern over growing income inequality. This development has received much attention from researchers, as well as the media, and has been heightened by the economic slump of the early 1990s.

According to Mayer and Jencks, while the official income statistics of the Census Bureau suggest a trend toward greater income inequality during the 1970s and 1980s, data on expenditures and other measures of material welfare do not reflect such a trend. The problem, they contend, is the income statistics and the methods used to measure inequality. According to them, the Current Population Survey (CPS), the source of the income data, has experienced a growing problem of nonresponse in recent decades. Furthermore, the Gini index and shares of aggregate income, the inequality measures used by the Census Bureau, do not reflect in what part of the distribution inequality is occurring. Consequently, conclusions based on the CPS data and analysis about a growing underclass and increasing disparities in material well-being are challenged by Mayer and Jencks.

The first major issue in this paper, of course, is the quality of the CPS income data and their usefulness as a measure of material well-being. This issue is not new. The measurement of material well-being over time, obviously, is no simple matter. Not only do difficult technical issues exist, but also theoretical and conceptual ones. These latter issues are really never addressed in the paper, and to my way of thinking, are no less problematic in the measurement of material well-being. For example, the inclusion of taxes and exclusion of capital gains in the CPS money income concept has always been controversial. More recently the exclusion of noncash benefits from the money income concept has raised questions about the Federal government's measure of poverty.

The Census Bureau has been not only very aware of these issues but responsive to them. In 1985, the Census Bureau sponsored a conference on the measurement of noncash benefits which addressed many of the conceptual issues regarding the money income concept

204

and its use in the measurement of poverty (U.S. Bureau of the Census, 1985). Experts on income measurement were invited. One of the results of this conference was the development of a recurring series of income estimates showing the effects of certain noncash benefits and taxes on the official income and poverty estimates (U.S. Bureau of the Census, 1988).

The issue of nonresponse – what Mayer and Jencks are most worried about – is obviously always a concern of the Census Bureau. The degree to which the CPS aggregate income estimates measure up to independent estimates, or benchmarks, of money income is periodically reported on in the Census Bureau's reports on money income (U. S. Bureau of the Census, 1991). In addition, special analyses of nonsampling errors in the CPS estimates also are periodically conducted, the most recent focusing on the wage and salary income distribution (Coder, 1991). This study, which involved matching CPS wage and salary income data to information from the Internal Revenue Service, found that while the most serious error problems were concentrated at the bottom and top of the distribution, the overall distributions of wage and salary income from both sources were very similar.

It may also surprise some readers of this paper to learn that the Census Bureau as well has initiated research into 'extended' measures of material well-being. In fact, a report on this topic is scheduled to be published in 1992 (U.S. Bureau of the Census, 1992). Consequently, the Census Bureau has acknowledged that measures of well-being, such as those discussed by Mayer and Jencks, can provide useful perspective when interpreting the official money income estimates derived from the CPS.

Related to the 'quality' issue is the issue of income inequality measures used by the Census Bureau. The Gini index and the shares of income received by fifths of households are the two principal inequality measures appearing in Census reports on income. However, income data are available in these reports for users to construct a variety of inequality measures which can focus on the bottom half or the top half of the distribution. Furthermore, Census Bureau researchers have used other inequality measures – the variance of the natural logarithm, the Gini index, the Theil index, and the Atkinson's measures of inequality – in their research (Green, Coder, and Ryscavage, 1992). This research revealed that these other measures corroborated the increases in U.S. wage inequality that were reflected in the Gini index and shares of aggregate wages measure. And, of course, many researchers have confirmed the increase in income inequality using other measures as well.

The second major issue concerns the apparent inconsistency between the trends in income inequality from the CPS and the trends in inequality of expenditures and aspects of material well-being. Regarding trends in expenditures, Mayer and Jencks create their expenditures trend line from various Bureau of Labor Statistics (BLS) consumer expenditure surveys. By their own admission, these surveys differed from one another in a number of important respects, such as response rates, definitions, and procedures. In my opinion, this seriously weakens the credibility of the comparison. But even if the data are accepted as valid representations of expenditure patterns, the trend lines presented in Figures 5.5a, 5.5b, 5.6a, and 5.6b, especially from the early 1970s to the 1980s, seem to contradict their conclusion of an inconsistency. After I 'eyeball' these trends, I would conclude that the expenditure trend lines are *more* similar to the income trend lines than dissimilar.

The information they present on disparities in material well-being, as reflected in housing conditions, automobiles, telephones, and health status, is interesting. These type of data and analysis may indeed be useful in identifying specific areas of material well-being which need to be addressed. However, this approach, I believe, has even more problems with it than the expenditure data approach when the issue is assessing changes in economic inequality. It is fragmentary. Even if one focuses on those items considered as basic necessities, as Mayer and Jencks attempt to do, the evidence is still incomplete. The specific array of goods and services considered to be necessities is large and no doubt changes over time.

More generally, I worry more about the confounding effects of relative price differences and taste differences over time. How does one control, for example, for substitution effects originating from price changes or changes in preferences across income classes? They concede that a measurement problem would exist with certain goods in different stages of the 'product cycle,' that is, products whose prices decline as they are introduced into the middle and low-income household markets. Problems such as these also make it difficult, in my opinion, to make judgments about trends in material well-being from specific consumption items.

In short, I am not convinced by the evidence presented in this paper that measures of expenditures and consumer goods provide us with a better sense of the course of material well-being in this society than the official money income estimates. Despite the problems with the CPS income data, they are the best indicators available to us as to the 'command over goods and services' of households.

References

Coder, John (1991) 'Exploring Nonsampling Errors in the Wage and Salary Income Data from the March Current Population Survey.' Washington: Housing and Household Economic Statistics Division, U.S. Bureau of the Census.

Green, Gordon, John Coder, and Paul Ryscavage (1992) 'International Comparisons of Earnings Inequality for Men in the 1980s,' *Review of Income and Wealth* (forthcoming).

U.S. Bureau of the Census (1985) *Conference on the Measurement of Non-cash Benefits, Proceedings . . . Vol. 1* (Washington: U.S. Bureau of the Census).

U.S. Bureau of the Census (1988) 'Measuring the Effect of Benefits and Taxes on Income and Poverty: 1986,' *Current Population Report*. Series P-60, No. 164-RD-1.

U.S. Bureau of the Census (1991) 'Money Income of Households, Families, and Persons in the United States: 1988 and 1989,' *Current Population Reports*. Series P-60, No. 172 (Washington: U.S. Government Printing Office).

U.S. Bureau of the Census (1992) 'Extended Measures of Well-being: Selected Data from the 1984 Survey of Income and Program Participation' (forthcoming).

Part II

Anatomy of Income Inequality

6 Social Security Annuities and Transfers: Distributional and Tax Implications

Edward N. Wolff

6.1. INTRODUCTION

The division of social security (OASI) benefits into an annuity portion and a transfer portion has been well documented. I have discussed this issue extensively in previous work (1987b; 1988; Greenwood and Wolff, 1990; and forthcoming), as did Burkhauser and Warlick (1981) previously. My methodology is quite similar to theirs. The annuity portion is defined as the benefit level the worker would receive on the basis of his (her) contributions into the social security system (OASI) if the system were *actuarially fair*. The calculation is based on the worker's estimated earnings history and actual social security tax rates. The transfer portion is the difference between the actual social security benefit received and the actuarially fair annuity equivalent. As we shall see below, it has been uniformly positive for workers who have retired on or before 1983.

Burkhauser and Warlick examined the relative proportions of annuity versus transfer benefits by income class and age group. However, they did not conduct an extensive examination of the overall distributional implications of the social security transfer portion. Nor did they consider the tax implications of treating social security transfers as taxable income. These are the principal subjects of the current paper.

With regard to the distributional implications of the social security system, I will examine three sets of issues. First, I will consider what the relative magnitudes have been of the annuity and transfer portions of social security income. Since I have data for three years, a related issue is whether the relative proportions have changed over time. Second, I will consider how the social security transfer portion has affected the distribution of income among elderly households. Has the transfer component been neutral or has it tended to redistribute income toward lower income elderly households? Third, the same issue can be addressed with regard to household wealth, in which social security benefit flows are transformed (capitalized) into wealth equivalents.

From a policy point of view, the more interesting issue is how do the total taxes of the elderly change with the removal of the exclusion of social security transfer income – that is, when social security transfer income is treated as taxable income. There are three questions of interest. First, how does the change in tax treatment affect the post-tax distribution of income. Second, which groups of elderly are most affected by the change in tax treatment. Third, what is the total change in the magnitude of tax revenues.

As a final point of policy interest, I will also consider whether the extra revenues generated by the new tax treatment of social security income can serve as a 'social security capital fund' to reduce the growing wealth gap among age groups in the U.S. As will become apparent in the analysis, the social security system has been quite generous to today's elderly, providing them with benefits far in excess of their contributions into the system. Moreover, young families have fared rather poorly over the last several decades in regard to their income and wealth accumulation. I will propose a policy vehicle below, called a 'social security capital fund', which can serve as an additional source of capital for today's young workers. The source of the funding can potentially come from the extra tax revenues from elderly households. It is thus also of interest to analyze whether the additional tax revenues are large or small relative to the wealth holdings of young households and whether such a fund can make a significant difference in the well-being of younger families.

My analysis will be based on the most recent comprehensive wealth survey currently available, the 1983 Survey of Consumer Finances (see Avery *et al.*, 1984). The file contains extensive information on the net worth of households at the microdata level. The sample also includes a high-income supplement. In my sample, the asset and liability figures are aligned to national balance sheet totals for the household sector (see Wolff, 1987a, for details).[1]

6.2 BACKGROUND AND MOTIVATION

Between 1962 and 1983 the mean net wealth of households in the United States showed a cumulative growth of 49 percent after accounting for increases due to inflation, an average annual rate of about 2 percent. During this period, there was substantial variation in how growth was spread among different sectors of the population, particularly with regard to age. In previous work (Greenwood and Wolff, 1988), we documented a fairly substantial shift in family wealth away from the young and old to the middle-aged.

The most significant finding is that the average wealth of younger age cohorts declined relative to the overall mean between 1962 and 1983. The mean wealth of households under 35 declined from 27 percent of the overall mean to 20 percent. The corresponding figures for households under 45 are 50 percent in 1962 and 40 percent in 1983. On net, over the two decades, younger families were worse off in relative terms. The average wealth of households under 35 grew by 0.58 percent per year in real terms, compared to 1.90 percent overall, and the mean wealth of families under 45 increased by 0.80 percent per year. The relative wealth of families 70 years and older also decreased over the two decades, from 46 percent above average in 1962 to 22 percent above average in 1983.

The big winners over the two decades were families between ages 45 and 69. Their average wealth increased from 1.35 to 1.74 of the overall mean, or at an annual rate of 3.10 percent. Families in the 45–49 age bracket improved their relative position the most over the 1962–83 period, from 0.98 of average in 1962 to 1.77 in 1983; families in ages 60–64 increased from 1.34 to 1.73; and those in ages 65–69 increased from 1.74 to 2.38.

The net result over the two decades was a redistribution of wealth from the young (under 45) and the old (70 and over) to the middle-aged (45–69). Between 1962 and 1983, peak wealth moved from the 55–59 age group to the 65–69 age group, and the peak became substantially higher. Over the two decades, the resulting age-wealth profile thus became 'humpier', with the peak higher (2.38 compared to 1.82) and occurring for an older age group (65–69 age bracket compared to the 55–59 age bracket).

This changing pattern of wealth holdings by age group has profound implications for the access to resources in our society. In particular, resources are shifting away from those most in need, namely younger families and the very old, to those of middle age.

Especially hard hit are young families with children. The shifting age-wealth profile thus has rather disturbing implications for the well-being of children. The most obvious is a falling homeownership rate among young families, and, indeed, a rising rate of homelessness. Rising poverty among children is another implication of the change in the availability to resources among age groups. Since childhood poverty also affects educational achievement, the shift in available resources may also result in a lower skilled labor force in the future, lower productivity, and a falling standard of living in our society.

6.3   POLICY ANALYSIS

This paper will examine one potential policy vehicle for tilting the age-wealth profile back in favor of the young. This involves a mechanism of taxing social security benefits and using the proceeds as a fund of available credit for younger workers. The proposal is directly related to a plan currently in effect in Singapore, which allows younger workers to borrow against accumulated pension savings. These two plans have the effect of increasing the resources available to younger families. My proposal will also provide a *redistribution* of resources from older families to younger ones. In addition, it may directly increase savings, since the funds can be earmarked for investment purposes only.

The proposed mechanism will work in the following way: Social security benefits received by workers consist of two components. The first is an annuity or 'pension equivalent', which is based on the individual's contribution to the social security system over his (her) lifetime. The pension equivalent can be imputed with available data. The second, or residual portion, is a direct transfer payment from the government to the individual. Current retirees, as well as workers in their 50s and early 60s, have benefited from legislative changes in the social security law which provide them with significantly greater social security income than would be justified by their contribution into the social security system. The government is, as it were, providing them with extra transfer income.

The annuity or pension component should be left untaxed, since this portion was already treated as taxable income when the individual received the wage or salary income. The other portion is simply a transfer payment, and this should be treated as ordinary taxable income like property income. Indeed, this portion was never taxed by the government, since it does not devolve from the social security contributions.

The proceeds can then be used as an investment fund for younger workers. In a sense, the worker is using his or her contributions for OASI as collateral for a loan. The loan may be restricted to housing, for educational purposes, or for other specified investments. Since the federal government has already set up loan programs for many purposes, including housing and student loans, this part of the proposal is by no means revolutionary. The only new provision is to treat OASI contributions as collateral for loans. However, it should be noted that the security of such loans is airtight, since it is the federal government itself which receives the OASI proceeds. Moreover, the funding for this program is made available by the increased revenues from taxing social security benefits. It is, of course, necessary to make the requisite calculations to determine the extent to which such increased revenues can provide investments for younger workers and the distributional consequences of such a program.

6.4 ACCOUNTING FRAMEWORK AND ESTIMATION PROCEDURES

A wealth accounting framework is employed in order to divide social security benefits into their constituent parts. Let us first define conventional household wealth, HW, as the sum of (i) owner-occupied housing and other real estate; (ii) bank deposits and other liquid assets; (iii) bonds and other securities; (iv) corporate stock; (v) equity in unincorporated business; (vi) trust fund equity; (vii) the cash surrender value of life insurance; and (viii) the cash surrender value of pension plans; less the sum of (i) mortgage debt and (ii) other household debt.[2]

There are two forms of social security 'wealth' considered here. The first is called social security entitlement wealth, *SSEW*. Following Feldstein (1974, 1976), I define SSEW as the present value of the discounted stream of future social security benefits. For symmetry, we can also define (private) pension wealth, *PW*, as the present value of the discounted stream of future (private) pension benefits. The second is social security annuity wealth, *SSAW*. This is defined as the accumulated contributions (OASI) made by employees and employers into the social security system. This represents the savings-equivalent of these social security contributions if the contributions were put into a pension reserve. Like a pension fund, these contributions are accumulated over time with the going interest rate. In effect, social security contributions are treated as if they are made into a 'defined contribution' pension plan, the benefits from which are based directly on the contributions. SSAW thus represents what the total wealth held by or for the benefit of the household sector would have been if social security contributions were placed in a pension reserve.[3]

Estimation. The imputation of social security wealth involves a large number of steps, which I will summarize here (see Wolff, 1987b, or Wolff, 1988, for further details). I begin with entitlement wealth. For retirees, (r) the procedure is straightforward. Let *SSB* be the social security benefit currently received by the retiree. Then,

$$SSEW = \int_0^{LE} SSB\ e^{(g - \delta)t}\ dt \tag{1}$$

where *LE* is the conditional life expectancy, *g* the expected average annual rate of growth of real social security benefits over time for retirees, and δ is the real discount rate.[4]

For pension wealth, the procedure is analogous. Among current beneficiaries, let PB be the pension benefit currently being received by the retiree. If it is assumed that pension benefits remain fixed in real terms over time for a particular beneficiary (as was generally true in 1983), then pension wealth is given by:

$$PW = \int_0^{LE} PB\ e^{-\delta t}\ dt \tag{2}$$

Social security accumulations consist of the accumulated contributions (OASI) made by employees and employers into the social security system on behalf of each individual. This is a hypothetical concept, since there are no actual reserves in the social security system that correspond to this amount.[5] It is first necessary to estimate social security accumulations for current workers. The first step is to estimate annual earnings for each worker from the start of working life to the present. These are based on earnings functions, which are estimated separately by sex, race, and schooling level. In particular, the sample is divided into 16 groups by the following characteristics: (i) white and non-white; (ii) male and female, and (iii) less than 12 years of schooling, 12 years of schooling, 13 to 15 years of schooling, and 16 or more years. For each group, an earnings equation is estimated as follows:

$$E_i = b_0 + b_1 A_i + b_2 A_i^2 + b_3 S_i + \epsilon_i,$$

where E_i is current annual earnings of individual i, A_i is current age, S_i educational attainment,[6] and ϵ is a stochastic error term. The earnings function for individual i is then adjusted so that it passes through the individual's earnings in the current year.[7] Then,

$$E_i^*(t) = [\hat{b}_0 + \hat{b}_1(A_i + t) + \hat{b}_2(A_i + t)^2 + \hat{b}_3 S_i] \cdot E_i / \hat{E}_i(t)$$

gives predicted earnings for individual i at age $A_i + t$, assuming no growth in overall real earnings. Accumulated earnings, AE, from the start of working life to the present, are then estimated on the basis of the actual real growth in average earnings and the real discount rate:

$$AE_i = \sum_{t=-t_0}^{0} E_i^*(t) \cdot K_y$$

where t_0 is the number of years at work (estimated as current age less years of schooling less 5), y_c is the current year (1983), y is the calendar year given by $y_c + t$, k_y is the real growth of average earnings in year y,[8] δ_y is the real discount rate in year y, and

$$K_y = \prod_{j=y}^{y_c} (1 + \delta_j - k_j),$$

which gives the present value of earnings in year y.[9]

Future earnings, FE, from current age to age 65, are estimated in analogous fashion.[10] Two values are assumed for future real earnings growth (k): one percent per year and two percent per year. Results are similar for the two values and are shown below for only k equal to 0.01. The total lifetime earnings of worker i, TLE_i, is then given by:

$$TLE_i = AE_i + FE_i.$$

In the second step, it is assumed that each worker was continuously employed from the end of schooling to the current year y_c (1983 in this case) and that the employment and coverage status of each person remained the same over the person's work life.[11] Let ζ_y be either twice the employee social security tax rate in year y or the self-employed tax rate in that year, depending on the employment status of the worker, and $SSMAX_y$ be the maximum taxable wage base in year y in constant (1983) dollars. The social security wage base, $SSWAGE$, in year y for a covered worker with earnings E_i^* is then given by:

$$SSWAGE(y) = \text{MIN} \, [E_i^* \, (y - 1983) \cdot H_y, SSMAX_y]$$

where MIN indicates the minimum value of the two arguments and

$$H_y = \prod_{j=y}^{y_c} (1 - k_j),$$

Then, social security annuity wealth for covered workers is given by

$$SSAW_{w,\,i} = \sum_{y=y_0}^{y_c} \zeta_y \, SSWAGE_i \, (y)F_y \tag{3}$$

where $y_0 = 1983 - t_0$, the year in which the person began working, and

$$F_y = \prod_{j=y}^{y_c} (1 - \delta_j),$$

For current beneficiaries, the appropriate concept is the present value of benefits that would be strictly calculated as an annuity on the person's accumulated contributions. Unfortunately, there is no information available on past earnings or contributions into the social security system in the SCF database. It is assumed that a retiree in the nth percentile of social security benefits for his age group was also in the nth percentile of the distribution of total lifetime earnings at retirement (assumed to be age 65). $SSAW_{w,\,n}$ is then computed for a worker of age 65 in the nth percentile of the earnings distribution. This value is then appropriately discounted, depending on the year of retirement of the beneficiary, to obtain $SSAW_b$.

The difference between $SSEW$ and $SSAW$ is what I will call 'social security transfer wealth,' $SSTW$. It can be defined formally as:

$$SSTW = SSEW - SSAW \tag{4}$$

Finally, we can define total household wealth, TW, as follows:[12]

$$TW = HW + PW + SSEW \tag{5}$$

Discount rate. Two sets of discount rates are used in the calculations. The first set is based on treasury bill rates. Before 1983, the discount rate is the real one-year treasury bill rate in each year, estimated as the nominal one-year rate less the change in the CPI. For 1983 onward, the real 10-year treasury bill rate is used, estimated as the current nominal rate less the average rate of increase of the Consumer Price Index (CPI) over the previous 10 years. The second is based on the average annual real rate of return on the average household portfolio over the 1962–83 period. I calculated that the average annual real rate of return for the average household portfolio over this period was 3.28 percent. (The source is Greenwood and Wolff, 1990.)

6.5 DISTRIBUTIONAL IMPLICATIONS

6.5.1 Relative Dimension of Social Security Transfers and Annuities

It is first of interest to examine the overall ratio of the social security transfer component to the total social security benefit. This is shown in the last line of Table 6.1 for all households 65 and over. Overall, social security transfers amounted to 66 percent of total social security income for households 65 and over in 1983 on the basis of the treasury bill discount rate. Burkhauser and Warlick (1981), whose results are based on the 1973 Social Security Exact Match file, which merges individual records from the 1973 Current Population Survey with OASI earnings and benefit records, calculated a ratio of 0.73. In previous work, I estimated a ratio of 0.85 for the 1969 data. Another study which attempted comparable calculations is Hurd and Shoven's (1985) paper. They computed an overall ratio of social security transfer income to total social security benefits of about 0.80 for 1969 on the basis of the Retirement History Survey. These results together indicate that social security transfers comprise a rather large (perhaps, surprisingly large) proportion of social security income. In other words, the benefits received from the social security system have far outweighed the annuity value of the social security contributions. Thus, much of the social security benefits received by retirees is a pure government transfer, over and above the actual contributions made into the system by the retirees.

Table 6.1   The ratio of social security transfer wealth (SSTW) to total
social security entitlement wealth (SSEW): Summary Table, 1983[a]

	T-Bill rate[b]	Portfolio rate[c]
1. *All*		
a. g = 0.01	0.63	0.57
b. g = 0.02	0.66	0.61
c. g = 0.03	0.69	0.65
2. *Age group[d]*		
a. 65–69	0.63	0.61
b. 70–74	0.65	0.60
c. 75–79	0.68	0.60
d. 80 and over	0.73	0.64
3. *Family type*		
a. Married couples	0.67	0.63
b. Single males	0.56	0.49
c. Single females	0.66	0.61
4. *Race[e]*		
a. Whites	0.66	0.62
b. Blacks	0.61	0.45
Addendum: Overall ratio of social security transfer income to total social security income	0.66	0.61

[a] *Source*: Own calculations from the 1983 SCF file. The parameter g is the
expected average annual rate of growth of real social security benefits over
time. Calculations are performed with g = 0.02 unless otherwise indicated.
[b] Based on the annual one-year real Treasury bill rate until 1983 and the
10-year real treasury bill rate from 1983 thereafter.
[c] Based on the average annual real rate of return on the average household
portfolio, 1962–83. The source is Greenwood and Wolff (1990).
[d] Age group is based on the age of the head of household.
[e] Based on head of household. Families with Hispanic surnames are classified
as white or black, depending on race. Whites include Asians and other races.

The three methodologies are quite different. Burkhauser and Warlick based their computations on actual earnings and OASI histories;
Hurd and Shoven based theirs on actual earnings histories, though
imputed social security contributions; whereas mine are based on
imputation techniques for both earnings histories and OASI contributions. Despite the differences, the results still strongly suggest
that the transfer component of social security income has been declining over time (that is, the annuity portion has been rising). This is

mainly a consequence of the fact that the system started up in 1937, so that older retirees payed into the system for fewer years and had much lower contribution rates than more recent retirees.

Another source of difference between my results and those of Burkhauser and Warlick is that they use a rate of return in accumulating social security benefits which is equal to the annual rate of return on government bonds plus the average annual increase in average stock prices. This return is higher than the straight treasury bill rates, which will have the effect of increasing the relative proportion of the annuity component in social security income. I also made a second set of calculations on the basis of the average annual real rate of return on the average household portfolio over the 1962–83 period. On the basis of this discount rate, I calculated an overall ratio of social security transfers to benefits among elderly households of 0.61. As predicted, this is lower than the 0.66 ratio based on the treasury bill rates, though the difference is not substantial.

It is next of interest to compare the sensitivity of the results to the value of g, the expected average annual rate of growth of real social security benefits over time (panel 1 of Table 6.1). For this, we look at the ratio of social security transfer wealth (SSTW) to total social security entitlement wealth (*SSEW*). The value of *SSEW* increases with g, since the value of future social security benefits are higher. Since *SSAW* does not vary with g, the value of social security transfers also rises with g. On net, the ratio of *SSTW* to *SSEW* is found to increase with g, though the differences are not great (0.63 to 0.69 in 1983 on the basis of the treasury bill rates for g varying from 0.01 to 0.03).

The ratio of *SSTW* to *SSEW* is also found to increase systematically with age group. In 1983, the ratio varies from 0.65 for those in age group 65–69 to 0.73 for those 80 and over on the basis of the treasury bill rates. Burkhauser and Warlick found a similar result for their 1973 data: The transfer component as a proportion of the total social security benefit varied from 0.52 for the 66–67 age group; 0.71 for age class 72–75; and 0.88 for the 81–85 age group. There are two reasons for this pattern. First, older beneficiaries paid into the social security system over a fewer number of years, since the system started up in 1937, and paid lower tax rates (OASI contribution rates for employees increased from 1 percent in 1937 to 4.8 percent in 1983). Second, Congress periodically increased OASI benefit levels for retirees over the last few decades.

The results also indicate some variation in the relative proportion of social security annuities and transfers by family type and race. The relative size of the transfer component is considerably greater for married couples than single males, though the results are comparable for married couples and single females. Moreover, the transfer component was proportionately greater for white families than black families, and the difference is particularly great on the basis of the household portfolio rate. At first glance, the results seem surprising, since married men have had, on average, higher earnings than single men, white families have had, on average, higher earnings than black families, and in addition, married couples who had worked are penalized by the social security benefit formula, which limits the spousal benefit. However, the explanation stems from differences in life expectancies, LE, between groups. On average, females have longer life expectancies than men, and whites have considerably higher life expectancies than blacks (particularly, as between males). As a result, the value of $SSEW$ is correspondingly lower for males than for females, and for blacks than for whites.[13]

Table 6.2 shows the ratio of social security transfers to the total social security benefit among elderly households by income and wealth class and for selected demographic groups. The results show that the relative size of the transfer component in social security benefits declines with income class over the lower income levels (up to $15 000 in 1983 dollars), remains relatively constant over the middle income range ($15 000 to $75 000), and then declines with income over the upper income classes. This pattern is quite similar by age group, family type, and race. These results are also comparable to those of Burkhauser and Warlick, who found that for all households 65 and over, this ratio generally declines with income for lower income levels (below $4000 in 1973 dollars) and then remains relatively constant above this level. I find an almost identical pattern for the 1983 data. These results indicate that the social security benefit formula is *redistributive* relative to the accumulated value of social security contributions. In other words, the system pays higher benefits relative to total social security contributions for lower income families than higher income ones.

However, interestingly, there is relatively little variation in the proportion of social security transfers in social security income by wealth class. This is most likely due to the less than perfect correlation between income and wealth among elderly families. A similar finding is reported by Hurd and Shoven (1985), who also found no variation in this ratio with wealth class.

Table 6.2 The ratio of social security transfers to total social security benefits by income and wealth class, and age group, family type and race, 1983[a]

	Percent of HH (65+)	Age group[b]					Family type (65+)			Race (65+)[c]	
		65+	65–69	70–74	75–79	80+	Married couple	Single male	Single female	White	Black
A. Income class											
Under $5 000	19.4	0.77	0.74	0.76	0.78	0.78	0.80	0.69	0.77	0.77	0.74
5 000–7 499	15.1	0.68	0.68	0.64	0.71	0.67	0.72	0.53	0.67	0.69	0.64
7 500–9 999	11.8	0.66	0.68	0.62	0.66	0.69	0.69	0.49	0.63	0.67	0.58
10 000–14 999	19.9	0.64	0.61	0.63	0.68	0.73	0.67	0.50	0.61	0.65	0.53
15 000–19 999	9.5	0.66	0.62	0.66	0.71	0.75	0.68	0.53	0.64	0.67	0.53
20 000–24 999	6.5	0.64	0.64	0.57	0.60	0.76	0.64	0.62	0.66	0.64	0.65
25 000–37 499	7.3	0.67	0.66	0.69	0.58	0.72	0.67	0.62	0.68	0.67	0.49
37 500–49 999	4.5	0.61	0.59	0.61	0.65	0.77	0.61	0.48	0.69	0.61	0.61
50 000–74 999	3.2	0.68	0.62	0.73	0.68	0.75	0.70	0.49	0.54	0.69	0.54
75 000–99 999	1.0	0.56	0.64	[d]	0.76	[d]	0.55	[d]	0.66	0.56	[d]
100 000 or more	1.8	0.57	0.44	0.66	0.66	0.67	0.56	0.68	0.56	0.57	0.66
B. Wealth class											
Under $10 000	20.9	0.67	0.65	0.64	0.69	0.70	0.67	0.59	0.69	0.69	0.63
10 000–24 999	10.5	0.68	0.65	0.70	0.67	0.77	0.69	0.48	0.71	0.69	0.64
25 000–37 499	6.7	0.67	0.65	0.65	0.67	0.71	0.69	0.48	0.70	0.69	0.57
37 500–49 999	6.9	0.68	0.66	0.69	0.69	0.72	0.70	0.46	0.68	0.69	0.61
50 000–74 999	12.4	0.66	0.66	0.64	0.70	0.74	0.68	0.49	0.65	0.67	0.51
75 000–99 999	7.3	0.66	0.61	0.64	0.69	0.73	0.66	0.58	0.67	0.67	0.61

continued on page 224

Table 6.2 (continued)

	Percent of HH (65+)	Age group[b]					Family type (65+)			Race (65+)[c]	
		65+	65–69	70–74	75–79	80+	Married couple	Single male	Single female	White	Black
100 000–249 999	19.5	0.65	0.62	0.61	0.67	0.74	0.66	0.61	0.63	0.65	0.59
250 000–499 999	7.9	0.63	0.60	0.66	0.56	0.75	0.63	0.57	0.69	0.63	0.59
500 000 or more	7.9	0.65	0.61	0.67	0.71	0.70	0.66	0.59	0.63	0.65	0.54
C. All	100.0	0.66	0.63	0.65	0.68	0.73	0.67	0.56	0.66	0.66	0.61
No. of HH (m)		16.13	5.59	4.57	3.20	2.77	8.19	1.54	6.41	13.90	2.23
Sample size		816	298	229	161	128	452	76	288	714	102

[a] *Source:* Own calculations from the 1983 SCF file, on the basis of the treasury bill discount rate.
[b] Based on the age of the head of household.
[c] Based on head of household. Families with Hispanic surnames are classified as white or black, depending on race. Whites include Asians and other races.
[d] The cell has fewer than 10 observations.

6.5.2 Social Security Transfers Relative to Total Income and Wealth

The distributional impact of social security transfers depends not on its size relative to total social security income but on its size relative to total income and wealth. These figures are displayed in Table 6.3. Here, considerable variation is evident by income and wealth class. Among all households 65 and over in 1983, the ratio of social security transfer income to total income averages 0.25. However, this ratio declines almost monotonically with income class, from a high of 0.59 for households with income between $7500 and $9999 (1983 dollars) to 0.03 for those with incomes of $100 000 or more.

The ratio of social security transfer income to total income is higher for older age groups (increasing from 0.19 for those aged 65–69 to 0.34 to those 80 and over). This is true despite the fact that average social security income is higher for younger ages, because other sources of income are proportionately lower for the more aged. Likewise, the ratio is lower for married couples than for singles, and for white families than black ones. The rationale is the same: though married couples have higher social security income than singles and white families receive greater social security benefits than black ones, other sources of income are proportionately greater.

The overall ratio of *SSTW* to total household wealth *TW* is 0.13 in 1983. For household 65 and over, the ratio declines monotonically with wealth class, from a high of 0.41 for the lowest to 0.03 for the highest. The ratio also shows a moderate decline by age class. This result is an artifact of the method for computing SSEW, which is partly based on conditional life expectancy. Since this is lower for older people, the value of *SSEW* is likewise smaller, as is the value of *SSTW*. The ratio is also smaller for single males than for married couples and single females. Again, this is a consequence of their lower conditional life expectancy. Finally, the ratio of *SSTW* to *TW* is greater for black households than white ones, because elderly black households hold much lower wealth in other forms.

6.5.3 Distribution of Income and Wealth among the Elderly

I next consider how the social security transfer portion has affected the distribution of income and wealth among elderly households. Has the transfer component been neutral or has it tended to redistribute income toward lower income elderly households? To do this, I

226

Table 6.3 The ratio of social security transfers to total income and wealth by income and wealth class, and age group, family type and race, 1983[a]

	Age group[b]					Family type (65+)			Race (65+)[c]	
	65+	65–69	70–74	75–79	80+	Married couple	Single male	Single female	White	Black
A. Social security transfer income/total income by income class										
Under $5 000	0.55	0.57	0.57	0.53	0.52	0.62	0.62	0.51	0.57	0.48
5 000–7 499	0.57	0.56	0.54	0.61	0.56	0.70	0.64	0.50	0.60	0.48
7 500–9 999	0.59	0.61	0.54	0.65	0.54	0.69	0.55	0.45	0.60	0.54
10 000–14 999	0.50	0.47	0.54	0.48	0.53	0.55	0.49	0.42	0.51	0.44
15 000–19 999	0.41	0.40	0.44	0.41	0.39	0.45	0.46	0.33	0.42	0.34
20 000–24 999	0.31	0.29	0.25	0.30	0.43	0.31	0.37	0.23	0.30	0.32
25 000–37 499	0.27	0.30	0.24	0.20	0.25	0.28	0.38	0.24	0.28	0.08
37 500–49 999	0.15	0.16	0.11	0.22	0.09	0.17	0.24	0.03	0.14	0.38
50 000–74 999	0.10	0.07	0.13	0.06	0.18	0.10	0.09	0.07	0.09	0.11
75 000–99 999	0.04	0.03	0.10	0.07	e	0.03	e	0.27	0.04	e
100 000 or more	0.03	0.02	0.05	0.03	0.02	0.03	0.04	0.05	0.03	e
All	0.25	0.19	0.28	0.31	0.34	0.22	0.33	0.35	0.24	0.35

B. Social security transfer wealth (SSTW) / total wealth (TW) by wealth class[d]

Under $10 000	0.41	0.46	0.40	0.38	0.32	0.50	0.26	0.35	0.43	0.37
10 000–24 999	0.39	0.41	0.46	0.28	0.24	0.45	0.23	0.27	0.41	0.32
25 000–37 499	0.32	0.40	0.35	0.23	0.23	0.41	0.12	0.19	0.35	0.25
37 500–49 999	0.31	0.40	0.34	0.18	0.16	0.40	0.14	0.17	0.32	0.13
50 000–74 999	0.29	0.35	0.23	0.24	0.15	0.35	0.11	0.22	0.29	0.21
75 000–99 999	0.22	0.22	0.20	0.24	0.16	0.26	0.08	0.13	0.21	0.28
100 000–249 999	0.17	0.22	0.16	0.11	0.11	0.20	0.03	0.13	0.17	0.13
250 000–499 999	0.11	0.12	0.10	0.04	0.14	0.11	0.13	0.05	0.11	0.07
500 000 or more	0.03	0.03	0.04	0.02	0.01	0.03	0.01	0.03	0.03	0.04
All	0.13	0.14	0.14	0.12	0.10	0.14	0.08	0.14	0.13	0.21

[a] *Source:* Own calculations from the 1983 SCF file, on the basis of the treasury bill discount rate.

[b] Based on the age of the head of household.

[c] Based on head of household. Families with Hispanic surnames are classified as white or black, depending on race. Whites include Asians and other races.

[d] Total household wealth $TW = HW + PW + SSEW$. The expected average annual rate of growth of real social security benefits, g, is assumed to be 0.02.

[e] The cell has fewer than 10 observations.

compare the actual distribution of income with one in which only the social security annuity is provided to retired households (that is, the transfer component is subtracted from total household income). These results are shown in Table 6.4.

Among all households 65 and over, the Gini coefficient for total family income less total social security income is 0.72. If we add only the social security *annuity* income, the Gini coefficient falls to 0.66. If we then include social security transfer income, the Gini coefficient falls to 0.58. Thus, the addition of total social security income to other income is highly redistributive among elderly households. However, the predominant equalizing effect comes from social security transfer income, not social security annuity income. The former accounts for about 60 percent of the reduction in inequality, and the latter for about 40 percent. The results are quite similar among different demographic groups.

The same issue can be addressed with regard to household wealth. In this case, the two effects are similar in magnitude. The addition of social security accumulations (*SSAW*) to household wealth (*HW* or *HW* + *PW*) has a sizable equalizing effect, as does the further inclusion of social security transfer wealth (*SSTW*). For all households 65 and over, the Gini coefficient for net worth (*HW*) is 0.77, that for *HW* plus *SSAW* is 0.71, and that for *HW* plus *SSEW* (with *g* equal to 0.02) is 0.64. Here, too, results are generally quite similar by age group, household type, and race. For black families, in particular, the effects are quite large. In 1983, the Gini coefficient for *HW* is very high, 0.84; the addition of *SSAW* reduces the coefficient to 0.71; and the further addition of *SSTW* reduces it to 0.62, the same level as white families.

6.6   TAX IMPLICATIONS

The tax analysis is conducted on the basis of 1989 personal income tax schedules. The procedure is as follows: First, 1983 income figures are inflated to 1989 values using the CPI. Second, adjusted gross income, AGI, is estimated as the sum of all income items, excluding social security income. The taxable portion of social security income is then added back in, according to the worksheet procedure outlined in the tax code. The rate is based on 'INC1', defined as the sum of all income, excluding *half* of social security income. If INC1 is less than $25 000 for single filers or $32 000 for joint returns, then all social

Table 6.4 The distributional effects of social security transfers: Gini coefficients for selected concepts of income and wealth, 1983[a]

	Age group[b]					Family type (65+)			Race (65+)[c]	
	65+	65–69	70–74	75–79	80+	Married couple	Single male	Single female	White	Black
A. Income										
1. Total income – social security income	0.716	0.690	0.706	0.701	0.669	0.709	0.710	0.557	0.714	0.603
2. Total income – social security transfer	0.661	0.641	0.638	0.638	0.616	0.656	0.631	0.508	0.659	0.554
3. Total income	0.578	0.571	0.550	0.539	0.533	0.565	0.561	0.433	0.574	0.485
B. Wealth[d]										
1. HH Wealth (HW)	0.771	0.778	0.743	0.740	0.772	0.768	0.766	0.695	0.754	0.840
2. HW + SSAW	0.708	0.714	0.671	0.673	0.712	0.705	0.684	0.624	0.693	0.711
3. HW + PW	0.713	0.710	0.682	0.681	0.726	0.712	0.697	0.614	0.700	0.690
4. HW + PW + SSAW	0.666	0.664	0.628	0.633	0.678	0.663	0.637	0.570	0.654	0.631
(a) $g = .01$[e]										
5a. HW + SSEW	0.647	0.638	0.604	0.617	0.679	0.624	0.655	0.570	0.633	0.628
6a. HW + PW + SSEW	0.616	0.600	0.571	0.587	0.651	0.592	0.617	0.534	0.604	0.583

continued on page 230

Table 6.4 (*continued*)

	Age group[b]					Family type (65+)			Race (65+)[c]	
	65+	65–69	70–74	75–79	80+	Married couple	Single male	Single female	White	Black
(b) $g = .02$[e]										
5b. HW + SSEW	0.641	0.629	0.597	0.613	0.676	0.615	0.651	0.565	0.627	0.623
6b. HW + PW + SSEW	0.611	0.593	0.565	0.583	0.649	0.585	0.615	0.531	0.599	0.580
(c) $g = .03$[e]										
5c. HW + SSEW	0.635	0.619	0.590	0.608	0.674	0.606	0.647	0.561	0.621	0.617
6c. HW + PW + SSEW	0.606	0.585	0.560	0.579	0.647	0.577	0.612	0.529	0.594	0.577

[a] *Source*: Own calculations from the 1983 SCF file, on the basis of the treasury bill discount rate.
[b] Based on the age of the head of household.
[c] Based on head of household. Families with Hispanic surnames are classified as white or black, depending on race. Whites include Asians and other races.
[d] Key: HW – fungible household wealth; PW – pension wealth; SSAW – social security accumulations; SSEW – social security entitlement wealth; and SSTW – social security transfer wealth, where $SSTW = SSEW - SSAW$.
[e] The parameter g is the expected average annual rate of growth of real social security benefits over time.

security income is excluded from taxable income. If INC1 exceeds these limits, INC1 is divided by two, and the lesser of this amount and total social security income is then included in AGI.

Third, the number of exemptions is computed. Fourth, the standard deduction is also computed. This is based on the filing status of the household and the number of persons 65 or older in the household. Fifth, taxable income is calculated as AGI less the number of exemptions multiplied by $2000 less the standard deduction. Sixth, federal income tax is then computed on the basis of the appropriate tax tables.

Several limitations of the estimation are apparent: (i) itemized deductions, particularly interest payments, cannot be included in the analysis; (ii) the data analysis cannot incorporate capital gains in family income; and (iii) tax-exempt interest income or any adjustments to income are not excluded from AGI. Despite these limitations, the results are quite encouraging. Total individual federal income taxes collected in 1989 amounted to $445.7 billion (the source is the *Economic Report of the President, 1991*, Table B-77). My tax estimation produces a total tax figure for all households of $410.2 billion (only a 8 percent discrepancy). The tax estimates are subsequently increased by 8 percent to align with the actual figure.

I then recompute the taxes in the same way, except that I now treat the transfer portion of social security income as taxable income. Moreover, I also ignore the worksheet adjustment to social security income incorporated in the 1989 tax code. These estimates are also increased by 8 percent for alignment purposes. It should be noted that one limitation of this analysis is that behavioral responses of social security beneficiaries to the new tax schedule are not considered. Despite this, the new tax calculations can give some guidance to their overall redistributional effects and magnitude.

The first point of interest is the distributional effects of the tax treatment change of social security income. This will depend on three factors: (i) the ratio of social security transfers to total income; (ii) the absolute level of the social security transfers; and (iii) the progressivity of the tax schedule. Though, as we have seen from Table 6.3, the ratio of social security transfers to total income is higher for lower income households, the progressivity of the tax schedule may make the tax treatment change equalizing rather than disequalizing.

Results on the relative incidence of the alternative tax treatment of social security income are shown in Table 6.5. The first panel shows the ratio of the new post-tax income to the original post-tax income.

Table 6.5 The ratio of alternative post-tax income to original post-tax income by income class, age group, family type and race, 1989[a]

	Age group					Married couple	Single male	Single female	White	Black
	65+	65–69	70–74	75–79	80+					
A. Income class: Treasury bill rate (1989 dollars)										
Under $6 250	0.94	0.94	0.94	0.94	0.94	0.94	0.94	0.94	0.94	0.95
6 250–9 274	0.94	0.94	0.95	0.94	0.94	0.93	0.95	0.95	0.94	0.96
9 275–12 499	0.94	0.94	0.95	0.94	0.94	0.93	0.96	0.95	0.94	0.95
12 500–18 749	0.95	0.95	0.96	0.95	0.94	0.94	0.96	0.96	0.95	0.96
18 750–24 999	0.95	0.96	0.95	0.95	0.95	0.95	0.96	0.96	0.95	0.97
25 000–31 249	0.97	0.97	0.98	0.97	0.95	0.97	0.96	0.98	0.97	0.97
31 250–46 874	0.97	0.97	0.98	0.98	0.98	0.97	0.96	0.98	0.97	0.99
46 875–62 499	1.01	1.02	1.01	1.00	1.00	1.01	1.03	1.00	1.01	0.97
62 500–93 749	1.01	1.01	1.02	1.01	1.02	1.01	1.02	1.02	1.01	1.02
93 750–125 499	1.01	1.01	1.04	1.01	–	1.01	–	1.04	1.01	–
125 000 or more	1.00	1.00	1.00	1.00	1.00	1.00	1.01	1.01	1.00	1.00
All	0.98	0.99	0.97	0.97	0.96	0.98	0.97	0.96	0.98	0.97
B. Total tax payments (billions, 1989$)										
1. Original taxes	59.5	34.4	14.0	6.7	4.4	48.8	4.1	6.6	58.6	1.0

(a) Treasury bill rate									
2a. Additional taxes	8.5	2.6	2.4	1.9	1.5	4.9	0.8	2.8	7.6	0.8
3a. Percentage Change in tax bill	14%	8%	17%	28%	35%	10%	18%	43%	13%	83%
(b) Household portfolio rate									
2a. Additional taxes	7.6	2.5	2.2	1.6	1.3	4.4	0.6	2.6	6.8	0.7
3a. Percentage Change in tax bill	13%	7%	16%	25%	31%	9%	16%	40%	12%	82%
C. Gini coefficients									
1. Pre-tax income	0.578	0.571	0.550	0.539	0.533	0.565	0.561	0.433	0.574	0.485
(a) Treasury bill rate									
2a. Original post-tax income	0.508	0.505	0.479	0.467	0.466	0.489	0.485	0.373	0.504	0.421
3a. Alternative post-tax income	0.520	0.517	0.491	0.479	0.476	0.504	0.495	0.381	0.517	0.429
(b) Household portfolio rate									
2b. Original post-tax income	0.508	0.505	0.479	0.467	0.466	0.489	0.485	0.373	0.504	0.421
3b. Alternative post-tax income	0.520	0.517	0.490	0.478	0.475	0.503	0.494	0.381	0.517	0.429

Source: Own calculations from the 1983 SCF file. See text for details on tax calculations.

Here, it is quite clear that the main losers are lower income households. Indeed, the ratio of the new to old post-tax income rises almost monotonically with income class. Families with incomes of $46 500 or more (1989 dollars) actually pay less taxes under the alternative treatment of social security income. The reason is that the actual 1989 tax code, by including a prorated portion of social security income for high income families, results in a greater proportion of social security income entering AGI than the alternative treatment, based on the transfer portion of social security income alone.

Moreover, older households lose out relative to younger ones. For those in age group 65–69, there is a 1 percent decline in after-tax income with the alternative tax treatment of social security income; for those between 70 and 79, there is a 3 percent decline; and for those 80 and over, there is a 4 percent decline. Single females do worse than single males under the new tax treatment, and single males do worse than married couples. Black households are slightly worse off than white households under the new tax treatment.

Panel B shows estimates of the total tax receipts under the actual tax code and the alternative tax treatment of social security income. Total personal income taxes paid by the elderly in 1989 are estimated to be 59.5 billion dollars. Under the new tax treatment of social security income (and estimation based on the treasury bill discount rate), total taxes are estimated to be 68.0 billion, or 14 percent higher. However, there is considerable variation in the incidence of the new tax burden. For households in age group 65–69, taxes would increase by only 8 percent under the new tax treatment of social security income; for those between 70 and 74, taxes would rise by 17 percent; for those 75–79, the increase would be 28 percent; and for those 80 and over, taxes would rise by 35 percent. Taxes of married couples would increase by 10 percent; those of single males by 18 percent; and those of single females by 43 percent. Black elderly households would see their tax bills rise by a staggering 83 percent! Results based on the household portfolio discount rate are very similar.

However, on net, the new tax treatment is only slightly disequalizing in comparison with the actual tax schedules (Panel C). For all households 65 and over, the Gini coefficient for pre-tax income is 0.58. The Gini coefficient for post-tax income based on the actual 1989 tax code is 0.51, while that based on the new tax treatment of social security income is 0.52. This pattern is very similar by age group, household type, and race. Thus, both the actual tax code and the alternative one are quite equalizing, though the redistributional effects of the former are slightly greater than that of the latter.

The other point of interest is to determine the relative magnitude of the new tax receipts originating from the alteration of the tax treatment of social security benefits. For this purpose, comparisons will be made between the new tax revenue and the actual wealth holdings of young households. The additional tax revenues emanating from the new tax treatment of social security income amount to 8.5 billion. In contrast, the total net worth (HW) of households age 30 and under is 458 billion (1989) dollars, and that of households in age group 31–39 is 746 billion dollars. Thus, if the new tax receipts were placed in a capital fund for young families, they would be quite insignificant compared to their actual wealth (amounting to 1.9 percent for families 30 and under, and 0.7 percent for families 35 and under).

6.7 CONCLUSIONS

With regard to the distributional effects of the social security system, one of the most important findings is that social security transfers have comprised the bulk of social security income. The relative proportion of the transfer component among all retirees 65 and over was 0.85 in 1969, 0.73 in 1973, and 0.66 in 1983. A similar pattern is evident when comparing these ratios among retirees of different age groups in a given year. Thus, most of the social security benefits received by retirees is a pure government transfer, over and above the actual contributions made into the system by the beneficiaries. In other words, the benefits have far outweighed the annuity value of the social security contributions. However, the figures also indicate that the transfer component of social security income has been declining over time (that is, the annuity portion has been rising). There are two reasons for this. First, because the social security system started up in 1937, with very low OASI tax rates, more recent retirees have contributed into the system for more years and at higher levels than older ones. Second, federal legislation has periodically increased OASI benefit levels for all retirees.

The redistributional effects of social security income are very strong among the elderly. The Gini coefficient for family income less (total) social security income is 0.72 in 1983, while that for total family income is 0.58. However, the social security benefit formula is strongly redistributive, paying out a higher benefit relative to accumulated contributions for lower income families. This is evident when comparing the distribution of pre-social security transfer income with that of post-transfer income. In 1983, the Gini coefficient for family income excluding social security transfers (but including the social security annuity portion) is 0.66, compared to 0.58 for total family income. Thus, the predominant equalizing effect of the social security system for retirees comes from social security transfer income, not social security annuity income.

With regard to the tax implications of treating the transfer portion of social security income as taxable income, the results are less than fortuitous. Within the elderly population, it is the poorer groups that are harder hit by the new tax treatment. Higher income families pay less tax under the alternative tax treatment than under the actual tax code, and lower income families pay more taxes. Older families, who are less well off in terms of both income and wealth, pay proportionately higher taxes than younger ones. While the total tax payments of families 65–69 increase by 8 percent, those of families 80 and over increase by 35 percent. Black families will see their tax bill grow by 83 percent, compared to 13 percent for whites. Thus, the tax incidence of the new treatment of social security income is far from equitable. However, it should be noted that, on net, the overall distributional effects of the new tax system compared to the actual code are minimal. The Gini coefficient for post-tax income under the actual system is 0.52, while that under the new system is 0.51.

Moreover, the new tax revenues raised by the new tax system would not be substantial, particularly in comparison to the wealth holdings of young families. Total taxes of families 65 and over would rise by 8.5 billion, 14 percent of their current taxes. The new tax revenues would amount to only 1.9 percent of the wealth of families 30 and under and 0.7 percent of the wealth of families 35 and under. Thus, as the funding source of a 'social security capital fund' for young families, the new tax revenues would have a minimal impact on the wealth of younger families.

However, it should be noted, in conclusion, that one can *unbundle* the loan portion of the proposed social security capital fund from the new social security taxes collected – that is, the loan program can be based on the actual contributions into the social security system (of the individual or family). New tax revenues are not necessarily needed in order to implement the loan portion of the proposed program. The loans could be provided from the accumulated surplus of the social security trust fund, which has now grown to substantial proportions.

Notes

1. Where appropriate, some comparative estimates will also be provided from the 1969 MESP database, created from a synthetic match of Internal Revenue Service tax records to the 1970 Census one-in-a-thousand Public Use Sample and the capitalization of selected income flows to corresponding asset types (for example, dividends to stock shares). The methodology is described in detail in Wolff (1980, 1982, and 1983).
2. The concept of wealth used is actually that of 'fungible wealth', i.e. that which is saleable and therefore has current market value. As a result, consumer durables and household inventories, which are included in some concepts of household wealth, are excluded here. The rationale for excluding them in this study is that their value represents consumption flows rather than income flows, the analysis of which is the principal objective here.
3. This treatment assumes that other forms of household savings would be unaffected by this new institutional treatment of social security contributions.

   It is also possible to define, in analogous fashion, pension accumulation wealth, based on actual contributions made by employees and employers into private pension reserves. However, this imputation is much more problematic and is not of direct interest here. See Wolff (1987b and forthcoming) for more discussion.
4. Separate imputations were performed for husband and wife and an adjustment in the social security benefit was made for the surviving spouse.
5. However, the social security system does keep track of these accumulations for each individual, and the benefit received depends on this record.
6. A schooling variable is not included for the high school graduate group.
7. This implicitly assumes that there is no transitory component to current income.
8. For the 1947–83 period, the figures used are average hourly earnings in private non-agricultural industries, adjusted for overtime and interindustry employment shifts. The data source is the *Economic Report of the President, 1990*, Table B-44. Before 1947, I use real total wages and salaries per employed person (computed from Tables B-24 and B-33).
9. It would be desirable to have separate values of g_y for each of the 16 groups enumerated above – or, at least, for each of the four schooling groups. Unfortunately, the data were not available. As a result, it is assumed that real earnings growth over time is the same for each group – that is, is equal to overall mean earnings growth in each year.

10. It is assumed throughout that current workers retire at age 65. In 1969 and 1983, 65 was the mandatory retirement age for most workers. It was also the normal retirement age as embodied in the social security and most private pension benefit formulae. Statistically, it has remained the modal retirement age since 1962, though the percent of the labor force retiring before age 65 has been increasing and the proportion retiring after 65 has been declining.

11. These assumptions will lead to greater equality in the distribution of social security accumulations than is likely to be the case in actuality.

12. Technically, the cash surrender value of pension plans is excluded from *HW*.

13. For married couples, the value of *LE* is the greater of the two spouses, with an adjustment in *SSB* for the survivor benefit (see equation (1)).

References

Avery, Robert B., Gregory Ellihausen, Glenn B. Canner, and Thomas A. Gustafson (1984) 'Survey of Consumer Finances, 1983,' *Federal Reserve Bulletin*, September, 679–92.

Burkhauser, Richard V., and Jennifer L. Warlick (1981) 'Disentangling the Annuity from the Redistributive Aspects of Social Security in the United States,' *Review of Income and Wealth*, Series 27, No. 4, December, 401–21.

Council of Economic Advisers (1990) *Economic Report of the President, 1990* (Washington, D.C.: Government Printing Office).

Feldstein, Martin S. (1974) 'Social Security, Induced Retirement and Aggregate Capital Accumulation,' *Journal of Political Economy*, **82** (October) 905–26.

Feldstein, Martin S. (1976) 'Social Security and the Distribution of Wealth,' *Journal of the American Statistical Association*, **71** (December) 800–7.

Greenwood, Daphne T., and Edward N. Wolff (1988) 'Relative Wealth Holdings of Children and the Elderly in the United States,' in John L. Palmer, Timothy Smeeding, and Barbara Boyle Torrey (eds), *The Vulnerable* (Washington, D.C.: Urban Institute Press).

Greenwood, Daphne T., and Edward N. Wolff (1990) 'Changes in Age-Wealth Profiles: Savings, Revaluation, and Inheritance,' C.V. Starr Working Paper No. 90–33, August.

Hurd, Michael D., and John B. Shoven (1985) 'The Distributional Impact of Social Security,' in David A. Wise (ed.), *Pensions, Labor, and Individual Choice* (Chicago: Chicago University Press).

Wolff, Edward N. (1980) 'Estimates of the 1969 Size Distribution of Household Wealth in the U.S. from a Synthetic Database,' in James D. Smith (ed.), *Modeling the Distribution and Intergenerational Transmission of Wealth* (Chicago: Chicago University Press).

Wolff, Edward N. (1982) 'Effect of Alternative Imputation Techniques on Estimates of Household Wealth in the U.S. in 1969,' in D. Kessler, A.

Masson, and D. Strauss-Kahn (eds), *Accumulation et Repartition des Patrimoines* (Paris: Economica).

Wolff, Edward N. (1983) 'The Size Distribution of Household Disposable Wealth in the United States,' *Review of Income and Wealth*, Series 29, June 125–46.

Wolff, Edward N. (1987a) 'Estimates of Household Wealth Inequality in the United States, 1962–83,' *Review of Income and Wealth*, Series 33, September, 231–56.

Wolff, Edward N. (1987b) 'The Effects of Pensions and Social Security on the Distribution of Wealth in the U.S.', in E. Wolff (ed.), *International Comparisons of Household Wealth Distribution* (Oxford: Oxford University Press).

Wolff, Edward E. (1988) 'Social Security, Pensions, and the Life Cycle Accumulation of Wealth: Some Empirical Tests,' *Annales d'Economie et de Statistique*, No. 9, Janvier/Mars, 199–226.

Wolff, Edward E. 'Methodological Issues in the Estimation of Retirement Wealth,' in D. Slottje (ed.), *Research in Economic Inequality*, Vol. 2 (forthcoming).

7 W(h)ither the Middle Class? A Dynamic View

Greg J. Duncan, Timothy M. Smeeding, and Willard Rodgers

7.1 INTRODUCTION

Increasing political attention is being paid to the status of middle-income or middle-class Americans. One of the major reasons for this increased attention is the results of research using cross-sectional survey 'snapshots' of household income taken over the past quarter century which reveal a growing inequality in the distribution of annual money income of households in the United States (Thurow, 1987; Levy, 1987; Levy and Michel, 1991; Michel, 1991; Karoly, 1990; Center on Budget and Policy Priorities, 1990; Easterlin, MacDonald and Macunovich, 1990). This research has prompted some to argue that the U.S. middle class is shrinking (Phillips, 1990; Bradbury, 1986). Aggregate data from the National Accounts and from wealth surveys (Wolff, 1989; Eargle, 1991) reinforce this conclusion by showing a growing share of income from capital, a falling share for earnings, and a slightly increasing concentration of wealth among upper-income groups. Also well-documented is greater inequality in the size distribution of earnings and wages in the late 1980s as compared to one or two decades before (Gottschalk and Danziger, 1989; Burtless, 1989; Blackburn et al., this volume, Chapter 8).

While these results create a consistent story, their almost universal reliance on data drawn from cross-sectional surveys leaves unanswered many important questions regarding the nature of the changes taking place in the distribution of income and wealth. Most importantly, cross-sectional snapshots provide information only on *net* changes in economic position and thus reveal little about the extent and nature of movement into and out of the middle class. For example, net increases in the number of low- relative to middle-income households occur when unfavorable transitions – families falling from middle- to low-income status – outnumber favorable transitions involving movement into the ranks of the middle class by previously low-income households. Surely it is important to track these two flows separately. Are increasing numbers of families 'falling from grace', as Katherine Newman (1988) puts it? If so, who are they and what events are linked to their income losses? Or is mobility into the middle class declining? And, if so, does this affect in particular young families? What avenues for upward mobility are disappearing? These are the types of questions we seek to address for adults crossing either the lower or the upper boundary of the middle class.

A second set of issues we address involves linkages between changes in income and changes in wealth. A recent Census Bureau study (Eargle, 1991) comparing population snapshots in 1984 and 1988 found that the median net worth of the most affluent quintile of households ranked by net worth increased by 14 percent, while overall median net worth declined slightly. However, this kind of study cannot tell us whether the increase was due to gains made by those moving into this quintile or gains made by those already among the richest fifth. Nor can it tell us whether changes in household income are reinforced by changes in wealth. Although one would expect such linkages, it still may be that many households apparently falling out of the ranks of the affluent into the middle class at the same time enjoyed substantial increases in, say, housing or stock-market wealth.

We address these issues by analyzing trends in the transitions of prime age (25–54 years old) adults into and out of the middle class using 22 years of data from the Panel Study of Income Dynamics. We begin by reviewing the methodology and measurement procedures that we employ to define the middle class and transitions into and out of middle-class status. Next we present our basic findings which, in fact, show a persistent 'withering' of the middle class since about 1980. We then search for clues as to who moved into and out of the middle-income groups and the source of such changes. Because notions of 'class' are usually based on measures of wealth as well as income, we also investigate longitudinal changes in the wealth distribution in the 1980s for these same individuals. Our findings on wealth reinforce those based on income. The paper concludes with a brief discussion of the policy implications of our findings.

7.2   METHODOLOGICAL APPROACH

Since we needed longitudinal data on income transitions in different periods of the recent past, we used the Panel Study of Income Dynamics, a panel survey of U.S. households begun in 1968 by the Survey Research Center (Hill, 1991). By following all members of its original sample households, the PSID provides (except for immigration and differential nonresponse) continuous representation of the U.S. population through time.

Low-income families were initially oversampled, but weights have been developed to adjust both for the differential initial sampling probabilities and for the differential nonresponse that has occurred since the beginning of the study (Hill, 1991). Assuming that differential nonresponse bias is eliminated through weighting, the adults in our PSID sample provide continuous representation of adults in the U.S. population with the sole exception of immigrants to the United States since 1968.

Our interest in middle-class transitions led us to focus on the prime-age population – men and women age 25–50 in the first year of the five-year period over which income transitions are observed (see below). The public discussion of the economic fate of the middle class generally concerns 'prime-age' adult Americans – individuals too young to have reached the conventional age of early retirement (55) but old enough to be living independently from their parents (25), thus, excising many of the life cycle movements up and down the distribution which are related to age – e.g., leaving school or retirement.

Sociologists argue that the concept of middle class (and 'class' in general) is based on far more than just income (Jencks, 1991). While this is true, the many unanswered questions regarding household income justify focusing on this dimension. To avoid confusion, we hereafter refer to our divisions of economic well-being as low-, middle- and high-income.

We gather information from annual interviews conducted from 1968 to 1989, which cover income received in calendar years 1967 through 1988, as well as wealth reported in the 1984 and 1989 interviewing waves. Income transitions are defined over all possible periods of five consecutive years observed in the data.[1] Each sample adult's 'initial' household economic position is defined by the two-year average household income (with and without adjustments for family size) over the first two years of the five-year interval. A 'final' position is defined by household income averaged over the fourth and fifth years of the interval. Two-year averages are used in order to provide a more reliable picture of change in economic status.[2] A transition occurs if average income in the fourth and fifth years was different enough from average income in the first two years to cross over one of the two thresholds that bound our middle-income category.

Aside from using two-year accounting periods, we departed from the conventional measurement of household income in two ways. First, since food-stamp income is arguably equivalent to cash income, we included the dollar value of food stamps as a component of household income. Second, since taxes reduce a household's disposable income, we subtracted estimates of federal income taxes and Social Security payroll taxes from each household's income.

Our search for upper and lower boundaries of 'middle income' began with a review of how several authors have defined the rich, affluent, well-to-do, upper class, etc., in recent studies and the issue of whether to adjust income for needs (e.g., family size) or not (see the appendix). Some adjust income for family size, others use income alone; some studies use after-tax income, most use Census (pre-tax, post-transfer) money income; some studies define affluence relative to a percentile point in the distribution, others have an absolute dollar figure that is subsequently adjusted for inflation using either the CPI-U or the revised CPI-UX1.

As detailed in the appendix, we developed two absolute measures of economic status, both of which are based on after-tax household income, and set the lower boundary of middle income at roughly the 20th percentile of the sample in the middle of our sample period and the upper boundary at the 90th percentile. The first measure is post-tax household income *not* adjusted for family size. The lower and upper boundaries are $18 500 and $55 000, respectively, in 1987 dollars, and are applied to all years using the CPI-UX1 price index.

Our second measure of economic status adjusts income for family size by dividing income by the U.S. poverty thresholds based on family size. The resulting 'income-to-needs' ratio equals 1.0 for a household with income just equal to its poverty threshold (which, in 1990, equaled roughly $13 000 for a family of four), 2.0 for a family with an income of twice its poverty threshold, etc. The lower and upper boundaries of middle income-to-needs are 2.0 and 6.0, respectively.[3] Because the basic patterns of income transitions appear similar for both measures, we concentrate on transitions based on unadjusted income but note differences between the two measures when they occur.

7.2.1 Wealth

Because notions of economic position and class depend on both long-term wealth and income, we were also interested in questions surrounding the movement of income and wealth in relation to each other. Do adults who move between income groups experience like changes in wealth? Do families falling from middle-income status experience declines in net worth and/or increases in debt, or are the wealth changes countervailing? While PSID wealth information is not available in most years, we were able to compare income transitions between 1984–5 and 1987–8 with PSID measures of net worth (total nonpension assets minus debt) taken in 1984 and repeated in 1989. Tax adjustments are not yet possible for all years of the income data, so we base income transitions on Census pre-tax, post-transfer money income.

7.3 SNAPSHOT COMPARISONS

We began by calibrating PSID data against the Census Bureau's Current Population Survey (CPS), the major data source of previous studies. To do this, we treated the PSID as if it were a series of cross-sections and compared pre-tax income from 1967–86 of all PSID households against published CPS data on the distribution of households with pre-tax incomes near our low- and high-income boundaries – $15 000 and $50 000 in 1989 dollars. (The CPS does not regularly record income or payroll taxes and has collected Food Stamp information regularly only after 1979.) The two data sources show very similar trends in the middle-income group – both time series show a slow but steady decline in the fraction of middle-income households from nearly 60 percent in the late 1960s to about 51 percent in the late 1980s (Figure 7.1). The simple correlation coefficient (r) between the PSID and CPS time series on middle-income households is quite high – 0.94.

Because the CPS consistently records less household income from its respondents than does the PSID, the CPS sample tends to produce higher estimates of households with incomes below $15 000 and lower proportions of households with incomes above $50 000. But here again the *trends* – an uneven rise in the proportion of high-income households, an unstable but essentially trendless time series on the proportion of households with low incomes, resulting in a

Figure 7.1 Distribution of low, middle and high income households in the Current Population Survey (1967–89) and in the Panel Study of Income Dynamics (1967–86)

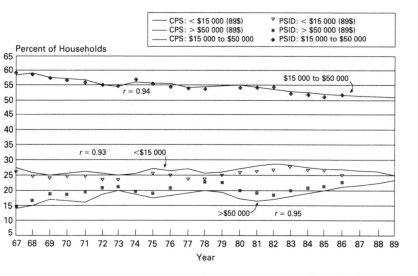

Source for CPS Data: U.S. Bureau of the Census; Current Population Reports, Series P–60, No. 168; Money Income and Poverty Status 1989, Table 2.

declining middle-income group – are quite similar in the two data series. Correlations between the PSID and CPS time series are 0.93 for the lower boundary and 0.95 for the upper boundary of middle income. Macroeconomic conditions account for much of the irregularity in the trends, with recessions around 1970, in the mid-1970s and again in the early 1980s temporarily increasing the proportion of low-income households and reducing that of high-income households. On balance, it appears that the PSID and CPS data tell very similar cross-sectional stories.[4]

7.3.1 Are There Fewer Middle-income Households?

We next examined cross-sectional trends in the size of PSID income groups, using the sample of 25- to 50-year-olds and our various adjustments to income. Figures 7.2 and 7.3 summarize the results.

As with CPS trends, there appears to be an irregular but clearly

Figure 7.2   Proportion of adults living in households with 'middle' income
and income/needs in the Panel Study of Income Dynamics, 1967–86

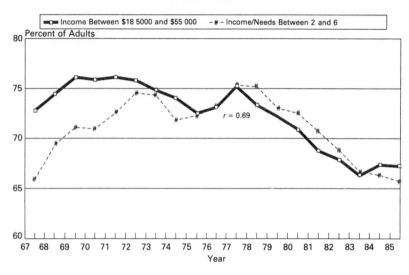

Note: Income data are post-tax 2 year averages.

discernible decline in the proportion of prime-aged adults with household incomes in the middle (the solid line in Figure 7.2). Thus, our
various adjustments to income and restriction of the sample to prime-
age adults changes the basic CPS household-income story very little.
However, unlike CPS trends, PSID proportions of adults with *size-
adjusted* incomes in the middle follow a rather different pattern (the
correlation between the PSID time series with and without family-
size adjustments is only 0.69), with the proportion in the middle
income-to-needs category increasing markedly during most of the
1970s and only then declining sharply.

Underlying the different trends is a sharp decline in family size in
the late 1960s and early 1970s, coupled with nearly flat real income
change, which reduced the number of low income-to-needs adults
(Figure 7.3) and increased the ranks of middle-income adults (Figure
7.2) between 1967 and 1973. However, in the late 1970s and throughout the 1980s, income changes became nearly as important as changes
in family size, making more nearly parallel the trends for the two
income measures.

Figure 7.3   Proportion of adults living in households with 'low' and 'high' income and income/needs in the Panel Study of Income Dynamics, 1967–86

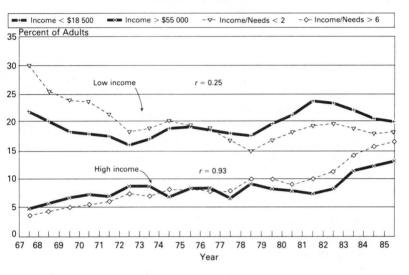

Note: Income data are post-tax 2 year averages.

The middle-income group shrank from a peak of about 75 percent of the population in the early 1970s and again in 1977–8 to a trough of 65 percent around 1983. Our most recent figures, for 1985–6 show just slightly more than two-thirds of the population – 67 percent – in the middle-income category. If anything, the recent decline in the size of the middle income-to-needs group is slightly steeper; only about 65 percent of the prime-age adult population can be termed 'middle-income' by this measure of well-being, down from a peak of 75 percent less than one decade before.

Whereas a family-size-driven decline in the low income-to-needs population accounted for most of the rise in the middle-income share during the early 1970s, the declining middle-income share in the late 1970s and, especially, during the 1980s resulted primarily from growth in the high-income and high income-to-needs population. Between 1979–80 and 1985–6, the proportion of high-income families grew by more than 50 percent – from about 8 to over 13 points. High income-to-needs grew by even more – from 10 percent in 1979–80 to over 16 percent in 1986. To paraphrase Michel (1991, p. 201), the rising tide of economic growth in the 1980s appears to have lifted the yachts, but neither the tugboats nor the rowboats.

7.4 TRANSITIONS

It appears that the fraction of adults with middle income, middle income-to-needs, and perhaps a middle class standard of living has withered. This is more pronounced when income is adjusted for family size and is occasioned by a substantial increase in the number of adults living in high-income households and unsteady growth in the number of low-income adults. Many questions remain unanswered about even the basic trends. What kinds of people are actually crossing the middle-income boundaries? What events are linked to their income losses or gains? How do periods of economic growth or recession affect flows across the income boundaries? To address these questions, we investigate actual transitions across our income boundaries using longitudinal data on our sample of adults.

The composition of a population's share of low-, middle- and high-income households is the product of offsetting flows across the middle-income boundaries. For example, growth in the number of high- at the expense of middle-income adults could result from increasing numbers of people making the transition from middle- to high-income status, decreasing numbers falling from high- to middle-income status, or to varying degrees both types of charges.

The first column of Table 7.1 shows the prevalence of transitions involving the three income groups. When averaged across all of the five-year observation windows afforded by the PSID's sample period, some 6.7 percent of adults whose two-year average post-tax household income was between $18 500 and $55 000 are found to have succeeded in garnering two-year average income above $55 000 two years later. A much larger fraction – 29.7 percent – of high-income individuals typically fell into the middle-income group. (The much smaller relative size of the high-income group translates these very unequal conditional transition probabilities into more nearly equal, overall *numbers* of people making the offsetting flows across the upper boundary line.)

Consistent with abundant research on flows across the poverty line (Bane and Ellwood, 1986; Duncan *et al.*, 1984), the third row of Table 7.1 shows that more than one third of low-income adults

Table 7.1 Percent of adults making key income transitions

	All years	Period effects		Cyclical effects	
		Before 1980	1980 and after	Nonrecession years	Recession years[a]
High-income transitions					
Percent of middle-income individuals Climbing out	6.7	6.3	7.5	6.9	6.2
Percent of high-income individuals Falling out	29.7	31.1	27.1	28.5	31.8
Low-income transitions					
Percent of low-income individuals Climbing out	33.6	35.5	30.4	35.0	30.4
Percent of middle-income individuals Falling out	7.0	6.2	8.5	6.2	8.5

[a] Recession years are defined by 5-year growth in per capita real disposable personal income. They include 1974, 1975, 1979, 1980 and 1981.

typically succeeded in making the transition over the $18 500 middle-income boundary, while 7.0 percent of middle-income adults typically fell below it.[5]

The importance of both calendar year and macroeconomic conditions is evident in Table 7.1. The second and third columns divide the transitions by whether the middle of the five-year observation window was before 1980, while the fourth and fifth columns divide the sample according to whether macroeconomic conditions (as measured by five-year trends in the U.S. Department of Commerce's series on per capita personal disposable income) were favorable or not.[6]

Relative to the late 1960s and 1970s, the 1980s were clearly a period in which *all four* of the transition probabilities tended to accelerate reductions in the size of the middle-income group. A higher percentage of individuals climbed into high-income status while a smaller percent fell out; a lower fraction of low-income individuals climbed into the middle class while a larger fraction of middle-income adults fell into the low-income group.[7]

Cyclical factors performed as expected with favorable transitions less prevalent and unfavorable transitions more frequent in recession years. Cyclical and period effects had very similar impacts on unfavorable transitions; period effects found in the 1980s were somewhat more important than business-cycle effects for favorable transitions.

Perhaps the most salient feature of these changing probabilities involves those adults who were middle class at the beginning of the decade. During the 1970s they faced roughly equal chances of moving up or down from the middle class. During the 1980s however, their probability of falling from middle income to lower income increased relative to their probability of moving up to the high income class. By the middle of the 1980s a middle class adult's chances of moving down the distribution were 85 in 1000 as compared to a 75 in 1000 chance of moving up the income distribution. This subtle change in the balance of middle class movements means that the middle class dreams of upward mobility which Levy (1987) wrote about are becoming ever more distant.

7.5 EXPLAINING TRANSITIONS

The next step in our investigation of transitions into and out of middle-income status was to see what demographic characteristics

Figure 7.4 Transitions into and out of middle-income

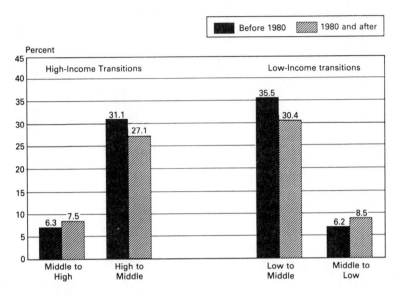

correlated most strongly with the transitions and whether characteristics such as advanced schooling and older age that are known to
have been more favored in the labor market in the 1980s were also
powerful in explaining household-income-based transitions. We do
this both with and without adjustments for the effects of business-
cycle and other demographic factors. We also present data on what
components of income – earnings of adult males, females, or other
family members – figured most prominently in the transitions.

7.5.1 Who Moved?

Table 7.2 helps to set the stage by showing the distribution of transitions according to the marital status of the adults undergoing the
transitions and the calendar year in which they occurred.[8] Our five-
year observation windows complicate the classification of marital
status somewhat, since someone may have been married for only a
portion of the five-year period. We concentrate on just three groups
of adults: husbands and wives living together throughout the five-year
period; all other men; and all other women.

Married couples dominate high-income transitions, particularly
prior to the 1980s, when they accounted for 90 percent of all

Table 7.2 The demographics of moving into and out of middle-income status: percent of each type of adult making transitions[a]

	Transitions into high-income status[b]			Transitions out of low-income status[c]		
	All	Before 1980	1980 and after	All	Before 1980	1980 and after
Married individuals[d]	86	90	74	56	65	37
Other men	8	5	13	14	12	20
Other women	6	5	13	30	23	43
Total	100	100	100	100	100	100
(Unweighted number of transitions)	(766)	(514)	(252)	(1704)	(1261)	(443)

	Transitions out of high-income status[b]			Transitions into low-income status[c]		
	All	Before 1980	1980 and after	All	Before 1980	1980 and after
Married individuals[d]	77	79	74	49	50	48
Other men	10	11	9	16	13	17
Other women	13	10	17	35	37	31
(Unweighted number of transitions)	(289)	(193)	(96)	(1240)	(828)	(412)

[a] Transitions and events are defined over five-year periods. The data covered 16 five-year periods, 1967–71 through 1982–6. The adult must be in the age range 25–50 in the first year of the given period. Five of those periods, starting with that for 1978–82, are defined as '1980 and after', while the other eleven are defined as 'Before 1980'.

[b] Transitions into (out of) high-income status are defined as occurring when the person's post-tax and -transfer family income is less (more) than \$55 000 (in 1987 dollars, using the CPI-UX1) in both the first and second years of the five-year period and greater than or equal to (less than) \$55 000 in both the fourth and fifth years.

[c] Transitions out of (into) low-income status are defined as occurring when the person's post-tax and -transfer family income is less than or equal to (greater than) \$18 500 (in 1987 dollars) in both the first and second years of the five-year period and greater than (greater than or equal to) \$18 500 in both the fourth and fifth years.

[d] The percent of transitions occurring to married couples is the sum of transitions experienced by husbands in the 25–50 age range and wives in the 25–50 age range. The within-group distribution of events shown in the table is that for married couples where the husband was required to be age 25–50. Results for couples where the wife was required to be age 25–50 were very similar.

transitions into high-income status and 79 percent of transitions from high- to middle-income status. Married couples were less likely to be involved in movements across the lower boundary of the middle-income category. Other men – mainly single men living without children – and other women – both single women and women heading families – were unlikely to experience high-income transitions, but more likely to experience low-income transitions. In fact, these 'other' women were the most likely group in the 1980s to move from low- to middle-income status.

The dominance of married couples among high-income transitions and the importance of unmarried women among low-income transitions is in large part a reflection of the fact that these groups are most *at risk* of making those transitions. Whether actual rates of transition differ for these and other demographic groups is the next question we address.

7.5.2 Demographic Correlates

A look at differential transition rates by schooling, race, household composition and age produced few surprises. Favorable transitions – both for middle- to high-income and from low- to middle-income status – were more frequent among adults with college educations and less frequent among female-headed families and, especially, among blacks. The incidence of unfavorable transitions was a mirror image: less frequent among the college-educated and more frequent among female-headed families and blacks. Transitions into high-income status were somewhat more prevalent among older adults while transitions from low- to middle-income status were more prevalent among younger adults. Aside from the drift toward middle-income-reducing transitions in the 1980s, these demographic patterns were quite similar both before and after 1980.

We performed a series of logistic regressions using each of our four transitions as a dependent variable in order to isolate the net contribution of business-cycle, period and demographic factors. Independent variables included schooling, race, household composition and age, macroeconomic conditions as measured by trend in per capita disposable personal income and a set of dummy variables measuring each person's distance between his or her own initial household income and the middle-income transition boundary line.[9]

We first combined all sample years and addressed the issue of whether the middle-income-withering differences in transition rates after versus before 1980 could be explained by differences in demographic characteristics, macroeconomic conditions or distance to the transition boundaries.[10] The answer was clearly negative, with the differences in all four regression-adjusted transition rates before and after 1980 generally as large as the simple differences displayed in Table 7.1.

We next ran regressions separately for the two periods before and after 1980 to gauge the changing importance of demographic factors. As before, we controlled for macroeconomic conditions as well as the gap between each person's household income and the income associated with the transition line. Results for the most interesting demographic variables are summarized in Figures 7.5 and 7.6.[11]

For making the transition into high-income status, a college education was a significant help, while being young (head of household under age 35) or black hurt (Figure 7.5). Blacks were only half as likely as the sample average to move into high-income status in both periods, even after adjusting for differences in schooling, family composition and the fact that the starting point for the typical black is further away from the high-income boundary. Interestingly, the regression-adjusted probability of female heads moving into the high-income group was significantly higher in the 1980s than before. (The *un*adjusted transition probabilities remained at a low 2 percent in both periods.) A closer look at transitions involving these women after 1980 showed that most were highly educated, young and childless. Their transitions were generally due to the much higher real earnings growth that such women experienced in the 1980s (U.S. Bureau of the Census, 1990).

As already mentioned, transitions out of low-income status (shown in the right half of Figure 7.5) were less likely in the 1980s for all groups. Only the college-educated had higher-than-average probabilities of moving out of low-income status. Being young lost its advantage in the 1980s, while blacks and female heads continued to be less likely to move into the middle class.

Downward mobility from high- to middle-income became less frequent in the 1980s than before. While all subgroups within the high-income class shared in this favorable development, younger families continued to have a higher-than-average risk of falling into the middle (Figure 7.6).

The probability of falling from middle-income status – falling from grace – increased significantly in the 1980s. Female heads and blacks maintained their already higher-than-average probability of falling

Figure 7.5 Adjusted fractions of various groups making favorable income transitions

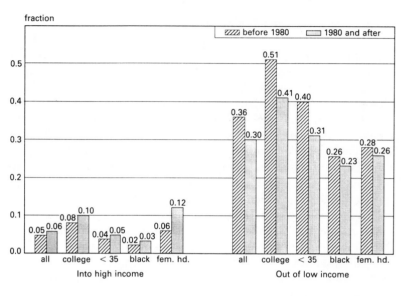

Figure 7.6 Adjusted fractions of various groups making unfavorable income transitions

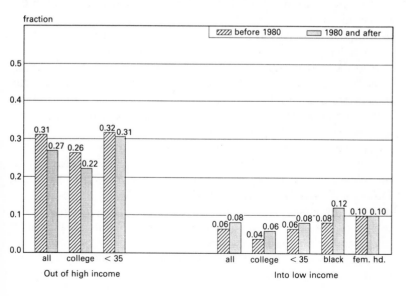

from the middle, while people with schooling beyond high school had lower-than-average risks.

7.5.3   Whose Income Changed the Most?

As with poverty transitions (Bane and Ellwood, 1986), it is also useful to isolate in our set of income transitions the income component that changed the most. We did this by calculating for each of our transitions the dollar changes in the earnings of adult men and women and in the income of other family members (principally older children). The component changing the most was designated 'most important', provided it accounted for at least half of the net change in total income. If the most important income component failed to account for half of the net change, then the given transition was assigned to an 'other income' category.

The results, shown in Table 7.3, clearly point to the importance of men's earnings; it was the most important income component in all four of the transitions, both before and after 1980. Women's earnings figured more prominently in high-income transitions during the 1980s, while the importance of the income of other adult family members declined for all four of the transitions.

The lessening importance of other earners held in particular for transitions between middle- and high-income status. Prior to the 1980s, increases in other family members' earnings were more important than women's earnings in explaining transitions into high-income status; after 1980 the relative importance of these two components reversed. Decreases in other family members' earnings, often due to the nest-leaving departure of a young adult from the family home, became less important in transitions from high- to middle-income status in the 1980s.

A more detailed look at the favorable transitions involving men's earnings (data not shown in Table 7.3) showed that they were more often associated with higher rates of pay rather than overtime hours or second jobs. Upward mobility linked to women's earnings was more evenly split between increases in wage rates and in hours. Downward transitions for men were more likely to result from changes in hours – job loss and unemployment – than declining rates of pay. For women, decreases in both wages and hours are important in explaining why earned income declined.

In general, our findings support those of Blackburn *et al.* (this volume, Chapter 8), Blank (this volume, Chapter 2), and Cancian,

Table 7.3 Relative importance of men's and women's earnings in favorable and unfavorable income transitions

Most important income component[a]	Favorable transitions (in percents)				Unfavorable transitions (in percents)			
	Into high-income		Out of low-income		Out of high-income		Into low-income	
	Before 1980	1980 and after	Before 1980	1980 and after	Before 1980	1980 and after	Before 1980	1980 and after
Men's earnings	51	50	50	53	50	57	60	63
Women's earnings	14	23	26	28	10	14	16	14
Income of other family members	26	15	11	6	30	22	15	13
Other income/mixed	9	12	13	13	10	7	9	10
Total	100	100	100	100	100	100	100	100

[a] Income of other family members consists of earnings plus any asset income of these other members. 'Other income/mixed' is the residual category from the family's total money income.

Danziger, and Gottschalk (this volume, Chapter 9). The widening of the income distribution and the withering of the middle class are mainly associated with growing inequality in men's earnings – in particular wage changes. Women's earnings are of increasing import-ance in explaining movements from middle to high income. How-ever, men's earnings still figure most prominently in at least twice as many transitions as do women's earnings.

7.6   THE ROLE OF WEALTH

Our discussion thus far has focused almost entirely on income, taking wealth into account only insofar as household incomes typically in-clude very small amounts of income from wealth in the form of interest, rent and dividends. Our belief that accumulated wealth or, more precisely, net worth constitutes a major difference between the lower, middle and upper classes leads us to investigate how taking wealth into account changes the income-based view chosen thus far. We examine recent changes in the distribution of net worth, joint distribution of income and net worth, and distribution of net worth among people making the kinds of income-based transitions analyzed in the first part of the chapter. Our measure of net worth includes the value of housing equity, other real estate, vehicles, farms and businesses, stocks, savings and investments and other assets, less other outstanding debt. Information on pension wealth was not avail-able, and even if it were, its illiquidity would lead us to treat it separately in our analyses.

The PSID contains only two waves with comprehensive wealth data – 1984 and 1989. Hence, we are limited to changes in net worth between the mid- and late 1980s – the period just beyond the final income transition year (1986) used thus far in this paper. We drew a sample of 25- to 50-year-olds in 1984 for this analysis, but were able only to use data on pre- rather than post-tax household income for our income measure. Income transitions are measured by averaging income over 1984 and 1985 to set initial position and 1987 and 1988 to set the final income position.

7.6.1   Changes in the Size Distribution of Wealth and Income

We begin with comparative snapshots showing changes in the size distribution of net worth between 1984 and 1989 (Table 7.4). In these

Table 7.4   Wealth inequality, 1984 and 1989

Net worth[a] distribution	1984 net worth	1989 net worth	Percent change in net worth	Change in net worth
20th percentile	$ 5 281	$ 8 162	55	$ 2 881
Median	38 083	50 894	34	12 811
80th percentile	117 478	175 537	49	58 059
90th percentile	207 582	321 555	55	113 973
Difference 90th–20th	202 301	313 393		
Ratio 90th/20th	39.3	39.4		

[a] Net worth is defined as the sum of the value of housing equity, real estate, vehicles, farm/business, stocks, savings/investment, and other assets, less other debt, inflated to 1987 dollars using the CPI-UX1.

two years the adults in our sample were ranked by net worth to determine the points separating the 20th, 50th, 80th and 90th percentiles of the wealth distribution.[12] Net worth at the 90th percentile was almost 40 times the net worth of the 20th wealth percentile in each year. In contrast, the ratio of the 90th percentile of two-year average incomes in 1984–5 to the 20th percentile was only 3.6. Thus, as has been shown with numerous sets of data, net worth in the PSID in the late 1980s is much less equally distributed than income.

The relative 90th to 20th percentile gap in net worth in 1989 was about the same as in 1984, suggesting that the 1984–9 period was marked by roughly equal percentage gains at the 20th and 90th percentiles. Similar results have been recorded for the 1983–6 period using the Federal Reserve Board's *Survey of Consumer Finances* by Avery, Elliehausen 1988 and Kennickell (1988). Percentage gains in the middle were somewhat smaller. Of course, the dollar changes in wealth at different points in the wealth distribution varied enormously, with the top decile gaining nearly $114 000 between 1984 and 1989 and the bottom two deciles gaining less than $3000.

As a second comparative cross-sectional tabulation, we ranked our prime-age adults according to income rather than wealth and calculated average income and wealth at the 20th, 50th and 90th percentiles of income (Table 7.5).[13] Not surprisingly, this ranking produces less extreme inequality in the distribution of wealth, but even here wealth inequality reinforced income inequality; the distribution of

Table 7.5 Trends in income and wealth inequality

Position in income distribution	1967–8 income	1977–8 income	Year 1984–5 Income[a]	Year 1984–5 Net worth[b]	Year 1987–8 Income[a]	Year 1987–8 Net worth[b]
20th percentile	$17 819	$19 683	$20 399	$ 12 546	$21 871	$ 18 533
Median	26 888	30 371	36 125	36 954	39 879	48 974
90th percentile	46 066	51 601	73 628	126 716	81 933	198 872
Difference 90th–20th	28 247	31 918	53 229	114 170	60 062	180 339
Ratio 90th–20th	2.6	2.6	3.6	10.1	3.8	10.7

[a] Income is defined as post-tax, post-transfer family income in 1967–8 and 1977–8, and pre-tax, post-transfer income in 1984–5 and 1987–8, inflated to 1987 dollars using the CPI-UX1.
[b] Net worth is defined as the sum of the value of housing equity, real estate, vehicles, farm/business, stocks, savings/investment, and other assets, less other debt. Median values of net worth between the 10th and 30th percentile of income are given for the 20th percentile of income, 40th and 60th percentile for the median, and 80th and 100th percentile for the 90th percentile.

wealth is still significantly less equal than is the distribution of income.

The ratio of the 90th to the 20th percentile of income rose from 3.6 to 3.8 over the 1984–5 to 1987–8 period, while the wealth ratios for these same people rose from 10.1 to 10.7. These increases imply that relative change at the upper end of the distribution (90th percentile) exceeded change at the lower end (20th percentile) in both absolute and percentage terms, producing a widening in the joint distribution. In other words, the group experiencing the largest gains in income is also enjoying the most substantial gains in net worth.[14]

7.6.2   Wealth Change Accompanying Income Transitions

Our final analysis combines income transitions with their concomitant wealth changes (Table 7.6). Individuals were first classified according to the income transition they experienced between 1984–5 and 1987–8. We then calculated median net worth, house equity as a fraction of net worth and debt as a fraction of income in both 1984 and 1989 for each subgroup defined by income change.[15]

The results clearly show that changes in net worth and debt closely mirror changes in income. Upwardly mobile individuals climbing into either the high- or middle-income class tended to enjoy more favorable changes in wealth than did those with downward income-based transitions. The change in net worth for adults who persisted in the middle-income group (+$14 400) was close to that of the entire sample (+$11 300, the row labelled 'All' at the bottom of table).

High-income groups experienced large increases in net worth in both absolute and relative terms. Moreover, the debt burden (relative to income) of those remaining in or climbing into the high-income category fell slightly as did their ratio of housing equity to net worth. Hence, the wealth gains for high-income, prime-age adults were largely in fungible nonhousing wealth, not in home equity. Debt as a fraction of income remained constant for the middle-income group but grew for people with low incomes. People climbing from low- to middle-income status (labelled 'climbed out of low' in the table) did relatively well, reducing their debt burden and enjoying the largest percentage gain in net worth. (However, the dollar amount associated with this change amounted to only $10 500.)

Sample sizes of people remaining in the middle- and low-income categories were sufficiently large to make possible separate estimates by race. Blacks had significantly lower net worth in both periods.

Table 7.6 Wealth and savings, 1984 to 1989, by 2-year average income class, for men and women in thousands of 1987 dollars

| 2-yr average income class in 1984-5 and 1987-8 | 1984 | | | 1989 | | | Change in Median net worth | Percent change in Median net worth | Percent of sample (Unweighted n) |
| | Median net worth | Mean ratio of | | Median net worth | Mean ratio of | | | | |
		House equity/ net worth	Debt/ 2-yr avg income		House Equity/ net worth	Debt/ 2-yr avg income			
High-income:									
Remained high-income	167.7	0.46	0.06	305.4	0.43	0.05	137.7	82	4.7(139)
Climbed into high-income	79.8	0.55	0.09	152.4	0.49	0.04	72.6	91	5.1(148)
Fell from high-income	115.2	0.33[a]	0.05[a]	164.7	0.41[a]	0.10[a]	49.5	43	1.7(49)
Middle-income:									
Remained middle-income									
All	39.9	0.57	0.07	54.3	0.56	0.07	14.4	36	52.3(1535)
Black	15.5	0.53	0.08	26.1	0.54	0.07	10.6	68	10.9(319)
Nonblack	41.5	0.57	0.07	55.7	0.56	0.07	14.2	34	40.9(1216)
Low-income:									
Remained low-income									
All	3.7	0.17	0.05	3.1	0.25	0.08	-0.6	-16	23.1(677)
Black	0.4	0.14	0.03	0.5	0.27	0.10	0.1	25	15.2(444)
Nonblack	7.3	0.18	0.06	6.3	0.24	0.07	-1.0	-14	7.4(233)
Climbed out of low-income	7.6	0.19	0.10	18.1	0.37	0.08	10.5	138	7.4(217)
Fell into low-income	22.6	0.41	0.07	12.6	0.43	0.08	-10.0	-44	5.6(162)
All	35.4	0.46	0.07	46.7	0.48	0.07	11.3	32	100 (2929)

Note: Data cover 5-year periods and compare mean pre-tax income in 1984 and 1985 to mean pre-tax income in 1987 and 1988. The 'high' income cutoff is $70 263. The 'low' income cutoff is $21 316. Incomes are inflated to 1987 dollars using the CPI-UX1. Net worth is defined as the sum of the value of housing equity, real estate, vehicles, farm/business, stocks, savings/investment, and other debt.

[a] Mean ratios of house equity to net worth and debt to 2-yr average income were calculated for all individuals between the 25th and 75th percentile of net worth in each group except 'Fell From High Income.' Mean ratios in this group were calculated for all individuals.

Middle-income blacks enjoyed larger percentage (but smaller absolute) gains than did whites. People remaining in or falling into the low-income group did the worst, posting declines in net worth of 16 and 44 percent, respectively. Among the low-income group, only blacks experienced an increase in net worth – and then it was only $100. Median net worth for those who continued to have low income fell by $600 ($3700 to $3100) over this period. In contrast, it grew by $137 700 ($167 700 to $305 400) for individuals remaining in the high-income group. All in all, the addition of wealth dramatically reinforces our picture of increasing income-based inequality.

7.7 CONCLUSIONS AND POLICY IMPLICATIONS

The middle of the income distribution among prime age adults in the United States has indeed withered over the past decade. A middle income adult's chances of falling from the middle to the bottom of the distribution increasingly exceeded their chances of moving from the middle to the top in the 1980s. If the seven percentage point decline in prime-aged adults from 1978–9 to 1985–6 continued until 1990, the middle-income group would constitute less than 65 and closer to 60 percent of the population. We find that cyclical and demographic factors explain little of the accelerated decline in the number of middle-income adults in the 1980s; all avenues of transition out of the middle-income group were more heavily travelled during the past decade. The withering of middle-income adult groups was marked by two major sets of forces: (1) the upward movement of prime-age men and women who first experienced and then maintained large real gains in their earnings during that period, and (2) the stagnation of real earnings among households in the low-income category. Wealth change in the latter 1980s clearly reinforced income change, particularly among individuals remaining in the high-income group and among those moving from middle- to high-income status.

Other analyses based on cross-sectional data and microsimulation models (e.g., Michel, 1991; U.S. House of Representatives, 1991, Appendices I, J, K; and U.S. Congressional Budget Office, 1991), confirm that the trends in our data continued through the late 1980s and are projected to persist into the early 1990s. If anything, the federal tax reform of 1986 solidified the gains in after-tax income reached by the well-to-do (Pechman, 1990), while the analyses in this paper indicate that the recession of 1990–91 should reduce upward mobility from the bottom while causing many of those most seriously affected to fall from middle-class status.

It appears, then, that the 1980s and, according to some prognosticators (e.g., Reich, 1991), the 1990s as well, will constitute an epoch in American life that was quite different from the post-war decades preceding it. Ours is a time marked by a significant increase in real income and wealth for those with already high incomes and substantial wealth. Of course, this change alone is one which policymakers should be most pleased with – if the trend was for upward mobility throughout the distribution. But again, large sustained income gains are apparent only for the yachts – not for the tugboats or the rowboats. When this upward mobility among the few is coupled with the persistently high and stagnant poverty rates of American families with children and the growing lack of upward mobility among our lower but still working class, a different policy picture emerges. As the Federal and state governments struggle to find funds to meet growing needs for human and physical capital, for health, education and related program areas – funds to extend the chance for upward mobility to all income classes – we believe that we have found a primary tax base to meet these revenue needs – the growing affluence of high-income middle-age Americans.

The policy discussions underlying the 1990 Deficit Reduction Act increasingly brought up the question of 'fairness' in the distributional effects of public tax and transfer policies at the Federal government level. These discussions brought policy changes which extended modest tax relief and additional health care benefits to low-income families. Because this coming decade will continue to be different from those that preceded it, we consider it vital to continue to re-examine the Federal income tax and to reconsider wealth taxation – in particular capital gains taxation of wealth at time of death or transfer – as a source of funding to meet America's human resource needs. Because the fruits of American economic growth are increasingly being concentrated among the privileged 10 to 15 percent of the population at the top of the middle-age income and wealth distribution, serious consideration should be given to modest sharing of this wealth, such as those suggested by Congressman Downey and Senator Gore in 1991 and by the National Commission on Children (see Steuerle and Jaffras, 1991) and their proposals to substitute a refundable child tax credit for the children's personal exemption, to expand basic health and human capital programs to cover all needy youth, and above all, to fund these expenditures via a modest increase in the top federal income tax bracket (from 34 to 37 percent). The significant secular changes in the size distribution of permanent income found in this paper make a strong case for the increased taxation of high income Americans as an answer to the oft heard question in Washington and in the state capitals. . . . 'but where will we raise the money?'

Appendix   Measures of Economic Status and Middle-Income Boundaries

Two important methodological issues arose in the transition analysis: (1) Should our measure of household income adjust for differences in family size? and (2) What income levels should define the boundaries of low-, middle- and high-income groups across time?

Adjust Income for Family Size?

It is common practice in poverty research to adjust income for family size to produce an income measure called 'income-to-needs,' usually obtained by dividing a household's income by the U.S. Government poverty threshold for the household's size. Well-being, it is argued, depends both on resources (usually income) and on the number and characteristics of individuals who must share those resources.

But what happens when we move beyond poverty to a study of middle- and high-income status? On the one hand, it can be argued that middle-income status also depends on both income and how that income is shared by the household. A household with two adults and an annual income of $35 000 has more income per person than does a household receiving the same income but consisting of two parents and two children. By this logic, a birth reduces well-being if it is not associated with an increase in income and the movement of a child from this household to a separate dwelling improves the well-being of the household left behind, so long as the departing child has 'eaten' more than he has earned.

However, others (e.g., Lambert, 1990; Fisher, 1987; Pollak and Wales, 1979) have argued that at some point in the income distribution, households may choose to add voluntarily to their 'needs' via the birth (or adoption) of children. In such cases, where children can clearly be identified as what economists call 'consumption goods,' the addition of a child does not necessarily decrease economic well-being. Particularly in a study of transitions from middle- to high-income, such adjustments to well-being can become arbitrary and misleading. Since we feel that both arguments have merit, we use two kinds of income boundaries: adjusting and not adjusting for family size. Size adjustments are accomplished by dividing income by the U.S. poverty line and its implicit equivalence scale.

Defining Middle (Income) Class

Our search for upper and lower boundaries of 'middle income' began with a review of how several authors have defined the rich, affluent, well-to-do, upper class, etc., in recent studies (Table A-1). Our choice of the boundary of 'high income-to-needs' was 6.0 (i.e., six times the poverty line). The 'high income' boundary was set at $55 000 (in 1987 dollars). These cutoffs came from examining the distribution of two-year average income and income-to-needs, expressed in 1987 dollars using the CPI-UX1, and the sample of adults (25–50) defined earlier. Income trends produce changing numbers of adults above and below these boundaries, but in the middle of the sample period (1977–8) each of these measures left roughly 10 percent (in fact 9 percent) of adults with high incomes.

Table A-1   Definitions of high-income status in other studies

Measure of 'richness'	Source
150 to 200 percent median; above 200 percent median	Kosters and Ross (1987)
Top one-third of distribution (affluent)	Rainwater (1974)
Disposable income-to-needs above 1.5 (well-to-do)	Coder, Rainwater, Smeeding (1989)
Pre-tax income-to-needs above 9.0 (rich)	Danziger, Gottschalk, Smolensky (1989)
Unadjusted money income $75 000 to $100 000 (moderately affluent); above $100 000 (very affluent)	U.S. Bureau of the Census (1990)
160 to 225 percent median (upper middle class); over 225 percent median (upper class)	Blackburn and Bloom (1986, 1987)
Above $50 000 in 1984 dollars (high income)	Bradbury (1986)
Variety of measures, adjusted and unadjusted especially 75th and 90th percentiles of income indexed relative to the median	Horrigan and Haugen (1988); Karoly (1990)

Following a similar procedure, we chose the 2.0 income-to-needs level and $18 500 (in 1987 dollars) as boundaries of the 'low income' groups. Each of these separated roughly the bottom quintile (actually the 18th percentile) of the distributions in 1977–8. The 2.0 level also appeals to us because of the recent work of Holden and Smeeding (1990) and Scholz and Maritato (1990), which used 2.0 as an income-to-needs level separating the economically 'insecure' and 'secure'. In addition we felt that cyclicity of income and earnings movements around the $20 000 threshold (e.g., Center on Budget and Policy Priorities, 1989; Levy, 1987) was an important phenomenon to capture in our analyses. Thus we arrived at our distributions of high- (6.0 and above; $55 000 and above), low- (below 2.0; below $18 500), and middle-income (2.00–5.99; $18 500–$55 000) groups.

Acknowledgments

The authors would like to thank William T. Dickens, Jerry Evensky, James Follain, Peter Gottschalk, Katherine Newman, Isaac Shapiro and Dorothy Duncan for helpful comments and Deborah Laren and Naomi Sealand for research assistance and Esther Gray for excellent secretarial support. The authors retain responsibility for all errors of omission and commission.

Notes

1. As explained below, as of late 1990, a consistent time series on post-tax household income is possible in the PSID only for calendar years 1967 through 1986. Incomes for 1987 and 1988 are used only in the wealth section of the chapter.
2. We also experimented with a transition measure that required household income to be in the low-, middle- and high-income categories for *both* the first and second or both fourth and fifth years. This restriction yielded presumably more reliable but fewer transitions, and did not fundamentally alter the conclusions of our analysis.
3. An alternative approach to the definition of boundaries, suggested by Peter Gottschalk, was to define the upper and lower bounds of the middle class at the same percentile points of the income distribution each year. We implemented this completely relative definition by setting the 'high income' line in each year at the 90th percentile and the lower bound of the middle class at the 20th percentile. With one minor exception (noted below) the results using this approach were very similar to those using the absolute approach.
4. As documented by the Center on Budget and Policy Priorities (1990), the 1989 CPS data show an all time high share of aggregate income for the top quintile and ventile and all time lows for the bottom two quintiles. The middle three-fifths of the family income distribution in 1989 received the lowest income share recorded by the Census since 1947, only 50.8 percent of total CPS money income, while the top fifth of families shared 44.6 percent of the total – their largest share ever recorded.
5. The comparable fractions of adults making the four transitions involving income-to-needs are 7.7, 27.5, 31.8 and 6.8 percent, respectively.
6. In calculating trends in disposable personal income per capita over each

five-year period, we regressed the natural logarithm of the per capita personal income measure on calendar year. The slope of the regression line has the interpretation as the average annual percentage growth. This produced a set of 'middle years' – 1974, 1975, 1979, 1980 and 1981 – with economic growth that was much below average.

7. Transitions based on income-to-needs showed very similar calendar-year patterns, as did transitions based on the completely relative definition of economic status. The single exception was that transitions into the high-income group (top 9 percent) were no more prevalent in the 1980s than before. We suspect that these differences are due to the fact that the top 9 percent had incomes that were growing so fast that they succeeded in pulling the lower boundary of the top income group up as fast as the incomes of those who would otherwise have joined the group. Hence, the extent of movement 'up' the distribution was no greater in the 1980s than before. A look at the inflation-adjusted dollar changes in income among adults grouped near the high-income cutoff point (e.g., $50 000–$55 000, $55 000–$60 000, etc.), showed all of the medians to be larger in the 1980s than before.

8. In contrast to the other transition based tables, the transitions in Table 7.2 are based on the 'both year' definition of income that required family income to be in a given income status in both years 1 and 2 or 4 and 5.

9. For example, in the analysis of transitions from middle- into high-income status, a person with an initial two year average household income of $27 500 would have an income that was 50 percent of the $55 000 transition line. In each set of regressions we expressed the distances to the transition lines as a set of dummy variables based on quintiles of the sample at risk of making the given transition. The exact regression results are available from the authors upon request.

10. If the entire income distribution were moving closer to the upper boundary of the middle-income group, then the typical person 'at risk' of making a transition into the upper-income group would be closer to the boundary after 1980 than before. Our dummy variables measuring a person's distance to the transition boundary adjust for this differential risk.

11. We calculated the effect of each demographic characteristic by estimating a regression-adjusted difference between the given demographic group and overall sample average. We then converted the logistic difference into an adjusted probability using the formula: $P_s = P_b\, e^{\beta \Delta x} / [(1 - P_b) + P_b\, e^{\beta \Delta x}]$ where P_s is the adjusted transition probability, P_b is the overall sample probability, ß is the logistic regression coefficient of interest and Δx is the change in the independent variable of interest.

12. Recall that we used roughly the 20th and 90th percentiles of the income distribution to define the boundaries of our middle-income group.

13. To determine pre-tax income cutoffs for the 1984–8 period we inflated the $18 500 and $55 000 amounts to 1984–8 levels using the CPI-UX1 and further increased these amounts by the average gap between pre- and post-tax income for households in 1984 with post-tax income around $18 500 and $55 000.

14. Another way to integrate wealth into our income-based analysis of

inequality is to substitute for reported property income (i.e., rent, dividends and interest) an imputed return on net wealth and to recalculate changes in the size of the low-, middle- and high-income groups based on this expanded definition of wealth. We also compared income transitions based on the two alternative treatments of income from wealth. Virtually never were favorable transitions based on one income definition accompanied by unfavorable transitions based on the other definition.

Using pre-tax income levels of $70 263 and $21 316 in 1987 dollars as boundaries of the middle-income group we applied the rate of return on U.S. government long-term bonds to net worth to obtain our alternative measure of income from wealth. With these boundaries, the group of middle-income adults shrank in size between 1984–5 and 1987–8 from 67.8 to 64.3 percent, but so did the lower-income group, from 18.9 to 16.4 percent. The big gainer was the high-income group, which grew from 13.2 to 19.1 percent.

15. In calculating house equity as a fraction of net worth and debt as a fraction of income, we took all individuals between the 25th and 75th percentiles and then found the mean of these ratios across these sets of individuals. Sample sizes for the 'fell from high income' group were sufficiently small that we took all such individuals in making the mean ratio calculations.

References

Avery, R. B., G. E. Elliehausen, and A. B. Kennickell (1988) 'Measuring Wealth with Survey Data: An Evaluation of the 1983 Survey of Consumer Finances,' *Review of Income and Wealth*, **34** (December) 339–69.

Bane, M. J. and D. T. Ellwood (1986) 'Slipping In and Out of Poverty: The Dynamics of Spells,' *Journal of Human Resources*, **1** (Winter) 1–23.

Blackburn, M. and D. Bloom (1987) 'Earnings and Income Inequality in the United States,' *Population and Development Review*, **13**, 575–609.

Bradbury, K. L. (1986) 'The Shrinking Middle Class,' *New England Economic Review* (September/October) 41–55.

Buhmann, B., L. Rainwater, G. Schmans, and T. Smeeding (1988) 'Income, Well Being, Poverty and Equivalence Scales: Sensitivity Estimates across Ten Countries Using the LIS Database,' *Review of Income and Wealth*, **34** (June) 115–42.

Burtless, G. (1989) *A Future of Lousy Jobs?* (Washington, DC: Brookings).

Center on Budget and Policy Priorities (1989) 'Drifting Apart' (Washington, DC: Center on Budget and Policy Priorities, July 1989).

Center on Budget and Policy Priorities (1990) 'Rich Poor Income Gap Hits 40 Year High' (Washington, DC: Center on Budget and Policy Priorities, October 1990).

Coder, J., L. Rainwater, and T. Smeeding (1989) 'Inequality among Children and Elderly in Ten Nations: The U.S. in an International Context,' *American Economic Review*, **79** (May) 320–24.

Congressional Budget Office (1991) unpublished tabulations.

Danziger, S., P. Gottschalk, and E. Smolensky (1989) 'How the Rich Have Fared, 1973–1987,' *American Economic Review*, **79**, 310–14.

Duncan, G. J. *et al.* (1984) *Years of Poverty, Years of Plenty* (Ann Arbor, MI: Institute for Social Research).

Duncan, G. J. and W. Rodgers (1991) 'Is Children's Poverty More Persistent?' *American Sociological Review*.

Eargle, J. (1991) 'Household Wealth and Asset Ownership: 1988,' Bureau of the Census, *Current Population Reports*, Series P-70, No. 22 (Washington, DC: U.S. Department of Commerce, December).

Easterlin, R. C., C. MacDonald and D. J. Macunovich (1990) 'How Have American Baby Boomers Fared? Earnings and Economic Well-Being of Young Adults, 1964–1987,' *Journal of Population Economics*, **3**, 277–90.

Fisher, F. (1987) 'Household Equivalence Scales and Interpersonal Comparisons,' *Review of Economic Studies*, **54**, 519–24.

Gottschalk, P. and S. Danziger (1989) 'Increasing Inequality in the United States: What We Know and What We Don't?', *Journal of Post-Keynesian Economics*, **11**, 174–95.

Hill, M. (1991) *The Panel Study of Income Dynamics* (Beverly Hills: Sage).

Holden, K. and T. Smeeding (1990) 'The Poor, The Rich and the Insecure Elderly Caught In-Between,' *Milbank Quarterly*, **68**, 191–219.

Horrigan, M. W. and S. E. Haugen (1988) 'The Declining Middle-Class Thesis: A Sensitivity Analysis,' *Monthly Labor Review*, **111**, 3–13.

Jencks, C. (1991) 'Is the American Underclass Growing?' in C. Jencks and P. Peterson (eds), *The Urban Underclass* (Washington, DC: Brookings).

Jencks, C. and S. Mayer (1990) 'Poverty and the Distribution of Material Hardship,' *Journal of Human Resources*, **24**, 88–113.

Karoly, L. (1990) 'The Trend in Inequality among Families, Individuals and Workers in the U.S.: A Twenty-Five Year Perspective' (Santa Monica: Rand Corporation, April) mimeo.

Kosters, M. H. and M. N. Ross (1987) 'The Distribution of Earnings and Employment Opportunities: A Re-Examination of the Evidence,' Occasional Paper (Washington, DC: American Enterprise Institute).

Kosters, M. H. and M. N. Ross (1988) 'A Shrinking Middle Class?' *The Public Interest*, **90** (Winter) 3–27.

Lambert, P. (1990) 'The Income Tax as a Tax on Equivalent Income' (York: University of York, October) mimeo.

Levy, F. (1987) *Dollars and Dreams* (New York: Russell Sage).

Levy, F. and R. Michel (1991) *The Economic Future of American Families* (Washington, DC: Urban Institute Press, January).

Michel, R. (1991) 'Economic Growth and Income Equality Since the 1982 Recession,' *Journal of Policy Analysis and Management*, **10**, 181–203.

Newman, K. (1988) *Falling from Grace* (New York: Vintage).

Pechman, J. (1990) 'The Future of the Income Tax,' *American Economic Review*, **80**, 1–20.

Phillips, K. (1990) *The Politics of Rich and Poor: Wealth and the American Electorate in the Reagan Aftermath* (New York: Random House).

Pollak, R. and T. Wales (1979) 'Welfare Comparisons and Equivalence Scales,' *American Economic Review*, **69**, 216–22.

Rainwater, L. (1974) *What Money Buys* (New York: Basic Books).

Reich, R. (1991) *The Work of Nations* (New York: Knopf).

Scholz, J. and A. Maritato (1990) 'Dimensions of Vulnerability Facing Young Families' (Madison, WI: Institute for Research on Poverty, September), mimeo.

Steuerle, E. and J. Jaffras (1991) 'A $1000 Tax Credit for Every Child: A Base of Reform for the Nation's Tax, Welfare and Health Systems,' Policy Paper (Washington, DC: Urban Institute, April).

Thurow, L. (1987) 'A Surge in Inequality,' *Scientific American*, **256**, 30–7.

U.S. Bureau of the Census (1988) 'Measuring the Effect of Benefits and Taxes on Income and Poverty: 1986,' *Current Population Reports*, Series P-60, No. 164-RD-1 (Washington, DC: U.S. Government Printing Office, December).

U.S. Bureau of the Census (1989) 'Money Income of Households, Families, and Persons in the United States: 1988,' *Current Population Reports*, Series P-60, No. 162 (Washington, DC: U.S. Government Printing Office, February).

U.S. Bureau of the Census (1990a) 'Money Income of Households, Families and Persons in the United States: 1989,' *Current Population Reports*, Series P-60, No. 168 (Washington, DC: U.S. Government Printing Office).

U.S. Bureau of the Census (1990b) 'Trends in Income by Selected Characteristics: 1947 to 1988,' *Current Population Reports*, Series P-60, No. 167 (Washington, DC: U.S. Government Printing Office, April 1990).

U.S. House of Representatives (1991) *Green Book*. Committee on Ways and Means, May 7, 1991.

Wolff, E. (1989) 'Trends in Aggregate Household Wealth in the U.S. 1900–1983,' *Review of Income and Wealth*, **35** (March) 1–30.

Comment

William T. Dickens

When graduate students come to me and tell me they are interested in income distribution I always experience an involuntary shudder. It is hard to think of another topic area that is as charged. It is also hard to think of one in which it is harder to define what constitutes an interesting question. At least in part this is because we have no clear definition of what constitutes a good or bad distribution of income. This paper typifies these problems for me. There is lots in it I find interesting but there are some things I find difficult to interpret and in these cases I have suggestions.

The first question for me is 'is there a problem?' My answer is yes, but you do not see it in this paper. From other studies we know that the real earnings of low-wage workers have been falling over the last decade. At the same time the real earnings of high-wage workers have been climbing. This, to my mind, represents a serious social problem which deserves policy attention. But, you do not see that in this paper. By focusing on incomes and choosing the cutoff point the authors do, we still have a disappearing middle, but it is only disappearing because the number of people with high incomes is growing faster than the number of people with low incomes is declining. Is this something we should be concerned about? It is not clear. There is more inequality, but on average people are better off and no one appears to be worse off. I would suggest the authors choose their measure of inequality to highlight the serious problem of declining real incomes in the low end of the distribution.

Of course the focus of this paper is on changes in income and not the static distribution. The authors motivate this question by saying they want to know how the changes are taking place. This impresses me as an interesting question. I would be more concerned if I knew that the decline of the middle class was associated with an increase in downward mobility as opposed to a slowing of upward mobility. I would not try hard to defend that view – like much in considering income distribution, it is mainly a matter of taste.

The problem is that this paper does not really get at these questions. The movements it analyzes are confounded in two ways. First, the periods analyzed are not periods of constant decline in the size of the middle class, so the movements we see are for both periods when the middle income group is growing and periods when it is declining. Second, even if the income distribution was stable we would see considerable movement. The transitions the authors report confound these steady state transitions with the changes that are responsible for the shift in the distribution.

A more interesting approach, from my point of view, would have been to pick two points in time and describe what movements of types of individuals account for the changes in the cross-section distribution between these two points in time. If it was possible to compare these changes with a period when the distribution was relatively stable, that would add some interest.

Something else that could be done with panel data (or with synthetic cohorts in repeated cross-sections) that I would find interesting would be an explanation of the extent to which increasing inequality reflects difference between as opposed to within age cohorts. This would allow us to answer the question of how much of the change is due to differences between individuals as opposed to being due to changes in life-cycle patterns. I would care less about increased inequality if it was mainly between rather than within cohorts.

The analysis of the wealth data I find very interesting, though I would stress different points than the authors do. First, everyone is getting wealthier. Second, the wealth distribution is being compressed – they note that the 20th and 90th percentiles had about the same increase, but the 80th percentile had a smaller increase than the 20th as did the 50th. Here a demographic breakout would be very interesting to me as I would again like to know how much of the increase in wealth might be due to aging of the population. It would also be interesting to know how much of the change in wealth was increased housing wealth. I suspect a lot. From what the authors report I suspect that changes in the distribution of non-housing wealth within cohorts would be surprisingly equalizing.

With respect to policy recommendations I am sympathetic to the authors' recommendation to change the deduction for children into a tax credit, but I do not see how it flows from their results. Before we make policy recommendations to deal with changes in the income distribution, we should consider what is causing those changes. From what we know from this and other studies, much of the increase in inequality is related to the increased return to schooling. This increase might be due to several causes. To the extent it represents temporary disequilibrium in the supply and demand for educated labor, increasing taxes on the wealthy will only exacerbate pre-tax income inequality by slowing adjustment. On the other hand, if the changes reflect a change in the return to innate ability as reflected in educational attainment, then such a tax change might have little effect on the efficiency of the economy while lowering the rents earned by those with high levels of innate ability.

8 Changes in Earnings Differentials in the 1980s: Concordance, Convergence, Causes, and Consequences

McKinley L. Blackburn, David E. Bloom, and Richard B. Freeman

The structure of earnings in the United States changed sharply in the 1980s. In contrast to the long-term trend of declining wage differentials between more- and less-skilled workers, the structure of earnings shifted against the less-skilled, with less-educated workers suffering sizable losses in real wages while more-educated workers enjoyed modest gains (see, e.g., Blackburn, Bloom, and Freeman, 1990; Bound and Johnson, 1989; Katz and Revenga, 1989; and Murphy and Welch, 1991). Increases in education-earnings differentials appear to account for part, though not all, of the rise in earnings inequality among males (see Blackburn, 1990; and Juhn, Murphy, and Pierce, 1989), which has in turn contributed to the rise in income inequality among families (Blackburn and Bloom, 1991).

Analyses of the changing pattern of earnings in the 1980s have generally focused on the magnitudes and causes of the increase in education-earnings differentials among white males. Only limited attention has been paid to the earnings structure among females and minority workers, or to the effects of changes in the earnings structure on school enrollment decisions.[1] Have the earnings structure and employment rates of these other demographic groups changed in the same manner in the 1980s as they did for white males? Within education groups, what happened to earnings and employment differentials between white males and other demographic groups? What can be learned about the causes of the changing earnings structure from differences in the experience of the various demographic groups? To what extent have the college-enrollment decisions of the different groups responded to changes in the earnings structure? Are market-supply responses likely to 'correct' the massive rise in differentials?

We address these questions using March 1980 and March 1989 CPS data on the earnings and employment status of workers in selected demographic groups. The March CPS provides information on workers' annual earnings for the calendar year preceding each survey, and on workers' labor-force status at the time of the survey. To capture primarily changes in annual earnings due to changes in wage rates, and not to changes in hours worked, we examine the earnings of full-time, year-round workers only. As our measure of employment, we use employment-to-population ratios rather than unemployment rates, although the fact that unemployment rates and employment rates move inversely for most groups suggests that a focus on unemployment would yield similar results. We focus on the earnings differentials of high school graduates (HS) relative to workers with less than high school education (LTHS) and of college graduates (CG) relative to high school graduates.[2] We also examine changes in the economic position of our specified demographic groups relative to white males, both in terms of earnings and employment.

We find that:

(1) Education-earnings and education-employment rate differentials widened for most, but not all, demographic groups. Education-earnings differentials rose more for whites (i.e., nonblacks, as defined in our analysis) than for blacks, while employment rate differences associated with education increased more for blacks than for whites. Most strikingly, the earnings differential between high school graduates and dropouts narrowed for black men while their employment-rate differential widened substantially. The fact that the change in education-earnings differentials varied across demographic groups in magnitude, and in some cases in direction, implies that distinct factors have affected the different groups. It also suggests that the overall increase in earnings inequality in the U.S. represents the net effect of sometimes discordant underlying currents.

(2) The earnings and employment position of white females improved relative to white males in the 1980s across all education groups. The change in the relative economic position of blacks, however, is less clear.

(3) Much of the change in education-earnings differentials for specific groups is attributable to measurable economic factors: to changes in the occupational or industrial structure of employment; to

changes in industry average wages; to the fall in the real value of the minimum wage, and the fall in union density; and to changes in the relative growth rate of more-educated workers. These factors also help in explaining the changes in demographic-group differentials within education categories.

(4) There has been a sizable college-enrollment response to the rising relative wages of college graduates. Females appear to respond more to male than to female earnings differentials, suggesting that they anticipate continued elimination of gender differentials within education groups over time. Looking to the future, the supply responses suggest that college-to-high school differentials will drop in the 1990s, barring accelerated shifts in the relative demand for college graduates.

8.1 CHANGES IN EARNINGS AND EMPLOYMENT DIFFERENTIALS FOR RACE/GENDER GROUPS

One of the most striking changes in the labor market for male workers in the 1980s was the massive increase in earnings and employment differentials across schooling groups. The increase was most marked for young workers, driven largely by sizable falls in the real earnings and employment of the less-educated rather than by any major improvements in the economic position of more-educated workers.

Table 8.1 records average real earnings for 24 demographic-education groups in 1979 and 1988, and the implied annual growth rates of earnings between those years. We distinguish between blacks and whites, men and women, and 25–64 and 25–34 year olds, in addition to the three education groups. The reported statistics are geometric means of annual wage and salary income for full-time year-round workers in the relevant March CPS, adjusted for inflation using the GNP personal-consumption-expenditure deflator. The table illustrates the well-known fall in real earnings for less-educated white males, and the modest rise in real earnings for white males with four or more years of college. The nature of changes in average earnings within education groups is similar for all prime-age white males (ages 25–64) and for those white males who have more recently entered the labor market (ages 25–34), although among the less-educated, real earnings have declined more rapidly for the young than for the old.

Table 8.1   Average earnings within demographic groups, 1979 and 1988

Demographic group	1979	1988	Annual growth rate
Age: 25–64			
All workers	23 445	23 297	–0.0%
White males			
LTHS	22 682	19 282	–1.8
HS	27 785	25 109	–1.1
CG	35 901	37 034	0.3
Black males			
LTHS	17 331	16 918	–0.3
HS	21 264	19 054	–1.2
CG	29 896	30 333	0.2
White females			
LTHS	13 005	12 647	–0.3
HS	15 800	16 225	0.3
CG	22 431	25 537	1.4
Black females			
LTHS	11 883	11 340	–0.5
HS	14 966	14 649	–0.2
CG	22 688	23 704	0.5
Age: 25–34			
All workers	21 823	20 678	–0.6%
White males			
LTHS	19 848	16 108	–2.3
HS	24 889	21 776	–1.5
CG	29 288	29 780	0.2
Black males			
LTHS	14 596	14 594	–0.0
HS	19 449	16 638	–2.0
CG	26 830	24 348	–1.5
White females			
LTHS	12 623	10 852	–1.7
HS	15 403	15 348	–0.0
CG	20 987	23 791	1.4
Black females			
LTHS	11 749	11 169	–0.6
HS	14 596	13 285	–1.0
CG	19 349	19 567	0.1

These statistics were calculated using the March 1980 and March 1989 Current Population Surveys. Earnings are defined as wage and salary income; only full-time, year-round workers with no self-employment earnings were included in the sample for this table. The average earnings statistics are geometric means, reported in 1988 dollars.

Whites include both the white and the 'other' racial group. The educational-group abbreviations are:

LTHS — less than high school education (completed schooling less than 12 years)
HS — high school graduates (schooling equal to 12 years)
CG — college graduates (schooling 16 years or greater)

This growth rate is calculated using the 1979 and 1988 endpoints only.

The results for white women show a pattern of change similar to that for white men, with a notable difference in the levels of change: greater increases in real earnings for the more-educated, and smaller decreases in real earnings for the less-educated (both compared to white men). The statistics for blacks, however, are more mixed. Among 25–64 year olds, black-male high school graduates suffered larger losses in real earnings than dropouts, producing a fall in the earnings differential between these educational groups. The earnings of 25–64 year-old black females increased more rapidly than those of white males, but less rapidly than those of white females, in all three education groups. Among 25–34 year olds, black-male college graduates suffered a real earnings loss of almost the same proportionate magnitude as that suffered by high school graduates, with both groups losing ground relative to high school dropouts. Among black women, high school graduates (though not college graduates) had larger losses in real earnings than dropouts. Taken at face value, the statistics in Table 8.1 suggest that different factors affected the job markets for blacks and whites.

To examine whether these changes in average earnings are due to changes in the labor-market characteristics of these broad demographic-education groups, we also estimated education-earnings differentials from regressions that control for the effects of age, marital status, and region on earnings.[3] The results of these regressions, reported in Table 8.2, reveal large increases in differentials for both white males and white females, but a mixed pattern of small increases, and some decreases, for blacks.[4] In particular, the rise in the CG/HS differential was much smaller for blacks than for whites, and the change in the HS/LTHS differential for blacks diverged qualitatively from the changes for whites. None of the estimated changes for blacks are statistically significant.[5]

Turning from earnings to employment patterns, Table 8.3 reports employment-to-population ratios in 1980 and 1989 by level of education for the various demographic groups. For white men, employment rates fell among 25–64 year olds, with a slightly greater fall for the less-educated, but were unchanged among 25–34 year olds (having fallen in the 1970s for that age group). Among black men, by contrast, employment rates dropped sharply – for all three education groups among 25–64 year-olds, but especially for the less-educated among 25–34 year-olds. The nature of changes in employment rates for women is different. Among whites, employment-population ratios rose; since they tended to rise more for the more-educated, employment differences between educational categories widened

Table 8.2   Regression estimates of changes in education-earnings differentials within demographic groups, 1979 and 1988[a]

Age: 25–64

	White males			Black males		
	1979	1988	Δ[b]	1979	1988	Δ
HS/LTHS[c]	0.23	0.29	0.06(0.01)	0.21	0.18	–0.03(0.04)
CG/HS	0.28	0.39	0.11(0.01)	0.34	0.40	0.06(0.06)

	White females			Black females		
	1979	1988	Δ	1979	1988	Δ
HS/LTHS	0.20	0.27	0.07(0.02)	0.23	0.25	0.02(0.04)
CG/HS	0.35	0.46	0.11(0.01)	0.45	0.49	0.04(0.05)

Age: 25–34

	White males			Black males		
	1979	1988	Δ	1979	1988	Δ
HS/LTHS	0.23	0.30	0.07(0.03)	0.30	0.15	–0.15(0.09)
CG/HS	0.17	0.33	0.16(0.02)	0.28	0.35	0.07(0.09)

	White females			Black females		
	1979	1988	Δ	1979	1988	Δ
HS/LTHS	0.21	0.36	0.15(0.04)	0.21	0.19	–0.02(0.09)
CG/HS	0.31	0.43	0.12(0.02)	0.32	0.38	0.06(0.07)

[a] These statistics are estimated differentials from logarithmic earnings regressions that include nine age dummies, three marital status dummies, and eight region dummies, as well as education dummies. The dependent variable is annual wage and salary income, and the sample is restricted to full-time, year-round workers.
[b] This is the estimated change in the differential from 1979 to 1988. The number in parentheses is the standard error for this change.
[c] HS/LTHS is the differential between high-school graduates and dropouts, and CG/HS is the differential between college graduates and high school graduates.

(except for the CG/HS differential for 25–34 year-olds). Among black females, the most striking change is a sharp drop in the employment rate for 25–34 year old high school dropouts.[6]

For groups whose relative earnings and employment moved in the same direction, or for which one statistic changed greatly while the other did not, the patterns of change in the two measures give a consistent picture of market changes. However, opposing changes in

Table 8.3   Measures of labor market activity within education groups, 1980 and 1989

Age: 25–64

	White males			Black males		
	1980	1989	Δ	1980	1989	Δ
E/POP[a]						
LTHS	0.75	0.71	–0.04	0.64	0.57	–0.07
HS	0.88	0.86	–0.02	0.84	0.76	–0.08
CG	0.94	0.93	–0.01	0.90	0.86	–0.04
HS-LTHS	0.13	0.15	0.02	0.20	0.19	–0.01
CG-HS	0.06	0.09	0.01	0.06	0.10	0.04

	White females			Black females		
	1980	1989	Δ	1980	1989	Δ
E/POP						
LTHS	0.40	0.42	0.02	0.43	0.41	–0.02
HS	0.58	0.65	0.07	0.64	0.68	0.04
CG	0.71	0.79	0.08	0.85	0.86	0.01
HS-LTHS	0.18	0.23	0.05	0.21	0.27	0.06
CG-HS	0.13	0.14	0.01	0.21	0.18	–0.03

Age: 25–34

	White males			Black males		
	1980	1989	Δ	1980	1989	Δ
E/POP						
LTHS	0.80	0.80	0.0	0.68	0.56	–0.12
HS	0.90	0.90	0.0	0.80	0.75	–0.05
CG	0.94	0.94	0	0.90	0.90	0
HS-LTHS	0.10	0.10	0	0.12	0.19	0.07
CG-HS	0.04	0.04	0	0.10	0.15	0.05

	White females			Black females		
	1980	1989	Δ	1980	1989	Δ
E/POP						
LTHS	0.43	0.44	0.01	0.41	0.29	–0.12
HS	0.59	0.67	0.08	0.64	0.64	0
CG	0.75	0.82	0.07	0.84	0.88	0.04
HS-LTHS	0.16	0.23	–0.07	0.23	0.35	0.12
CG-HS	0.16	0.15	–0.01	0.20	0.24	0.04

[a] E/POP is the employment-to-population ratio. The statistics were calculated using the March 1980 and March 1989 Current Population Surveys.

relative earnings and employment in the HS/LTHS differentials for 25–34 year old blacks (a 15 point drop in the earnings differential coupled with a 7 point increase in the employment rate difference) leave open the question of whether the overall economic position of the more-educated improved or worsened relative to the less-educated. One way to combine the two statistics to reach an overall assessment is to multiply the earnings and employment rates to yield earnings per member of the population.[7] In this case, the overall change would be equal to the change in the logarithmic earnings differential plus the change in the logarithm of the ratio of employment rates. For example, comparing young black-male high school graduates to high school dropouts, this calculation suggests that the change in employment rates had an effect on the 'total earnings' differential that is equivalent to a 13 log-point increase in the education/wage differential between these two groups. This essentially offsets the estimated 15 log-point decline in the annual-earnings differential (reported in Table 8.2). The impact of changes in employment rates on the HS/LTHS 'total earnings' differential for young black females is even larger – a 34 log-point increase – suggesting that the labor market for high school graduates may have improved relative to dropouts among this group.

One way to highlight the cross-group variation of earnings and employment experiences is to reorganize the earnings and employment data to show differentials by demographic group within educational categories. Table 8.4 does this by reporting changes in earnings and employment rates for black males, white females, and black females relative to changes for white males in the same education category.

Among 25–64 year olds, white and black women gained relative to white men in both earnings levels and employment. However, the earnings position of black men did not improve relative to that of white men, except among dropouts. With the employment rates of black men falling relative to those of white men in all education groups, more-educated black men fell further behind whites. Among 25–34 year olds, white women gained relative to white men in both earnings and employment. Among college graduates, black men and women had modest falls in relative earnings, while among high school graduates, black males lost ground in both their relative earnings and employment rates. There are remarkable black–white differences among 25–34 year old high school dropouts, as both black men and women gained in earnings but lost in employment. In sum, the

Table 8.4 Changes in earnings and employment rates of demographic groups relative to white males – within education categories

Age group:	25–64		25–34	
	Change in		*Change in*	
Group	*Earnings*[a]	*E/POP*[b]	*Earnings*	*E/POP*
College Graduates				
Black males	–0.02(0.04)	–0.03	–0.06(0.06)	0
White females	0.09(0.02)	0.09	0.09(0.02)	0.07
Black females	0 (0.04)	0.02	–0.02(0.06)	–0.04
High school graduates				
Black males	0 (0.02)	–0.06	–0.03(0.04)	–0.05
White females	0.12(0.01)	0.09	0.13(0.02)	0.08
Black females	0.07(0.02)	0.06	0.03(0.04)	0
Less than high school				
Black males	0.09(0.03)	–0.03	0.19(0.07)	–0.12
White females	0.12(0.02)	0.06	0.08(0.05)	0.01
Black females	0.09(0.04)	0.02	0.14(0.09)	–0.12

[a] This is the estimated change (from 1979 to 1988) in the earnings differentials between the specified race/gender group and white males, within the specified education category. The differentials are from regression estimates that include region and age dummies as independent variables. Standard errors are reported in parentheses.
[b] This is the change (from 1980 to 1989) in the difference in the employment-to-population ratio between the specified group and white males.

economic position of white females clearly improved relative to white males, but the change in the status of blacks relative to white males is less clear.

Can the complex changes in earnings across demographic-education groups be summarized parsimoniously? The following identity links the earnings (W_{ij}) of workers in the ith education category and jth gender–race group to the earnings of white males in the same education group ($W_i.$):

$$W_{ij} = W_i. + D_{ij},$$

where D_{ij} is the difference of the average earnings of workers in the ijth race/gender group with those of the reference group of white males. Focusing on changes over time (Δ), we have

$$\Delta W_{ij} = \Delta W_{i.} + \Delta D_{ij}. \tag{1}$$

If the labor market treats all race-gender groups similarly, save for fixed differences due to discrimination, changes in $W_{i.}$ would be associated with identical changes in W_{ij} over time, producing similar changes in educational differentials for all demographic groups. We refer to this as the *concordant* change hypothesis. If market forces were putting equal pressure on non-competitive labor-market differentials to disappear, we would further expect within-group differences to narrow more rapidly the greater the initial differential. This suggests that $\Delta D_{ij} = BD_{ij}$, with $-2 < B < 0$; with this relationship, average earnings will increase more rapidly for groups with the largest initial earnings differences relative to white males, while variation in the average level of earnings across groups will decline over time. We refer to this as the *convergent* change hypothesis. The following estimable version of equation (1) links observed changes in a particular group's earnings to the changes in earnings of the reference group, and to the initial deviation of its earnings from those of the reference group:

$$\Delta W_{ij} = \alpha + \gamma \Delta W_{i.} = BD_{ij} + e, \tag{2}$$

where e is an error term, and the coefficient γ is allowed to differ from unity in order to capture imperfect transmission to other demographic groups of the factors that alter the relative earnings of white males.[8]

To examine the extent to which changes in the earnings structure among demographic groups can be represented by a simple combination of concordant and convergent changes, we estimated equation (2) using the 1979-to-1988 changes in earnings for 9 education/demographic groups (3 education groups for each of 3 race/gender groups). For 25–64 year olds, the estimated regression is (standard errors in parentheses)

$$\Delta W_{ij} = -1089 \quad +0.41\ \Delta W_{i.} \quad -0.19\ D_{ij} \quad R^2 = 0.67$$
$$\phantom{\Delta W_{ij} =}\ (1196) \qquad (0.16) \qquad\quad (0.11)$$

which is consistent with both the concordance and convergence hypotheses. For 25–34 year olds, the estimated regression is

$$\Delta W_{ij} = -2460 \quad +0.35\ \Delta W_{i.} \quad -0.34\ D_{ij} \quad R^2 = 0.39$$
$$\phantom{\Delta W_{ij} =}\ (1691) \qquad (0.28) \qquad\quad (0.21)$$

which, though less precisely estimated, also provides some support for both hypotheses. However, the strong version of the concordance hypothesis ($\theta = 1$) is not supported, and the R^2s suggest that substantial variation in wage changes is not accounted for by concordance and convergence. We turn next to explore the reasons for the concordant and convergent changes in earnings differentials, as well as the reasons for the non-concordant and nonconvergent variation.

8.2 DIFFERENTIAL FACTORS

Studies of rising earnings differentials among white males have considered several measurable economic factors as potential contributors to this rise: the inter-industry distribution of employment, the inter-occupation distribution of employment, the real value of the minimum wage, union density, immigration, educational quality, and relative labor supplies. These studies have accounted for some of the increased differentials, though a sizable residual remains.[9] In this section, we use a regression decomposition analysis to examine how a number of these factors have contributed to the trends in both education-earnings differentials and race/gender differentials. (See Blackburn, Bloom, and Freeman, 1990, for a full description of this method of analysis.)[10]

Table 8.5 reports our estimates of the contribution of selected factors to changes in education-earnings differentials. The upper panel refers to 25–64 year olds, the lower panel to 25–34 year olds. The first column repeats the estimated change in the regression-corrected earnings differentials reported in Table 8.3; the middle columns report the contributions of each of the five factors; the penultimate column reports the sum of these contributions; and the final column reports the residual change.

Our estimates of the effects of changes in occupational and industrial mix and the inter-industry wage structure are based on a simple regression decomposition. We pool our 1979 and 1988 samples for all workers in a demographic group and estimate a log earnings equation for the pooled sample. In controlling for the effects of education, age, region, and marital status on earnings, we allow these factors to have separate coefficients for 1979 and 1988. However, when we add dummy variables for occupation as independent variables, we constrain the coefficients on the dummy variables to be the same in both years. In this way, we measure the effect of occupational shifts holding constant the occupational wage structure (at its average level for the two years). The magnitudes by which the estimated changes over time in the regression–corrected education-earnings differential are lowered when the occupation dummies are added is our measure of the occupational-mix effect; these numbers are reported in the second column of Table 8.5.[11] Starting with a specification that includes occupation dummies, we then add industry dummy variables as controls, again estimating only one set of coefficients for the industry variables for both 1979 and 1988.[12] Finally, we estimate the effect of changes in the industrial wage structure on earnings-education differentials by allowing the industry wage coefficients in the earnings regression to vary from 1979 to 1988. The effects of industry shifts and industry-wage changes are reported in the third and fourth columns of Table 8.5.

Because union status is not available for jobs in the previous calendar year in our data, our measures of the impact of changes in union status are based on separate calculations using current-job information in the May 1979 CPS and the March 1989 CPS.[13] We first calculated the percent unionized in 1979 and in 1989 for each demographic-education group; these statistics (in columns 1 and 2 of Table A-4) illustrate the well-known fall in union density, particularly among less-educated workers. We then estimated union premia in 1979 for the various groups, by including union dummy variables interacted with education categories in our specifications for a usual-hourly-earnings regression.[14] The estimated premia we obtained for men are consistent with those from other studies, showing a larger union effect on wages for the less-educated. For women, our analysis shows little difference in union premia by education group, the one exception being a very large estimated union effect for 25–34 year old black female college graduates (i.e., 32 percent). Because we doubt the validity of this estimate, we have replaced it with the estimated premium for 25–34 year old white female college graduates. We estimate the effect of deunionization on the average earnings of the relevant education-demographic group by multiplying the decrease in the groups' proportion unionized by the relevant union wage premium. Estimates are reported in the sixth column of Table 8.5.

Our estimate of the effect of the change in the real minimum wage on the relative earnings of different groups of workers is also based on calculations using the May 1979 and March 1989 CPS. We compared the differentials from the actual distribution of hourly earnings in 1989 to the differentials from a simulated distribution constructed

Table 8.5 Contribution of changes in the occupational and industrial mix, the minimum wage, and unionization to changes in earnings differentials within demographic groups

| Differential | Actual change | Change due to:[a] | | | | | | Not Expl.[b] |
		Occ.	Indus.	I. Wage	Minim.	Union	Total	
Age: 25–64								
White males								
HS/LTHS	0.06	0.01	0	0.01	0.01	0.05	0.08	–0.02
CG/HS	0.11	0	0.02	0	0	0.01	0.03	0.08
Black males								
HS/LTHS	–0.03	–0.02	0.01	–0.01	0.01	–0.02	–0.03	0
CG/HS	0.06	0.01	–0.02	–0.02	0	0.05	0.02	0.04
White females								
HS/LTHS	0.07	0	0.01	0.02	0.02	0.01	0.06	0.01
CG/HS	0.11	0.01	0.03	–0.01	0	–0.01	0.02	0.09
Black females								
HS/LTHS	0.02	0	0.01	0	0.04	0	0.05	–0.03
CG/HS	0.04	–0.01	0.02	0.02	0.01	–0.03	0.01	0.03
Age: 25–34								
White males								
HS/LTHS	0.07	0.02	0	0.01	0.01	0.03	0.07	0
CG/HS	0.16	0	0.03	0	0	0.03	0.06	0.10
Black males								
HS/LTHS	–0.15	–0.01	–0.02	0.02	0.01	–0.03	–0.03	–0.12
CG/HS	0.07	0	0.02	0.03	0	0.06	0.11	–0.04
White females								
HS/LTHS	0.15	0.02	0	0.01	0.01	0.01	0.05	0.10
CG/HS	0.12	0	0.05	0	0.01	–0.01	0.05	0.07
Black females								
HS/LTHS	–0.02	–0.04	0	0.01	0.04	–0.02	–0.01	–0.01
CG/HS	0.06	–0.3	0.02	–0.02	0.01	–0.02	–0.04	0.10

[a] These are the estimated effects of the change on the specified earnings differentials. The changes refer to: Occ. – the occupational mix of the demographic group, Ind. – the industrial mix of the group, I. Wage – the interindustry wage structure, Minim. – the real value of the minimum wage, Union – the percentage of the group unionized, Total – the sum of the five estimated effects.

[b] The portion 'not explained' is the actual change in the differential minus the total change explained by the five effects listed in note *a*.

under the assumption that from 1979 to 1988 the nominal minimum wage increased at the rate of inflation (so that the minimum wage had the same real value in 1989 as it did in 1979.)[15] Our procedure for simulating the effect of raising the 1989 minimum wage to the real value of the minimum in 1979 is straightforward: first, if a worker's wage is between the actual minimum wage in 1989 ($3.35) and the simulated minimum ($4.61), their wage was raised to the simulated minimum; second, if a worker's wage was below the actual minimum in 1989, their wage was multiplied by the ratio of the simulated minimum to the actual minimum; and third, if a worker's wage was above the simulated minimum, it was not changed.[16] Our estimate of the impact of the fall in the real minimum wage on an earnings differential (reported in the fifth column of Table 8.5) is simply the difference between the actual change in the earnings differential and the change in our simulated data that hold the real minimum constant.

Changes in the occupational structure of employment appear to explain little of the changes in educational differentials, more often suggesting decreases rather than increases in earnings differentials. The estimated effects of shifts in industry employment are, on the other hand, generally in the 'right' direction and moderate; the effects of industry-wage shifts also tend to help explain the observed changes. Taken together, the shifts in occupation and industry employment and in the industry-wage structure can account for 20 to 40 percent of the increase in differentials for whites, but often suggest declines for blacks. Changes in union density have substantial effects on the pattern of differentials for male workers, while the minimum wage has a sizable effect primarily for the differential involving the lowest paid group – black female dropouts. The drop in unionization is the dominant factor explaining the change in the HS/LTHS differential among white males, and the change in the CG/HS differential among black males.[17]

There are a large number of decomposition statistics in Table 8.5. In some cases the statistics suggest that our decomposition analysis explains a sizable proportion of the observed changes; in other cases, our analysis 'over-explains' changes; and in yet others, it fails to explain much of the change at all. Can we summarize this diverse set of results using a single measure of the overall success of our analysis in accounting for the observed changes in education-earnings differentials? We propose a pseudo-R^2 measure that contrasts the sum of the squared changes in relative earnings after our analysis (the residual changes in the final column) to the sum of the squared changes in relative earnings for all groups before our analysis (in the first column). If $\Sigma(\Delta W)^2$ is the sum of the squared changes in actual earnings differentials, and if $\Sigma(\Delta W_r)^2$ is the sum of squared residual changes, we measure the proportion of the earnings-differential changes explained by our analysis as

$$1 - [\Sigma(\Delta W_r)^2 / \Sigma(\Delta W)^2].$$

If we explain all of the change in relative earnings for all groups, this statistic will equal unity. However, because the decompositions can increase rather than decrease the squared residuals, the statistic can be negative. Measuring the goodness-of-fit of our analysis in this way, we find that our analysis accounts for 53 percent of the squared changes in relative earnings for 25–64 year olds, and for 48 percent of the squared changes in relative earnings for 25–34 years olds.[18]

8.2.1 Demographic Differentials Within Education Groups

Table 8.6 reports the results of analyses designed to explain changes in differentials between various demographic groups and white males. The estimated effects of occupation and industry on changes in between-group differentials are from log earnings regressions estimated separately by educational group.[19] The estimated effects of unionization and minimum wages are calculated as the estimated effect of each factor on the average earnings of the specified group minus the effect on average earnings for white males. Using our pseudo-R^2 measure of the explanatory power of the model, our analysis accounts for 39 percent of the variation in changes between groups among 25–64 year olds, and 62 percent of the variation in changes across groups among 25–34 year olds.[20] This result for 25–34 year olds mainly reflects the effect of deunionization on the relative earnings of high school dropouts, since white males were the most highly unionized group in this education category. Note also that occupation, which explains little of the changes in education-earnings differentials, helps explain several of the changes in demographic differentials within education categories, particularly for LTHS workers. Changes in industry employment are also an important factor. By contrast, changes in the inter-industry wage structure often work in the opposite direction to the actual changes. As before, the decline in the minimum wage has its major effect on black female dropouts.

Table 8.6   Contribution of changes in the occupational and industrial mix, the minimum wage, and unionization to changes in earnings differentials relative to white males

Differential	Actual change	Change due to:						Not Expl.
		Occ.	Indus.	I. Wage	Minim.	Union	Total	
Age: 25–64								
College graduates								
B. Males	−0.02	−0.03	−0.02	0	0	0	−0.03	0.01
W. Females	0.09	0.02	0.02	0	0	−0.02	0.02	0.07
B. Females	0	0.01	0.04	−0.01	0	−0.05	−0.01	0.01
HS graduates								
B. Males	0	−0.02	−0.01	0	0	−0.04	−0.07	0.07
W. Females	0.12	0.01	0.01	0.01	0	0	0.03	0.09
B. Females	0.07	0.01	0.02	0.01	−0.01	−0.01	0.02	0.05
Less than HS								
B. Males	0.09	0.03	0	0.01	0	0.03	0.07	0.02
W. Females	0.12	0.03	0	−0.02	−0.01	0.04	0.04	0.08
B. Females	0.09	0.02	−0.01	−0.02	−0.03	0.04	0	0.09
Age: 25–34								
College graduates								
B. Males	−0.06	−0.03	0	0	0	0	−0.03	−0.03
W. Females	0.09	0.01	0.04	−0.01	0	−0.02	0.02	0.07
B. Females	−0.02	−0.02	0.04	−0.02	0	−0.04	−0.04	0.02
HS graduates								
B. Males	−0.03	−0.01	−0.02	0	0	−0.03	−0.07	0.04
W. Females	0.13	0	.01	0.02	−0.01	0.02	0.04	0.09
B. Females	0.03	0.01	0	0.03	−0.01	0.01	0.04	−0.01
Less than HS								
B. Males	0.19	0.03	0.02	0	0	0.03	0.08	0.11
W. Females	0.08	0	.01	−0.01	−0.01	0.04	0.03	0.05
B. Females	0.14	0.01	0	0.03	−0.03	0.06	0.07	0.07

8.2.2   The Effect of Relative Labor Supplies

Several recent analyses have stressed the slowdown in the relative growth of more-educated to less-educated white males, and the actual decline in the relative proportion of more-educated workers among 25–34 year old white males, as contributing to the rise in education-earnings differentials (see Blackburn, Bloom, and Freeman, 1990; Katz and Revenga, 1989). It seems natural to explore the

Table 8.7   Annual growth rates of the relative supply of labor force
participants, 1980–89

A: Relative supply within demographic groups

Age:	25–64		25–34	
	HS/LTHS	CG/HS	HS/LTHS	CG/HS
White males	0.04	0	0.01	–0.02
Black males	0.06	0.03	0.05	–0.02
White females	0.04	0.04	0.02	0.01
Black females	0.07	0.02	0.08	0.02

B: Supply relative to white males, within education categories

Age:	25–64			25–34		
	LTHS	HS	CG	LTHS	HS	CG
Black	0.01	0.02	0.04	–0.02	0.02	0.03
White females	0.01	0	0.06	–0.02	0.00	0.03
Black females	0	0.03	0.04	–0.07	0	0.04

extent to which the relative supplies of workers with differing levels
of schooling have changed within demographic groups. To what
extent, if at all, are cross-group differences in the change in the
relative supply of more-educated workers – taken as predetermined
by earlier market conditions due to the time lag involved in obtaining
schooling – related to differences in the change in relative earnings?
To address this issue, we estimated the annual growth rate of the
relative number of labor-force participants in specified education
groups. The results of these tabulations for 1980–89 are presented in
the top panel of Table 8.7. There was an increase in the ratio of more-
to less-educated workers for most demographic groups, with two
exceptions: declines among both white males and black males in the
number of college graduates relative to high-school graduates among
25–34 year olds. In addition, the table reveals considerable variation
across groups in the change in relative supplies in the 1980s.

To determine whether supply changes help explain changes in the
residual earnings differentials, we calculated correlation coefficients
between the 1980–89 annual growth rates of relative supply (from
Table 8.7) and both the actual changes in the HS/LTHS and CG/HS
differentials, and the residual earnings changes after correcting for
the five factors in Table 8.5.[21] If differences in rates of growth of

Table 8.8   Correlation of changes in earnings differentials and relative supply

Differential	Age:	Correlation coefficients[a] 25–64	25–34
Education differentials[b]			
Actual change		–0.64*	–0.69*
Residual change		–0.69*	–0.37
Group differentials[c]			
Actual change		–0.48	–0.69**
Residual change		–0.46	–0.45

[a] These are correlation coefficients of the growth rate in relative supply and the change in the relevant earnings differential. Tests of the hypothesis that the correlation coefficient differed from zero were conducted using an F-test for independence. One star denotes statistical significance at the 10 percent level, two stars at the 5 percent level.
[b] These correlations are for the actual and residual changes in the education-earnings differentials (both HS/LTHS and CG/HS) from Table 8.5.
[c] These correlations are for the change in race/gender earnings differentials within education groups, from Table 8.6.

relative supply contributed to the differing changes in education-earnings differentials, these correlation coefficients should be negative. The estimated correlation coefficients, presented in Table 8.8, are uniformly negative, supporting this conclusion.

Finally, we also examined the correlation between the growth rate of relative supply and the change in earnings differentials between white males and our other race/gender groups. These correlations, presented in Table 8.8, are also uniformly negative, but tend to be smaller than the correlations for the education differentials.

8.3   MARKET RESPONSES

The preceding analyses provide evidence that the relative economic position of more-educated workers improved during the 1980s within race, gender, and age groups. However, the form of the improvement exhibits some cross-group variation. The relative earnings of more-educated white males and more-educated white females increased sizably and significantly (both for 25–64 and 25–34 year olds), though their relative employment rates increased only slightly (if at all). By contrast, the relative earnings of more-educated black males and black females tend to show small and statistically insignificant increases, though the relative employment rates for these groups tended to increase sizably.

Our results also provide some evidence of convergence during the 1980s between the wages of white females in different educational categories and those of white males in corresponding categories. But there is little evidence of similar convergence between the wages of either black males or black females and those of white males.

Our analyses suggest that multiple factors are required to explain changes in the relative earnings of more-educated workers and that a number of plausible explanations are not borne out by the data. In particular, deunionization and changes in the industrial composition of employment account for small, but non-negligible, portions of relative earnings increases for college graduates in different demographic groups. On the other hand, we find little evidence that changes in the occupational distribution of employment or (except for black females) the fall in the real value of the minimum wage are associated with the widening of education-earnings differentials. Since the variation across demographic groups in the change in the supply of more-educated workers supports a negative association between supply changes and the change in relative earnings, changes in relative supply also appear to be a contributor to changes in the wage structure observed in the 1980s.

Thus far, our analysis has focused almost exclusively on the comparison of 1979 and 1988 data. In Figures 8.1a and 8.1b we plot the 1967–87 time series of education–earnings differentials for males and females aged 25–34 – of all races.[22] These plots suggest that the data for 1979 and 1988 are not anomalous in any obvious way; they also reveal that the level that education–earnings differentials reached in the 1980s is not unprecedented, at least for men.

What are the future consequences for the U.S. labor market of recent increases in education-earnings differentials? The most important consequence one might expect would be a supply response to the change in relative wages. In order to examine this hypothesis, we have plotted in Figures 8.2a–8.2d time-series data from 1965 to 1989 on school enrollment rates for 18–19 and 20–21 year olds in four race/gender groups. For 18–19 year old white males and white females, enrollment rates track changes in relative earnings fairly closely throughout this time period. Though weaker, there is also some correspondence between the time series patterns of relative

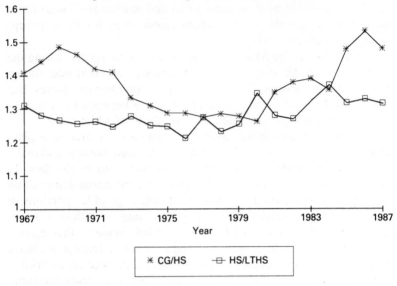

Figure 8.1a   Earnings ratios for males, 25–34

Source: Current Population Reports, P–60.

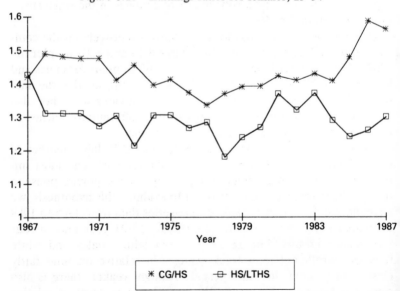

Figure 8.1b   Earnings ratios for females, 25–34

Source: Current Population Reports, P–60.

Figure 8.2a   Enrollment rates among 18–19 year-olds. by race/gender group

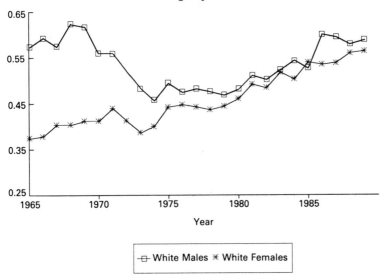

Source: Current Population Reports, Series P–20.

Figure 8.2b   Enrollment rates among 18–19 year-olds. by race/gender group

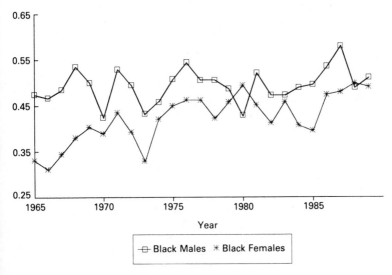

Source: Current Population Reports, Series P–20.

Figure 8.2c   Enrollment rates among 20–21 year-olds. by race/gender group

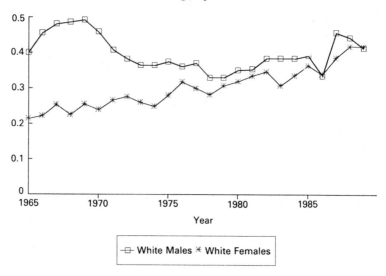

Source: Current Population Reports, Series P–20.

Figure 8.2d   Enrollment rates among 20–21 year-olds. by race/gender group

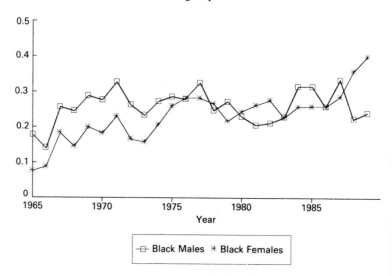

Source: Current Population Reports, Series P–20.

earnings and school enrollment rates among white males and white females aged 20–21. For black males and black females, enrollment rates exhibit too much year-to-year variation (mainly because the rates are calculated from much smaller samples than for the whites) to draw any firm conclusions. Since enrollment rates can be viewed as leading indicators of changes in the relative supply of more-educated workers, we may expect that an accelerated growth rate of more-educated workers will depress education–earnings differentials in the coming years.

The closeness of the time-series patterns in Figures 8.1 and 8.2 suggests that individuals are responding in their schooling investment decisions to signals being sent from the labor market about the private returns to schooling.[23] But schooling decisions would also be expected to depend upon the private costs of schooling investments. One component of the direct costs of attending college – tuition and fees – is plotted in Figure 8.3 (in inflation-adjusted terms for two- and four-year public institutions combined). Especially notable in this series is the sharp rise in tuition and fees from 1980 to 1987, a trend that would, all else equal, be expected to discourage school enrollment.

To test this idea, we estimated probability models of the school enrollment behavior of college-age youths using the CG/HS differential, corrected for tuition costs, and a linear trend variable as explanatory variables.[24] The results are reported in Table 8.9 for white males and white females.[25] For white males, enrollment rates tend to increase when the earnings differential for males rises; the enrollment-rate elasticity with respect to changes in the differential is 0.34 (evaluated at the average enrollment rate). For white females aged 18–19, enrollment rates also tend to increase when relative earnings increase, though the magnitude of the response is less than that among males. In addition, females aged 18-19 appear to treat male relative earnings as a more relevant factor than female relative earnings in their decision to enroll in school. (The elasticity with respect to changes in the male differential is 0.25.) The results for white females aged 20–21 do not suggest a strong connection between enrollment decisions and the relative earnings differentials of females or males. Holding constant the earnings differential, enrollment rates have been increasing over time for white women, but falling for white men.[26]

These results provide evidence that school enrollment decisions are quite sensitive to changes in the net return on schooling, particularly for white men. If the difference in real earnings between college graduates and high-school graduates had not increased over the

Figure 8.3   Average undergraduate tuition and fees. All Public
Institutions (1987 dollars)

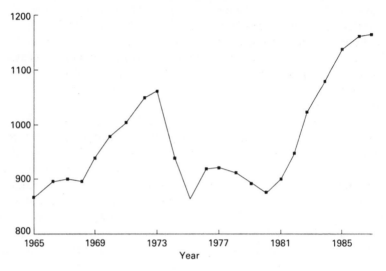

Source: *Digest of Education Statistics*, 1989.

1980s, our probit estimates suggest that the school enrollment rate for
18–19 year old white males would have been 8 percentage points
lower than it actually was in 1987. Alternatively, if tuition had not
increased as it did over the 1980s (see Figure 8.3), school enrollment
rates would have been higher, though by less than one percentage
point.[27]

What do these responses portend for changes in education-
earnings differentials in the near future? One of the primary factors
causing differentials to decline in the early 1970s was the increase in
enrollment rates in the late 1960s – itself a result of the high level of
differentials that existed in the late 1960s. In similar fashion, one
might expect that the high enrollment rates of the late 1980s (particularly among whites) will cause education-earnings differentials to fall
in the 1990s. A dependable forecast of changes in the differentials in
the near future would require a careful model of the impact of supply
changes on earnings differentials, something that we have not provided. But it does appear from the results we have provided that the

Table 8.9 Estimates of enrollment equations for white males and females[a]

Dependent variable:	% Enrolled of 18–19 year-olds				% Enrolled of 20–21 year-olds			
Independent variable	Males		Females		Males		Females	
	(1)	(2)	(3)	(4)	(5)	(6)	(7)	(8)
Constant	−0.32	−0.33	−0.51	−0.49	−0.51	−0.49	−0.78	−0.78
	(0.06)	(0.07)	(0.07)	(0.06)	(0.08)	(0.08)	(0.06)	(0.07)
D^* for males[b]	0.87	0.78		0.46	0.73	0.98		0.10
	(0.11)	(0.31)		(0.15)	(0.13)	(0.35)		(0.17)
D^* for females[c]		0.18	0.43	−0.37		−0.51	0.06	−0.11
		(0.58)	(0.16)	(0.30)		(0.65)	(0.15)	(0.34)
Trend	−0.006	−0.007	0.014	0.019	−0.13	−0.10	0.016	0.017
	(0.002)	(0.004)	(0.002)	(0.002)	(0.002)	(0.004)	(0.002)	(0.003)
R^2	0.79	0.79	0.84	0.90	0.77	0.78	0.86	0.86
DW	1.73	1.63	1.08	1.60	1.54	1.56	2.57	2.45

[a] The dependent variable is the inverse of the cumulative normal function evaluated at the percentage enrolled in school among the specified age group. The estimation method is ordinary least squares, with standard errors for the coefficient estimates reported in parentheses. The sample consists of annual observations for 1967–87. Over this period, the average enrollment percentage was 0.52 among white males aged 18–19, 0.46 among white females 18–19, 0.38 among white males 20–21, and 0.30 among white females 18–19.
[b] This is the average-earnings differential between male college graduates and male high-school graduates (both aged 25–34), divided by one plus the ratio of tuition to high-school-graduate earnings for males 18–24. Tuition costs are the average undergraduate tuition in public institutions of higher education. When this differential appears in enrollment equations for females, the denominator in the correction uses female, not male, high-school-graduate earnings.
[c] This is the corrected differential for females. When it is used in equations for male enrollment rates, the denominator uses male high-school graduate earnings.

market is responding, and responding strongly, to the increased incentive to acquire a college education.

Can government policy influence education–earnings differentials? Given that the value of a college education has increased, policymakers may consider it socially beneficial to promote investment in this area. As our analysis of enrollment-rate behavior suggests that college-age individuals do respond to financial incentives, government could attempt to amplify this response by increasing the after-tax return to a college education. Whether this would be done most efficiently by increasing tuition subsidies, adjusting marginal tax rates, or providing wage subsidies to college graduates is not clear.

While it appears that the government can influence college-enrollment behavior, it is not obvious from our analysis whether it would be appropriate for it to do so. It is true that the social value of a college education increased in the 1980s, but we see no reason to believe that the value of a college education to private individuals has not increased by a similar amount.[28] If there was no strong argument for increasing the subsidization of college education in the late 1970s, there would appear to be no strong argument for doing so now. Also, further increasing the number of college graduates would have uncertain effects on earnings variation across individuals – reducing the earnings differences between college graduates and high school graduates but increasing the number of individuals at the top end of the earnings distribution. Given these uncertainties, and the strong market response to the increased differentials, the case for increased tuition subsidies does not appear to be all that compelling.

Acknowledgments

An earlier version of this paper was presented at the Jerome Levy Economics Institute of Bard College in June 1991. The authors thank Melissa Binder and Pravin Krishna for computational assistance, and Alan Blinder and Kevin Lang for helpful comments.

Appendix

Table A-1   Changes in education–earnings differentials within demographic groups, 1979 and 1989
Hourly earnings, all employed individuals[a]

Age: 25–64

	White males			Black males		
	1979	1989	Δ	1979	1989	Δ
HS/LTHS	0.19	0.27	0.08(0.02)	0.18	0.17	–0.01(0.08)
CG/HS	0.22	0.42	0.20(0.02)	0.28	0.37	0.09(0.08)
	White females			Black females		
	1979	1989	Δ	1979	1989	Δ
HS/LTHS	0.17	0.27	0.10(0.03)	0.14	0.41	0.27(0.08)
CG/HS	0.34	0.48	0.14(0.02)	0.45	0.58	0.13(0.07)

Age: 25–34

	White males			Black males		
	1979	1989	Δ	1979	1989	Δ
HS/LTHS	0.23	0.31	0.08(0.04)	0.18	0.13	–0.05(0.13)
CG/HS	0.15	0.38	0.23(0.03)	0.31	0.37	0.06(0.11)
	White females			Black females		
	1979	1989	Δ	1979	1989	Δ
HS/LTHS	0.15	0.25	0.10(0.05)	0.08	0.25	0.17(0.13)
CG/HS	0.33	0.48	0.15(0.04)	0.38	0.57	0.19(0.09)

[a] These statistics are calculated using the 'usual' earnings and hours information available for one-quarter of the CPS sample. We use the May 1979 and March 1989 surveys. Standard errors for the changes are reported in parentheses.

Table A-2 Sample sizes for data on full-time, year-round workers[a]

Age:	25–64		25–34	
Demographic group	1979	1988	1979	1988
All workers	36 135	35 505	13 113	12 703
White males				
LTHS	4 159	2 479	846	730
HS	7 806	7 119	2 773	2 771
CG	5 653	5 994	2 328	1 954
Black males				
LTHS	559	329	108	65
HS	624	622	252	254
CG	180	300	88	84
White females				
LTHS	1 722	1 177	331	258
HS	5 256	5 557	1 721	1 857
CG	2 391	3 489	1 213	1 508
Black females				
LTHS	378	232	73	41
HS	602	744	262	291
CG	226	346	101	142

[a] These are the sizes of the annual earnings samples drawn from the March 1980 and March 1989 Current Population Surveys.

Table A-3   Earnings differentials for white females within age cohorts,
1979 to 1988
Annual earnings, full-time year-round workers

Cohort age in:		CG/LTHS earnings differential	
1979	*1988*	*1979*	*1988*
18–24	27–33	—	0.81
25–30	34–39	0.52	0.76
31–36	40–45	0.60	0.77
37–42	46–51	0.50	0.70
43–48	52–57	0.50	0.70
49–54	58–63	0.63	0.71

Table A-4   Impact of deunionization on changes in average hourly
earnings from 1980 to 1989
Hourly earnings, all employed individuals aged 25–64

Demographic/ education group	*Percent unionized:*[a]			*Union premium*[b]	*Effect on Δ in wages*[c]
	1979	*1989*	*Δ*		
Age: 25–64					
White males					
LTHS	0.48	0.24	−0.24	0.24	−0.06
HS	0.47	0.32	−0.15	0.10	−0.01
CG	0.24	0.17	−0.07	−0.01	0
Black males					
LTHS	0.42	0.29	−0.13	0.22	−0.03
HS	0.56	0.30	−0.26	0.18	−0.05
CG	0.41	0.42	0.01	−0.12	0
White females					
LTHS	0.27	0.11	−0.16	0.14	−0.02
HS	0.19	0.12	−0.07	0.11	−0.01
CG	0.35	0.25	−0.10	0.15	−0.02
Black females					
LTHS	0.32	0.18	−0.14	0.17	−0.02
HS	0.43	0.24	−0.19	0.10	−0.02
CG	0.52	0.28	−0.24	0.21	−0.05
Age: 25–34					
White males					
LTHS	0.37	0.12	−0.25	0.25	−0.06
HS	0.46	0.25	−0.21	0.16	−0.03
CG	0.24	0.13	−0.11	0.03	0
Black males					
LTHS	0.28	0.17	−0.11	0.31	−0.03
HS	0.55	0.22	−0.33	0.18	−0.06
CG	0.48	0.51	0.03	0.03	0

White females					
LTHS	0.18	0.06	–0.12	0.19	–0.02
HS	0.17	0.11	–0.06	0.16	–0.01
CG	0.32	0.18	–0.14	0.14	–0.02
Black females					
LTHS	0.30	0.14	–0.16	–0.03	0
HS	0.40	0.16	–0.24	0.08	–0.02
CG	0.53	0.25	–0.28	0.14[d]	–0.04

[a] This statistic is the number of wage and salary workers who are members of a labor union or employee organization.

[b] This is the estimated effect of being a union member on hourly wages, from log wage regressions using the 1979 data. Separate union effects were estimated for the different demographic/education groups.

[c] This number is equal to the change from 1979 to 1988 in the percent unionized multiplied by the estimated union coefficient for that race/gender/education group.

[d] Since the estimated union premium for black female college graduates aged 25–34 was likely an overestimate, we use the estimated union premium for white female college graduates.

Notes

1. Katz and Revenga (1989) focus on women as well as men, while Blackburn, Bloom, and Freeman (1990) present earnings differentials for four race/gender groups.
2. The educational grouping of the sample is actually based on completed years of schooling: college graduates are individuals with 16 or more years of completed schooling; high school graduates are individuals with exactly 12 years of schooling; and individuals with less than a high school education have less than 12 years of schooling. We will sometimes refer to LTHS workers as high school dropouts, even though a substantial portion of these workers never reached high school.
3. The differentials are taken from coefficient estimates for education dummy variables in a log-earnings regression. Therefore, the differentials are in log points, and can roughly be interpreted as measuring percentage differences in (geometric) means between the two groups being compared.

   We also estimated education–earnings differentials using the hourly wage data in the May 1979 and March 1989 CPS surveys; the results are presented in Table A-1. One advantage of the hourly wage data is that we do not need to restrict the sample to full-time, year-round workers; however, it has the disadvantage that the data are available for only one-fourth of the sample, resulting in higher standard errors for the changes.
4. In terms of magnitudes, the table suggests a greater absolute log-point increase in the CG/HS differential than in the HS/LTHS differential for most groups. This pattern should not, however, be interpreted as indicating

a greater increase in the educational premium per year of schooling for the CG/HS than the HS/LTHS differential: college graduates have on average more than four years of additional schooling compared to high school graduates, while high school graduates have about two more years of schooling compared to dropouts.

5. This is likely due to the relatively smaller samples available for blacks in the March CPS (see Table A-2): there are only 65 LTHS black males aged 25–34 in our samples for 1988, and only 41 LTHS black females aged 25–34.

6. The 12 point fall in employment rates for 25–34 year old black male dropouts raises the possibility that their increased real earnings (reported in Table 8.1) reflect a change in the selection process into employment, with the fall in employment concentrated among those with the lowest earnings. The identical 12 point fall in the employment rate for 25–34 year old black female dropouts does cast some doubt on this interpretation, however, as the real earnings of young female dropouts fell. Nevertheless, testing this hypothesis more carefully for the 1980s would be a useful subject for future research.

7. This procedure is valid under the assumption that the differential in average hours worked between education groups has not changed over time. There is also an implicit assumption that the extra leisure associated with a fall in the employment rate for a particular group has no value to individuals in the group. If this latter assumption is not true, we will tend to overstate the impact of changes in employment rates on changes in the relative position of the more- and less-educated.

8. The changes in earnings within demographic groups, and the initial earnings differences, are calculated using the average earnings statistics reported in Table 8.1.

9. The residual may at least partly be accounted for by technological change, or changing patterns of international trade. For attempts to measure these influences, see Allen (1991), Krueger (1991), Mincer (1991), and Murphy and Welch (1991).

10. Table A-3 presents the white-female CG/LTHS differentials in 1979 and 1988 within age cohorts. The results show that education-earnings differentials have increased for both young and old cohorts, suggesting that changes in educational quality do not appear to be an important factor increasing earnings differentials. (A similar result for white males was reported by Blackburn, Bloom, and Freeman, 1990.)

11. For example, the change from 1979 to 1988 in the regression-corrected HS/LTHS differential for white males aged 25–34 is 0.06; when we add occupation dummies to the regression, the estimated change is 0.05, implying that 0.01 of the change is due to the effects of occupational employment shifts.

12. In our analysis, we add occupation dummies, then industry dummies, to the regression. Since the two are likely to be correlated, it could be the case that occupation picks up part of the industry-shift effects, so that we overstate the occupation effect and understate the industry effect. However, our measured contributions are essentially invariant to the order in which we add these two sets of variables to the regression –

which is not surprising, given the small estimates we obtain for the occupation effects.

13. For the details of these calculations, see Table A-4.
14. The hourly-wage regressions were estimated with industry dummies as independent variables in order to avoid double-counting the industry-shift effect as part of the union effect. One might also suspect that the declines in unionization rates are also partly due to industrial shifts, which would again imply double-counting; however, calculations made for Blackburn, Bloom, and Freeman (1990) suggest that the estimated impact of industrial shifts on unionization rates is very small.
15. We utilized the usual hourly earnings data in the March 1989 CPS instead of the annual earnings data because the usual earnings figures likely provide more reliable information on hourly pay.
16. As noted in Blackburn, Bloom, and Freeman (1990), this simulation will not capture any effects that changing the minimum may have on the employment or unemployment rates of workers above and below the minimum, or the effect it might have on the wage distribution above the minimum.
17. One odd result is the union effect for black females, where a larger drop in density for college graduates than for high school graduates acted to reduce rather than increase the CG/HS differential.
18. Our goodness-of-fit measure uses squared deviations of the estimated differentials (and residuals) from zero, rather than from their sample averages. A pseudo-R^2 measure could also be constructed using the deviations from the sample average, i.e., one minus the ratio of the variance of the residual changes to the variance of the actual changes. These alternative R^2s are 11 percent for the 25–64 year-olds, and 36 percent for the 25–34 year-olds. However, this alternative R^2 does not take into account the extent to which our analysis explains changes that are operating in a similar fashion for all four demographic groups, but rather only measures the extent to which we account for discordant changes in differentials.
19. Since marital-status effects on wages tend to be very different for males and females, we omitted marital-status dummies from these regressions.
20. The alternative pseudo-R^2's are even higher for the changes in demographic-group differentials – 62 percent for the 25–64 year-olds and 72 percent for the 25–34 year-olds. This implies that much of our 'explanation' of the changes in these differentials pertains to how the changes in differentials vary across groups, and less to why the changes are different from zero.
21. Since the analysis combines two different education groups, with elasticities of substitution that presumably differ, the correlations should be viewed as giving crude indicators of the direction of the effects.
22. These differentials were calculated using arithmetic means reported in the Current Population Reports P-60 series. They are for all races combined, since average earnings statistics within races were not available in all years. Two adjustments were made to the pre-1975 statistics: one, for changes in the imputation procedure for income that were first implemented with the 1975 data; and, two, for using average income in

our pre-1975 calculations rather than average earnings (since the latter was not available). For more detail on these adjustments, see Blackburn, Bloom, and Freeman (1990).

23. This type of response would be suggested by a recursive, or 'cobweb,' model of enrollment decisions. Cobweb models have been used successfully in the past in analyzing enrollment behavior (e.g., see Freeman, 1975).

24. The differential we use as an explanatory variable in our enrollment equations is constructed as:

$$D^* = (C - H) / (H + T),$$

where C is college-graduate earnings, H is high-school-graduates earnings, and T is tuition. Under several simplifying assumptions, the internal rate of return to investing in a college education can be shown to be reasonably approximated by a linear function of D^*, i.e.,

$$r = \theta_0 + \theta_1 D^*.$$

In our estimations, we use the college-graduate and high-school earnings for 25–34 year-olds in the numerator of D^*, and high-school earnings for 18–24 year-olds in the denominator.

Among individuals, we assume the best alternative rate of return $r_A \sim N(\mu, \sigma^2)$, so that the probability of enrolling in school is

$$P_E = P(r > r_A) = \Phi[(r - \mu)/\sigma].$$

We use grouped-probit methods to estimate θ_1/σ and $(\theta_0 + \mu)/\sigma$ from time-series estimates of P_E and D^*, i.e., we estimate, by least-squares

$$\Phi^{-1}(P_E) = (\theta_0 + \mu)/\sigma + (\theta_1/\sigma)D^* + \epsilon.$$

We also add a linear-trend term as a right-hand-side variable, which can be thought of as measuring changes over time in μ. The error term (ϵ) arises in part because P_E is an estimate of the true percentage attending school, and so will necessarily be heteroskedastic (see Maddala, 1983). However, a weighted-least-squares estimator that takes this problem into account left the coefficients and standard errors virtually unchanged from our OLS estimates.

25. We do not report results for blacks because the published data used to estimate these equations do not report average earnings figures by race, and the apparent differences between blacks and whites in the pattern for education-earnings differentials in the 1980s suggests that the combined differentials in Figure 8.1 would be a much poorer proxy for blacks.

26. There is no apparent reason to believe that young males are 'under-responding' to the increased differentials. In fact, estimates allowing the coefficient for the corrected differential to vary before and after 1979 suggest that the response to the differential was higher after 1979 (though the change in the coefficient is not statistically significant).

27. This is because tuition is a very small part of the overall cost of a college education, even after the tuition increase. Our analysis likely understates the impact of tuition changes, since it does not take into account the fact that tuition costs are certain but the CG/HS earnings difference over one's lifetime is varying and uncertain. However, estimates that allowed the $C-H$ and $H+T$ to enter linearly provided highly imprecise coefficient estimates for $H+T$ that were also not robust to the years used for estimation.
28. It is true that private tuition costs increased in the 1980s, but over the same period the average real expenditures per college student were also increasing.

References

Allen, Steven (1991) 'Technology and the Wage Structure.' Unpublished manuscript, North Carolina State University.

Blackburn, McKinley (1990) 'What Can Explain the Increase in Earnings Inequality Among Males?' *Industrial Relations*, **29**(3), 441-56.

Blackburn, McKinley, and David Bloom (1991) 'Changes in the Structure of Family Income Inequality in the U.S. and Other Industrialized Nations During the 1980s.' Unpublished manuscript.

Blackburn, McKinley, David Bloom and Richard Freeman (1990) 'The Declining Economic Position Less Skilled American Men,' in Gary Burtless (ed.), *A Future of Lousy Jobs? The Changing Structure of U.S Wages.* (Washington, D.C.: The Brookings Institution).

Blackburn, McKinley, David Bloom and Richard Freeman (1991) 'An Era of Falling Earnings and Rising Inequality? *The Brookings Review*, **9**(1), 38–43.

Bound, John and George Johnson (1989) 'Changes in the Structure of Wages During the 1980s: An Evaluation of Alternative Hypotheses.' National Bureau of Economic Research Working Paper no. 2983.

Freeman, Richard (1975) 'Overinvestment in College Training?' *Journal of Human Resources*, **10**(3), 287–311.

Juhn, Chinhui, Kevin Murphy, and Brooks Pierce (1989) 'Wage Inequality and the Rise in Returns to Skill.' Unpublished paper, University of Chicago.

Katz, Lawrence, and Ana Revenga (1989) 'Changes in the Structure of Wages: The United States vs Japan.' *Journal of the Japanese and International Economies*, **3**, 522–53.

Krueger, Alan (1991) 'How Computers Have Changed the Wage Structure.' Unpublished manuscript.

Madalla, G. S. (1983) *Limited-Dependent and Qualitative Variables in Econometrics* (Cambridge: Cambridge University Press).

Mincer, Jacob (1991) 'Human Capital, Technology, and the Wage Structure: What Do Time Series Show?', NBER Working Paper no. 3581.

Murphy, Kevin and Finis Welch (1991) 'Wage Differentials in the 1980s: The Role of International Trade.' Forthcoming in *Economic Inquiry*.

Comment

Alan S. Blinder

Some empirical papers have a clear theme and tell a more or less linear story. These are the easy ones for discussants to handle. You can evaluate the evidence the authors bring to bear on the question and give your own version of the story. Other papers simply throw a massive amount of data at you, often regression-processed data. These are much harder to handle because the trees sometimes conceal the forest. The paper by Blackburn, Bloom and Freeman (henceforth, BBF) is – unfortunately for me – of this second genre. It deals with males and females, blacks and whites, two different age groups, and offers findings on both wages and employment rates. When you have a sixteen-fold classification like this, no simple theme is likely to emerge; and none emerges here.

When I get a paper of this second type, I usually ask myself how I would have organized the inquiry. In this case, I think there are four steps I would have taken.

Step One would be to give 'the big picture,' which in this case is one of widening inequality in the distribution of wage rates. Research has by now established that, if you want to understand the rise in *income* inequality in the 1980s, the place to start is with the rise in *wage* inequality. In this context, a brief look at a consistent time series on, say, the log variance of wages since 1979 would have been a useful way to start the paper. BBF do not offer us this look, however – perhaps because the overall story is so well known to conference participants. I think it would have been an appropriate way to frame the issue.

Step Two would be to divide the population into groups in interesting ways, and then to study changes in inequality both *between* and *within* the groups so defined. Why? Because doing so would focus attention on the most important *dimensions* of the 'rising inequality' story, and that, hopefully, would offer some hints about the most important *causes*. BBF do half of this job extremely well: a good portion of the paper consists of carefully examining increases in between-group inequality with groups defined by race, sex, education, age, occupa-

308

tion, industry, and union membership. Of these, education appropriately receives the greatest emphasis, though falling unionization rates are also highlighted as a significant cause of rising inequality.

Unfortunately, within-group inequality is totally ignored. This, I think, is a mistake because it leaves the reader with a somewhat distorted picture. The reason is that, in several cases, between-group inequality actually *fell* between 1979 and 1988 even though total inequality was rising. For example, black females generally gained on the other three race-sex groups. So, if our goal is to understand why inequality *rose*, findings that between-group wage differentials were narrowing are not terribly helpful. Indeed, they suggest we may be barking up the wrong tree.

Fortunately, however, BBF direct most of their fire on educational differentials. And there, with one important exception, the between-group story is definitely one of widening inequality. The exception is interesting, disturbing, and the most important new fact I picked up from this paper. It is by now well known that educational differentials widened noticeably in the 1980s; for example, the wage advantage for college graduates over high school graduates increased markedly. But BBF document a stark exception to this rule: Among black males, the wages of high school graduates actually dropped relative to those of high school dropouts.

Simple grouping of the data, of course, enables us to look at only one division of the population at a time: males versus females, blacks versus whites, etc. In *Step Three*, I would put all these splits together in a regression format by estimating a wage equation like:

$$\ln (w_i) = bX_i + e_i, \tag{1}$$

which implies the following decomposition of the log variance:

$$\text{var}(\ln w) = \sum b_i^2 \, var\,(X) + \text{var}(e) + \text{covariance terms.} \tag{2}$$

Equation (2) enables us to parse out the rise in wage inequality, to its constituent causes: changes in the distributions of the Xs, changes in the slope coefficients, and changes in var(e) (here the covariance terms are a big annoyance that defy classification). The last of these is the aforementioned increase in within-group inequality, which BBF ignore; they look only at the first two.

Equation (1) has at least one major shortcoming: it allows no interactions among the Xs. One obvious approach would be to estimate (1) separately for each race-sex group. Now we are getting close to what BBF do. With separate wage equations for white males, black males, white females, and black females in hand, you could: (i) analyze changes in within-group inequality; (ii) examine how the coefficients (e.g., the returns to education) changed over time; (iii) conduct a complete decomposition of inequality such as found in Blinder (1973) or Oaxaca (1973).

I have already noted that BBF do not do (i). They also do not do (iii), although their tables give us much of the same information. They do, however, offer a thorough version of (ii).

The final step would be to provide some behavioral models to explain the findings in Steps Two and Three. Here BBF do some quite interesting things on the question of college attendance. (Unfortunately, their decision to work with group averages rather than micro data leaves them precious few degrees of freedom.) They find evidence for two types of supply response. First, looking across the four race-sex groups, they find that wage differentials by education seem to have risen less where relative supplies have risen most (Table 8.8). Second, looking at time series changes in college enrollment rates, they find (Table 8.9) that enrollments generally respond positively to wage differentials (the benefit of education) and negatively to tuition costs (part of the costs).

To what policy conclusion does this lead? Many would unthinkingly jump to the conclusion that such high apparent returns to college education suggest serious underinvestment, and would therefore prescribe a corrective subsidy. But BBF are properly circumspect on this point. As they note, college attendance was already heavily subsidized a decade ago. To rationalize an increase in the subsidy, we would have to believe that the gap between the social and private returns to college education increased in the 1980s. Why should we believe that?

BBF's point is well taken. But I can think of at least two cogent arguments for increasing the subsidy. First, BBF tacitly assume that society was using the right subsidy rate in 1979. If we were under-subsidizing college attendance then, there is probably a case for raising the subsidy now. On the other hand, perhaps we were over-subsidizing it then. Second, divergence between social and private benefits is not the only rationale for subsidizing the costs of college education. It seems quite likely, for example, that a number of students who should be going to college on pure efficiency grounds are prevented from doing so by their inability to borrow enough money. Since tuition costs rose faster than most other prices in the 1980s, it is plausible that such capital market constraints are now a more serious problem than they were a decade ago. If so, an expanded program of students loans is probably warranted as a corrective device.

References

Blinder, Alan S. (1973) 'Wage Discrimination: Reduced Form and Structural Estimates,' *Journal of Human Resources*, Fall pp. 436–55.

Oaxaca, Ronald (1973) 'Male Female Wage Differentials in Urban Labor Markets,' *International Economic Review*, **14**, October, pp. 693–709.

Comment
Kevin Lang

Empirical labor economists tend to divide into two groups – those who provide convincing answers to minor questions and those who tackle major questions but inevitably provide less convincing answers. This paper and its authors definitely fall into the latter category. The authors have taken on one of the central problems of economics – the distribution of income – and have generated stimulating results but cannot hope to overcome all of the inevitable problems they face.

There has been a long series of papers pointing to the increased return to education over the 1980s. Blackburn, Bloom and Freeman (BBF) extend this literature by examining how this return varies among sociodemographic groups. By explaining differences among these groups, the authors can generate a more credible explanation for the general trend.

Table 8.5 which summarizes the authors' efforts in this direction is quite striking. The combination of changes in the occupational and industrial structure, wages by different industries, the real decline in the minimum wage and union density can account for a significant part of the change. Indeed in a couple of cases, these factors can more than account for the change in the education wage differential.

Some caution is required in assessing the success of this exercise. Only in the case of the college/high school differential for black males does the combined effect of the change in the occupational and industrial structures and interindustry wage differentials account for more than half of the change. The two remaining variables, the decline of the minimum wage law and the decline in union density are not independent ('orthogonal' in the technical jargon of statisticians) of each other or of the first three variables. Thus there is a danger of double-counting.

To summarize their success in explaining the changes in the education wage differential, the authors develop a pseudo-R^2. A value of 1 would mean that they had explained the changes perfectly. A value of 0 would mean that after all their work, they had not explained the changes at all. The way the pseudo-R^2 is constructed, it can be negative. If it were, and if one believed that the factors they measure

312

had the impact they estimate, the mystery would be even greater than previously recognized. Their pseudo-R^2 estimates are striking. BBF explain 53 percent of the variation across groups among the 25–64 year olds and 48 percent among 25–34 year olds. For these familiar with the values of R^2 typical of labor economics, these values are indicative of considerable success.

However, again there is reason for caution. The pseudo-R^2 is not comparable to what we are used to seeing in labor economics. At a minor level, the errors we make in assessing the wages of high school graduates will affect the comparison between high school graduates and dropouts and between high school graduates and college graduates. In addition an R^2 of 0.5 with five regressors and eight observations would not be impressive if it were based on ordinary regression with maximizes the R^2. (A mini-Monte Carlo study in which a standard normal was regressed on five other independent standard normals gave an R^2 in excess of 0.45 six out of ten times.) It is harder to assess what constitutes success with a method which does not.

Perhaps most significantly, the method by which the pseudo-R^2 is calculated captures not only the success of the authors in explaining differences across groups but also their success in explaining the average change for all groups (the constant term). They point out in note 18 that their pseudo-R^2s for explaining differences across groups are much lower – 0.11 for 25–64 year olds and 0.36 for 25–34 year olds.

Viewed in this way, it appears that BBF have done a much better job of explaining the cross-group trend than of explaining the inter-group differences. This is unfortunate since success in explaining the inter-group differences would have given us much more confidence in their explanation of the source of the common trend.

Of course the idiosyncratic differences among groups may simply be large. One factor which is essentially impossible to take into account within the framework used by the authors is the changing composition within groups. Labor force participation rates for low-wage workers appear to have declined over the period studied by BBF. Note for example that for almost every group, the change in the employment–population ratio is less positive or more negative for those with less than a high school degree than for the college-educated. Increased nonemployment rates of low education workers will attenuate estimates of the increase in the return to education. Similarly, increased nonemployment rates for low-wage blacks will attenuate the decline in the wages of blacks relative to whites.

Moreover, as high school graduation and college attendance have become more common, those who fail to graduate high school increasingly consist of the least capable. At the same time the average high school and college graduate also becomes less capable. How this affects the high school graduate/dropout and college/high school comparisons cannot be determined a priori, but there undoubtedly is some bias.

Composition effects become even more important for comparing blacks and whites and men and women. High school dropout rates declined over this period, but when comparing 25–34 year olds in 1979 and 1988, the change is among blacks not whites. As Table 8.C1 shows, the fraction of 35–44 year olds in 1988 (roughly the 25–34 year old age group in 1979) who were dropouts in 1988 was 12.8 percent. The fraction of 25–34 year olds in this age group was almost identical (12.7 percent). Among blacks the dropout rate in the older group was 22.3 percent; in the younger group it was 19.5 percent.

What is even more striking is that in the older age group, blacks were somewhat more likely than whites to have no high school education. In the younger age group, the opposite is true. As a consequence, especially in the younger group, black high school dropouts are much more educated than white high school dropouts, and this difference has been increasing over time. In Table 8.6, we see a huge (11 percent) unexplained increase in the earnings of black male high school dropouts relative to white male high school dropouts. It is plausible that this within group change in composition accounts for some of the unexplained variation.

Table 8.C1 High school and pre-high school dropout rates by race and age (1988)

| | Dropout rate (%) | Fraction of dropouts with | |
		No high school (%)	Some high school (%)
Whites			
25–29	13.4	29.1	70.9
30–34	12.1	34.7	65.3
35–44	12.8	42.2	57.8
Blacks			
25–29	19.1	14.1	85.9
30–34	19.8	21.7	78.3
35–44	22.7	26.9	73.1

Source: *Statistical Abstract of the United States*, 1990, p. 134.

Another potential explanation for the increased relative wages of young blacks with little education is the effect of affirmative action and equal pay laws. Equal pay laws tend to raise wages of blacks relative to whites. If not supported by laws enforcing employment equality, this will tend to generate a movement along the labor demand curve and reduce employment of blacks. One of the goals of affirmative action laws is to increase employment by shifting the demand curve for labor. Thus to the extent that equal pay laws have been enforced, we would expect wages and employment to move in opposite directions for blacks. To the extent that affirmative action has been enforced, we would expect wages and employment to increase simultaneously.

In fact, one of the most striking results is the very large increase in the wages of young blacks with less than a high school degree. Equally striking is the sharp decline in the employment–population ratio among this group. Yet the pattern of surprisingly low employment–population ratios is not limited to blacks with little education. For every group except young college-educated black men, the increase in the employment–population ratio is smaller or the decrease larger for black men than for white men and for black women than for white women. It is tempting to attribute this to a movement along the labor demand curve. If, in fact, we are observing movement along the labor demand curve for blacks as a whole or for some sub-groups, this suggests that the relative wages of blacks would have fallen further in the absence of a decline in the relative employment–population ratio. Even if we reject the notion of movement along a labor demand curve, the differences in the evolution of the employment–population ratios signal the need for caution.

These quibbles aside, perhaps the major shortcoming of the paper is a failure to clearly outline the theoretical structure which underlies it. This may appear to be an unfair charge to level at a paper which is clearly intended as an empirical exercise and where the ultimate goal is policy-relevance. Yet I find it troubling that the authors move seamlessly between explanations which rely on supply and demand and those which rely on some nonmarket-clearing mechanism such as union coverage and minimum wage laws. Perhaps it is possible to add together demand shifts in a market-clearing framework and factors which push wages above the market-clearing level, but it is not obvious, to me at least.

For example, the authors provide evidence that the supply of highly-educated labor responds to the return to education. This is an important finding which suggests that the return to education is likely to return to historical levels in the not too distant future. This point and the ensuing policy discussion are eminently sensible. As long as we believe that the changing return to education reflects shifts in demand towards more educated workers, it is unlikely to be challenged by mainstream economists.

However, if the change in relative wages reflects a decline in the minimum wage and in union density, then the declining wages for workers with relatively little education will be accompanied by an increase in employment opportunities and, possibly, by decreased unemployment. If the labor market does not clear for low-wage workers, the 'return to education' is not a sufficient statistic for its benefits.

I suspect that it would not be too difficult to write down the model which the authors implicitly use. The authors have done a remarkable job of organizing a vast quantity of data in a manner which is interesting and informative, but I would have found it even easier to assimilate the information with an explicit model to organize my thoughts.

9 The Changing Contributions of Men and Women to the Level and Distribution of Family Income, 1968–88

Maria Cancian, Sheldon Danziger, and Peter Gottschalk[1]

9.1 INTRODUCTION

In 1968, the typical married couple had annual earnings of $25 633 (in constant 1988 dollars)[2] from a husband who averaged 47.7 weeks of work, and $4913 from a wife who worked 21.0 weeks. By 1988, the typical husband earned somewhat more, $28 350 per year, while working somewhat less, 45.5 weeks. The typical wife worked substantially more, 32.1 weeks, and earned substantially more, $10 369. For the typical couple, real earnings increased by $8173 per year, of which about two-thirds was attributable to the increased earnings of wives. The typical wife increased her weeks worked by more than half and earned about one-third more per week.[3]

Income inequality also increased substantially between 1968 and 1988, with the Gini coefficient of total family income for all couples rising from 0.305 to 0.336. Growth in the mean earnings of husbands was even slower and the increase in inequality even greater between 1978 and 1988, than in the prior decade. The largest singe factor contributing to the increased inequality in family income was the rising inequality of husbands' earnings.

This experience of slow growth in husbands' earnings (an increase of only 11 percent in mean earnings over two decades) and rising income inequality contrasts sharply with the previous two decades, over which time real earnings almost doubled and inequality declined somewhat. During those decades, all families, throughout the income

317

distribution, gained as economic growth and rising productivity raised real wages and hence, family income.

The past two decades are characterized by uneven growth, with inequality increasing during both recessions and economic recovery. In fact, many families had lower real incomes at the end of the 1983–90 recovery than at the beginning. During these last two decades, the increased work effort of married women has taken over the role previously played by economic growth. Increased wives' earnings have accounted for a substantial portion of the rise in family income, and have prevented income inequality from rising to an even greater extent. Working wives, and not economic growth, have been the 'rising tide that lifts all boats'.

In this paper, we focus on changes in the level and distribution of earnings of men and women and their impacts on the distribution of family income among married couples, and among all households. This topic has received a modest amount of attention over the past several decades. Economists and journalists have speculated that because a woman's decision to work is now less dependent on her husband's earnings, wives' earnings, which were once a factor leading to an equalization of family incomes, are now 'becoming a source of family inequality' (Thurow, 1975, p. 12).

This speculation seems to derive from a popular stereotype – the increasing numbers of young couples in which both the husband and the wife earn very high salaries in a variety of professional, technical and managerial jobs. In this case, inequality increases relative to past decades when the highest-earnings husbands expected their wives not to work in the market. In the earlier period, two-earner couples were more typically ones in which the wife worked not to further her own career, but because her husband earned too little for her to remain at home. If this were true on a large scale, then the increased labor force participation of wives married to highly-paid husbands might be a major cause of the recent increase in inequality.

While such dual-career high-earnings couples are clearly more common today than in the past, they are, as our empirical work shows below, still relatively rare. They are relatively rare, in part, because many of the wives who do work, work only part time, and, in part, because very few women are in highly paid jobs.[4]

Our primary focus is on changes in the distribution of income among married couples. However, to place these changes in context, we begin with an examination of trends in labor force participation for all women and men. In addition, we examine the impact of wives' earnings on the distribution of income among all families, since working wives affect inequality not only *among* couples, but also increase income differences *between* married couples and other households. We also analyze how these impacts differ for white, black and Hispanic families.

We use data from the March Current Population Survey (CPS) computer tapes for income years 1968, 1978, and 1988.[5] Our sample includes persons 18 to 64 years old. We divide our sample into three mutually-exclusive demographic groups: married persons, heads of household, and other adults.[6] We present data for all families (including whites, blacks, Hispanics, and others), but our discussion emphasizes disaggregation by race and ethnicity. For 1968, the CPS data are reported for whites and blacks; for 1978 and 1988, we examine white non-Hispanics, black non-Hispanics, and Hispanics.[7]

9.2 TRENDS IN MARRIAGE AND LABOR FORCE PARTICIPATION RATES FOR MEN AND WOMEN

Table 9.1 shows the percentage of men and women who are married, household heads, or 'others' for each of the three race/ethnic groups. For married persons and heads, we distinguish among those who have any young children present (less than 6 years of age), those who have only older children present (between 6 and 17 years of age), and those with no children residing with them.

Of particular importance for our analysis of changes in the level and distribution of husbands' and wives' earnings is the decline in marriage rates, especially for blacks. Table 9.1 shows that by 1988, about 60 percent of white women, about half of Hispanic women, and only about a third of black women between the ages of 18 and 64 were married and living with a spouse. This raises an important issue relevant to this and past studies that analyze the effect of wives' earnings on the distribution of income among married couples.[8] That is, this decline in marriage rates may have indirectly affected income inequality. If the women (or men) who are no longer married have above-average or below-average earnings, then the selection of who marries will affect inequality among married couples, even if the participation and wages of all women (all men) do not change. Selection issues are, therefore, potentially important if the trends in labor force participation and earnings of married women (men) differ significantly from those of other women (men).[9]

Table 9.1 Percentage of persons in each demographic category, by gender, race and ethnicity

	All			White			Black			Hispanic		
	1968	1978	1988	1968	1978	1988	1968	1978	1988	1968	1978	1988
All men	100.0	100.0	100.0	100.0	100.0	100.0	100.0	100.0	100.0		100.0	100.0
Married men	73.1	63.8	57.9	75.0	66.3	61.3	56.8	44.6	39.1		61.8	51.2
w/ children < 6	23.6	17.1	16.0	23.9	16.9	16.1	20.5	13.6	11.0		27.0	20.4
w/ children 6–17	25.0	21.4	17.4	25.7	22.1	17.9	19.8	16.5	13.6		19.7	16.6
no children	24.5	25.3	24.5	25.4	27.3	27.3	16.4	14.5	14.5		15.1	14.2
Male heads	9.0	16.3	22.4	8.1	15.3	21.4	15.7	23.3	28.7		17.6	23.0
w/ children < 6	0.1	0.2	0.5	0.1	0.2	0.4	0.2	0.6	1.1		0.3	0.6
w/ children 6–17	0.6	0.7	1.0	0.5	0.6	0.9	1.5	1.2	1.5		0.8	1.0
no children	8.3	15.4	20.9	7.5	14.5	20.0	14.0	21.4	26.1		16.5	21.4
Other men	17.9	19.9	19.7	16.8	18.4	17.3	27.5	32.1	32.3		20.6	25.8
All women	100.0	100.0	100.0	100.0	100.0	100.0	100.0	100.0	100.0		100.0	100.0
Married women	68.4	61.6	56.7	70.9	65.5	61.1	48.0	36.0	32.6		58.2	53.1
w/ children < 6	22.1	16.5	15.7	22.6	16.6	16.0	17.3	11.0	9.2		25.4	21.1
w/ children 6–17	23.4	20.6	17.0	24.3	21.8	17.8	16.8	13.3	11.3		18.6	17.2
no children	22.9	24.4	24.0	24.0	27.0	27.3	13.9	11.7	12.1		14.2	14.7
Female heads	16.7	23.8	28.4	15.0	21.1	25.6	31.0	42.3	46.7		24.0	27.6
w/ children < 6	2.0	3.0	3.9	1.3	1.9	2.4	7.1	9.8	11.5		6.2	6.6
w/ children 6–17	3.9	5.4	5.7	3.2	4.2	4.2	10.2	12.9	13.8		6.6	7.4
no children	10.8	15.4	18.8	10.5	15.1	19.0	13.6	19.6	21.4		11.2	13.6
Other women	14.9	14.7	14.9	14.1	13.4	13.3	21.1	21.7	20.7		17.8	19.3

The percentage of men and women within each category who worked at some time during the year is shown in Table 9.2.[10] Figures 9.1a and 9.1b illustrate these labor force participation rates for all men and all women, by marital status. For white men there was relatively little change in labor force participation – the percentage of married men working declined modestly from about 97 to 93 percent between 1968 and 1988. The participation of male heads remained about the same, while that of other men fell slightly, from about 89 to 86 percent.

For white women, labor force participation increased by a large amount for each category. The increase was especially large among married women – the percentage working increased from about half to about three quarters over the two decades. The gains were even larger for those with young children. In 1968, only 42.4 percent worked, but in 1988, 68.2 percent worked.

The fact that the labor force participation of both white married women and white female heads increased, suggests that for white women selection was probably not an important issue – if the increased work among married women reflected the fact that women not working were not getting married, then participation among unmarried women would have fallen. This did not happen.

The data in Table 9.2 also show a convergence in labor force participation rates for women with young children, and women with older children. Married mothers were substantially less likely to work than their unmarried counterparts in 1968, but by 1988 this was no longer the case.

For black men there has been a substantial decline in the percent working during the year. As can be seen in Table 9.2, the participation of male heads declined by about 10 percentage points between 1968 and 1978, and then stabilized, while the participation of married men fell by about 7 percentage points over the entire period. However, there was a 16 percentage point decline for other black men, indicative perhaps, of their inability to earn enough to either head their own household or support a family (Wilson, 1987). These trends imply that selection into marriage may make our analysis of trends in the income distribution for black couples problematic.

The trend in the percentage of black women working also varies substantially by marital status and raises the selection issue. Over the twenty-year period, the participation rate of married black women rose from 67.6 to 79.3 percent, while that of female heads fell from 71.3 to 67.9 percent. The rates for black mothers varied more by

Table 9.2 Percentage of persons working positive weeks during 1968, 1978, 1988

	All			White			Black			Hispanic		
	1968	1978	1988	1968	1978	1988	1968	1978	1988	1968	1978	1988
All men	95.1	91.7	89.9	95.5	92.8	91.5	91.7	82.6	80.0		91.5	89.3
Married men	97.1	93.9	92.7	97.3	94.1	93.2	95.2	91.3	88.1		94.5	93.6
w/ children < 6	99.1	97.9	97.3	99.3	98.3	98.2	97.7	95.3	93.5		96.5	97.1
w/ children 6–17	97.5	95.6	95.1	97.9	96.1	96.0	93.5	91.7	89.5		94.3	94.1
no children	94.9	89.7	88.1	94.9	89.8	88.5	94.1	87.1	82.5		91.3	87.8
Male heads	92.1	90.3	89.5	92.4	92.0	91.2	91.5	81.3	81.3		92.3	88.6
Other men	88.3	85.6	81.9	88.9	89.0	85.5	84.7	71.5	69.0		81.7	81.6
All women	61.3	67.9	75.0	60.3	68.9	77.3	69.1	65.1	70.2		58.9	61.9
Married women	54.7	63.1	72.8	53.6	62.9	73.4	67.6	70.6	79.3		56.6	60.1
w/ children < 6	44.0	55.7	67.4	42.4	55.3	68.2	61.2	66.2	77.4		49.9	56.3
w/ children 6–17	57.8	65.5	76.9	56.6	64.8	77.8	71.7	75.6	82.4		60.5	62.7
no children	61.8	66.1	73.5	61.1	66.0	73.7	70.6	68.9	76.2		63.5	62.6
Female heads	76.0	76.4	78.8	77.4	80.9	83.9	71.3	64.4	67.9		60.0	65.0
w/ children < 6	62.5	61.1	61.6	65.8	71.2	70.9	59.0	53.7	54.8		38.3	50.1
w/ children 6–17	71.2	73.9	77.8	72.8	80.2	84.5	68.5	64.2	71.7		53.4	62.4
no children	80.2	80.2	82.7	80.3	82.3	85.4	79.7	69.8	72.6		76.0	73.6
Other women	75.0	74.3	75.7	76.0	79.1	82.5	69.3	57.5	61.0		64.8	62.3

Figure 9.1(a) Percent of men working by marital status, 1968, 1978, 1988

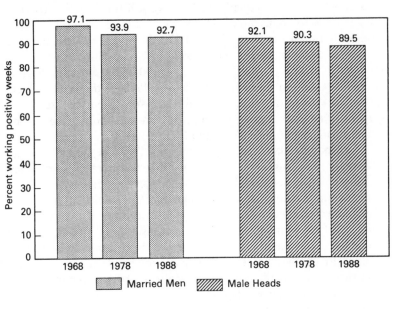

Figure 9.1(b) Percent of women working by marital status, 1968, 1978, 1988

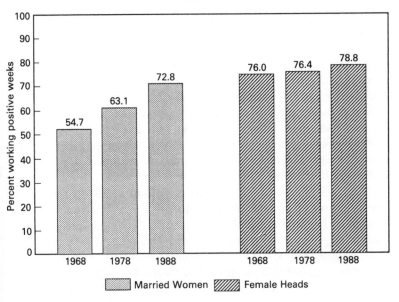

marital status in 1988 than in 1968. In 1968, mothers of young children where almost equally likely to work if they were married or female heads of household. The same was true of mothers with children between the ages of 6 and 17. However, by 1988 married mothers were substantially more likely to work. This pattern is the opposite of that for white mothers, who showed substantially less variance by marital status in 1988 than in 1968. If those most likely not to work were the ones who did not marry, then the rise in the propensity to work among married women and the decline among female heads could reflect selection.

For Hispanics, data are unavailable for 1968. Between 1978 and 1988 there was a modest decline in the percent of Hispanic men working positive weeks.[11] Their participation rates in every year are much closer to those of whites than blacks. Participation among Hispanic women increased, but their rates are lower than those of white or black women. The largest increases were among married and unmarried women with children under six, and among unmarried women with children 6 to 17. For women with children, the difference in participation according to marital status narrowed somewhat over the period. Selection is, therefore, probably less of a problem for Hispanics than for blacks.

9.3   TRENDS IN ANNUAL EARNINGS FOR MARRIED MEN AND WOMEN

The data reviewed in the previous section suggest that selection into marriage may not bias an analysis of trends in the level and distribution of income for white and Hispanic married men and women. However, we caution that changes in earnings within marital categories for blacks may reflect changes in who has married as much as marital-specific changes in earnings. Given this caveat, we now turn our attention to changes in the distribution of earnings for husbands and wives in married-couple families.

Table 9.3 and Figures 9.2(a) to 9.2(h) show the distribution of annual earnings in 1988 constant dollars for all married men and women by race and ethnicity.[12] We classify all persons into one of six categories – nonearners, those earning less than $12 000 per year, those earning $12–$24 000, $24–36 000, $36–48 000, and those earning more than $48 000 per year. For married women, we also show the percent with positive earnings who earn over $36 000 per year.

Table 9.3 Annual earnings of married men. Percent with earnings in each category, 1968, 1978 and 1988

	All			White			Black			Hispanic		
	1968	1978	1988	1968	1978	1988	1968	1978	1988	1968	1978	1988
Annual earnings												
zero	3.3	6.6	7.7	3.0	6.5	7.3	5.3	9.0	12.4		5.6	7.0
<12k	10.6	10.4	12.4	9.3	9.2	10.6	26.2	18.6	18.3		18.6	26.5
12k–24k	38.2	27.0	25.1	37.2	25.6	23.5	50.4	34.5	32.4		42.4	35.9
24k–36k	31.3	30.7	26.8	32.7	31.4	28.1	15.0	28.4	23.0		22.9	18.9
36k–48k	10.3	14.6	13.8	10.9	15.5	14.9	2.1	6.7	8.7		7.4	7.2
48k +	6.4	10.7	14.2	6.8	11.7	15.7	1.1	2.8	5.3		3.1	4.5
Mean earnings	25 633	27 692	28 350	26 429	28 751	29 872	16 479	19 898	20 497		20 315	19 228
CV squared	0.443	0.440	0.561	0.428	0.425	0.524	0.379	0.426	0.634		0.422	0.663

Annual earnings of married women. Percent with earnings in each category, 1968, 1978 and 1988

	All			White			Black			Hispanic		
	1968	1978	1988	1968	1978	1988	1968	1978	1988	1968	1978	1988
Annual earnings												
zero	48.8	38.7	28.0	50.0	39.1	27.5	34.5	29.7	21.1		44.3	40.4
<12k	33.6	35.8	34.4	32.4	35.5	34.4	47.9	36.6	34.8		37.0	35.5
12k–24k	15.6	20.3	24.6	15.6	20.2	24.8	15.0	25.6	29.6		16.1	18.1
24k–36k	1.8	4.3	9.6	1.7	4.1	9.9	2.4	7.2	11.6		2.2	4.7
36k–48k	0.2	0.6	2.2	0.2	0.6	2.3	0.1	0.8	2.2		0.2	0.9
48k +	0.1	0.3	1.1	0.1	0.3	1.2	0.0	0.1	0.6		0.1	0.5
% earners of 36k+ *	0.6	1.5	4.6	0.6	1.5	4.8	0.2	1.3	3.5		0.5	2.3
Mean earnings	4913	6890	10 369	4870	6794	10 491	5344	8773	11 730		5387	6984
CV squared	2.154	1.707	1.335	2.212	1.740	1.329	1.599	1.147	0.877		1.860	1.955

* Percent of women with positive earnings, who earn over $36 000.

Figure 9.2

(a) Earnings of married men

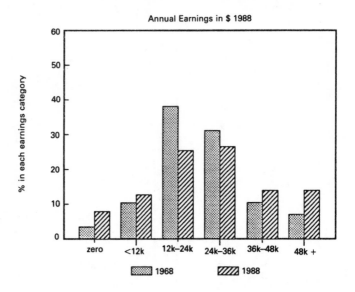

(b) Earnings of married women

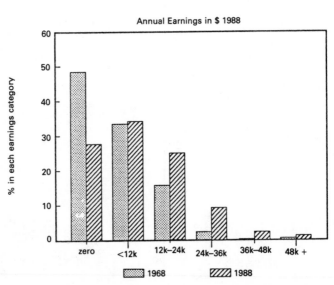

(c) Earnings of white married men

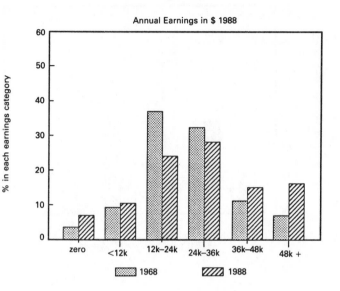

(d) Earnings of white married women

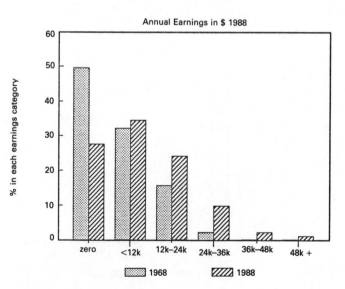

(e) Earnings of black married men

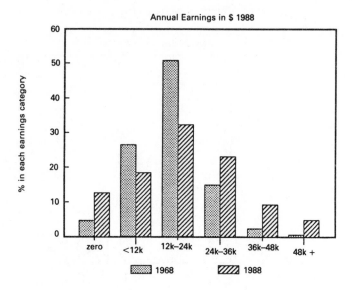

(f) Earnings of black married women

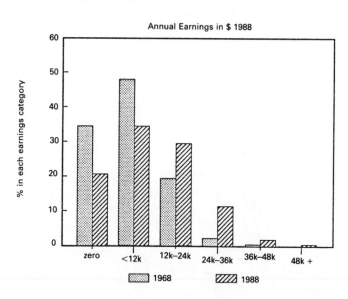

(g) Earnings of Hispanic married men

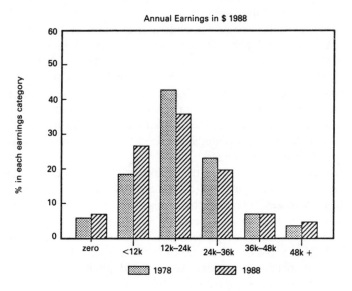

(h) Earnings of Hispanic married women

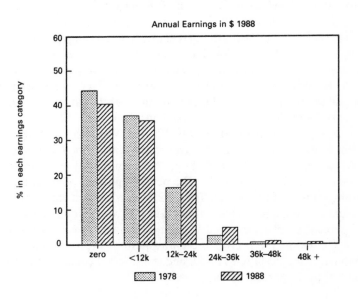

The earnings categories are arbitrary, but $12 000 is about equal to the poverty line for a family of four, and $24 000 is close to the mean annual earnings of married men.[13]

The earnings distribution for white married men has grown in both tails. As Table 9.3 and Figure 9.2(c) show, the percent of white married men earning between $12 000 and $36 000 (in constant 1988 dollars) has fallen substantially, while the percent earning less than $12 000 and more than $36 000 has grown. Their mean annual earnings increased by 13 percent, from $26 429 in 1968 to $29 872 in 1988. As evidenced in the figure, inequality increased. The squared coefficient of variation of husbands' earnings for whites increased by 22 percent from 0.428 to 0.524.[14]

For white married women, the dominant factor was the decline in zero earners (see Figure 9.2(d)) from 50.0 to 27.5 percent. The greatest increases were in the categories between $12 000 and $36 000, from 17.3 to 34.7 percent. As a result of these changes, mean annual earnings of white married women more than doubled from $4870 to $10 491. As discussed in the next section, this was due both to an increase in weeks worked and an increase in weekly earnings. However, the percentage of working married women who earned over $36 000 remained remarkably low: only 4.8 percent 1988. By comparison, about one-third of married white men earned more than $36 000. Inequality among all white wives also decreased substantially because of the decline in zero earners. The squared coefficient of variation fell by 40 percent, from 2.212 to 1.329.

For black married men, the percent with no earnings for the entire year rose from 5.3 to 12.4. However, there was also a substantial increase in the percent earning more than $24 000, from 18.2 to 37.0 percent. These increases in the upper and lower tail caused earnings inequality to increase for blacks. In fact, both the mean and inequality increased more for black than white men. Mean earnings rose 24.4 percent, from $16 479 to $20 497, while the squared coefficient of variation increased by over 65 percent, from 0.379 to 0.634.

As with white married women, the earnings of black married women increased significantly. The percentage with zero earnings or earnings under $12 000 fell from 82.4 to 55.9 percent, while the percentage in each category above $12 000 rose. Nonetheless, only 3.5 percent of black married women with nonzero earnings earned over $36 000 in 1988. Over the entire period, the mean more than doubled, from $5344 to $11 730, and the squared coefficient of variation fell by 45 percent, from 1.599 to 0.877.

Figure 9.2(g) illustrates the changes in the distribution of Hispanic married men's earnings between 1978 and 1988. The percent with zero earnings increased modestly, from 5.6 to 7.0 percent, those with positive earnings less than $12 000 increased, from 18.6 to 26.5 percent. There was a decline in the middle income ranges – from 12 000 to $36 000 – and not much change at higher levels. This recent decade was particularly difficult for Hispanic married men. Their mean earnings fell by 5 percent, from $20 315 to $19 228.[15] In contrast, the mean for white men increased by about 4 percent, and that of black men, by about 3 percent over the decade. Their experience, although better than that of Hispanic men, was much worse than their respective gains in the 1968–78 decade.

The level and distribution of earnings among Hispanic married women also changed less between 1978 and 1988 than among white and black women, though the differences were not as great as for men. The percent of married Hispanic women with no earnings fell from 44.3 to 40.4 percent. There were small increases (of two to three percentage points) in those earning between $12 000 and $36 000. As a result, mean earnings rose from $5387 to $6984, or by 30 percent over the decade. However, Hispanic women also gained less than black and white women, whose earnings rose by 34 and 54 percent, respectively.

In sum, the last two decades have been characterized by slow growth in mean earnings and rising inequality for husbands and rapid growth in the mean and falling inequality for wives. The rising inequality in earnings among husbands has been documented in a number of recent studies. As Karoly (1993, p. 77) notes, 'among men, [labor income] inequality has been increasing since the 1960s, with growing dispersion in both the lower and upper tail.' The increased earnings inequality reflects increasing returns to education and experience (Katz and Murphy, 1992; Murphy and Welch, 1993; Acs and Danziger, 1991). The differential in earnings between high school and college graduates, and between blue collar and white collar workers has risen over time. Inequality of earnings among men has also increased within skill groups (Juhn, Murphy and Pierce, 1989; Karoly 1993).

There is also evidence of increasing returns to education for women (Katz and Murphy, 1992). However, the distribution of earnings among married women has grown more equal, due to increases in the percent of married women who work. Nonetheless, given substantial positive assortative mating based on education, these trends may have important implications for the distributional impacts of married women's earnings. We now turn to an examination of whether changes in labor force participation and the earnings of wives differed for women married to men who were lower versus higher earners.

9.4 PARTICIPATION RATES AND WEEKLY EARNINGS OF MARRIED WOMEN: WHICH WIVES WORK?

As shown above, the labor force participation rates and annual earnings of married women have risen substantially. These increases are consistent with a pattern of rising labor force participation among married women since 1950. Several studies suggest that the increased work effort can be attributed primarily to substantial increases in real wages for women (Mincer, 1962; see Killingsworth and Heckman (1986), for a review of this literature). Analysis of long-term trends in participation by Claudia Goldin (1990) suggests, however, that increased labor force participation since 1960 is also due to such 'supply-side' factors as 'reduced numbers of children, increased probability of divorce, reduced barriers to various occupations, and changes in social norms' (Goldin, 1990, p. 137).

We do not consider possible causal connections between changes in the wages and participation of men and women. However, there is little evidence that the increased participation of women was caused by the stagnation of male earnings or that it, in turn, substantially affected the rate of growth of male earnings. In particular, married women's labor force participation began to increase in the 1950s, considerably before men's wages began to stagnate. Moreover, the participation of women married to men with higher earnings has grown disproportionately, although their husbands generally experienced significant increases in earnings.

Katz and Murphy (1992) examine the changing relative wages of men and women. They find that among high school graduates, the gains of women relative to men reflect sharp declines in demand for production jobs typically held by low-skilled men, as well as substantial increased demand for jobs dominated by high school women. In the case of college graduates, they find smaller increases in demand for traditionally female college jobs, and note the substantial increase of women in traditionally male occupations and industries. Thus, the greatest impact of women substituting for men should have been in college jobs, the sector which experienced relatively large wage gains.

To begin to understand how changes in labor force participation and earnings have affected family income inequality, we examine how married women's participation and earnings vary by husbands' earnings levels. Table 9.4 shows the percentage of white, black, and Hispanic couples with working wives, classified according to the level of husbands' earnings.[16] In general, the higher was the husband's earnings, the lower was the probability that the wife worked, although the differences were not large in the two ranges in which most husbands were concentrated (positive earnings less than $24 000). For example, the first number in Table 9.4 shows that in 1968, 41.9 percent of wives whose husbands' had no earnings worked at some time during the year. In contrast, only 29.7 percent of the wives whose husbands' earned more than $48 000 worked.

Over the next two decades, there were substantial increases in the percent of married women working, regardless of their husband's place in the earnings distribution. The largest increases for whites occurred in the labor force participation of wives of men with high earnings. For example, over the entire 1968 to 1988 period, the percentage working in the lowest positive earnings category increased by 18.1 percentage points (from 56.0 to 74.1 percent), but by more than 30 points for wives whose husbands were in the two categories above $36 000. Thus, the differences in participation between wives of low and high earning men narrowed considerably.

There was a similar convergence in participation rates for Hispanic wives of men with low and high earnings. The percentage of black wives who work does not vary as much by husbands' earnings level as it does for whites. There was also a very rapid growth in labor force participation for minority wives whose husbands earned more than $48 000, but there are very few husbands in this category.

By 1988, white and Hispanic married women joined black married women in having labor force participation rates that varied relatively little with husbands' earnings. This suggests that the equalizing effect of their earnings on family inequality may have eroded, as the negative correlation between wife's work and husband's earnings became much smaller. However, to this point, we have examined only the variation in participation, not how the earnings of wives vary with the earnings of their husbands. We now examine how the weekly earnings of working wives vary across the distribution of husbands' earnings.

Table 9.4   Percent of married women working

All	1968	1978	1988	*Percent change*	
				1968–78	1978–88
Husband earns 0	41.9	45.1	49.0	3.2	3.9
Husband earns <12k	58.0	65.1	71.8	7.1	6.7
Husband earns 12k–24	55.2	67.8	77.7	12.6	9.9
Husband earns 24k–36	48.1	64.2	75.9	16.1	11.7
Husband earns 36k–48	39.4	57.1	71.8	17.7	14.8
Husband earns 48k+	29.7	45.0	66.3	15.3	21.3
All wives	49.8	61.0	71.9	11.2	10.9
White	1968	1978	1988	*Percent change*	
				1968–78	1978–88
Husband earns 0	41.1	44.3	48.3	3.2	4.0
Husband earns <12k	56.0	64.9	74.1	8.9	9.3
Husband earns 12k–24	54.2	68.4	79.2	14.2	10.7
Husband earns 24k–36	47.5	63.6	76.1	16.1	12.5
Husband earns 36k–48	38.8	56.7	72.1	17.9	15.4
Husband earns 48k+	29.6	44.8	66.0	15.1	21.3
All white wives	48.6	60.5	72.5	11.9	12.0
Black	1968	1978	1988	*Percent change*	
				1968–78	1978–88
Husband earns 0	47.5	55.6	62.8	8.1	7.2
Husband earns <12k	67.9	72.6	75.8	4.7	3.2
Husband earns 12k–24	64.0	71.4	81.4	7.4	10.0
Husband earns 24k–36	63.6	73.1	83.3	9.5	10.2
Husband earns 36k–48	66.8	70.2	78.6	3.4	8.4
Husband earns 48k+	35.4	58.1	79.1	22.7	21.1
All black wives	63.9	70.3	78.3	6.4	8.0
Hispanic	1968	1978	1988	*Percent change*	
				1978–88	
Husband earns 0		38.4	40.6	2.1	
Husband earns <12k		56.7	56.4	–0.3	
Husband earns 12k–24k		57.2	63.1	5.9	
Husband earns 24k–36k		60.0	65.4	5.4	
Husband earns 36k–48k		49.3	59.0	9.7	
Husband earns 48k+		45.5	58.8	13.3	
All Hispanic wives		55.8	59.8	4.0	

Table 9.5 presents the mean weekly earnings of working wives (in constant 1988 dollars), classified by husbands' earnings level.[17] There is relatively little variation in mean weekly earnings across the distribution. The mean for wives rises with husband's income, but at a much slower rate. For example, the men in the highest income

Table 9.5   Mean weekly earnings of working married women

All	1968	1978	1988	Change 1968–78	Change 1978–88
Husband earns 0	234	279	311	45	32
Husband earns <12k	207	237	254	31	17
Husband earns 12k–24	231	252	284	21	32
Husband earns 24k–36	261	283	332	22	48
Husband earns 36k–48	275	299	366	24	67
Husband earns 48k+	318	335	415	17	81
All wives	243	274	323	31	49

White	1968	1978	1988	Change 1968–78	Change 1978–88
Husband earns 0	246	281	319	35	37
Husband earns <12k	223	243	266	20	23
Husband earns 12k–24	233	252	284	18	33
Husband earns 24k–36	259	279	325	20	46
Husband earns 36k–48	273	291	362	18	71
Husband earns 48k+	317	327	408	11	81
All white wives	247	273	325	26	52

Black	1968	1978	1988	Change 1968–78	Change 1978–88
Husband earns 0	163	268	268	106	–1
Husband earns <12k	136	216	231	81	15
Husband earns 12k–24	213	261	307	48	46
Husband earns 24k–36	290	329	382	39	53
Husband earns 36k–48	351	389	380	37	–9
Husband earns 48k+	353	459	488	106	29
All black wives	206	288	326	82	38

Hispanic	1968	1978	1988		Change 1978–88
Husband earns 0		255	296		41
Husband earns <12k		216	205		–11
Husband earns 12k–24k		236	253		17
Husband earns 24k–36k		281	327		46
Husband earns 36k–48k		292	368		77
Husband earns 48k+		389	450		60
All Hispanic wives		252	277		25

category have mean earnings that are about 10 times those of men in the lowest category, but their wives earn less than twice as much as the wives of the lowest-earning husbands.

For whites, the positive relationship has increased somewhat over time, as the wages of wives of higher earning men have risen more rapidly than average. While the average white married woman's weekly wages rose by about $78, they rose about $89 for women married to men earning $36 000–$48 000 and by about $92 for those married to men earning more than $48 000.

Among black couples, the gap between the earnings of women with high and low earning husbands is greater than for whites. However, this positive relationship weakened somewhat over the two decades. For example, the average black wife's weekly earnings rose by $120, while they rose by approximately $90 for the wives of men earning $12 000-$24 000 and $24 000-$36 000, and by only about $28 dollars for those whose husbands earned $36 000-$48 000. The gains made by women with low-earning husbands are even more dramatic in percentage terms. Wives of the highest earning men had the highest wage increases, but the number of couples in this category is very small.

Among Hispanics, the greatest gains in weekly earnings were generally experienced by women married to men with higher earnings. Mean weekly earnings of women married to men with positive earnings less than $12 000 actually fell.

9.5   THE IMPACT OF WIVES' EARNINGS ON FAMILY INCOME INEQUALITY

Over a period when husbands' earnings rose very little, wives' earnings increased substantially. Between 1968 and 1988, married men's mean annual earnings rose 13.0 percent for whites and 24.4 percent for blacks, while married women's earnings more than doubled for both whites and blacks. Over the 1978 to 1988 decade, married men's mean annual earnings rose 3.9 percent for whites, 3.0 percent for blacks, and actually fell by 5.4 percent for Hispanics. At the same time, married women's mean earnings rose 54.4 percent for whites, 33.7 percent for blacks, and 29.6 percent for Hispanics.

As discussed above, the rise in married women's earnings reflects an increase in the proportion of married women who work as well as increased weekly earnings for working wives. In order to more fully understand the impact of married women's earnings on the distribution of family income, we first examine how they change the percentage of families living in various categories defined as multiples of the official poverty line. This provides a measure of how wives' earnings affect the absolute income levels of couples.[18] Then, we examine their effects on measures of relative inequality, such as the Gini coefficient and the squared coefficient of variation (CV^2).

Table 9.6 shows the distribution of income in categories defined in terms of the official poverty line – that is, the percentage of families with incomes less than the poverty line, between one and two times the poverty line, etc. The highest category includes those with incomes greater than seven times the poverty line. Because the official poverty line increases with family size and is adjusted annually for inflation, this income measure adjusts both for changes in prices over time and for differences in family size.[19] We define 'the rich' as couples whose incomes exceed seven times their poverty lines. This is analogous to the official poverty definition which counts as poor those below a fixed threshold. Of course, any such measure for defining the rich is arbitrary (see Danziger, Gottschalk and Smolensky, 1989).[20]

The proportion poor and rich are both affected by changes in the level and the shape of the income distribution. For example, if every wife worked and earned an amount equal to her husband's income, then the entire distribution would shift to the right. There would be fewer families in each of the lower income categories and more in the higher income categories. The mean would increase, but measures of relative income inequality would not change.

The first panel of Table 9.6 shows the distribution of total family income from all sources. In addition to the earnings and self-employment income of husbands and wives, total family income, as reported in the Current Population Survey, includes the earnings of other family members, property income (interest, dividends, and net rents), government cash transfers (Social Security, welfare, etc.), and other income (private pensions, child support, etc.).[21] The second panel shows the distribution of total family income less wives' earnings.[22]

The first two numbers in the first column show that 5.8 percent of married couples had total family income less than the poverty line in 1968, and 20.5 percent had total family income between one and two times the poverty line. The equivalent numbers in the second panel show that without wives' earnings, 9.2 percent of families would have been below the poverty line, and 26.4 percent would have had income between one and two times the poverty line.

The change in the distribution of income due to wives' earnings is shown in the third panel, and illustrated by Figures 9.3(a)–9.3(d). Figure 9.3(a) shows that in all three years, wives' earnings signifi-cantly reduced the percentage of all families with income below three

Table 9.6 Percent of married couples in each poverty line category

Total family income

Times Poverty line	All couples			White couples			Black couples			Hispanic couples		
	1968	1978	1988	1968	1978	1988	1968	1978	1988	1968	1978	1988
<1	5.8	4.5	4.8	4.9	3.7	3.4	16.9	8.5	8.8		10.8	14.2
1-2	20.5	13.5	11.7	19.3	11.8	9.8	34.9	22.7	18.6		30.2	24.6
2-3	26.9	20.6	15.3	27.2	20.0	14.5	22.9	24.5	18.2		25.0	21.2
3-5	31.0	35.2	30.5	31.9	36.2	31.5	19.6	30.4	28.6		25.0	24.7
5-7	10.6	16.3	18.6	11.0	17.4	19.9	4.3	10.3	14.9		6.6	9.4
7+	5.3	9.9	19.1	5.6	10.8	20.9	1.3	3.7	10.9		2.4	5.8
Mean	33 329	40 154	44 595	34 037	41 301	46 391	24 359	33 201	36 883		29 557	31 481

Total family income less wives' earnings

Times Poverty line	All couples			White couples			Black couples			Hispanic couples		
	1968	1978	1988	1968	1978	1988	1968	1978	1988	1968	1978	1988
<1	9.2	7.9	9.2	7.9	6.6	7.0	25.1	16.4	18.2		16.6	21.3
1-2	26.4	20.0	18.4	25.3	17.8	16.3	39.8	33.2	28.3		37.5	31.8
2-3	30.0	25.5	21.1	30.6	25.6	21.2	23.0	25.7	21.8		25.3	20.8
3-5	25.4	31.5	29.7	26.6	33.3	31.5	10.6	20.8	22.2		16.5	19.3
5-7	5.8	9.8	12.1	6.2	10.7	13.3	1.1	2.8	6.2		3.2	3.9
7+	3.2	5.3	9.5	3.5	6.0	10.7	0.4	1.1	3.3		1.0	2.9
Mean	28 594	33 229	34 425	29 352	34 463	36 104	19 127	24 396	25 375		24 258	24 587

Percentage point change due to wives' earnings

Times Poverty line	All couples			White couples			Black couples			Hispanic couples		
	1968	1978	1988	1968	1978	1988	1968	1978	1988	1968	1978	1988
<1	-3.3	-3.4	-4.4	-2.9	-2.9	-3.6	-8.1	-7.9	-9.4		-5.8	-7.1
1-2	-5.9	-6.5	-6.8	-6.1	-6.1	-6.5	-4.9	-10.6	-9.8		-7.3	-7.2
2-3	-3.2	-4.9	-5.8	-3.4	-5.5	-6.6	-0.1	-1.3	-3.5		-0.3	0.4
3-5	5.6	3.7	0.8	5.3	2.9	-0.0	9.0	9.6	6.4		8.5	5.4
5-7	4.8	6.5	6.5	4.9	6.7	6.6	3.2	7.5	8.7		3.4	5.5
7+	2.0	4.6	9.6	2.1	4.9	10.2	0.9	2.7	7.6		1.4	2.9
Mean	4735	6925	10 170	4685	6838	10 287	5232	8806	11 508		5299	6894

times the poverty line, and increased the percentage with incomes in the middle range, from three to seven times the poverty line.

The role of wives' earnings in moving families into the highest categories has grown over time. White wives increased the percent of families with earnings over seven times the poverty line by only 2.1 percentage points in 1968, but by 10.2 points in 1988. White wives increased the percentage of families above 9 times the poverty line by only 0.7 percentage points in 1968, but by 5.2 points in 1988. Thus, by 1988, wives were not only raising a greater percentage of lower-income families out of poverty and near-poverty into the 'middle class', but they were also increasingly likely to move families out of the middle class and into the ranks of the rich.

Black married women had a similar impact on the distribution of black families' income, as illustrated in Figure 9.3(c). They played an even greater role in reducing the number of low earning families, reducing the percent of families with income below three times the poverty line by 13.1 percentage points in 1968 and by 22.7 percentage points in 1988. As was the case for whites, black wives had a much larger impact on the percent of families with higher income in 1988. In 1968, only 1.3 percent of all black couples had an income over seven times the poverty line, and 0.9 percentage points of this were due to wives' earnings. This figure increased to 10.9 percent by 1988, with 7.6 percentage points due to wives.

The earnings of Hispanic wives reduced the percent of Hispanic married couples with earnings below three times the poverty line by about 14 percentage points in both 1978 and 1988. Wives' earnings moved a substantial proportion of Hispanic families from the lower income categories to the middle range. Relatively few Hispanic married couples were rich – 5.8 percent in 1988. This figure would have only been about one-half as large had it not been for wives' earnings.

Wives' earnings clearly play a major role in reducing the percent of married couple families with incomes below three times the poverty line. In later years they also increase the percent of higher earnings families, especially for whites and blacks. The earnings of married women have shifted the entire distribution of married couples' income to the right. Working wives have taken the place of economic growth as the engine of growth in family income.

To summarize the overall impact of working wives' earnings on the relative distribution of family income, we turn to an analysis of two commonly-used summary measures of inequality, the squared coefficient of variation and the Gini coefficient. Table 9.7 presents the

Figure 9.3

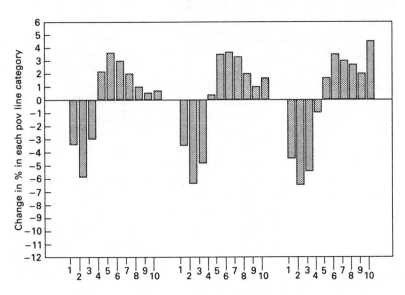

(a) Change due to all wives' earnings, 1968, 1978, 1988

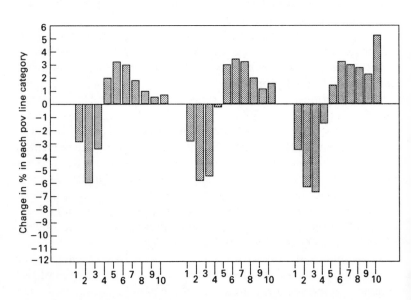

(b) Change due to white wives' earnings, 1968, 1978, 1988

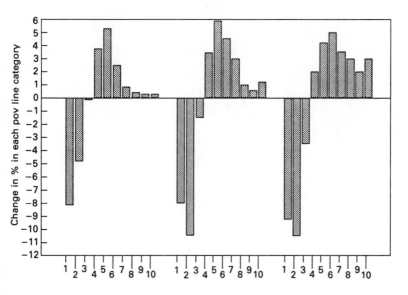

(c) Change due to black wives' earnings, 1968, 1978, 1988

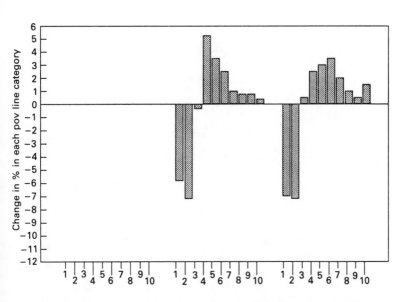

(d) Change due to Hispanic wives' earnings, 1968, 1978, 1988

Table 9.7 Percentage change in the squared CV and Gini of total family income due to wives' earnings

	All			% Change		Black			% Change	
	1968	1978	1988	1968–88	1978–88	1968	1978	1988	1968–88	1978–88
All families										
Squared CV of:										
Total family income	0.51	0.51	0.66	29.4	29.4	0.58	0.72	0.84	44.8	16.7
Less wives' earnings	0.56	0.55	0.69	23.2	25.5	0.53	0.63	0.77	45.3	22.2
%Change	-8.9	-7.3	-4.3			9.4	14.3	9.1		
Gini of:										
Total family income	0.359	0.381	0.422	17.5	10.8	0.405	0.440	0.474	17.0	7.7
Less wives' earnings	0.366	0.384	0.420	14.8	9.4	0.386	0.417	0.451	16.8	8.2
%Change	-1.9	-0.8	0.5			4.9	5.5	5.1		
All couples										
Squared CV of:										
Total family income	0.38	0.32	0.41	7.9	28.1	0.35	0.35	0.38	8.4	7.0
Less wives' earnings	0.46	0.40	0.52	13.0	30.0	0.37	0.38	0.48	30.2	26.8
%Change	-17.4	-20.0	-21.2			-5.4	-6.7	-21.2		
Gini of:										
Total family income	0.305	0.300	0.336	10.2	12.0	0.322	0.302	0.339	5.1	12.3
Less wives' earnings	0.325	0.328	0.368	13.2	12.2	0.319	0.317	0.368	15.4	16.1
%Change	-6.2	-8.5	-8.7			1.1	-4.7	-7.9		

	White			% Change		Hispanic			% Change	
	1968	1978	1988	1968–88	1978–88	1968	1978	1988	1968–88	1978–88
All families										
Squared CV of:										
Total family income	0.48	0.47	0.59	22.9	25.5		0.55	0.83		50.9
Less wives' earnings	0.54	0.51	0.63	16.7	23.5		0.53	0.83		56.6
%Change	−11.1	−7.8	−6.3				3.8	0.0		
Gini of:										
Total family income	0.347	0.364	0.401	15.6	10.2		0.397	0.453		14.1
Less wives' earnings	0.355	0.370	0.401	13.0	8.4		0.389	0.446		14.7
%Change	−2.3	−1.6	0.0				2.1	1.6		
All couples										
Squared CV of:										
Total family income	0.37	0.32	0.38	2.0	17.7		0.34	0.58		70.6
Less wives' earnings	0.45	0.39	0.49	8.9	25.6		0.38	0.68		78.9
%Change	−17.8	−17.8	−23.0				−10.5	−14.7		
Gini of:										
Total family income	0.300	0.295	0.325	8.2	10.2		0.314	0.380		21.0
Less wives' earnings	0.320	0.323	0.358	11.8	10.8		0.328	0.396		20.7
%Change	−6.2	−8.7	−9.2				−4.3	−4.0		

squared coefficient of variation (CV^2) and the Gini for total family income and for total family income less wives' earnings for all families and for married couples.[23] These two summary measures of inequality show similar trends for both income concepts.[24] As a result, our discussion emphasizes changes in the Gini coefficient.

Turning first to total family income, inequality increased for whites and blacks between 1968 and 1988 for all families and for married couples. Most of the increase occurred during the 1978 to 1988 decade.

For all white families, the Gini coefficient rose by about 16 percent, from 0.347 to 0.401, between 1968 and 1988, with most of the increase occurring after 1978. The Gini coefficient for white couples rose from 0.300 to 0.325, by about 8 percent, over the two decades. For couples, this reflected a slight decline in the Gini in the first period, followed by a more substantial increase in the second.

Among all black families, the Gini coefficient of total family income grew by 17 percent over the two decades, from 0.405 to 0.474. Again, income inequality among couples increased by a smaller amount, from 0.322 to 0.339, about 5 percent. As was the case for white couples, this increase was a result of a decline in the first decade, offset by a greater rise in the second decade.

The greatest increase in income inequality in the last decade was among Hispanics. Between 1978 and 1988, the Gini coefficient for all families increased by about 14 percent, from 0.397 to 0.453. Over the same period, the Gini for married couples increased by 21 percent.

Between 1968 and 1988, wives' earnings increased substantially, but the labor force participation of wives married to men with above-average earnings increased the most. What was the net impact of these changes on the distribution for all families and for couples?

One common measure of the impact of wives' earnings on family income inequality is the percentage change in income inequality due to wives' earnings.[25] Table 9.7 also shows the percentage change in the CV^2 and the Gini coefficient due to the inclusion of wives' earnings; that is, the distribution of total family income is compared to what it would have been if the earnings of all wives had been zero.[26] This calculation is made for all families and for married couples.[27] As discussed earlier, it is especially important to consider the impact of wives' earnings on the distribution of income of all families as the proportion of households headed by married couples has fallen over time.

The earnings of white married women have an equalizing impact on the distribution of income for all white families and for all white couples in each of the three years. The impact on married couples has grown modestly. In 1968, wives' earnings reduced the CV^2 by 17.8 percent and the Gini coefficient by 6.2 percent, while in 1988 these figures were 23.0 and 9.2 percent, respectively. However, over the same period, the equalizing impact among all families has fallen, from 11.1 to 6.3 percent when measured by the CV^2, and from 2.3 to 0.0 percent when measured by the Gini.

Given the disproportionate increases in the participation and earnings of women married to higher earning men, why has the equalizing impact of wives' earnings on the distribution of income of married couples risen over time? First, because the level of wives' earnings has risen dramatically (mean earnings of white married women more than doubled between 1968 and 1988, while those of white married men increased by only 13 percent). Second, because the distribution of earnings among all white wives has grown more equal (the CV^2 of white wives' earnings fell from 2.212 to 1.329, see Table 9.3).[28]

For blacks, the equalizing impact of married women's earnings on the distribution of income among married couples has risen substantially. The earnings of black wives reduced the CV^2 of total family income of married couples by only 5.4 percent in 1968, but by 21.2 percent by 1988. Over the same period, wives' earnings went from increasing the Gini coefficient by 1.1 percent to decreasing it by 7.9 percent.

In contrast, black wives' earnings increased the inequality of income among all black families, between about 9 and 14 percent when measured by the CV^2, and about 5 percent when measured by the Gini coefficient. This difference is due to the fact that black married couples are a much more advantaged group than black female-headed families, and this advantage has increased over the two decades at the same time that the percentage of couples has fallen and the percentage of female headed families has increased.[29]

Hispanic wives equalized the distribution of income among couples, but made the distribution among all families somewhat less equal. For Hispanic married couples, wives' earnings decreased the CV^2 by 10.5 percent in 1978 and by 14.7 percent in 1988; they decreased the Gini coefficient by about 4 percent in both years. The impact of married women's earnings was relatively minor for the distribution of income among all families, increasing the CV^2 by 3.8 percent in 1978, and the Gini by 2.1 percent in 1978 and 1.6 percent in 1988. Their earnings had no effect on the CV^2 for all families in 1988.

9.6   POLICY IMPLICATIONS

Wives have increased their work effort despite the disincentives of federal income tax policies. Women are discouraged from entering the labor market, as they must earn not only enough to offset the loss in home production, but also enough to pay the taxes on their market earnings (plus any additional work expenses).

Under the current tax system, two families with equal ability to pay face different tax levies depending on whether or not the spouse works in the market. Consider two families with similar consumption patterns but different money incomes. In one family, the wife works in the home. In the second, the wife works in the market where she earns just enough income to buy the same goods that the first wife produces at home. The members of each family work an equal number of hours and would consume at the same level were it not for the tax system. However, while the first family does not pay taxes on the home production, the second must pay Social Security tax and federal and possibly state income taxes on the wife's market earnings.

We believe there are a number of changes in the tax law which could redress the imbalance between the treatment of home and market production. First, child care expenses associated with both parents working in the market should be treated more favorably, especially for families with low incomes. Under current law, a family may deduct 20 to 30 percent of child care expenses under the Dependent Care Credit.[30] Because the credit is not refundable, few of the benefits accrue to low-income families.[31] The credit should be made refundable. In addition, the credit rate should be raised, especially for families with lower income.

An additional means of compensating two-earner families for the loss of tax-free home production would be a two-earner deduction, similar to the one available in the mid-1980s. For example, one could exempt from income taxes 10 percent of the first $25 000 of earnings of the lowest earner in the family.

We believe that there are a variety of changes in the tax law that would result in the more equal treatment of home and market production. We are not wed to any single proposal but rather support changes that would cease to penalize spouses who enter the labor market, especially low-income spouses.

9.7 SUMMARY

Married women are more likely to work and are likely to earn more when they work, than they were twenty years ago. This growth in married women's earnings has been very important because it co-incided with a period of relatively stagnant earnings for married men. To place this period, and the role of working wives, in historical context, consider the following scenario which suggests the extent to which the growth of wives' earnings 'have made up' for the slow real earnings growth for husbands.

Between 1968 and 1988, the mean earnings for husbands and wives combined grew (in 1988 dollars) by $8173. If husbands' earnings had grown as fast in these two decades as they did between 1949 and 1969, the annual real growth rate would have been about 3 percent, and their earnings alone would have increased by almost $20 000. Thus, even if wives had not worked and earned more, family income in 1988 would have been substantially higher than it was. From this perspective, the increased mean earnings of wives, about $5000 over the 1968–88 period, were only able to offset a small part of the decline in the growth of their husbands' earnings.

Thus, family income growth is likely to remain modest unless there are unforseen changes in the structure of labor markets that would accelerate earnings growth for men or lead more women to work in different occupations or increase the wages paid for 'women's work.' In addition, at least two trends suggest that we cannot depend primarily on the growth of wives' work effort, as a substitute for higher wages, to increase family income. First, the proportion of all adults living in married couple households continues to decline. Thus, fewer families can benefit from the earnings of two spouses. In addition, the participation of married women cannot increase indefinitely.

Some writers have expressed concern that changes in the participation and wages of married women would cause their earnings to have less of an equalizing impact on the distribution of income among married couples. The data above suggests that the opposite is true. While income inequality among couples increased over the past twenty years, it would have increased to an even greater extent were it not for the increased earnings of wives.

Nonetheless, as married couples came to represent a smaller proportion of all households, the impact of wives' earnings on the distribution of income among all families has changed. Income inequality among all families has increased for all groups. However, the impacts of married women's earnings were different for whites, blacks and Hispanics. For whites, inequality would have been greater in the absence of married women's earnings. However, married women's earnings actually increased the inequality of income among all black families. Their impact on the distribution of income among Hispanic families was relatively minor.

We have shown the importance of increases in wives' earnings on the level and distribution of family income. Without increases in market work by wives, family income gains would have been much smaller and income inequality would have increased considerably more than it actually did.

Notes

1. Jon Haveman and Cathy Sun provided computational assistance; Gregory Acs, Jon Bound, Gary Burtless, Laura Dresser, Sanders Korenman, Robert Schoeni, Matthew Shapiro, Daniel Weinberg and participants in the Demography Seminar, Population Studies Center, University of Michigan, provided helpful comments on earlier drafts.
2. All dollar figures in the text and the tables are in constant 1988 dollars using the CPI-X1.
3. The Current Population Survey data do not provide good enough information on hours for us to decompose the change in annual earnings into changes in hours and changes in hourly wage rates. Some portion of the increased weekly earnings of wives is due to increased hours worked per week. This issue is discussed further in endnote 17.
4. In fact, most previous studies (e.g., Smith, 1979; Danziger, 1980; Bergmann *et al.*, 1980; Lehrer and Nerlove, 1981 and 1984; Treas, 1987; Wion, 1990) found wives' earnings to be inequality-reducing.
5. Tables 9.1, 9.2 and 9.3 do not include farmers or farm managers, or their spouses. Also excluded from these tables are persons reporting positive earnings and zero weeks worked.

   See Cancian, Danziger and Gottschalk (1993) for a related analysis which includes five observations over the same period: 1968, 1973, 1978, 1983, 1988. That analysis reveals little cyclicality in wives' participation or earnings.
6. Married persons live with a spouse and head a family or unrelated subfamily, or are the spouse of a head of a family or unrelated subfamily. Heads of families do not have a spouse present, but are the head of a family or unrelated subfamily that contains relatives. We also include unrelated primary and secondary individuals as heads; in effect, they head a single person family. Persons who do not head their own family are classified as 'other.' Most people in this category would be adult children living with their parents, or persons living with other relatives.

The CPS counts two nonmarried individuals who share a housing unit as two unrelated individuals. We did not attempt to simulate which of these cases were cohabiting couples, who might more appropriately be classified as married persons. Declines in marriage rates over the period discussed here may, in part, be due to increased cohabitation. However, Bumpass and Sweet (1989) demonstrate that cohabitation is a short-lived state, with a median duration of only 1.3 years. Thus, 'despite the high levels of lifetime experience, cohabiting couples are a small proportion of all couples' (1989, p. 620). Moreover, given their short duration, it is questionable whether these unions involve the same economic relationships as marriage. For example, one might expect labor force participation of women who are cohabiting, to be less dependent than that of wives' on their partners' earnings.

7. In the text and tables that follow, 'whites' ('blacks') refers to all whites (blacks) in 1968, and to white (black) non-Hispanics in 1978 and 1988. Non-Hispanic persons who respond 'other,' rather than white or black (for example, Native Americans or Asian Americans), are included only in 'all.'

  In Tables 9.1–9.3, persons are categorized according to their own race/ethnicity. In Tables 9.4–9.7, couples are categorized according to the husband's race/ethnicity.

8. Blackburn and Bloom (1987) is an exception.

9. Over the period, the proportion of white and black married women without children present has also increased. However, by 1988, the labor force participation rate of these women was not very different from that of married women with children.

10. Table 9.2 includes all persons working positive weeks, including those with zero, or negative, earnings.

11. The Hispanic category is very heterogeneous. It includes persons of Mexican, Cuban, Puerto Rican, Central and South American origins. Analysis of Census data (see Bean and Tienda, 1989) reveals very different patterns of work and family structure among the various Hispanic subgroups. However, the CPS sample size is not large enough to analyze the groups separately. As a result, any given trend for all Hispanics, as shown here, may mask different trends for the various subgroups.

12. We include wages, salaries and non-farm self-employment income as earnings in Table 9.3.

13. Danziger (1989) classifies those earning less than $12 000 per year as low earners, as on their own they earn too little to keep a family of four out of poverty.

14. The squared coefficient of variation is the ratio of the variance to the squared mean.

15. The fall in earnings can, in part, be attributed to the relatively large proportion of Hispanic men with low education levels, and the growing proportion of less educated men that have low earnings (see Acs and Danziger, 1991). Mean earnings may also have been affected by the arrival of immigrants with low earning potential, or by changes in the extent to which these immigrants were sampled by the CPS.

16. In Tables 9.4 and 9.5, women are considered to be working if they report positive weeks worked and positive earnings. Husbands' and wives' earnings include wages, salaries, farm and non-farm self-employment.

   Tables that present data on the percent of wives working and mean weekly wages for the subsamples white, black, and Hispanic couples with children under six are available from the authors on request.

17. Weekly earnings are computed as the ratio of annual earnings to annual weeks worked. Fuchs (1988) found that among married women aged 25 to 64 who worked, 22 percent worked less that 30 hours per week in 1960, while 25 percent worked less than 30 hours per week in 1986. Blank (1989) finds a similar proportion of all working women worked part time throughout the 1980s. Thus, the weekly wage figures presented here understate the mean weekly wage for full-time workers.

   When we examined the data presented in Tables 9.4 and 9.5 only for those wives who worked full-time full-year, the magnitude of this downward bias did not vary substantially over the period.

18. Implicit in our analysis is the assumption that changes in husbands' earnings are independent of wives'. For a discussion of alternative models of husbands' and wives' labor supply see Lundberg (1988).

19. In 1988, the poverty line for a couple was $7958, while it was $12 092 for a family of four and $24 133 for a family of nine or more. Consider, for example, three couples, with identical incomes of $24 000, but with zero, two and seven children. They would be counted in Table 9.6 in three different categories. The couple with no children would be categorized with income between 3 and 4 times the poverty line; the one with two children, as between one and two times the poverty line; and the one with seven children, as less than the poverty line. We use the CPI-X1 to adjust these measures back in real terms to the earlier years.

20. Danziger *et al.* (1989), in an analysis of all families, defined the rich as those families whose incomes exceed 9 times the poverty line. We use 7 times the poverty line here because so few black and Hispanic families have incomes above 9 times the line.

21. The CPS does not gather information on noncash income, such as Food Stamps, Medicare, or employer-provided health insurance, capital gains, or taxes paid.

22. Implicit in this simple subtraction of wives' earnings is the assumption that the distribution of the remaining sources of income would not change if wives did not work. While this assumption might be questioned for any single year, it will not effect our analysis of changes over time, if the responsiveness of the other incomes sources to wives' earnings was stable over the entire period.

23. Unrelated individuals are considered one-person families. The category 'all families' includes couples, unrelated individuals and families headed by nonmarried men and women.

24. The CV^2 is equally sensitive to transfers at all income levels, while the Gini coefficient is more sensitive to transfers near the mode (Kakwani, 1980, p. 87).

25. This analysis treats two families with equal money incomes as equal.

Because we use money income as a proxy for economic well-being several caveats are in order. Increased market work for wives typically comes at the expense of home production and/or leisure. For example, consider two couples, A and B. Husband A earns $40 000, while wife A does not work in the market; husband B earns $25,000, while wife B works full time and earns $15 000. Both families have $40 000 total earnings, but A may be better off since wife A may provide child care, housework, etc., which family B may need to purchase. On the other hand, family B may benefit if the participation of the wife leads to a preferable distribution of resources within the family, and/or increases the wife's labor market opportunities in the event of divorce. Moving beyond a comparison of money income to a comparison of economic well-being is beyond the scope of this paper.

26. The percentage change in the CV^2 (Gini) due to wives' earnings is calculated by computing the CV^2 (Gini) of total income less wives' earnings, and comparing this with the CV^2 (Gini) of total income. This measure of wives' impact is an upper-bound estimate, because the implicit counterfactual is that wives do not work and that husbands' earnings are not responsive to changes in wives' labor force participation or earnings.

27. The inequality measures in Table 9.7 are not adjusted for family size, as the data were in Table 9.6. Thus, a single individual and a family of 9 earning $24 000 are considered to have an equivalent income. Because families headed by married couples are larger on average, the figures may understate the equalizing (or overstate the disequalizing) impact of wives' earnings on the distribution of income among all families. To see whether our analysis was sensitive to differences in family sizes, we prepared a similar table for our measure of income divided by the poverty line. Using this adjusted measure, the equalizing impact of wives' earnings is stable over time for all white families, while for all black families, the disequalizing impact shown in Table 9.7 is substantially reduced. See endnote 29.

28. A formal decomposition of the change in the CV^2 of total family income shows that the equalizing impact of growth in mean wives' earnings and the fall in the CV^2 of wives' earnings, more than compensates for the inequality-increasing impact of the rising correlation of spouses' earnings. See Cancian, Danziger, and Gottschalk, 1993.

29. However, when incomes are adjusted for family size using the poverty line (see the discussion of Table 9.6), the disequalizing impact for blacks is substantially reduced. In this case, black wives' earnings increase the CV^2 by 5.5, 0.0, and 1.3 percent, and the Gini by 3.1, 1.4, and 1.8 percent, in 1968, 1978 and 1988.

30. The percent deductible depends on the family's income level. The maximum amount that can be subsidized is $2400 for one child, and $4800 for two or more children.

31. For example, a family of four earning about $13 000 (the federal poverty line) will owe no federal income tax. Thus, if it spent, for example, $1000 on child care, it would not be able to claim the $300 credit.

References

Acs, G. and S. Danziger (1991) 'Educational Attainment, Industrial Structure, and Male Earnings, 1973–1987.' Institute for Research on Poverty Discussion Paper no. 945–91, University of Wisconsin-Madison.

Bean, F. D. and M. Tienda (1989) The *Hispanic Population of the United States* (New York: Russell Sage Foundation).

Bergmann, B. R. *et al.* (1980) 'The Effect of Wives' Labor Force Participation on Inequality in the Distribution of Family Income,' *Journal of Human Resources*, 15, 452–6.

Betson, D. and J. van der Gaag (1984) 'Working Married Women and the Distribution of Income,' *Journal of Human Resources*, 19, 532–43.

Bumpass, L. and J. Sweet (1989) *American Families and Households* (New York: Russell Sage Foundation).

Blackburn, M. and D. Bloom (1987) 'Family Income Inequality in the United States: 1967–1984,' *Industrial Relations Research Association Series*, Proceedings of the Thirty-ninth Annual Meeting, 349–56.

Blackburn, M. and D. Bloom (1990) 'Changes in the Structure of Family Income Inequality in the U.S. and Other Industrialized Nations During the 1980s.' Unpublished paper.

Blank, R. (1989) 'The Role of Part-time Work in Women's Labor Market Choices Over Time,' *American Economic Review*, 79(2), 295–9.

Cancian, M. and S. Danziger, and P. Gottschalk (1993) 'Working Wives and the Distribution of Family Income,' in S. Danziger and P. Gottschalk, *Uneven Tides: Rising Inequality in America* (New York: Russell Sage Foundation).

Danziger, S. (1980) 'Do Working Wives Increase Family Income Inequality?' *Journal of Human Resources*, 15, 444–51.

Danziger, S. (1989) 'Education, Earnings, and Poverty.' *Institute for Research on Poverty Discussion Paper*, no. 881–89, University of Wisconsin-Madison.

Danziger, S. and P. Gottschalk, and E. Smolensky (1989) 'How the Rich have Fared, 1973–1987,' *American Economic Review*, 79, May, 310–14.

Fuchs, V. (1988) *Women's Quest for Economic Equality* (Cambridge, MA: Harvard University Press).

Goldin, C. D. (1990) *Understanding the Gender Gap: and Economic History of American Women* (New York, NY: Oxford University Press).

Juhn, C., K. M. Murphy, and B. Pierce (1989) 'Wage Inequality and the Rise in Returns to Skill.' Mimeo, University of Chicago.

Kakwani, N. C. (1980) *Income Inequality and Poverty: Methods of Estimation and Policy Applications* (esp. chapter 5, Measures of Income Inequality) (Oxford: Oxford University Press).

Karoly, L. A. (1993) 'The Trend in Inequality Among Families, Individuals and Workers in the United States: a Twenty-five Year Perspective,' in S. Danziger and P. Gottschalk, *Uneven Tides: Rising Inequality in America* (New York: Russell Sage Foundation).

Katz, L. F. and K. M. Murphy (1992) 'Changes in Relative Wages, 1963–1987: Supply and Demand Factors.' *Quarterly Journal of Economics*, 107, 35–78.

Killingsworth, M. and J. J. Heckman (1986) 'Female Labor Supply: a Survey,' in O. C. Ashenfelter and R. Leyard (eds), *Handbook of Labor Economics* (Amsterdam: North-Holland).

Lehrer, E., and M. Nerlove (1981) 'The Impact of Female Work on Family Income Distribution in the United States: Black-white Differentials,' *Review of Income and Wealth*, 27(4), 423–31.

Lehrer, E. and M. Nerlove (1984) 'A Lifecycle Analysis of Family Income Distribution,' *Economic Inquiry* 22, 360–74.

Lundberg, S. (1988) 'Labor Supply of Husbands and Wives: a Simultaneous Equations Approach,' *Review of Economics and Statistics*, 52, 224–35.

Mincer, J. (1962) 'Labor Force Participation of Married Women: a Study of Labor Supply,' in H. Gregg Lewis (ed.), *Aspects of Labor Economics*. Universities-National Bureau Committee for Economic Research (Princeton, NJ: Princeton University Press).

Murphy, K. M. and F. Welch (1993) 'Industrial Change and the Rising Importance of Skill,' in S. Danziger and P. Gottschalk, *Uneven Tides: Rising Inequality in America* (New York: Russell Sage Foundation).

Smith, J. (1979) 'The Distribution of Family Income,' *Journal of Political Economy*, 87, S163–S192.

Thurow, L. (1975) *Generating Inequality: Mechanisms of Distribution in the U.S. Economy* (New York: Basic Books).

Treas, J. (1987) 'The Effect of Women's Labor Force Participation on the Distribution of Income in the United States,' *Annual Review of Sociology*, 13, 259–88.

Wilson, W. J. (1987) *The Truly Disadvantaged* (Chicago: University of Chicago Press).

Wion, D. A. (1990) 'Working Wives and Earnings Inequality among Married Couples, 1967–84,' *Review of Social Economy*, 48, 18–24.

Comment

Daniel H. Weinberg*

This is a superb paper – many careful analyses and a discussion of alternate hypotheses. The tables are very well done and very informative. The authors have realized that it is not enough to tell us that men have had slow earnings growth and increasing inequality and women have had fast earnings growth and decreasing inequality. They have also tried to tell us why. I want to thank the authors for a very careful job and their responsiveness to my earlier suggestions.

Two sources of decreasing earnings inequality are more working women (fewer zero earners) and increasing education, while a particular source of increasing inequality is demographic changes. Additional hypotheses they might have examined and did not are discrimination and job characteristics. As women face less discrimination in the working world, perhaps women are displacing less competent men, men whose income is now lower than it might have otherwise been, increasing inequality. Perhaps some of it has to do with the industrial and occupational distribution of men versus women in the 1980s versus the 1960s.

I think that more studies ought to use a relative income measure, that is, income corrected for economies of scale resulting from household and family formation. Most common (and the way Cancian *et al.* do it) is to use the equivalence scale implicit in the poverty thresholds; Ruggles (1990) among others has pointed out the problems with that. We all need someone to do careful work on coming up with a more sensible alternative. Perhaps one of the things that the new Committee on National Statistics panel on poverty measurement can do is to investigate that issue.

Reference

Ruggles, Patricia (1990) *Drawing the Line* (Washington, DC: Urban Institute Press).

* The views expressed here do not necessarily reflect those of the Census Bureau or the Department of Commerce.

Part III

Policy Discussion

10 Policy Forum: Prospects for Future Policy

The policy forum characteristic of all Levy Institute sponsored conferences was scheduled as a debate for or against the major public policy issues raised in the individual chapters of this volume. The panelists were Robert B. Avery, Professor of Economics at Cornell University; Sheldon Danziger, Professor of Economics at the University of Michigan; William T. Dickens, Professor of Economics at the University of California-Berkeley; Robert Haveman, Professor of Economics at the University of Wisconsin-Madison; Timothy M. Smeeding, Professor of Economics at Syracuse University; Edward N. Wolff, Professor of Economics at New York University; and Dimitri B. Papadimitriou (moderator), Professor of Economics at Bard College and executive director of the Jerome Levy Economics Institute.

DIMITRI PAPADIMITRIOU   This conference volume is the culmination of a multifaceted project that was undertaken by the Levy Institute focusing on the economic inequality and maldistribution of wealth and income in the United States at the close of the twentieth century. The goal was for each facet to analyze a particular perspective of inequality and income or wealth disparity and to ultimately prescribe practical recommendations for improving current tax, transfer and other policies that affect the division of the economic pie.

Most of the chapters in this book provide policy-oriented conclusions in addition to identifying policy problems. Some of these are analyzed and critiqued by formal commentaries. The purpose of this roundtable discussion is to concentrate on the policy recommendations drawn from the research findings. In so doing, it is necessary to distinguish public policy problems from research problems. One needs to be concerned with the cost of the policy problems, i.e. the cost of doing nothing being demonstrably serious enough to warrant government action. In addition, given the US federal budget difficulties, recommendations to use resources more efficiently and fairly obviously have far more political potential than do those requiring new resources. Finally, the values and principles reflected in the solutions must be politically acceptable to voters. In the discussion that follows, each of the panel members focuses on poverty and distributional problems, policy issues and possible government responses.

ROBERT AVERY   I would like to talk about three areas. First, how we as economists are functioning in our role as scientists and what we can contribute. Then I shall discuss two public policy areas, household structural change, and wealth.

I spent eight years at the Federal Reserve in Washington; in terms of how close an economist can come to actually making policy, the Fed is one of the best places to be. Looking back, I can say that my view when I left was quite different from that which I had when I started. I now fundamentally believe that our role as research scientists is to provide information from which policy makers, who are drawn from the public at large, can make decisions. Even though we do have the privilege of providing information directly to the policy maker, we can derive no more right to advocate a particular policy position than anybody else.

In this regard, what we do as a profession is sadly deficient. The ills of banking deregulation, for example, were obvious to most people who thought about them, yet we failed to provide information to help make better policy decisions.

One reason has been the significant depletion of the federal statistical agencies over the last fifteen years as is the reason of the quality of the staff working at the various agencies including the Federal Reserve Board. And it is much more pronounced in agencies like Health and Human Services, and the Department of Labor. Everywhere, it seems there is an eroding ability to think about policy even a year or two years ahead, much less do any kind of in-house analysis. Indeed, most of the surveys that have been referenced in the various chapters are surveys that have been in place for the last fifteen years. A lot of this can also be traced to the declining value our society places on public service.

I would like to make some observations on policy. I have increasingly become aware that we have not thought enough about the issue of structural change at the household level. For example, we have paid too little attention to the long-run consequences of divorce and the changing nature of the extended family. This, in terms of long-term health care, requires that we ask questions about the relationship between divorced parents and children, and other intergenerational relationships. It is not clear that we can extrapolate from previous generations, since people who were divorced in the 1950s, were not as likely to have anticipated it or developed their human capital as insurance protection. This is an area in which there is enormous need for study and where there may be implications for institutional change.

Similarly, we need to ask questions involving family leave policy and child care, part-time and flexible-time jobs, as well as labor productivity. We have developed stereotypical views of household structure – with one wage earner – even though this structure has changed. Our profession has not provided information and guidance to industry on how to accommodate new family structures that might have very different needs than from those of thirty years ago.

The role of young adults is another area that needs to be analyzed. Each quarter, individuals move in and out in 15 percent of households, an unbelievably high number. How do we treat young adults who once unemployed instantly move in with their parents. Who is responsible? Does society have a role in supporting these young adults? We have steered away from these kinds of questions because they do not involve well defined concepts or structures.

Finally, I would like to touch on the concept of wealth. Income is much more highly related to short-run well-being and, as it should be, has been a more greatly weighted factor in determining public policy. Because we have not collected wealth data, we have tended to steer away from policy questions that are highly related to wealth. There are areas of taxation in particular, where wealth is extremely relevant. The best example I can think of is society's decision to have a high real rate of interest in response to budgetary deficit. This decision will have major distributional impacts which need be explored. For example, it was Paul Volcker's unilateral decision in 1979 that caused real interest rates to be as high as they were, and we did not have the data that would have been helpful in assessing such a decision. Yet, that decision had a major distributional impact on wealth; we however, chose to focus on income instead.

SHELDON DANZIGER   In 1971, Robert Lampman wrote a book in which he said, given the programmes and policies in place, and given the expected growth in the economy, there should be no poverty as officially measured by 1980. Contrary to that publication, we are now in a situation where we have more poverty than in 1970, and where we are about to get more poverty because of the effects of the current recession.

Most of the essays in this book, have utilized peak or close-to-peak data for the 1979 to 1989 decade. The focus has been on why did not things get better as the economy grew in the 1980s. In some ways, what we now have is a 'pseudo-social experiment'. The economic recovery, combined with President Reagan's policy of cutting back on income transfer programs, has generated a broad consensus on the diminished ability of the economy alone to alleviate poverty.

Historically, one of the initial motivations for the 'War on Poverty' was the realization in the 1960s that, even as the economy grew rapidly, there was a large group of poor people being left behind. Similarly, we need an active anti-poverty policy now because many poor people were left behind by the healthy economy of the late-1980s. The big political success of the Reagan era was in generating large deficits so that now, despite a broad consensus that additional anti-poverty spending is needed, there is no money to fund them.

Normally you assume that in a recovery everybody is moving up the standard of living escalator. In this recovery, while one group started to move up, it is as if somebody turned around and gave a push and the people toward the bottom of the distribution got knocked down a number of steps. The Reagan changes in unemployment insurance, AFDC, tax policies, etc, pushed them even a little further down the steps. As Alan Blinder has mentioned in his comments at the end of Chapter 8, in almost all areas, the groups that were already disadvantaged fell back. The one exception is that women's wages rose relative to men's.

For most being pushed back, it was the result of adverse changes in labor market policies and practices. Even if the government policies of the 1970s had been in place, the poor and low-educated workers would still have lost ground in the 1980s. It is not that people are staying unemployed because unemployment insurance and AFDC are increasingly generous; rather that they are increasingly poor, in many cases, even though they are working as much. For example, take black non-Hispanic males in the prime working ages of 25 to 54, who were putting in 50 to 52 weeks of work in north central cities. No one would define them as the underclass because of this work effort. In 1979, 8 percent of them earned less than $12 000 a year; by 1989, the number had doubled to 16 percent.

In addition, consistent with the Blackburn *et al.* in Chapter 8 in this book, a high school diploma is no longer enough to guarantee an escape from poverty. Indeed, there was an increase in low earnings among both black and white college graduates in the prime working ages.

Labor markets have undergone large changes. We, as economists see the symptoms, but do not really understand the causes. Many recent studies have concluded that the increased inequality in the labor market is a demand phenomenon, and that the causes are declining unionization, the changing industrial structure, and global competition. Yet, to cure the problem, instead of treating the symptoms, we need a set of policies in areas where I think there is enormous consensus. In other words, we do not have a direct policy response to the increased lower earnings that could lead to more higher paid jobs. But we do know how to offset hardship among those whose real earnings have fallen.

An example consistent with what Robert Avery indicated and what Lawrence Lindsey mentions in his book is to expand the subsidy for low income families for child care. In particular, the dependent care tax credit should become refundable. Unlike higher income families, many of the working poor and near poor cannot get subsidies. The Tax Reform Act of 1986 has taken them out of federal income taxation, but leaves them without a day care credit because the current credit is not refundable.

The law should be changed to make it refundable. This is very attractive to economists, far superior to setting up a national day care system. Phil Robins, for one, would propose changing the current law where the credit is 30 percent and nonrefundable to 80 percent refundable for the poor and the near-poor.

In another area, the National Commission on Children has proposed turning the personal exemption for children into a refundable tax credit. Again, there is broad consensus that this would be beneficial to low earners. The Far Right would like to raise the child care exemption very high because they want women to stay at home and have more kids, while the Left would subsidize both working and nonworking mothers. It would be enormously important for low income families.

I wrote a paper back in 1979 with Robert Haveman in which, we actually proposed turning the exemption into a $600 refundable tax credit. Our figure would be presently the equivalent of $2000. So, contrary to Robert Avery's remarks, the failure to enact policies has not been for lack of knowing what to do.

The big question is of course, 'where do we get the money to fund these changes'? With the Downey–Gore bill Timothy Smeeding referred to, we could easily get the money to make the child care tax credit refundable, as the bill proposes by raising the top bracket tax rate from 34 to 37 percent. However, the consensus I have talked about breaks down when we mention tax rate increases. There are other areas that could be changed. The earned income tax credit is another example. The whole health care area, particularly child health, is an important one that relates to Steven Hill and Barbara Wolfe's chapter. Finally, if one believes that there is a serious labor demand problem – which reminds me of the point I made about the different labor market problems of black males of prime working ages in north central cities – I think one will need to consider some sort of a guaranteed employment policy. There is not anywhere near as much consensus on these sort of proposals because of the costs and difficulties in implementing them. Nevertheless, although we do not know how to prevent the economy from generating low wages even for full-year workers, we certainly do know how to subsidize people in a way that would not produce adverse consequences of the kind we observe now.

WILLIAM T. DICKENS   I find many interesting things occurring in the distribution of income and the changes in household income due to the family composition. What is more important however, is the observation of the very large changes in the earnings distribution and the fact that the relatively less well off, in terms of earnings, have gotten worse off in the 1980s. This is not just high school drop-outs, but also high school graduates who have had the particularly bad fortune of entering the job market in the 1980s.

About half of the change in the 1980s can be attributed to the increasing returns of two factors: college education and experience. This has also been shown in the research by Katz and Murphy and is basically reconfirmed, by a rough estimate, by Blackburn *et al.*, in their findings. The increase in the return to experience is concentrated among the less well educated. But, is it really an increase in return to experience? We do not know, because we are looking at cross sections. What it might be instead, is a decrease in the return to education primarily concentrated on factors of labor market entry because there might be an over-supply of people relative to the labor market demand in the 1980s. These studies show that with just a constant trend increase in the demand for skilled labor, one can explain most of the observable increased fluctuations in return to education over the 1970s and the 1980s. If one also adds that there may have been a substantial increase in the 1980s, then one can tell a very consistent story about increasing returns to education having to do with increasing demand for more highly skilled workers. The total effect of this increasing return to skills is probably greater than the reported 50 percent because the Population Surveys only measure a very, very small part of the total skill acquisition.

What are the policy implications? First, let me refer to the question of whether we should tax the wealthy. We probably should, but this may not be the right reason. If it were the case that what we were seeing was an increase in the return to a native ability that was just being signaled by the acquisition of higher education, that would be a different story. However, if the difference was due to a change in an acquired trait, then one would think that one of two things will be true. It is either transitory because the high return to education is due to everybody deciding to go to school or not transitory. As I have shown, during the 1970s and 1960s there was a pattern of the return to different types of education going up because people entered particular fields. This was transitory, and if in the 1990s everybody decides to go to college, this phenomenon will be observed again. On the other hand, it might not be transitory. Blackburn *et al.*, have shown in their data and estimates that there have been changes in the supply side, making this phenomenon not transitory.

The fact is that costs of education have been going up during the 1980s. This is not because of avarice or greed on the part of the education sector, but rather the pure and simple economics of a very labor intensive industry. The cost of educated labor, the primary input, has been going up.

What has also increased the costs of getting a college education, is the big drop in the amount of student aid or loans that are now available. There is much more money being given out on the basis of ability and much less for need.

Alan Blinder talked about the fact that many people going to school are capital constrained. It is not easy for them to borrow to cover all of the costs of education. Even if they can borrow the money to pay the education related expenses, they cannot borrow the money to make up for the opportunity costs of getting a job. If one is from a poor family where the previous generation did not have a college education, one is faced with a two-fold problem not only dealing with education costs going up, but also with income or family earnings going down. So there is a greater probability that this inequity will be perpetuated intergenerationally.

What conclusions do we draw from that? Do we want to subsidize education as a way of solving these problems? First, let me point out that we do not want to tax the higher incomes resulting from a college education since all we shall be doing is increase the distortion and the number of people who are not going to school. In my view, this is not the way to solve the problem.

So what do I think determines one's level of education? Probably a lot of sociological factors. Cost factors certainly matter. We know it is going to push the distribution around, but I doubt it is determining the mean of the distribution. What we need is cost benefit analyses other than the ones already done, which look only at incomes and conclude that whether a college education is worth it depends on the discount rate used. Parenthetically, let me mention, there is a study by Robert Lucas at Boston University, in about 1978, in which he did add into the cost or the value of higher education all of the non-pecuniary benefits that one gets. We know, for example, that pensions go up when one's money income increases and there are a lot of other benefits like that. One's job gets savory and more pleasant. All of these are essentially consumption goods that add positively to one's income. So, the return to a college education is tremendously undermeasured when the measurement is only based on money income. It seems to me that a cost benefit analysis will suggest that the increase in the expenditures on higher education might not be a bad policy, and moreover it might be a good way of addressing the problem of inequality.

On the other hand, one hears about the fact that subsidizing higher education would have adverse effects on the income distribution, in the sense that it would promote an increase in the disparity of income so as to move those who are educated out of the middle class and into the upper-class. In addition, the claim is made that when higher education is subsidize, for the most part the subsidy benefits people who are already relatively well off. Let me point out, however, that when the supply of high school educated labor is decreased, the return relative to what it would be otherwise, is increased. In this sense policy addressing this issue results in bringing the bottom of the distribution up. So I am not convinced that the distributional consequences are fully thought out and would be so terrible, even if the aid is not particularly well directed. In my view, I would like to see it directed to the areas of technical training. There, it might be better utilized for intergenerational mobility.

Finally, I would like to make some observations about the relationship of income disparity and nonmarket factors affecting labor. In my work, I support the notion that nonmarket clearing views of labor markets should be taken seriously. In particular, my view is that an awful lot of what determines blue-collar wages is unions, even when unions are not present. All sorts of evidence shows this point. Anecdotal evidence shows that if you ask compensation specialists in large nonunion firms what they think they are doing when they set their wages, they say they are looking at the wages of union plants and that their primary concern is that they do not want to see any union coming in. On the other hand, one could tell another story with the same facts. That instead during the 1980s there was a lot of union bashing. Not only the wages of people who stayed in them or left them were lowered, but also those of workers who were never in unions and could previously use the threat of unionization. Actually, I expect the latter workers's wages to fall even more than the union workers. This view might explain why blue-collar wages, essentially those of high school graduates and the less-educated, have fallen relative to nonunion white-collar workers's wages. It also can be observed in a number of other countries that have experienced recent union bashing, such as Great Britain and Argentina. Countries that have had relatively strong and stable unions movements, like Germany and Japan, seem not to have experienced the same change in income or earnings distribution.

Why then am I not saying we should promote unions as a potential counter to the problem of income and earnings distribution? Because I have been convinced that there is enough other evidence against it to make it unconvincing, even though I would like it to be the correct explanation. First, it should be noted that the decline in unionization started in 1953, which was the peak year. Though the rate of decline accelerated in the 1970s and even more in the 1980s, one would still expect to see some of this effect before the 1980s. And yet it is not seen. And second, when regressions for income distribution testing the relative effects of education and changes in occupation and industry are performed, education is always vastly significant; one would think that if it were unions that mattered, education would not be the winner. Even though occupation is, it should be noted not particularly well measured, in my view it is the increasing returns to skills and particularly, acquired skills that matter in these estimates. Thus, if I were to propose a policy prescription, I would be in favor of addressing the increasing costs of education.

ROBERT HAVEMAN   My purpose is to make some summary state-ments with respect to the findings of the research work included in the previous chapters of this book, and then to suggest a menu of policies that I think are targeted on the groups that we have identified as being the most in need.

First the general thrusts. In almost all chapters of this book one will read about the increasing earnings inequality among males over time, along with stagnation in the increase of mean earnings. The source of the growing inequality in male earnings was in dispute – as to whether or not it rested with the wage rate or labor force participation and work hours – with Rebecca Blank having one position and Black-burn, Bloom and Freeman, a quite different one. Nevertheless, the phenomenon of increasing inequality in male wages was not in question.

Sheldon Danziger and his coauthors (Chapter 9) have shown that the falling earnings inequality among women coincided with increas-ing earnings inequality for men and families. As was revealed in a number of occasions, the overall result was increased income in-equality for families, even though wives were contributing more than before. From the essays in this book and the commentaries, one gathers that this has led to a long-term slow down in the reduction of poverty as we officially measure it.

Within this poverty population, we learned that the composition of the poor has also changed. The winners – those who have tended to move out of poverty – have tended to be older people and intact families, including black families. Those who have moved in have tended to be mother-only families, minority singles, young people, and those with extremely low education. When an alternative view of poverty is used, one which focuses on those who are poor in capabili-ties and in their long-term productive characteristics, the changes in this bottom tail of the distribution is even more severe. Increasingly the hard core of the nation's population of economically dependent people is minority, single male, and single mother. It increasingly has a low level of education, indeed a very low level. It is increasingly populated by children. As a result, one could conclude that this hard core of the nation's poverty population is the first which is not able to work itself out of poverty or to use the labor market effectively.

It is dominated by a set of groups that I now want to identify and use as the basis for a discussion of a targeted set of policies: (i) Working age single-mothers who are largely black. (ii) Working age, single youths, who are predominantly black and Hispanic. (iii) Heads of household and children with less than nine years of education, and these too are mainly non-white. Because people with these characteristics have filtered to the bottom of the capability distribution, a number of targeted policies seem increasingly worthy of attention and analysis.

First, a marginal employment subsidy policy ought to be targeted on the working age population with low skills. In other words, I am talking about labor market reform. This is quite consistent with the central theme of this book that public policy concerns for this population have to be designed to decrease the nonemployment of the people at the bottom of the income and capability distributions.

If one is talking about reform of a market, one is talking about changes in both the supply and demand sides of the market. I suggest a two-pronged policy which has been modestly studied and indeed, modestly tried.

On the demand side, there is substantial potential in thinking through an employer-based marginal employment subsidy. We had one a dozen years ago that was modest in size and short-lived. It was called the New Jobs Tax Credit, and a number of research studies indicated it was a potential instrument for employing low-skilled workers. The idea here to target employer-based, marginal employment subsidies on lower-skilled workers. This would make it more attractive for employers to hire disadvantaged workers, shifting the demand curve for the disadvantaged to the right.

A second prong would operate on the supply side. I suggest a wage rate subsidy in which the subsidy rate is larger for those workers who can only be employed at very low (if not minimum) wage rates, with the subsidy decreasing as a worker's wage rate rises. Such a subsidy would increase the take-home wages of workers relative to the market wages that they are paid. As a result, it becomes more attractive for disadvantaged workers to supply their labor to the labor market. In effect, this would shift the supply curve of low-skilled labor to the right.

There are a number of questions about these two policies that need to be answered: displacement effects, the degree of response by both employers and employees, and the impacts on the overall market wage. Nonetheless, let me suggest that it has potential and is worthy of consideration and testing.

Other policies that I would propose are targeted on families with children. Let me mention several that deserve further thought:

- Child care subsidization for low skill, non-employed single parents conditional upon their working or taking training. It would be meant for people who would supply labor to the market, were they able to provide adequate child care for their dependent children. It is, again, designed to shift the supply curve of disadvantaged workers to the right.

- Universal child support. This was talked about a lot a few years ago, but is not discussed extensively in this book. It would substitute support from the absent parent for public welfare support. Professor Irwin Garfinkel has done much of the basic design work on such a program, which is certainly targeted in the right direction.

- A variety of policies targeted directly on youth. Edward Wolff, in his chapter, talks about the desirability of shifting the wealth distribution in favour of young workers. One possibility here is a capital account for youths. There have been other people who have written about this concept in recent years, Professor Michael Sherraden, Isabel Sawhill, and myself. These proposals draw attention to the leveraging effect on behavior and aspirations of providing assets and stakes in assets to low skill poor people.

- Policies targeted on schoolwork, vocational training, and the quality of education at the K through 12 level. I shall only mention this as I do not feel qualified to speak about it in detail. In my view, however, it is a potentially fruitful area for policy.

- Finally, policies targeted on individuals with multiple problems. In this respect, Steven Hill and Barbara Wolfe's Chapter (4) has the effect of making me at least think through the incredible disadvantages of people who have several problems afflicting them simultaneously. Here is a population that deserves special attention.

This then would be my catalog of potentially fruitful redirections in policy that I think were guided and enlightened by the research chapters in this book.

TIMOTHY SMEEDING   No one disagrees about the worsening of inequality in the 1980s, whether it is observed in terms of wages, earnings, income or wealth. Since there is agreement on this, the obvious question is if this finding is bad or good.

The bad part, as Sheldon Danziger and others indicated, is that the disadvantaged groups have not and are not doing as well as they did prior to the 1980s. Upward mobility from below (lower class) and from the very bottom (poverty) has been low, and it probably will not get much better in the short term. Unlike William Dickens, I am not unhappy that a lot of people are moving up and out of the middle class. I think that is great. But to find the money to finance and implement all of the policies that have been suggested to help the underprivileged, would require increasing federal revenues.

As Chapter 7 shows, wealth inequality has not increased over the decade of 1980s. What has been observed was that there was a gain of $3000 to $6000 at the bottom of the income distribution to somewhere around $100 000 at the top. I ask you then, whose kids are going to have greater access to college? Whose grandparents are going to be able to help kids get into the housing market when they need it? Which particular racial and minority groups have characteristically not had much wealth and will continue not to. This is why Robert Haveman is recommending the policies he outlined.

Inequality increased in all countries in the 1980s, but from comparative work it is very clear that United States's public policies were less responsive than were those in any other country. Other systems do a much better job of leveling the inequality outcomes of market related outcomes than does ours. In addition, we incurred a big debt and a continuing deficit during the 1980s. Generationally, I think this is going to have an important effect. Let us not forget that during the decade, taxes became less progressive. At the state level, revenue needs have increasingly been met by less progressive instruments such as sales, gas or property taxes, and similarly, at the federal level, income tax progressivity declined while payroll taxes increased.

As Sheldon Danziger pointed out and Rebecca Blank showed in Chapter 2, the economic recovery of the 1980s did not exactly have the same distributional impact as growth in the 1960s did. In fact, quite the opposite. In answering the question about what will happen in the 1990s, I cannot help but think that this current recession can only exacerbate the problems we have seen. Furthermore, as the Blackburn, Bloom and Freeman findings indicated in Chapter 8, there is a problem of falling salaries and ages prepared for jobs. Even tight labor markets will not help them.

Furthermore, increased foreign trade will not help our lesser skilled workers. What will happen to their jobs if Ford Motor Company and other companies decide that since their biggest markets are in Europe or Korea or Spain, that is where their manufacturing should be done? Free trade agreements with Canada and Mexico can only make the consumer better off because products can be bought cheaper; yet most routine jobs will move to low wage areas and across the US border. Together with the lack of a clear federal domestic agenda and a coherent education policy which existed previously, there will be a problem. Thus, I am not too hopeful for the upward mobility of the unskilled.

Let me also underscore the argument that children are in trouble and need help. The consensus Sheldon Danziger mentioned is certainly there. I do not know however, if I would advocate Robert Haveman's almost Swedish active labor policy. The call for a modest policy action to help poor children via Head Start and child health programs need to be made.

The question that one needs to answer is where would the resources to finance these programs be found? As it has been shown in Chapter 7, there is a group of people who can now afford to help other people. This feeling is not just shared by social policy engineers on the Left; Kevin Phillips wrote about it too.

What is needed is an income tax structure that is a little more progressive. I am not suggesting going back to 70 percent marginal tax rates or even 50 percent or 40 percent, but moving from 34 to 37 percent is not that bad. The tax base can be expanded to include fringe benefits and transfer payments such as social security. Because of the exemptions and other built-in features of the Federal Tax System, taxes on transfers would not be paid by people receiving AFDC and most people receiving other means tested benefits. It certainly would mean that the elderly would pay a larger share of their income in tax, but I think those living on $30 000 a year could afford it.

Finally, wealth taxation at death or transfer is another useful revenue measure to consider. Again, I am not advocating confiscatory taxation, but a wealth tax that would be targeted on capital gains at death and wealth transfer. I would suggest a tax rate of 10 to 15 percent. In fact, if one believes that people are dumping assets to qualify for nursing homes and Medicare, a wealth tax at death of the surviving spouse may even have some positive behavioral effects. Valuing capital gains should be done along an Alan Blinder-like adjustment for price increases, from the time of purchase to the sale of an asset, thus levying a real tax. Revenues must be found to meet the nation's needs, and this seems to me, to be the least costly way of doing it with as little burden as possible.

EDWARD WOLFF   The policy proposal I would make is what Robert Haveman and Barbara Wolfe have advocated, that I have called a social security capital fund. This approach has a number of virtues and may also redress some of the intergenerational imbalances that have been occurring over the last several decades.

As it has been shown in Chapter 6, since the early 1960s, middle-aged groups have become wealthier while younger age groups, those under the age of 35 particularly, have become less well off in terms of wealth. We know from the work of Frank Levy and others, that the same thing has been happening with income. Part of the reason is that the younger generation, the baby boom generation in particular, has experienced a very sluggish labor market and depressed wages. Part of the reason is apparently also that the savings rates of the younger age groups have fallen tremendously over the last generation. Meanwhile, it has been observed that the older generation has accumulated so much wealth that there is no feasible way that it can run down its assets before death. Almost by default, the children of the current elderly will be inheriting substantial sums.

Perhaps, the expectation of bequests is one reason why the younger generation has not saved very much, but whatever the reason I think there is some rationale for trying to transfer some wealth back to the younger generation. One mechanism is through a social security capital fund. Such a plan is currently in effect in Singapore. It would be tied directly into the social security system. The plan provides very strong collateral – social security contributions. Even if they do not go into an actual fund, the expectation of benefits provides a fairly strong guarantee that a loan taken out will be repaid.

The banking system might be involved or the federal government could manage some kind of banking operation, as it does now implicitly with the various housing loans it guarantees. In any case, the federal government has had a history of setting up loan programs for specific purposes and this part of the proposal is by no means revolutionary. The only new provision is to treat the OASI contributions as collateral to these loans.

As to funding, let me say that part of the reason why I undertook this research was to see if taxing social security transfers would provide sufficient loanable funds to establish the kind of program and whether it would have a reasonable effect on the wealth of the young. The answer turns to be *no*. It produces a fairly low level of additional tax revenues. The additional tax revenue raised as a proportion of the current wealth of families of the head of which is age 30 and under, it would amount to only 2 percent of their current wealth; for families of age 35 and under, it would amount to only 0.7 percent. So there would be some problems in finding funding. On the other hand, a solution could be to cut defense expenditures. Compared to other OECD countries, the US spends a much higher percentage of its budget on defense spending. Even, if there were not a peace dividend as a source of funding, the fund could operate like any other kind of loan fund with a reasonable interest rate attached to it.

Such a fund could also provide a supplement to unemployment insurance. As is well known, both the unemployment coverage and the unemployment insurance benefit levels have declined rather drastically during the 1980s. In any case, this kind of plan has a lot of virtues and it does help to alleviate the kind of imbalance that is occurring now between the generations. This is one kind of a program which although not entirely new, has a lot of possibilities and deserves to be explored further.

ROBERT AVERY   At the risk of being placed over the other side of Sheldon Danziger, let me be the devil's advocate for a moment. If one was to go back to the decade of the 1980s and tell us that during President Ronald Reagan's administration that there would be, (i) 21 percent rates of interest – making them the highest real interest rates of the past century, (ii) the worst recession since the depression, (iii) a major cut in or essentially eliminate the corporate income tax, (iv) dramatic cuts in the personal income tax rates to the extent to which they have, (v) severe decreases in funding of programs to the extent that is believed they have, and (vi) an increase of our national debt by 250 percent over that period of time, most of us would have said that this will be a disaster and that it would bring the country back a hundred years. But, if one looks at the truth of the matter, in terms of the changes in both the wealth and income distribution, it would be observed that these were remarkably small.

One can probably conclude that society and individuals are a lot more resilient than we think they are; they adjust and change. They realize that circumstances change. Thus if they decide they need more education, they go and get it. When they realize they should change their job, they acquire new skills. If this were true, it might be useful to rethink the proposals for change that have been mentioned above. Perhaps, they are not necessary and maybe some of the lessons are that fundamental forces that move society cannot be changed by the kinds of policies that have been suggested.

SHELDON DANZIGER I should like to say that the changes in inequality are largely historical standards. Alan Blinder wrote a marvelous paper starting with the famous line that 'the more things change, the more they remain the same'. Income inequality was mostly stable from 1950 to 1980. Some of the consequences that Robert Haveman and Edward Wolff have mentioned, will not be seen until the next generation. I am not an economic historian, but if you look at Oliver Williamson's book on the history of American inequality, this decade is unlike any others, except the 1920s, when inequality last increased substantially.

If one is to ask what would it cost to implement a set of public policy changes to reduce inequality back to its 1980 level, the answer would involve a modest set of proposals such as expanding Head Start and the Women, Infants and Children's Program (WIC), increasing spending on employment and training programs, and enlarging the tax credits for the working poor. Such a policy package is much more modest than those that Edward Wolff and Robert Haveman have advocated. Yet, this modest package could cost as much as $30 to $50 billion per year.

DIMITRI PAPADIMITRIOU If one is to ask for a cost/benefit analysis on the existing programs, are there any that should be abandoned or recrafted because they are bad and do not deliver the results?

SHELDON DANZIGER I do not think you heard anyone say that welfare benefits for the able-bodied, nonworking recipient should be raised. That is a major difference between now and 20 years ago. When I first started in this profession, people like Robert Haveman were saying we ought to have a negative income tax that provided a near-poverty line income for all families. You do not hear that now from many economists. We have learned a lot and the focus is now on investments in kids, in areas where benefits can be gotten, and in trying to encourage more people to get into the labor market rather than to continue receiving cash transfers.

DIMITRI PAPADIMITRIOU Aside of defense expenditures, are there any other government expenditures in programs that could be eliminated in favour of those that have been proposed?

TIMOTHY SMEEDING Yes, farm subsidies. The federal government spends twice as much on farm subsidies as it does on food stamps, and they are distributed exactly in the opposite ends of the distribution. There is a real need to develop an output measure for education in order to determine how well children are doing. A national standard is needed by which one can judge how well the system works. Once this standard is devised, then at least a target can be established and comparisons as to whether one is getting better or worse can be drawn. I think this is incredibly important and would use the farm subsidy money for it.

WILLIAM T. DICKENS   I will disagree with what Robert Haveman has introduced in the discussion as subsidies for low wages. Although I agree with just about every other policy recommendation that he has proposed, I think it is a bad idea from the standpoint of mainstream economics because if one subsidizes low wages, the result will be to succeed in changing the relative return, if that return is due to acquired skill. All it will do is to increase the number of people who will not seek to get higher education and thus, make the distortion worse. I tend to think that what determines wages is the ability of labor to extract rents from capital. If low wages are subsidized, as opposed to subsidizing low skill employment, then there will be an increase in the number of people employed in the low wage, low productivity industry, a decrease in the number of people employed in general and thus have a negative shift. One can at least somewhat undo that by subsidizing low skill as opposed to low wage unemployment, but even that has a problem of a negative shift too.

Why not subsidize high wage employment? If one subsidizes high wage employment, then people shift from low productivity jobs to high productivity ones. The people who are left behind have lowered the supply of workers to those sorts of jobs and might increase the wages there. That seems to me to be the preferable policy. A way to increase national revenues would be to introduce a Value Added Tax (VAT). It might be regressive, if one looks at it on the surface. A colleague of mine at Berkeley is fond of pointing out that if one observes the number of countries that have had major tax revolts, they have been countries that have primarily funded their national expenditures from income taxes. Countries that have instead funded their expenditures by VATs have not had tax revolts. Thus, in a sense, the VATs are actually progressive. They can go along with persistent maintainable progressive social policies because VATs do not appear on people's paychecks.

ROBERT HAVEMAN   I welcome William Dickens's comments on the possibility of subsidizing either the demand side or the supply side of the labor market for disadvantaged workers. His perspective on this is quite unorthodox.

It was about a decade ago, in fact, when there was a lot of attention paid by, what I would say, the mainstream labor economics wing of the profession to the thought that employment subsidization of one kind or another had high potential. Some of the benefits of it were benefits that I alluded to in my comments, in addition to other benefits such as shifting the Phillips curve. The major objection to it then was the traditional union-oriented objection: if you subsidize low wage workers, you are going to displace union workers. Perhaps, this is why William Dickens takes such exception to the proposals.

There was research of a serious kind 10 or 15 years ago by people such as James Tobin and Robert Eisner that concluded that such policies had real potential for both macroeconomic and economic efficiency gains. I think it is worthy of study and experimentation to see if this kind of labor market reform has potential for those people trapped at the bottom of the capability distribution.

WILLIAM T. DICKENS   In response to Robert Haveman, just briefly, let me say that I do not think there is anything nonmainstream about human capital which is the basis of my objection. It is one thing to propose general wage subsidies as ways of creating aggregate employment which can be debated drawing from the experiences of the Swedish active labor market policies.

ROBERT HAVEMAN   It seems that Professor Dickens looks narrowly at a particular policy proposal, finds one component of it and places a negative sign in front of and says, that let us discard further thought about it because it tends to provide a relative disincentive for additional higher education and training expenditures. I say that it is worthwhile listing all benefits and costs and then determine if the policy makes sense.

WILLIAM T. DICKENS   Most of the previous discussion about this issue in the active labor market literature, on which you are supporting your argument, was not about a specifically low wage employment subsidy but was about a general employment subsidy. I am suggesting that if the cause of the change in the income distribution has been the sort of response to the supply-side factors that I described, then it will not have the desired effect by doing this. It will only exacerbate the underlying problem.

TIMOTHY SMEEDING   I would like to remind everyone that there exists one such subsidy right now, called the Earning Income Tax Credit. In the State of New York, if employers hire low wage workers and train them, then they can give out checks at the end of the week that included approximately one dollar an hour more in subsidy. No one knows what effect this EITC is really having. No one knows how many employers are aware of this and how many are utilizing it. No one is pointing out to their employees or potential employees with children that, in fact, they can get an extra dollar an hour if they take it. No one knows exactly who is participating, how eligible they are and who they are. All we know is that in 1991, it will have a net effect of $8 million and about $10 million in 1992.

DIMITRI PAPADIMITRIOU   I would like to ask each one of the panelists, what he would have advocated as a first policy priority should he have had the opportunity to implement it.

TIMOTHY SMEEDING   Refundable child credit and universal Head Start.

ROBERT AVERY   I agree with Timothy Smeeding on child care. I would move to increase the various taxes, taxes on the elderly, taxes on social security, and I clearly would move to reduce expenditures in defense and other areas as well. Compared to the overwhelming nature of the revenue and expense side, most policies that have been discussed, in my view, would be of secondary concern.

ROBERT HAVEMAN   I would set up a task force to study the feasibility of a personal capital account for youths, perhaps, on the same order as Edward Wolff mentioned, and I would set up another one to look at ways of making work by less skilled disadvantaged workers more attractive, both to them and to potential employers.

EDWARD WOLFF   My number one priority would be universal health insurance, but I would also pursue social security capital funds and cut defense spending and federal spending for intelligence operations.

SHELDON DANZIGER   In this discussion I proposed a package that I thought would cost $30 or $50 billion. Let me add something else. One of the things that stopped in the 1980s, in addition to spending on the poor, was social experimentation. I would like to experiment with various kinds of wage rates subsidies, various public employment programs, etc., so it would be possible to know how well they operate.

WILLIAM T. DICKENS   The specific programs that I would mention, have been mentioned already, i.e., national health insurance and various sorts of improvements to our family policies. In addition, I am very concerned about the federal deficit, and I would be concerned with a weak economy and the monetarist preoccupation of the Federal Reserve who seem to be more concerned about the slightest hint of inflation than they are about the 7 or 8 percent unemployment. With specific respect to the distributional issues that have been discussed, it seems to me that something needs to be done for education. If one is particularly worried about the low end, then perhaps one should be concentrating on preparing people with less advantaged backgrounds better for college, so that they can make that transition. It will be necessary, however, to start children's preparation – especially those in the inner city schools – all the way back to matters that involve family policy in order to make certain that children have enough to eat and reasonable access to programs like Head Start.

FLOOR DISCUSSION

A participant asked the panelists whether national health insurance policy should include prenatal care, while another participant suggested that federal revenues can be increased by $70 million annually, if the mortgage interest reduction on personal income tax is disallowed.

Edward Wolff responded that mortgage interest deduction, at least inter-generationally, has an equalizing effect. Younger people pay higher prices for their houses and have much higher interest rates than did older people. Thus, in a sense, the deduction is an intergenerational subsidy from older households to younger ones.

Another participant commented on the policy about Head Start citing recent analyses in which there seems to be a low take-up rate because the problem with Head Start is that it is not a full day program. Thus, in order for it to be successful it would need to be expanded. Furthermore, he pointed out that one cannot advocate one policy here, one policy there, but rather a set of coordinated policies. Head Start and concern for working parents is a good example. There was also the need to take into account the changing demographic composition and that if one is to look at children, in particular, it will be noticed that the nature of today's children is changing. Part of the reason the poverty rate has gone up is because children are now living in single-parent families, and more of them are not white; these are increasing trends, and must be carefully considered in the policy design.

Another participant suggested that we need a new GI Bill of Rights. The social experiment known as GI Bill of Rights enabled hundreds of thousands of poor people to get to college; it enabled hundreds of thousands of young GIs to buy homes; it enabled hundreds of thousands of GIs to get subsidies as a premise in their employment. The participant found similarities in the panelists's policies with the GI Bill of Rights which worked well and was very successful. He wondered why it has been overlooked by economists over all these years.

Both Dickens and Wolff agreed that such a program would probably work better under the present circumstances.

Papadimitriou raised the issue of the multiplicity of poverty indices used in the various chapters of this book and asked if it would be possible to devise a single and objective index of 'well-being' which would be relatively easy to compute and able to withstand the arbitrariness of individual value judgments and thus be widely accepted. Nowadays, there is evidence that families even though they are above the official poverty level yet, are not able to afford adequate housing and health insurance, let alone child care.

Barbara Wolfe responded by mentioning the survey performed by the Leiden School, conducted among people who were in different income levels, on what they think they would need to live at a decent standard of living. The survey was taken among people of different ages and different characteristics to try to get a type of index that would incorporate particular needs for health care or housing.

Papadimitriou indicated, however, that such surveys might be problematic since responses relate to particular peoples's income, and people are usually very sensitive to such questioning. For example, for people living in $350 000 homes, the answer to the question of how much is needed, will probably be in the neighborhood of $5000 per month. Such responses are worrisome in devising a generally accepted index.

Papadimitriou (moderator) thanked all the panelists and other participants and noted that a related issue not covered in the discussion, was to focus on creating opportunities for employment. An important area of research, in his view, was the analysis of the problems of unemployment and employment growth and decline in both the public and private sectors, the quality and creation of jobs, and the structure of supply and demand in the labor markets. An examination of these issues might point to solutions to combat earnings inequality and poverty.

Index

account balancing, CEX and 184
Acs, G. 331
activities of daily living related to work
(ADLs) 9, 92, 115
    single mothers: earnings
    capacity 100, 101, 103, 104, 108,
    113; SSI program 110–11, 118
affirmative action 72, 315
age
    education–earnings differentials
    277–83
    income transitions 253–6
    social security transfers 220, 221,
    223–4; distributional effects
    229–30; relative to total income
    and wealth 225, 226–7; taxation
    232–3, 234, 236
age of building 154, 159, 163, 167
age–wealth profile 2, 12–13, 213–14,
    371
    see also social security transfers
Aid to Families with Dependent
    Children (AFDC) 118–19
    compared with SSI 110–11
    policy changes and poverty rates 35–7
    single mothers 107, 109; health 97–8;
    policy recommendations 10,
    109–10, 112, 119
    stereotyped family 85; and poverty
    rates 67, 68, 70, 71
air conditioning 154, 157, 159, 162–3,
    167
Anderson, W. H. L. 21
Ando, A. 59
Annual Housing Survey (AHS) 150–1,
    153, 160, 180, 199
annuity portion of social security see
    social security annuity portion
automobiles 138, 198
    measure of material well being 153,
    154, 158, 159, 165–7, 167
    see also trucks
Avery, Robert B. 212, 259
    policy forum 358–9, 372, 376

Bane, M. J. 248, 256
bathrooms 154, 157, 159, 160–1, 162,
    167
Becker, G. S. 59

'bed days' 168–73
Blackburn, M. 240, 275, 285, 290
blacks
    earnings: gender gap 335, 336;
    husbands' earnings and wives'
    employment 333, 334; male city
    workers 360; trends for married
    men and women 325, 328, 330;
    wives' earnings and family
    income 338, 339, 341, 342, 344,
    345, 348, 351
    labor force participation 321–4
    marriage trends 319, 320
    poverty prevalence 64–6
    poverty rate 26, 27, 66
    prototypical families 85; poverty
    patterns 70, 71; poverty
    probabilities 67–9
    see also race
Blank, R. M. 5, 22, 42
Blinder, A. S. 5, 22, 310, 363, 370,
    373
block grants 34–5
Bloom, D. 275, 285, 290
blue-collar family 67, 68, 70, 85
Bound, J. 275
Bradbury, K. L. 240
building, age of 154, 159, 163, 167
Burkhauser, R. V. 211, 219, 220–1,
    221, 222
Burtless, G. 240
business cycle
    income transitions and 249, 250
    wages and 42

capital fund for young workers see
    social security capital fund
Census 29, 53, 181, 201
    income data compared with
    CPS 132–5, 188, 195–7; trends in
    inequality 179–80
central heating 154, 157, 159, 161–2,
    167
chief executive officers (CEOs) 130,
    135–6
child care costs
    NEC 63, 87
    single mothers' earnings
    capacity 103–5

child care subsidies 17, 72, 368, 376
  taxation and 346, 351, 361;
    refundable credit 346, 361–2
child support 72
  universal 368
children 378
  contribution to family economic
    status 86–7
  doctor visits 174–5, 176
  material well-being 131, 195
  parents' labor force
    participation 319–24
  policies to aid 4–5, 370
  poverty rates 26
  shifting age–wealth profile 214;
    policy recommendations 264, 273
  single mothers 89; effect on earnings
    capacity 99–105; with disabled
    child 89, 91–2, 99, 103, 105–7,
    107–8; *see also* single-mother
    families
Coder, J. 205
cohabitation 349
college-enrollment rates 277, 293–300,
    306, 310
Consumer Expenditure Survey
    (CEX) 11, 137, 198
  compared with CPS 138–40
  design changes 182–6, 201; account
    balancing 184; definition of
    consumer unit 182–3; fluctuating
    response rates 185–6; missing
    expenditure data 184; missing
    income data 183–4; movers
    184–5; newly-formed CUs 186;
    recall period 184
  expenditure and consumption
    inequality 141–8, 189–91;
    trends 179, 180, 206
consumer units (CUs) 139–40
  defining 182–3
  newly-formed 186
  see also Consumer Expenditure
    Survey
consumption 121, 122
  and economic well-being 59–60
  inequality 123, 136–49, 179–80,
    190–1
  and material well-being 149–51,
    206–7
  migration and patterns of 167–8
  see also net earnings capacity
cost benefit analysis 364

cross-sectional snapshots *see* 'snapshot'
    comparisons
crowding 155–60, 161, 200
current income poverty measurement
    (CY) 58–9, 64, 81–2
  changes in poverty incidence 66
  comparison with NEC 66, 69–71
  poverty composition and
    incidence 64–6, 79–80
  poverty probabilities for families
    66–8; changes in rates 68–9
Current Population Survey (CPS) 35–6,
    37, 60–1, 194
  compared with CEX 138–40
  income inequality 123–36, 187–8,
    205–6; CEX and 141–8; compared
    with Census 132–5, 188, 196–7;
    quality of income data 132, 204–5;
    trends 179–80, 206
  poverty rates 31, 32, 33
  PSID correlation with 244–5, 267
  single mothers and health 93–6,
    117–18
Cutler, D. 147–8, 198
CV^2 (squared coefficient of
    variation) 339–45, 350, 351

Danziger, Sheldon 240, 331, 337
  policy forum 359–62, 373, 377
debt 261, 262, 269
defense expenditures 372, 376
Deficit Reduction Act (1990) 264
demographic change
  income inequality 136
  income transitions 253–6
  poverty rate and economic
    growth 37–41
dentists, use of 177, 178
dependent care credit 346, 351, 361
Dickens, William T. 362–6, 374, 375,
    375–6, 377, 378
disability
  children with and single mothers 89,
    91–2, 99, 103, 105–7, 107–8
  women with 92–8, 114
  see also health
discrimination 354
doctors, use of 173–7, 181, 200–1
domestic workers, live-in 127, 194
Doolittle, F. C. 34–5
doubling up 160, 200
Douglass, E. B. 92
Downey, Congressman 264

Duncan, G. J. 248
durables, expenditure on 138, 198

Eargle, J. 240, 241
Earned Income Tax Credit
    (EITC) 181, 376
earnings 240, 272, 362
    education–earnings differential *see*
        education–earnings differential
    income transitions and 256–8, 263
    married couples' 317
    married women's: impact on family
        income 336–45; labor participation
        rates and 332–6; trends 324–32,
        366
    men's: inequality 3, 256–8, 275, 366;
        trends for married men 324–32
    mobility and middle class *see* middle
        class
    responsiveness to macroeconomy
        6–7, 41–50, 51; income and
        economic growth 43–5; labor
        market involvement and wages
        45–50
    sources of gender inequality 354
    subsidies 72
    see also income; wages
earnings capacity
    net *see* net earnings capacity
    single mothers' and health 99–105,
        108, 113; and poverty 105–7
earnings capacity poverty 60–3
    see also net earnings capacity
Easterlin, R. C. 240
economic growth 1–2, 21
    poverty rates and 5–6, 22–8, 50–2;
        policy changes and 34–7; regional
        location of poverty 30–4;
        responsiveness of wages 7, 22,
        45–50, 51
    see also poverty rates
economic uncertainty 135
economists, role in policy-making 358
Edin, K. 137
education 303–4, 360–1
    costs 363–4
    government policy and return to
        15–16
    income inequality and return
        to 273–4, 331, 362–5
    income transitions and 253–6
    level and poverty 65, 66;
        prototypical low-education

families 67, 68, 69, 70, 71, 85
    need for output measure 374
    policy recommendations 364–5,
        365–6, 368, 377
    single mothers' earning capacity 101,
        102
    and women's earnings 331–2, 332–3
    see also education–earnings
        differentials
education and training programs 5, 72
education–earnings differentials 3,
    14–16, 275–316
    differential factors 285–92;
        demographic 289–90; relative
        labor supplies 290–2
    employment differentials by race and
        gender 277–85
    market responses 292–300
    policy recommendations 4, 15–16,
        299–300, 310–11
elderly
    distribution of income and
        wealth 225–8, 229–30; *see also*
        age–wealth profile; social security
        transfers
    poverty rate 26
Elliehausen, G. E. 259
Ellwood, D. T. 248, 256
employment 379
    education–earnings differentials 276,
        276–7, 279–85, 304, 315; industry-
        shift effects 285–6, 287, 288, 289,
        290, 304–5, 312; occupational
        structure 285–6, 287, 288, 289,
        290, 304–5, 312
    policy of guaranteed 362
    probability and poverty rate 45, 46,
        47, 49, 50
    status and health 90
    subsidies 367, 374–5, 375–6
    see also labor force participation
enrollment rates, school/college 277,
    293–300, 306, 310
equal pay laws 315
expenditure 121, 122, 206–7
    changes in distribution of 123,
        136–49, 190, 197–8
    data and CEX 184, 201
    trends and income inequality 179–80,
        206
    see also Consumer Expenditure
        Survey

families
  poverty rates 26–7
  prototypical 85; NEC and CY
    poverty probabilities 66–9, 81–5;
    poverty patterns 69–72
  structural change 358–9
  type and social security
    transfers 222, 223–4; distributional
    effects 229–30; relative to total
    income and wealth 225, 226–7;
    taxation 232–3
  see also family income; family size;
    family units
family income
  CPS 124; inequality 125–7, 193–4
  men's and women's contributions
    317–48; impact of wives' earnings
    336–45, 366; married women in
    employment 332–6; policy
    recommendations 346; trends in
    earnings for married men and
    women 324–32; trends in marriage
    and labor force participation
    319–24
  see also family units; income
    inequality
family size
  dentist visits 178
  doctor visits 173, 174–5, 176
  middle class income 243, 265
  see also household size
Family Support Act (1988) 9, 89, 107,
    118
family units 53
  changes to AFDC program 35–6
  changing demographic
    composition 37–41
  earnings and the macroeconomy
    41–50
  regional distribution of poverty 31–4
farm subsidies 373–4
Federal Reserve 377
Feldstein, M. S. 215
female-headed families *see* single-
    mother families
fertility, declining 136
Fisher, F. 265
food stamps 28–30, 138, 243
Freeman, R. 275, 285, 290
Friedman, M. 140
'full income' measure 59

Garfinkel, I. 7, 60, 368
Garner, T. 140

gender differences
  education–earnings differentials
    292–3, 294, 332–3; college
    enrollment 295–6, 297, 299;
    employment differentials 276,
    277–85
  marriage trends and labor force
    participation 319–24
  trends in annual earnings 324–32
ghetto youth 67, 68, 69, 70, 71, 85
GI Bill of Rights 378
Gini coefficient 124, 192
  social security transfers 228, 229–30,
    234, 235–6
  wives' earnings and family
    income 339–45
Goldin, C. 332
Gore, Senator 264
Gottschalk, P. 240, 337
government transfers 52
  growth in non-cash programs 180–1
  poverty rate and 23–5; in-kind
    income 28–30; policy
    changes 34–7
  and standard of living 1
  see also Aid to Families with
    Dependent Children; food stamps;
    social security; Supplemental
    Security Income
Green, G. 205
Greenwood, D. T. 12, 211, 213, 219
gross earnings capacity 61, 62–3
  see also net earnings capacity
gross national product (GNP) growth,
    poverty rate and 25–7, 37, 39–41
  earnings' responsiveness 43–8

hardship, material 130, 150, 195
  see also material well-being
Haveman, Robert 7, 58, 60
  policy forum 366–8, 375, 376
Haveman-Wolfe measure 93, 116
Head Start 376, 377–8
health
  single mothers 9–10, 89–119;
    earnings capacity 99–105; earnings
    capacity and poverty 105–7;
    measuring health status 92–8;
    policy recommendations 107–12;
    poverty 90–2
  status and material well-being 150–1,
    168–73
health insurance 376, 377
  single mothers 108, 110, 118

Health Interview Survey (HIS) 150–1, 168–9, 173
Heckman, J. J. 332
Hill, M. 242
Hispanics 349
  earnings of married men and women 329, 331, 349
  labor force participation 322, 324
  trends in marriage rate 319, 320
  wives' earnings 335, 336; and family income 339, 341, 343, 344, 345, 348
  wives' labor force participation 333, 334
Holden, K. 266
home ownership 154, 158, 159, 163–5, 214
homelessness 181, 201, 214
'hot deck' 132, 184
hourly earnings 300–1, 302–3
  see also earnings; wages
hours worked, single mothers earnings' capacity and 99–102, 102–3, 104, 113, 118
house equity 261, 262, 269, 273
household income
  CPS 123, 127–8; adjusting for size 130–2, 136, 195; weighting individuals 128–30
  and health status 169, 170–1
  income inequality 123–36, 187–8; trends 179–80
  and material well-being 153–5
  middle class *see* middle class
  per capita and total compared 131–2
  see also family income; income
household size
  health status and income 169, 170–1
  and household income 130–2, 136, 195
  and material well-being 153–5
  see also family size
household wealth 215, 218
  total 218, 225, 226–7
households, structural change in 358–9
housing conditions 150–1, 153–65, 179–80, 181, 199
housing subsidies 29–30, 52, 181
Hurd, M. D. 219, 220, 222
husbands' earnings
  trends 324–32, 332, 336
  and wives' earnings 334–6
  and wives' labor force participation 333–4

income 121–2, 240, 359
  current as poverty measurement *see* current income
  data: CEX and missing 183–4; CPS compared with Census 132–5, 195–7; quality of CPS data 132
  distribution among elderly 225–8, 229
  family *see* family income
  'full income' measure 59
  household *see* household income
  inequality *see* income inequality
  and material well-being 121–2, 150
  middle class *see* middle class
  relative measures 354
  responsiveness to economic growth 43–5
  social security transfers relative to total 225, 226–7
  see also earnings; wages
income inequality 10–11, 204–7, 369
  anatomy of 11–17
  increase in 1980s 1, 121
  trends 123–36, 177–8, 179–80; and expenditures 136–49; and material well-being 149–77; policy recommendations 180–1
  see also earnings; education–earnings differentials; family income; income; middle class; social security transfers; wages
'income-to-needs' ratio 243, 265
income tax
  mortgage interest deduction 377
  negative 373
  progressive 370
  see also taxation
income transitions 13–14, 240–1, 248–58, 263–4, 267–8, 272–3, 369
  demographic correlates 253–6
  distribution 251–3
  income component with most change 256–8
  policy recommendations 14, 264–5
  wealth change accompanying 261–3
individuals, household income and 128–30, 194–5
industry employment changes 285–6, 287, 288, 289, 290, 304–5, 312
inflation 23–7
in-kind income 52
  growth in 180–1
  measuring poverty and 28–30
  see also food stamps; government

transfer programs; Medicaid
interest rates 359
inter-industry wage differentials 285,
    286, 287, 288, 289, 290, 312
investment fund for young workers *see*
    social security capital fund

Jaffras, J. 264
Jencks, C. 59, 121, 137, 150, 242
Johnson, G. 275
Juhn, C. 3, 7, 275, 331

Karoly, L. 132, 240, 331
Katz, L. 275, 290, 331
    gender differences and wages 332
    income inequality and consumption
        inequality 147–8, 198
Keane, M. 42
Kennickell, A. B. 259
Killingsworth, M. 332
kitchens, complete 165, 166, 167

labor force participation
    education–earnings differentials 313,
        362–3; market response 293–300,
        310, 315–16; relative labor
        supplies 290–2, 310
    health and single mothers 90–1, 93–4,
        95; earnings capacity 99–107, 113
    marital status and 319–24
    married women 332–3, 334, 346;
        policy recommendations 346
    poverty rate and economic
        growth 42, 51; wages and 22,
        45–50
    see also employment
labor market
    changes 360–1
    nonmarket clearing approach 365
    reform recommendations 367, 374–5
labor productivity growth 2
Lambert, P. 265
Lampman, R. 359
Lazear, E. 131
Leiden School survey 378
Levy, F. 240, 248, 267
Lillard, L. 132
live-in domestic workers 127, 194
living conditions 1, 10–11
    see also expenditures; material well-
        being
lodgers 127, 194

loans
    social security capital fund 215,
        236–7
    student 215, 310–11, 363

MacDonald, C. 240
macroeconomy, poverty and 22–8
    see also economic growth; poverty
        rates
Macunovich, D. J. 240
Maddox, G. L. 92
mailback questionnaires 132–3, 133,
    196
managers' pay 130, 135–6
marginal employment subsidies 367
marital status
    and income transitions 251–3
    and labor force participation 321–4
Maritato, A. 266
marriage rate trends 319–20
material hardship 130, 150, 195
    see also material well-being
material well-being 10–11, 121, 122,
    123, 378–9
    adjusting household income for 131,
        195
    disparities 149–77, 206–7; age of
        building 163; automobiles 165–7;
        bathrooms 160–1; complete
        kitchens 165; dentists 177;
        doctors 173–7; health status 150–1,
        168–73; home ownership 163–5;
        space 155–60; telephones 167;
        temperature control 161–3
    trends and income inequality 179–80,
        204
Mayer, S. E. 59, 121, 150
measurement of poverty 3–4, 7–8,
    58–9
    in-kind income and 28–30
    see also net earnings capacity; poverty
        rates
Medicaid 52, 90, 111, 118
    measurement of poverty and 28–30
    use of doctors 176, 181
Michel, R. 36, 131, 240, 248, 263
middle class 2, 3, 13–14, 240–71, 272–4
    defining by income 242–3, 266–7
    income and family size 265
    income transitions 13, 248–58;
        demographic correlates 253–6;
        distribution 251–3; income
        components with most
        change 256–8

policy recommendations 14, 264–5, 273–4
snapshot comparisons 244–8; shrinkage 245–8
wealth 240, 241, 244, 258–63, 268–9, 273; change accompanying income transitions 261–3; distribution 258–61
Midwestern farm family 67, 68, 69, 70, 71, 85
migration 167–8
Mincer, J. 332
minimum wage 286–8, 289, 290, 305, 312
mobility, class *see* income transitions
Modigliani, F. 59
Moffitt, R. 36, 42, 108
Moon, M. L. 59
mortgage interest tax deduction 377
motor vehicles *see* automobiles; trucks
movers, data collection and 184–5, 201
multiple problems, policy targeting for 368
Murphy, K. 3, 7, 275, 331, 332

Nathan, R. P. 34–5
National Commission on Children 264, 361
National Income and Product Accounts (NIPA) 196
necessities, defining 153
need, adjusting income for 130–2
see also material well-being
negative income tax 373
net earnings capacity (NEC) 7–8, 60, 69
comparison with current income measurement 66, 69–71
estimation 60–3
poverty composition and incidence 64–6, 79–80
poverty probabilities for families 66–9, 71, 83–4
Newman, K. 241
non-cash transfer programs *see* in-kind income

Oaxaca, R. 310
occupational structure of employment 285–6, 287, 288, 289, 290, 304–5, 312
Old Age and Survivors' Insurance (OASI) *see* social security system; social security transfers

owner-occupation 154, 158, 159, 163–5, 214

Panel Study of Income Dynamics (PSID) 13, 242
correlation with CPS data 244–5
see also middle class
Papadimitriou, Dimitri viii, 357–8, 373, 378–9
part-time employment 46, 47
Pechman, J. 263
pension wealth 215, 216, 218
Phillips, K. 240
Pierce, B. 3, 7, 275, 331
policy, costs to return inequality to 1980 level 373
policy changes, poverty rates and 34–7
policy recommendations 4–5
to aid children 4–5, 370
and education–earnings differentials 4, 15–16, 299–300, 310–11
to aid families 4–5, 8–9, 72; wives' labor force participation 17, 346
policy forum 357–79
redistributive 5, 11, 181, 273–4; children's tax deduction 264, 273; social security capital fund 12–13, 236–7; taxation of social security transfers 12–13, 214–15; wealth taxation 14, 264–5, 274
single mothers with health problems 9–10, 72, 107–12, 113
Pollak, R. 265
poverty
composition 5–11, 63–6, 79–80, 366
definition 7, 58–9
earnings capacity poverty 60–3; *see also* net earnings capacity
economic growth and 359–60
incidence 63–6, 79–80
measurement *see* measurement of poverty
poverty probabilities for families 66–9
trends and sources 5–11
poverty line, official 337, 350
poverty rates 1, 2, 3, 5–6, 21–57, 58
current income and NEC compared 64–6, 79–80
demographic changes 37–41
macroeconomy and 22–8
policy changes and economic growth 34–7

problems in poverty measurement
   28–30
regional location of poverty 30–4
responsiveness of earnings to the
   macroeconomy 41–50; income and
   economic growth 43–5; labor
   market involvement and wages
   45–50
preferences 59, 60
productivity growth 2
pseudo-R^2 288–9, 305, 312–13

race
   education–earnings differentials 276;
      affirmative action and equal pay
      laws 315; college enrollment
      295–6, 297; employment differentials
      277–85, 304
   income transitions and 253–6;
      wealth accompanying 261–3
   poverty rate 64–6, 66, 69, 71–2
   school dropout rates 314
   social security transfers 222, 223–4;
      distributional effects 228, 229–30;
      relative to income and wealth 225,
      226–7; taxation 232–3, 234, 236
   see also blacks; Hispanics
Rainwater, L. 131
recession 130, 249, 250, 263–4
Rector, R. 59
regional variations in poverty rates 30–4
Reich, R. 264
relative income measures 354
rent, reported 197
rental value 138, 198
'restricted activity days' 168–73, 176
retirees see age–wealth profile; social
   security transfers
retirement age 238
Revenga, A. 275, 290
Rickets, E. R. 34
rooms, number of 154, 155, 156, 159,
   161, 199
Ruggles, P. 7, 36, 59, 354
Runkle, D. 42
rural families 67, 68, 69, 70, 71, 85
Ryscavage, P. 205

savings 371
Sawhill, I. V. 34, 368
Scholz, J. 266
school dropout rates 314
school enrollment rates 277, 293–300,
   306, 310

self-reported health measures 9, 92
   women 92–7; single mothers 97–8
Shoven, J. B. 219, 220, 222
single-mother families 4, 85, 89–120
   earnings capacity 99–105, 108, 113;
      and poverty 105–7
   health status 91, 92–8
   income transitions 253–6
   policy recommendations 9–10, 72,
      107–12, 113
   poverty rate 37, 65, 66; economic
      growth and 26–7; policy changes
      and 35, 36; poverty probabilities
      67, 68, 69, 70, 71
skills 362–3, 365
   low-skilled workers 369–70
   see also education
Slesnick, D. 147–8, 198
Smeeding, Timothy 240, 266
   policy forum 368–70, 373–4, 376
Smith, J. P. 132
Smolensky, E. 59, 131, 337
'snapshot' comparisons 240, 244–8
social experimentation 377
social security annuity portion 12, 211,
   214, 215–16
   distribution of income and wealth
      228
   estimation 216–18
   proportion rising 220–1, 235
social security capital fund 12–13, 368,
   376
   funded from defense cuts 372
   funded from social security trust
      fund 13, 236–7
   funded from taxation of transfers
      212, 215, 235, 236, 371–2
social security entitlement wealth 215,
   216, 218, 225
social security system 11–13, 211–39
   see also social security transfers
social security transfers 12–13, 211–12,
   218, 219–37
   distributional effects 225–8, 229–30,
      235–6
   proportion of total benefit 219–24,
      235
   relative to total income and
      wealth 225, 226–7
   taxation 12, 212, 214–15, 371–2;
      implications 228–35, 236–7; see
      also social security capital fund
space, housing 154, 155–60, 161
standard of living 1, 10–11

see also expenditures; material well-being
statistical agencies, depletion of 358
Steuerle, E. 264
student loans 310–11, 363
students, independent 67, 68, 70, 71, 85
subsidies
    child care *see* child care subsidies
    education 299–300, 310–11, 364
    employment 367, 374–5, 375–6
    farm 373–4
    housing 29–30, 52, 181
    wages 72, 367, 374–5
suburban families, poverty and 67, 68, 69, 70, 71, 85
Supplemental Security Income (SSI) program 110–12, 118–19
Survey of Income and Program Participation (SIPP) 91–2, 97–8, 117–18

targeted programs 5, 7, 51
tastes 59, 60
Tax Reform Act (1986) 263, 361
taxation
    children's exemption as credit 264–5, 273–4, 361–2
    decline in progressivity 369
    EITC 376
    and income inequality 1
    refundable dependent day care credit 361
    social security transfers *see* social security transfers
    VAT 374
    wealth 14, 264–5, 273–4, 370
    wives and labor force participation 17, 346
    see also income tax
technical innovations 167–8
telephones 154, 158, 159, 167, 168
temperature control 161–3
    see also air conditioning; central heating
Thurow, L. 240, 318
trade 369–70
trade unions
    education–earnings differentials 286, 287, 288, 289, 290, 305, 312; hourly earnings 302–3
    and wage-setting 365
training 364–5, 368
    see also education

transfer portion of social security *see* social security transfers
transitions, income *see* income transitions
'trickle down' 21, 51–2
trucks 158, 166, 200
    see also automobiles
tuition costs 297–8, 307
    subsidies 299–300, 310–11

underclass 32–3, 124, 130
unemployment 30–1
    poverty rate and 22–7, 45, 46, 47
unemployment insurance 372
universal child support 368
universal programs 5
urban poverty 32–4

Value Added Tax (VAT) 374
Van der Gaag, J. 131
Vaughan, D. 131
Volcker recession 130, 359

wages 240
    and business cycle 42
    declining real 22
    education–earnings differentials:
        industry wage changes 285, 286, 287, 288, 289, 290, 312; minimum wage 286–8, 289, 290, 305, 312
    gender differences 332–3
    inequality 22, 240, 308
    lack of responsiveness to economic growth 7, 22, 45–50, 51
    productivity and 2
    single mothers' earnings capacity 99–101, 102
    subsidies 72, 367, 374
    trade unions and 365
    see also earnings; income
Wales, T. 265
Warlick, J. L. 211, 219, 220–1, 221, 222
wealth 359
    fungible 237
    household wealth *see* household wealth
    inequality 1, 240, 369
    middle class *see* middle class
    social security 215–18
    social security transfers: distributional effects 225–8, 229–30; relative to 225, 226–7
    taxation of 14, 264–5, 273–4, 370

wealth–age profile 2, 12–13, 213–14, 371
　see also social security transfers
weeks of work 45–6, 47, 49, 50, 54
Welch, F. 132, 275
'well-being', proposed index of 378–9
　see also material well-being
Wilson, W. J. 32, 321
wives' earnings 317
　and family income 4, 16–17, 318, 336–45, 347–8; policy recommendations 17, 346
　labor participation rates and 332–6
　trends 324–32
Wolfe, B. 108
Wolff, Edward N. 12, 211, 212, 213, 216, 219, 240

policy forum 371–2, 376, 377, 378
women
　earnings and income transitions 256–8; *see also* wives' earnings
　health status 92–8, 114; *see also* single-mother families
　labor force participation 318, 321–4, 332–6

young people
　capital fund for *see* social security capital fund
　ghetto youth 67, 68, 69, 70, 71, 85
　policies for 368
　role of society 359
　see also children; students